Dreams for Sale

400

00026954

Dreams for Sale

Popular Culture in the 20th Century

Edited by

Richard Maltby

HARRAP

London

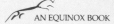
Volume editor Peter Furtado
Art editor Ayala Kingsley
Designers Frankie Macmillan,
Niki Overy, Linda Reed, Janet
McCallum, Tony De Saulles
Picture editor Christine Vincent
Picture research Jan Croot

Art direction John Ridgeway

AN EQUINOX BOOK

Planned and produced by
Equinox (Oxford) Ltd, Musterlin
House, Jordan Hill Road, Oxford,
England

Copyright © Equinox (Oxford) Ltd
1989

Published in this edition 1989 by
Harrap Books Ltd
19–23 Ludgate Hill
London EC4M 7PD

ISBN 00-245-54883-1

Printed by Gorenski Tisk, Kranj,
Yugoslavia

ADVISORY EDITORS

Lord Briggs
Worcester College, Oxford

Dr M.L.H.L. Weaver
Linacre College, Oxford

CONTRIBUTORS

Jennifer Hargreaves
Roehampton Institute, London

David Horn
University of Liverpool

Keith Lyons
London School of Economics

Penny Sparke
Royal College of Art, London

Elizabeth Wilson
North East London Polytechnic

CONTENTS

PREFACE

Fashion, entertainment, design, leisure, recreation pervade our daily lives, but we seldom take them very seriously. They form the surface gloss around the more important matters of our work, politics and home life. And yet these forms which make up modern popular culture have an important role to play in helping us to recognize ourselves, at work, as citizens, in our families. The media – press, radio, television, films – supply not simply information and entertainment but images and impressions which instruct us in the conduct of our lives. In the present century our manners and our morals are increasingly taught us by the movies, television programs, and advertisements that surround us.

Think of a fashion advertisement: its purpose is to persuade us to buy. But in making us want the dress on the model, it also attracts us to the chair on which she sits, the cup in her hand, the house behind her, her pose, her smile. These form part of a constant stream of images and incitements which remind us continually of what it means to be beautiful, or well-respected, or sexy, or a "happy family" – assuming, of course, that we wish to conform to what our culture promotes as normal. Such images define not what we *are*, but what we *desire*; they encourage us to imitate the ideals of behavior which they represent.

Their influence shows most in their significant details: in the cut of a hemline or a catchphrase from a movie. Their representations of larger issues, such as family, or heroism, or sexuality, or law, or class, or race, are less evident because they are also the currency of contemporary culture. In its images, popular culture reproduces the common ideas and dominant beliefs of a particular society in a particular period.

To explain why popular culture takes the form it does, we must ask not only how things were, but how they came to be so. If we want to understand why the New Look took over the fashion world in 1947, for instance, we need to know more than the name of the designer who tailored it. We need to know how the fashion industry worked, and how Paris couturiers sought to regain international prominence after World War II. Beyond this, we also need a more general knowledge of fashion's commitment to change for its own sake and of the ways in which styles of dressing can reflect broader cultural attitudes: we can ask why this reassertion of impractical and decorative femininity emerged in the aftermath of World War II and at the start of the Cold War.

The present book seeks to analyze the popular culture it describes, rather than simply to celebrate it. In doing so, it lays emphasis more on consumption than production. The topics it covers – film, popular music, design, fashion, the media and sport – are those areas where we consume most avidly. The transient, fashionable objects of our lives are bought, sold, used and thrown away; and an understanding of this process explains how they relate to contemporary culture more clearly than a simple record of their production.

Richard Maltby   University of Exeter

INTRODUCTION

When we look nostalgically at the recent past, we often recognize it by the things we used to buy, or else by such modern "heroes" as movie stars and sports celebrities. The movies, music, fashions, sport and designs provide a vivid map of our past, because they all share ephemerality. They are all things of the moment, designed to have a brief life, to burn brightly for the instant and disappear, but are always replaced by other, even more gaily colored things of the hour.

An athletic record or popular song is replaced by another which is little different from it. These pass us in an endless parade with similar functions but different details. In the details of this parade is contained a history of our century. At one level it is a history of skirt lengths and Top Ten hits, a history of the ephemera in which we wrap our sentimental memories of lost loves and long-ago summers. But it is also a history of how modern society has created images of itself and expressed its fantasies, its fears, its ambitions.

This is also the history of the economic system by which the images are manufactured and distributed and sold. We talk of the entertainment *industry*, of show *business*, of the dream factory. Industrial societies turn the provision of leisure into a commercial activity, in which their citizens are sold entertainment, recreation, pleasure and appearance as commodities that differ from the goods at the drug store only in the way they are used. For 70 years, Hollywood, "The Metropolis of Make Believe", "the entertainment capital of the world", has manufactured and marketed a non-durable consumer commodity: the experience of "going to the movies" rather than any particular film. In going to the movies, people do not buy anything tangible. They merely consume *time* by renting seats in the cinema for an hour or two. What we are really buying is perhaps something different, something already our own. As a name for Hollywood, the Dream Factory has long been a cliché, but no-one has yet found a more evocative analogy for the experience of cinema-going than that of the dream. As spectators we sit, spellbound in darkness, sharing a public privacy with our fellow viewers, all of us engaged witnesses in a fantasy that is not under our control, but is nevertheless ours to make of what we will. The people who run what Italian critic Umberto Eco has called "the heavy industry of dreams" are in the business of selling us desires we already have. They steal our dreams, and then sell them back to us for entertainment.

The marketing of leisure

The buying and selling of time is the central activity of the leisure industry in a capitalist economy. This is what differentiates modern popular culture from the folk culture which preceded it, and from which it borrowed many of its forms. Football, for instance, developed in the 19th century into its various modern forms out of local, traditional games, but by 1900 had become a professional sport. The players earned their living by the game, and their spectators paid for the pleasure of watching. Throughout the present century, adults have berated their children for preferring to buy the products of popular culture rather than "make their own entertainment". This offers a clear distinction between folk culture and popular culture: folk culture is something you make; popular culture is something you buy.

Among the many fundamental social changes brought by the Industrial Revolution was the way in which leisure was systematized. The factory system regulated time in a new way, making time-at-work different from time-not-working. In a sense that had not been true in preindustrial culture, time-not-working became an empty period that needed to be occupied. For much of the 19th century leisure, which can be defined as the non-productive use of time, remained the prerogative of the propertied classes. But by the early 20th century the notion of leisure spread down through the social system in Europe and North America and new activities came into existence to occupy leisure time.

The city amusements of the late 19th century were prototypes for ephemeral consumption: saloons, dance halls, pool rooms and roller-skating rinks; dime novels and illustrated papers, circuses, amusement parks, burlesque shows and professional sports; melodrama and cheap seats in the theaters and concert halls. Most spectacular of all were the great exhibitions of the second half of the 19th century, beginning at London's Crystal Palace in 1851 and culminating in the Chicago World's Columbian Exposition in 1893 and the Paris Exhibition of 1900. These architectural extravagances, thrown up for a summer to display the new wonders of the worlds of industry and commerce, were available to anyone who could pay.

This was not enough. By the turn of the century industrial production had developed to the point where the economy required consumption, as well as production, to be managed. 19th-century industrialists had regarded their labor-force as a necessity for production, but in the early 20th century it was recognized that capitalism must encourage the workers to be purchasers as well. Mass advertising developed out of a need to persuade people to buy. Manufacturers merely made products, but advertisers "manufactured consumers". Advertising involved a shift in cultural values away from a Victorian Protestant ethic which demanded that production, property, and personal behavior be controlled. It encouraged an ethic which permitted pleasure and even sensuality. Advertising came to concentrate not on describing the product it was selling, but on the emotional satisfactions that its consumption would afford its purchaser. It preached the new, "therapeutic" doctrine of 20th-century capitalism, that its citizens should seek self-realization through the intense experiences brought about through buying products for their leisure time. In 1899 the American economist Thorstein Veblen argued that "the conspicuous consumption of valuable goods" became the principal means by which members of the Leisure Class demonstrated their social standing to each other and to the rest of society. As he was describing the nature and implications of a consumer culture, American capitalism was spreading that culture, and the idea of leisure, to far larger sectors of the population. Several years later, a writer on fashion noted that as wealth or social status were the basic selling points of most clothes, "the styles should go as far as possible in proving that the owner does not have to work for a living". From the 1920s onward, the idea of stylistic obsolescence in which annual models introduce new season's fashions spread out from automobiles to other types of

▶ St Louis World's Fair, 1904.

consumer goods as the way to maintain a constant demand, through what Charles Kettering of General Motors called "the organized creation of dissatisfaction". In 1929 Christine Frederick wrote, "Consumptionism is the name given to the new doctrine; and it is admitted today to be the greatest idea that America has to give to the world; the idea that workmen and masses be looked upon not simply as workers and producers, but as consumers....Pay them more, sell them more, prosper more is the equation."

This was the American Dream: an economic perpetual-motion machine which made everyone appear equally prosperous. It drew immigrants with the fantastic visions seen, as novelist Michael Gold described in 1930, "In the window of a store that sold Singer Sewing Machines in our (Romanian)

village. One picture had in it the tallest building I had ever seen. It was called a skyscraper. At the bottom of it walked the proud Americans. The men wore derby hats and had fine mustaches and gold watch chains. The women wore silks and satins, and had proud faces like queens. Not a single poor man or woman was there; everyone was rich."

America leads the world

The image of the Americans as the "people of plenty" is with us still, as alluring in a slum in Manila or Buenos Aires as ever it was in a Romanian village. What the history of our popular culture tells above all is how many of our fantasies have been sold to the rest of the world by Americans; how much people all over the world have all been influenced, in the details of

In the 1960s media theorist Marshall McLuhan proclaimed that electronic communications had turned the world into a "Global Village", in which "our central nervous system is technologically extended to involve us in the whole of mankind and to incorporate the whole of mankind in us". McLuhan argued that the electronic media were more "organic" than mechanical forms such as print; thus the new media could become quite literally, "the extensions of Man." His writings enjoyed an enormous vogue at the time of their publication, and he contributed a collection of slogans by which the media would be discussed and categorized – "the medium is the message"; "Culture is our Business", "hot" media, such as film or radio, that concentrated attention on a single sense, against "cold" media like television that he claimed required more participation on the part of the consumer. But McLuhan's theories were only another version of the popular excitement which has accompanied every new development in communications' technology in this century. In McLuhan's media fantasy, "We are certainly coming within conceivable range of a world automatically controlled to a point where we could say, 'We can program twenty more hours of TV in South Africa next week to cool down the tribal temperature raised by radio last week'." What was missing from this monstrous scenario was any suggestion about who might be doing the controlling. McLuhan's mythology ignored the historical forces that actually shaped the world's media institutions.

American popular culture has formed so many of our contemporary images of "civilization" in part because the United States has been the great economic power of the century, and in part because the characteristic forms of each new medium of popular culture have first been fixed in America, and then copied elsewhere. If popular culture in its modern form was invented in any one place, it was at the turn of the century in the great cities of the United States, and above all in New York. The forms by which a mass population would talk to itself, and what it would talk about, were tested and refined in the newspaper print rooms of Park Row, where Joseph Pulitzer and William Randolph Hearst fought circulation battles for tabloid newspaper readers; in the primitive film studios in the Bronx where Edison, Vitagraph and Bioscope were learning how to mass-produce movies; in the piano rooms of Tin Pan Alley where songs for the city were being mass-produced; in the advertising offices of Madison Avenue, where the stylish agencies dreamed up ways to spend other people's money. All of them unconsciously modeled their mode of working on the tailoring sweatshops of the Lower East Side of New York.

A similar phenomenon might have been witnessed in Paris five years earlier, for the cinema, the mass-circulation daily newspaper, the press and advertising agencies and the fashion houses were already there. But popular culture needed not only the body heat of a metropolis and the blood of capitalism, but the oxygen of American democracy to bring it to life. Workers there could choose how to spend their leisure; American laborers campaigned for "eight hours for work, eight hours for sleep, and eight hours for what we will". Leisure was a social leveler, and popular culture has always, on its surface, been an enemy of class distinction. In 1898 the *New York Tribune* explained why relatively poor garment workers spent all their money on fashionable clothes: "In the matter of dress, it is natural that the East Side should be strictly up to date, for it does not furnish clothes for the rest of the town."

their daily lives, by the United States; how, if the rest of the world has not been colonized by the United States in the 20th century, it has all, certainly, been Coca-Colonized: "If the United States abolished its diplomatic and consular services, kept its ships in harbor and its tourists at home, and retired from the worlds' markets, its citizens, its problems, its towns and countryside, its roads, motor cars, counting houses and saloons would still be familiar in the uttermost corners of the world... The film is to America what the flag was once to Britain. By its means Uncle Sam may hope some day, if he is not checked in time, to Americanize the world." What the *New York Morning Post* said of the movies in 1923 has become only more true since, as the instruments of Americanization have become more and more effective.

This was the great American cultural promise, a "democracy of surfaces" brought into being through the mass production and distribution of images. The realities of the distribution of economic and political power within the culture could thus be disguised, to the satisfaction of capitalist and worker alike. Mass fashion allowed everyone to appear upwardly mobile. In the "democracy of goods", the best things in life appeared available to all at reasonable prices. The American city was a world of strangers, where the individual needed to construct an impressive appearance and to disguise him- or herself: for the immigrant masses, an old culture was being discarded and a culture of novelty adopted. Immigrants were the first customers and the first proprietors of the nickelodeons. Their involvement in the new leisure industries came about in part because conventional business activities were seldom open to them, in part because the entertainment industries required little capital, and in part because, as new citizens of a New World, they were well placed to develop new forms of expression and commerce.

American popular culture has been so successful above all because it has been able to absorb and assimilate forms and material from anywhere, and yet reproduce them as specifically "American". One advertiser claimed in 1929 that his profession was bringing about "the growth of a national homogeneity in our people". He came close to describing what was at the same time the great boon and the great vice of American popular culture. By acting as the means through which the enormously varied cultural traditions that immigrants brought with them were assimilated into American life, it worked to level differences between ethnic groups and social classes. At the turn of the century American popular music began to borrow rhythms and dances from black and other ethnic groups. In doing so, it awarded these socially inferior musical forms a degree of legitimacy they had previously been denied, and in the process also provided one of the few means of genuine upward mobility for this group of the American poor. One of its other effects was to help spread what psychologist William James called "The Gospel of Relaxation" among the white American middle-class. Danced to ragtime rhythms, the "Bunny Hug" and "Grizzly Bear" brought a new sensuality to middle-class life, and eventually made it respectable. That process has continued ever since.

The "homogeneity" that advertisers sought, the cultural equivalent of the Melting Pot of different nationalities that America described itself as being, was a diluted version of each of its mixed ethnic origins. Many of its critics argued that it was not only homogeneous, and acceptable to everyone, but also homogenized, watered-down and blended until it had no taste, no life, no soul. In the 1940s young whites took up another black dance form, the jitterbug. But for all their increased abandon, they still looked inhibited to black writer Malcolm X: "The white people danced as though somebody had trained them, as though somebody had wound them up. But those Negroes – nobody in the world could have choreographed the way they did whatever they felt."

Popular culture and high art
The Industrial Revolution had taken work out of the home into the factory and office. The home became a place of male leisure, serviced by women, at the same time that many things that had once been made at home were now bought in stores. Offering objects for leisurely use in the home, advertising – the form of popular culture that is most concerned to sell the

◀ Entertaining the troops, 1944.

satisfactions it promised – was primarily addressed to women.

The consumer was usually viewed by producers and critics alike as female. In part there was good reason for this: women were responsible for as much as 85 percent of consumer spending. Middle-class women constituted a new leisure class, spending their time at shops, theater matinées and hairdressers. The ethos of sensuality cooperated with the cosmetic industry to insist on the "natural right" of American woman to be beautiful. In the 1920s the "flapper" as a beautiful American woman was a ubiquitous advertising image. She was, as social historian Stuart Ewan put it, "Pure consumer, busy dancing through the world of modern goods. She was youth, marked by energy not judgement. Her clothes, her vehicles, her entire milieu was mass-produced – and she liked it."

It was because "mass culture" was addressed particularly to women that it was a matter of anxiety. The "masses" were taken to have exclusively "feminine" characteristics: they were irrational, capricious, passive, and conformist. Like women, the masses would respond only to emotional appeals and "raw sensation". The cultural objects designed for them could not, in the eyes of elite male critics such as Dwight Macdonald or the poet T.S. Eliot, qualify as art. Macdonald was disturbed by what he called Gresham's Law in Culture, by which "bad stuff drives out the good by mimicking and debasing the forms of High Art". His colleague Clement Greenberg, writing in 1946, argued in similar terms, that "Mass Culture pre-digests art for the spectator and spares him effort, provides him with a short-cut to the pleasures of art that detours what is necessarily difficult in genuine art". Although in some respects this argument echoed the position of blacks who claimed that "whitening-up" their music had deprived it of its essence, it was more forcefully a defense of cultural elitism against the contamination from the hands of a larger and more "vulgar" audience.

The debates over "mass culture" arose from the occupation, by commercial enterprises such as the cinema, of territory previously reserved for elite culture by its designation as art. The description of mass culture as feminine depended on the actual exclusion of women from high culture and its institutions. Thus mass culture could be declared trivial and dangerous at the same time, symptomatic of and responsible for all the social ills of life under capitalism. Veblen had described how "expensive vices" were reserved for the rich and forbidden to others.

What was at stake in this debate, as in the recurrent concerns of critics over the censorship of what their social inferiors consumed, was the question of where cultural power was situated in Western democracies. The "democracy of images" protected the political and economic elite from social criticism, but it equally endangered their role as protectors of "culture". So they constantly disparaged the effects of "mass culture" as morally corrupting. That argument was applied equally to dime novels and to skirt lengths or movies, but it was always couched in terms of a discussion of the effects on the mentally and morally deficient – children and "morons" – of objects that were not fully under the control of the cultural elite. At its root was a middle-class fear that there was no control over the behavior and values of the lower orders. Against this denunciation of "nickel madness", there arose a counter-argument, couched in terms of the definition of "entertainment" as "harmless". In 1916 the Supreme Court adjudged that movies were not to be permitted the free speech protections of the First Amendment, because they were "a business pure and simple, originated and conducted for profit...not to be regarded as part of the press of the country or as organs of public opinion. They are mere representations of events, of ideas, and sentiments published or known, vivid, useful, and entertaining, no doubt, but...capable of evil, having power for it, the greater because of their attractiveness and manner of exhibition."

The activity of regulating entertainment, whether through censorship, mechanisms such as the Motion Picture Production Code, or less official devices, constituted an attempt to render the potentially harmful object harmless, but throughout, this was a debate conducted among the cultural elite about what might be permitted to the lower classes, whose opinions were seldom directly requested.

As capitalist producers, the major companies and the financial forces behind them had strong vested interests in having their product regarded as merely a harmless form of entertainment too inconsequential to merit state interference or regulation. As advertising had to argue that it influenced consumer choice but did not otherwise affect people's lives, the movies had to bluff their way through the contradictory arguments that while they provided their audiences with immediate pleasurable experiences, they did not cause people to behave differently in any important way. Such an argument was even more convincing if movie content appeared superficial, "escapist" and irrelevant to the world outside the movie theater.

Art and escapism

Any distinction between art and entertainment is far from precise, because entertainment lacks a firm definition. It is usually defined through negatives: that which fails to be art or socially significant is entertainment. We may not know what entertainment or popular culture is, but we know it when we see it. Its connotations are triviality, ephemerality, and an absence of seriousness. Unlike Art, entertainment is not "about" anything outside itself, but is self-enclosed. Play, whether it is called "sport" or "entertainment", has been made into an area of activity sealed off from our engagements with power, ideology and politics. It is therefore usually escapist.

Mark O'Dea, a leading New York advertising executive, wrote that the key to successful advertising copy was the ability to "release people from the limitations of their own lives". Helen Woodward suggested that fashion had a similar role. But it was from the movies, above all, that writers and critics came to see the consumer audience as trapped in a humdrum existence, secretly desiring the illusion of romance.

Like such other fictional forms as radio soap opera or pulp fiction magazines, "the world of entertainment" the movies presented was one of heightened experience, in which the complexity of their audience's daily lives was replaced by an intensity of focus on particular dramatic events. In their films Clark Gable, Gary Cooper or Bette Davis seldom endured the minor irritants of ordinary life. Life in the movies was not so much simpler than elsewhere as less cluttered. Most moviegoers recognized Hollywood's perfectible world, where problems were cured by a dose of romantic love at the end of the plot, as escapist, but it might be better described as utopian, an attempt to project, as one critic has suggested, "what utopia would feel like rather than how it would be organized".

Escapism is far too simple a description of the complex relationship between our mundane realities and the heightened realms of experience made available to us by Hollywood or television. A stenographer in the 1930s going to a screwball comedy set in the art deco world of the very rich might seem to be indulging in an "escape" from her drab daily life. But what is she doing, the next week, when she goes to her local department store and buys a copy of the dress worn by the star in that same movie? Escapism usually suggests to us that we must be escaping from somewhere where we ought to be, the daily world of work and responsibility, and escaping to somewhere make-believe, a Shangri-La, a utopian fantasy-land over the rainbow. But that does not explain why the stenographer buys the dress. Sportswriter Hugh McIlvaney came closer to the mark when he wrote, "Sport has no validity, no worth whatsoever, if it is not governed by utopian ethics, by a code of morality infinitely superior to anything likely to be found in everyday life".

But sport *is* part of everyday life; like the movies and the songs about perfect love and the party dresses we wear for special occasions, sport is the utopian part of our daily existence, the part in which we dream we are at our best. Science tells us, as individuals, that we need to dream when we sleep, that we suffer if we are not allowed to. Our culture tells us, every day in myriad ways, that we need to dream, to let our secret, holiday selves escape. And escapism that is not an escape from or to anywhere, but an escape of our utopian selves, has always been present in the idea of Carnival, where the inhibitions which bind us to conventional roles are loosened. It is our Carnival selves that we take on holiday, and the holiday resort – from Atlantic City to Blackpool to Pattaya – has always been a place of loosened inhibitions. If it is the crime of popular culture that it has taken our dreams and packaged them and sold them back to us, it is also the achievement of popular culture that it has brought us more and more varied dreams than we could otherwise ever have known.

The interplay between our public and private worlds which popular culture invokes by the moment suggests that the artefacts of popular culture should be seen as a form of public fantasy. Frank Sinatra crooned "I'll be seeing you" to a million "you's", and his sentiment was put to personal use by each viewer. The world of private imaginings is a shared commodity that everyone can purchase, and it takes place in public spaces like picture palaces, around communal property, such as the images of movie stars. Marilyn Monroe, for example, served as the public fantasy of American sexuality in the 1950s and early 1960s. In some senses, popular culture and entertainment involve the escape of those elements of ourselves and our culture that are normally kept under restraint – what Freud termed "the return of the repressed".

Popular culture and social change

Because popular culture charts social change exactly and swiftly, it is commonly held responsible for the changes it reflects, and denounced as the harbinger of social dislocation. In the early years of the century, jazz and the movies were held responsible for juvenile delinquency, as television continues to be today. Cultural conservationists blame the spread of popular culture for their discomfort, believing that if only it could be kept under proper control, then the stability of the old ways of life might return. But this is to punish the messenger for the news he delivers. The media of popular culture are not themselves the origin of social change, although they encourage its novelties by making them appear desirable. In one important respect popular culture is itself conservative, since, to be popular, it must speak a language that is already common to its consumers. To sell the people what they want to sell, the producers of popular culture must say what they think people most want to hear. In this sense popular culture is a form of dialog which a society has with itself.

The debates over censorship reflected a widespread belief that popular culture was an instrument of informal education and influence, and that as a result care needed to be taken over

its content. Non-capitalist countries supervised their information and entertainment media at least as closely as they supervised their state education systems. In the United States, by contrast, the industries of leisure accepted "escapism" as a definition of their activities, since it has provided them with an easy means of avoiding responsibility for what they represent.

Entertainment, industry and politics

Throughout the 20th century the industries of leisure have expanded to constitute an ever greater part of the economies of industrialized nations. From the Korean factory worker producing television sets to the part-time saleswoman in Stockholm who sells them, ever-increasing numbers of people are employed in the production and servicing of leisure activities.

All these activities are couched in the idioms of advertising and entertainment: they all respond to real needs, but as they do so, they define what constitute the legitimate needs of the people of their society. As critic Richard Dyer has expressed it, "The ideals of entertainment imply wants that capitalism itself promises to meet...entertainment provides alternatives to capitalism which will be provided by capitalism." Yet such ideals and alternatives, dismissed as merely entertainment, are held to be unworthy of serious consideration. As a result, we are alienated from our own dreams and utopian desires, persuaded instead that they can be fulfilled, or just disposed of, by two hours at the movies or a new dress and in the process

▲ The hula-hoop craze of the mid-1950s.

15

reassured that, like the commodities that have replaced them, the dreams were never "about" anything important in the first place.

Broadcasting has been one of the most predictably profitable commercial enterprises of the century. Within 15 years of its appearance, television became an integral part of American culture: not simply recording or reflecting in distorted form, but its dominant medium of social expression. To watch was an act of citizenship, participation in the national culture. On a typical autumn evening in the late 1970s, over 100 million people, in 60 percent of American homes, chose between the programming output of the three national television networks. The particular genius of the medium came not from its intensity but from its sheer volume, its pervasiveness, and its extraordinary capacity to integrate everything – news, entertainment, talk, sport, comedy, commercials, action – into a single entity. To an even greater extent than movies, sport or radio, television filled its consumers' lives with drama, so that, as the British literary critic Raymond Williams wrote in 1972, "More drama is watched in a week or a weekend, by the majority of viewers, than would have been watched in a year or in some cases a lifetime in any previous historical period."

Politics and show business became increasingly entangled; it became ever harder to disentangle "the media" from political or social history. Subjected to increasingly sophisticated advertising pressure, viewers have been constantly presented with politics as a drama of personalities in which the object of the game has been to pick the winner. Certainly television obliged politicians to become performers in a way radio never had, and the "image" they presented was scrutinized as intensely as their policies. The coverage of elections by television has grown to concentrate increasingly on campaign strategies and the techniques of voter manipulation, and less on the substantive political issues at stake. One consequence has been an increasing apathy towards the political process, a lower regard for the ethics and integrity of politicians and a greater volatility in voting behavior. The extent of media influence is reflected in the observation that when an industrially developed country is occupied or liberated today, whenever there is a coup d'état or a revolution, the new regime will take over the radio and television stations, the telephone and telex exchanges, and the printing presses. But the most striking way in which the media, and television in particular, have come to set the political agenda in the last quarter of the century can be seen in the extent to which the politics of personality and image have come to predominate in American and European politics. Whether in the election in 1980 of Ronald Reagan, whom novelist Gore Vidal called "the Acting President", whose most effective skills have been in communications rather than administration, or in the increasing employment of advertising agencies by political parties of all persuasions in the West, issues of style and image have come to dominate issues of political substance. The impact of Mikhail Gorbachev's more acceptable face of communism is evidence that such notions are not limited to the West.

Hollywood and cultural imperialism

The United States has remained the dominant influence on world culture throughout the century, and this position has hardly been challenged. It has been by far the largest exporter of cultural commodities – larger than the rest of the world combined. Every national cinema has defined itself in relation to Hollywood, even when that self-definition has been a conscious rejection of American commercial practice, for the United States has exported not only the products of its popular

culture, but its forms, too. Japanese movies in the 1930s were composed and edited in accordance with Hollywood conventions; Brazilian or Nigerian advertisements, soap operas and game shows have been written to the formats of American practice, with which their audiences were already familiar. The content might take on a local coloring, but the shape of the media package changed far less from country to country, and the overwhelming source for the model has been the United States. In large part the dominance of American popular culture throughout the world is simply a manifestation of raw economic power. But it also reflects decisions made within the importing countries.

Few governments have regarded culture as an economic commodity. By comparison with trade in raw materials or manufactured goods, the global trade in cultural commodities is not especially large, although satellite and computer

technology have produced dramatic increases in its volume in the 1980s. Its relatively small economic importance is one reason why few Third World countries have made a priority of controlling American imports, or developing national culture industries based on models other than imitations of American practice. But, as the American film industry has argued almost from its infancy, cultural products play a crucial role in opening export markets for other goods and the way of life they promote. On the other hand the very existence of American-dominated popular culture has been responsible for the development of national styles in fashion or media, as governments try to resist the encroachment of a homogenized "world" culture, whether it emanates from New York, Hollywood, Paris or Tokyo.

In Europe, popular culture has been derided not only as "feminine" and as the inferior cultural goods of the working class, but also as "American". The word has implied an excessively democratic society where classes do not know their proper place in a hierarchy of social order. European experience has made clear that the crucial difference between high culture art and popular culture is that high culture is sold to a small elite audience. European film and television reflect specifically middle-class values and are directed much more firmly toward an elite audience than the products of Hollywood and the networks. The middle classes, used to paying higher prices for their cultural commodities, have always seen their purchases as qualitatively superior to those available to the masses. This is ultimately not an argument about esthetic quality, but a demonstration of real cultural, social, and finally economic power. Since the cultural elite in European societies has

▲ Miss World contestants in 1965.

corresponded closely to the economic and political elite, it has been able to dictate the terms of the debate. This has, for example, been a powerful influence on British broadcasting, whose patrons insist, against all evidence except cultural prejudice, that it provides the "least worst television in the world". The adaptations and documentaries which give British television its envied reputation for "quality" reproduce the "worthiest" remnants of British culture. As in Germany, television has absorbed writing and directorial talent which might have contributed to a cinematic renaissance. Innovation has been contained within the hierarchies of television. Elsewhere in Europe the formal experimentation of the avant-garde and international Art Cinema has been rendered harmless by being kept within a cultural ghetto of small metropolitan theaters for a middle-class elite, where its power to disrupt or subvert has been reduced to an untroublesome minimum.

On occasion, as in the *Cinema Novo* movement in the 1960s in Brazil, cultural resistance has been linked to opposition to the political and economic dominance of the United States as well as to its cultural influence. *Cinema Novo* used the history, mythology and imagery of traditional Brazilian culture as the basis on which to revive a national culture free of North American domination. Much Third-World cinema has derived its impetus from an opposition to the cultural colonialism of Western countries, which has often dominated distribution and thus hindered or prevented the emergence of an indigenous film industry.

The most enduring forms of cultural nationalism have been those able to integrate imitations of American media forms with a culturally specific, preferably traditional content: the martial arts films of Hong Kong; Japanese "home dramas"; or, largest and perhaps most spectacularly successful of all, the Indian cinema.

only in scale, from the complaints against Hollywood's influence in the 1920s. As the mass audience for the electronic media began to decline and fragment in the West, broadcasting became increasingly internationalized through coproduction arrangements, seeking its audience in many countries simply to pay the bills. The media have been important forces in maintaining Western influence and interests in Third World countries after independence from colonial rule: into the 1980s the majority of journalistic and technical staff continued to be trained by American or European agencies, and, partly as a result, to adopt Western values in regard to media content. Equipment and programs have enabled broadcasting services to be established, but have inhibited local production because of its high cost by comparision to American programming of much more ostentatious production qualities.

The revolutions in information technology in the 1980s have made the media more immediate – when American marines in Beirut were killed by a bomb in 1983, a CBS producer proudly exclaimed, "this week we have brought grief into American homes – fast." The escalating cost of satellites and other hardware has concentrated ownership of the means of media distribution in fewer and fewer hands.

This phenomenon is not limited to single media or separate countries: we all now live in the "Global Village" which McLuhan predicted in 1964. It is not like a real village: we can see and enjoy the carnival colors of our different cultures, but only a very few can speak, and the rest must merely listen. The power of the media – political, economic, cultural – now belongs to a handful of multinational corporations, who colonize the rest of the world, sometimes benignly, sometimes not. Throughout the century, Western popular culture has caused intense social disruption in the Third World, inculcating new patterns of behavior, new desires and new dissatisfactions. The pervasiveness of the electronic media increases the efficiency of this process.

Many analysts argue that only the pursuit of international mass audiences can sustain the investment in both equipment and programming, and envisage with dread a diet of Least Objectionable Programming, sport, music videos, news and reruns. What is undoubtedly clear is that a central feature of the Third Age of Broadcasting will be that, however increased the range of choice available to consumers may be, fewer organizations will own the means of distribution and determine what is offered to consumers.

For most people in the industrialized countries, the consumption of media has come to occupy more time than any other activity except sleeping and working – on average six hours per day in the United States, four hours in Europe. Home video recording, video games, remote-control television, cable and home computers have increased the amount of media available for consumption in the 1980s exponentially. But, contrary to the claim of a cable television company to provide "over 70 hours a day" of programming, the proliferation of media sources did not increase viewing times significantly. Time spent in front of a home computer screen tends to be at the expense of television time – saturation was reached in the mid-1970s. So far the fantasies of futurologists who predicted the electronic home, where people would shop, bank and work through interactive video, or the paperless office where all data would be computerized, have remained fantasies, like earlier overenthusiastic predictions of the changes new communications technologies would bring. As one television executive put it, "I have seen the future. And it's still in the future."

Curiously, the American film industry is required to be most sensitive to the demands of audiences outside its own cultural boundaries, since it is dependent on foreign sales for more than half its income. This heavy dependence on foreign markets is one explanation for the continuing ability of American popular cultural forms to absorb and assimilate almost anything. Polish filmmaker Andrej Wajda caught the other basic ingredient of their success: "The paradox is that because the American cinema is so commercial, because the pressure of money is so strong, everything in a film has to be the very best. That means the most expensive, but it also means the most authentic, the most honest. No half measures, everything on the edge of excess.... The amount the Americans are prepared to spend on making their films is in a way a sign of respect for the audience."

Essentially the argument has changed little in substance,

1900 · 1914
THE CONSUMER SOCIETY

Time Chart

	1900	1901	1902	1903	1904	1905	1906
Film	● Color photography simplified by Dugardin (Fr) ● *Cinderella*, directed by G Méliès, magician and theater-manager (Fr) ● Vaudeville strike; some theaters kept open by film shows (USA)	● 24 Oct: Incorporation of Eastman Kodak Co. (USA)	● First film-show area in an arcade opened in Los Angeles by T Tally (USA) ● 1 May: *A Trip to the Moon*, first science fiction film, released by G Méliès (Fr)	● *The Great Train Robbery* by Edwin Porter, running to 12 minutes (USA)		● Opening of first nickelodeon in Pittsburgh (USA)	● First animated cartoon released by Vitagraph ● *The Story of the Kelly Gang*, the first full-length film ● Legislation on the minimum distance between cinemas, to curb proliferation (Rus)
Media		● 11 Dec: Wireless telegraphy messages sent across Atlantic by G Marconi	● Voice modulator of "practically continuous waves" patented by R Fessenden (Can)	● Mar: Regular news service started by radio between London and New York (UK/USA) ● 4 Jul: Message from President Roosevelt circled world in 9½ minutes via Pacific Cable ● *Daily Mirror* was the first paper to have photos throughout (UK)	● Mar: Color photos published in London *Daily Illustrated Mirror* (UK) ● Offset lithography process became commercially available (USA) ● Three-electrode valve (audion) patented by Lee De Forest (USA)		
Music	● Patent granted on first molded recording cylinder (USA) ● First jazz band claimed by Buddy Bolden (USA) ● International craze for the cakewalk	● Shellac 10in (25cm) diameter gramophone record with spiral-groove introduced ● "Rags" popular (USA) ● Adoption of Victor trademark (USA)	● Enrico Caruso's first recording (It)	● First amplifier patented, by Charles Parsons (UK) ● *Babes in Toyland*, an operetta by Victor Herbert, opened (USA)	● First music radio broadcast (Aut)	● First double-sided disks released ● First preselective jukebox (USA) ● Franz Lehar's opera *The Merry Widow* opened (Aut)	● 17 Oct: Photographs sent by telegraph over 1000 miles (1600km) (Ger) ● Typecasting machine allowed large display type for headlines and bills (USA)
Fashion and Design	● Brownie camera introduced (USA) ● 14 Apr: Opening of the Paris International Exhibition (Fr) ● Button-down shirt introduced to USA by Brooks Bros (from UK) ● Glassmaker and designer LC Tiffany created Tiffany Studios, New York (USA)	● Apr: The first mass-produced gasoline-driven car, an Oldsmobile, introduced (USA) ● Société des Artistes Décorateurs founded (Fr)	● Cartier (Fr) opened its first London branch ● Turin International Exhibition (It) ● Sew-on press studs invented (Fr) ● Pepsi-Cola Co. founded (USA)	● The first Harley-Davidson motorcycle built (USA) ● Safety razor with disposable blades manufactured by King C Gillette (USA) ● Wiener Werkstätte founded as a craft cooperative (Aut) ● Jun: Foundation of Ford Motor Co. (USA)	● Electric machine that permanently waved hair introduced (UK) ● 30 Apr: Opening of St Louis World's Fair (USA)	● Fauvist paintings exhibited at annual Salon d'Automne in Paris, introducing fashion for bright colors (Fr) ● *Die Brücke* magazine founded to revive the graphic arts (Ger) ● Alfred Stieglitz opened a gallery in New York to exhibit photography as a fine art (USA)	● Saddlery shop opened in Florence by Guccio Gucci (It)
Sport	● Jul: Second modern Olympic Games held in Paris (Fr) ● 10 Aug: Davis Cup competition (tennis) held for first time; won by American team ● First motorcar race with international competitors, Paris to Lyon (Fr)	● Boxing recognized as legal sport in Britain	● First French soccer team played in England ● Jan: Inaugural Rose Bowl game between leading college teams (American football) ● Rubber-cored golfball invented (USA)	● First Tour de France cycling race held ● 13 Oct: First World Series in baseball, won by the Boston Red Sox (USA)	● 21 Jul: Rigolly (Fr) became first man to drive at over 100mph (160km/h) ● Aug: Olympic Games held in St Louis (USA) ● Foundation in Paris of Fédération Internationale de Football Association (FIFA)	● Jul: May Sutton (USA) became first non-Briton to win a Wimbledon tennis title	● First Victorian Football League (Australian rules) final at Melbourne (Aus) ● Jun: First Grand Prix motorcar race held, near Le Mans (Fr)
Misc.		● 22 Jan: Death of Queen Victoria (UK)		● 17 Dec: The Wright brothers made first flight in a heavier-than-air machine (USA)			

22

1907	1908	1909	1910	1911	1912	1913	1914
• Slow-motion film invented by A Musger • Foundation of Hollywood as filmmaking center (USA)	• 11 Feb: Patent rights over moving-picture camera granted to Edison and major companies (USA) • Florence Lawrence became known as "The Biograph Girl" (USA) • May: Movies placed within copyright laws (USA)	• 1 Jan: US Motion Picture Patents Co. set up, licensing nine producers, including two French (USA)	• First movie publicity stunt, with Gertrude Lawrence mobbed after reports of her death • Biograph made its first films in Hollywood (USA) • Opening of largest cinema yet built, the 5000-seat Gaumont Palace in Paris (Fr) • Aug: Kinetophone, with moving picture and simultaneous sound, demonstrated by TA Edison (USA)	• 1 May: Color talkie released, with sound on Biophon synchronized disk (Swe)	• Jun: Universal Studios founded by Carl Laemmle (USA) • Sep: Keystone Co. founded by Mack Sennett (USA) • Motor-driven movie cameras introduced (USA)	• Charlie Chaplin's first film for Keystone Co. released (USA) • First films from Paramount Co. were released (USA)	• *The World, the Flesh and the Devil* – the first full-length color film (UK)
• First regular studio radio broadcasts, by De Forest Radio Telephone Co. (USA)		• First newsreels released (USA) • May: First radio press message, from New York to Chicago (USA)	• Metropolitan Opera, with Caruso, broadcast on radio (USA) • First radio receivers in kit form on sale to public (USA)		• May: First issue of *Pravda* (Rus)	• First crossword puzzle published, in *New York World* (USA)	
• *Ziegfeld Follies* revue opened in New York (USA)		• First transcription of blues – WC Handy's *Memphis Blues* (USA)	• Craze for the tango • March band leader John Philip Sousa (USA) toured world	• *Alexander's Ragtime Band*, by Irving Berlin	• Dixieland Jazz Band opened at Reisenweber's Cabaret, New Orleans (USA)		• Feb: Foundation of American Society for Composers, Authors and Publishers (ASCAP)
• Nov: Maiden voyage of HMS *Mauretania*, largest and fastest ocean liner for 20 years (UK) • First Cubist paintings shown in Paris, influencing avant-garde fashion (Fr) • Deutscher Werkbund (German Association of Craftsmen) founded in Munich to promote industrial design (Ger) • First Rolls Royce Silver Ghost produced (UK)	• Dance triumphs of Isadora Duncan in London and New York, in flowing costumes based on ancient Greek styles (UK) • Aug: Model T Ford, first successful mass-produced car (USA) • Hoover company founded to market vacuum cleaner invented in 1902 (UK) • Sep: General Motors founded (USA)	• Sergei Diaghilev's Ballets Russes opened in Paris, creating a fashion for oriental dress and decor (Fr) • Process for manufacturing bakelite developed by L Baekeland (USA) • CR Mackintosh's Glasgow School of Art completed (UK) • Silk-pleating process patented in Paris by Mariano Fortuny (Sp) • *Vogue* magazine bought by Condé Nast (USA)	• Hairdresser Antoine (Pol) created bobbed hairstyle in his Paris salon	• Atelier Martine (Fr) founded by Paul Poiret, as design studio modeled on Wiener Werkstätte (Fr)	• Fashion designer Coco Chanel opened her first salon, in Deauville (Fr) • Foundation of arts and fashion magazine *La Gazette du Bon Ton* (Fr)	• First electric refrigerator for home use (USA) • Oct: Moving-belt conveyor used in assembly of Ford cars (USA) • Slide fastener (later called a zipper) developed (USA) • *Harper's Bazaar* magazine bought by WR Hearst	• First major exhibiton of industrial art by Deutscher Werkbund, in Cologne (Ger) • Jun: Le Syndicat de Défense de la Grande Couture Française founded, to protect copyright (Fr) • Live models used in US fashion shows for the first time • Edna Woolman Chase became editor of *Vogue* (USA) • First brassière patented, by Caresse Crosby (USA)
• May: First Isle of Man TT motorcycle race (UK) • Jun: Start of first long-distance motorcar rally, Paris to Beijing	• Jul: Olympic Games held in London (UK) • Dec: Jack Johnson (USA) became first black world heavyweight boxing champion • WG Grace retired from first-class cricket (UK) • International Swimming Federation (FINA) formed	• Imperial (later International) Cricket Conference founded (UK)		• May: Inaugural Indianapolis 500 motorcar race (USA) • First Monte Carlo motorcar rally (Mon)	• Jul: Stockholm Olympic Games, with the first women's swimming events (Swe) • International Lawn Tennis Federation founded in Paris (Fr)	• First Far Eastern Games held in Manila (Phil) • Charter for International Amateur Athletic Federation (IAAF) drawn up in Berlin (Ger)	
• More than 1 million immigrants entered USA		• R Peary reached North Pole (USA)			• 15 Apr: Sinking of the SS *Titanic* (USA)		• Aug: Outbreak of World War I

23

Datafile

In the final years of the 19th century the dominant design esthetic had been related to the arts and crafts movement, which valued crafts and skills and traditional design. The Art Nouveau movement of the 1890s developed this by the adoption of organic and irregular forms in opposition to the mechanical modern world. This movement also involved the reassertion of traditional European values over those of America.

Skyscrapers were beginning to appear in New York and Chicago, and came to be seen as symbolic of the new world of technology and industrial organization. They expressed the idea that the form should derive from the structure – in this case from their crude metal frame – and that surface decoration was a mere embellishment to justify an object's cultural pretensions. In the early years of the century, however, this idea was challenged by the search for modernism via an undiluted functionalist machine esthetic. This movement was to gain supremacy in the 1920s.

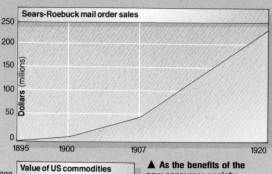

Sears-Roebuck mail order sales

US per capita consumption

Total $446
1909

Total $508
1919

☐ Food, clothing, housing
☐ Leisure
▨ Medical, education

Value of US commodities
☐ 1900 ☒ 1914

▲ As the benefits of the new consumer society became widely known, rural dwellers were reluctant to forgo the advantages of those who lived in towns. The mail-order catalog was the result. The Sears-Roebuck catalog was the largest, but similar selling techniques were employed at every rung in the social scale.

◀ Even in the United States the new consumer electrical goods accounted for a relatively small proportion of total consumer spending, despite advertising. The decline in sewing-machine sales was a temporary phenomenon: by 1919 they had risen to near their 1900 level (though sales of refrigerators continued their dramatic rise).

▲ Per capita income rose in the United States during the 1910s, and the proportion available for spending on leisure remained fairly constant. This meant, in effect, that leisure spending rose and provided new opportunities for the development of an entertainment industry, in which immigrants could play an important role.

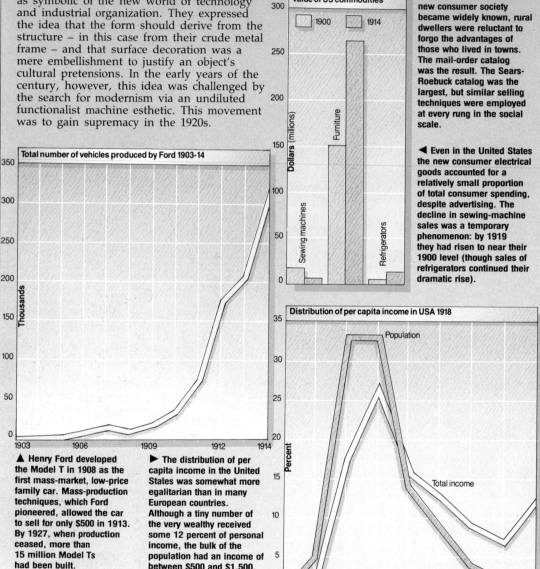

Total number of vehicles produced by Ford 1903-14

Distribution of per capita income in USA 1918

Population

Total income

Income (thousand $)

Average incomes 1914

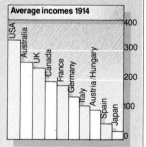

▲ Henry Ford developed the Model T in 1908 as the first mass-market, low-price family car. Mass-production techniques, which Ford pioneered, allowed the car to sell for only $500 in 1913. By 1927, when production ceased, more than 15 million Model Ts had been built.

▶ The distribution of per capita income in the United States was somewhat more egalitarian than in many European countries. Although a tiny number of the very wealthy received some 12 percent of personal income, the bulk of the population had an income of between $500 and $1,500.

▲ The graph of average personal incomes in leading countries in 1914 emphasizes the importance of the United States, even at this early period, in the development of the culture of consumption. The image of America as the land of plenty was borne out for many in their material wellbeing.

LEARNING TO BUY

By 1900 all major industrial countries had become aware of the importance of the consumption of goods by their citizens as well as production. As a result a "culture" of consumption emerged, which played an important role in the shaping of a country's social, economic and cultural identity. One feature of this new culture was a heightened awareness of social status and a strong desire at all levels of society to show off newly acquired wealth. New social aspirations were expressed most visibly in the "world of goods", and the concept of style became increasingly significant as a measure of social status.

This culture of consumption grew as a direct result of the process of industrialization within capitalist economies. It became increasingly necessary for manufacturers to produce and sell more and more goods to more and more people in order to guarantee their company's profits. The

▼ **By 1900, advertising signs on stores, billboards and public transport urged people to identify themselves through what they consumed.**

success of this formula also depended on the growth of the mass market. As the general level of affluence rose, there were increasing numbers of new consumers who sought new goods to reflect their enhanced social status. Most of them emulated their "social superiors" by imitating their purchases and as far as possible reproducing their lifestyles. The approach varied: in Britain the middle classes aspired to the lifestyle of the country gentry, whereas in the United States the new industrialists and businessmen sought to overturn the values of the traditional aristocracy. Everywhere, the new consumers displayed their new-found wealth and demonstrated the nature of their social ambitions through the many goods they bought.

One of the ways in which manufacturers tried to encourage consumption was by identifying a particular market and deliberately making their

goods look attractive to their potential customers. Even in the 18th century, when Britain was showing the first signs of becoming a consumer society, some entrepreneurs had achieved this by employing fine artists to design products for them. Goods that offered obviously "artistic" qualities conformed to the fashionable styles of the day and were particularly appealing to the newly affluent, status-conscious consumers for whom they were intended.

Adding style to goods

By the late 19th century manufacturers were addressing a sizable fashion-conscious mass market that included members of the working classes. The guarantee of taste or status was still connected with the visible presence of "art" in a product. This was a period of rampant estheticization in which almost any and every consumer product – in particular those that fell into the category of the traditional decorative or applied arts – could be seen to have an "artistic" content. This led to an extensive use of surface ornamentation that seemed to guarantee allegiance to the world of style for a market that was unfamiliar with fine art. The great vogue for "art furniture" and "art

pottery" in the 1880s and 1890s produced not only a spate of expensive, exclusive items designed for a middle-class market by such craftsmen as William de Morgan and E.W. Godwin, but also countless ranges of cheaper, mass-produced "art goods".

The dissemination of goods to a mass market depended on more than the efforts of manufacturers and designers to inject style into products. It also required a whole network of activities and institutions. These included changes in production methods so that more goods could be manufactured; the development of new kinds of retailing outlets; and the expansion of advertising and activities to promote sales. The introduction of a credit system of buying which was initiated by the Singer Sewing Machine Company in the United States in the 1860s, and adopted some decades later by the manufacturers of furniture and electrical appliances in Europe and the United States, also went a long way toward making more goods available to more people.

There were also changes in retailing. The department stores established in the second half of the 19th century – Bon Marché in Paris, Macy's in New York, and Derry and Toms, Whiteleys, and Harvey Nichols in London – were joined, at

▶ Trade cards provided one of the most direct forms of marketing at the turn of the century. They served to advertise a shop and to indicate, through the graphic style employed, the kind of market at which its goods were directed.

▶▶ This spread from a Sears Roebuck catalog, showing the wide variety of boots and shoes on offer by that company, would have been seen by a large sector of America's rural population at the turn of the century. Unable to make frequent shopping trips to the cities, these customers relied upon mail-order companies which brought an enormous range of goods to them.

▼ The cosmetics and drug department in an American store at the turn of the century. By this time the department store had become a vital means of retailing. Grandiose styling transformed these shops into the "temples" of the modern age.

about the turn of the century, by multi-branch retailing firms appealing to the lower end of the market, such as John Jacobs' furniture stores in England. American department stores appealed to as wide a market as possible through dramatic visual means. Interior spaces expanded and large shop windows were introduced to show off the new products to their best advantage. Electric lighting increased their visual appeal. The idea was pioneered in 1877 by John Wanamaker who persuaded Thomas Edison to install electricity in his store. The techniques of window dressing were also refined.

In the United States, where there were large distances between urban centers, the mail-order catalog became a vital means whereby the rural population could acquire goods that they would not otherwise have been able to buy. Montgomery Ward pioneered the concept, producing a single-sheet catalog in 1872. Three years later the catalog had nearly four thousand items listed in it. Sears followed suit, producing his first catalog in 1891 and moving on to become, with Roebuck, the largest mail-order company in the 20th century. They offered goods as diverse as agricultural machinery, applied art products, clothing and other utility goods. By 1900 electrical appliances had joined these earlier items.

The most direct way of making goods desirable was by modifying their appearance. Britain had gone a long way toward making the products of the traditional "art" industries available to the mass market through improved production techniques and distribution methods, but it was in the United States that the first consumer machines – automobiles, sewing machines, typewriters and domestic appliances – were made generally available. From the 1860s these began to take over from furniture as primary status symbols. Mass consumption of these consumer durables developed very quickly after their first

appearance on the market, as a result of the consumer boom that took place in the United States in the last decades of the 19th century. The market was quickly saturated with these new goods, however, and as supply began to exceed demand new ways were needed to market and sell these products. Credit buying was joined by aggressive sales programs in which salesmen toured the country offering demonstrations in their customers' homes.

Like the Singer sewing machines of the 1860s, which had gold scrollwork on their metal surfaces to give them greater domestic appeal, the first Hoover suction cleaner, a crude workshop-produced model, was adorned with decorative motifs in the fashionable Art Nouveau style. Product elaboration was thus transferred from ceramics and furniture to electrified machinery for the home. Electric fans, toasters, hot-plates and coffee-makers soon appeared on the market displaying the same decorative motifs as more traditional goods. Coffee pots resembled silver samovars and kettles looked like silver teapots from an earlier era.

The relationship between mass production and mass consumption was crucial in these years. High capital investment in a product meant that it had to sell in vast numbers to justify its initial costs and as a result marketing, advertising and design became increasingly important. However, the one product that dominated mass production and consumption in the first decades of the 20th century – the automobile – did not rely on "art" input to appeal to the mass market. Henry Ford's formula for mass production was based on product standardization; hence his famous statement that his cars were available in any color – providing it was black. The appeal of the Model T Ford lay less in its appearance than in its low price. Ford also used advertising and other marketing techniques to increase sales.

The spread of fashion

The "flapper" of the 1920s has long been considered the symbol for women's emancipation in the 20th century. In fact the freedom of manners and morals that she represented had begun to erode the old, stiff codes and conventions well before World War I. By the late 19th century middle-class and respectable working-class women were to be seen unchaperoned in city streets. One reason was that many more young women were now employed in offices, shops and department stores, while these department stores themselves – temples of 19th-century commerce – were places in which leisured women might wander alone or with their friends. Their refreshment rooms and cloakrooms, and sometimes even reading rooms and libraries, were social havens that even unaccompanied women could

frequent without damaging their reputations.

One result of the growth of cities was the advance of fashion as a popular pursuit. Anonymity in the crowd was one new result of urbanization, and fashionable clothes provided an opportunity for people to express themselves in their daily business. The enormously increased demand for smart apparel at a reasonable cost found a solution in the mass production of fashionable garments. The mass production of clothes had begun with the making of uniforms in the early 19th century, but this had been extended well before 1900 as the independence and consumerism of city life fostered the growing appetite for fashionability. The factory process was first extended, in the 1830s and 1840s, to urban daywear for men – young clerks and shop assistants in London and other large cities whose pretensions to style were made possible by ready-made outfits.

It was between 1890 and 1910, however, that the mass production of fashionable clothing really took off. Blouses or shirtwaists and petticoats began to be made in bulk. Department stores sold ready-made women's suits, dresses and coats, which could be altered slightly for each customer, echoing the moves towards standardization and product variation pioneered in other areas of mass-market manufacture, such as furniture.

The great cities of the industrial world gradually took on a different air. Although the gulf between rich and poor remained, and although a whole underclass of the very poor still barely had clothes enough to keep them warm, women and men from the lower and upper middle classes now dominated city pavements, and among the vast urban masses clothes became as much an index of personality and of purpose as of simple social status. Dress in the city street was a performance, a subtle indicator of calling or leisure activities, hinting at sexual proclivities as

▼ By the early 1900s the S-bend figure had superseded the previous tight-laced look. The new corset still nipped in the waist and thrust the bosom upwards, but stretched lower down over the stomach, tilting the whole body backwards. In the Edwardian period too, the corset did not so much produce a cleavage as a "monobosom". To our eyes today the finished effect is of a human lampstand rather than a woman's body.

▶ The middle-class woman of the 1900s was less constrained than her mother would have been in the 1870s. She was still stiffly corseted and usually her blouse did up high at the throat. Her appearance would be completed with a towering edifice of hat and hair. Hair was often padded out artificially while hats were vast and often covered with flowers and fruit, or more gruesomely with dead birds.

WARNER BROS.

CORALINE.

CORSETS.

much as at rank, and symbolizing countless allegiances. For men as well as women, to dress in fashion was to make a statement about yourself and your aspirations.

At the beginning of the 20th century women's clothing was changing more rapidly than men's. The growth in popularity of women's sports – particularly tennis and bicycling – meant that women were no longer quite so rigidly confined within the tight, voluminous garments that they had been wearing since the 1820s. Initially women laced themselves tightly even when running about the sportsfield; the bicycle at last made bloomers, or breeches, acceptable for women – if still rather "fast", or daring. A fashion for exercise, dance and calisthenics indicated the evolution of a new attitude toward the body. Women's exploits at hockey and cricket, on the bicycle and at the wheel of that most glamorous of fashion accessories, the motor car, inaugurated a new ideal of beauty that was soon to become dominant: the youthful, lissom, boyish woman. By the second decade of the 20th century her hair might well be bobbed (cut short), while long, loose clothes had replaced the hourglass figure.

STYLE BOOK

FALL 1911
The Ladies' Home Journal Patterns

◄ A new esthetic for street wear was the "coat and skirt", developed by Redferns and other British tailors from hunting and riding dress, but so functional for urban life that as a concept it has never really gone out of fashion.

▼ Some of the most daring women cyclists took to a cycling outfit which consisted of breeches, sometimes worn with a man's shirt, jacket and tie. It was widely accepted in France, as shown in this painting of the Bois de Boulogne, Paris, by Béraud.

▲ The American "Gibson Girl", drawn by Charles Dana Gibson, modified the severe tailored look of the New Woman and she became acceptably feminine, while retaining an air of dash and independence to typify the new woman of the 1900s.

Luxury and severity

Sportswear, the artistry of the great dress designers, and the ideas of dress reformers combined to create a new esthetic of dress to match the evolving new style of beauty. "Reform dress" had long been preached, and sometimes worn, in radical and artistic circles. Dress reformers objected to corsets, and to fashions such as the crinoline and the bustle which distorted the figure, for they believed that dress should follow the natural shape of the human form. The most famous example of reform dress was Amelia Bloomer's trousered costume of 1850 – named "bloomers" after its originator. Similarly reformers disliked men's trousers and preferred breeches, since they revealed the calf; the Irish playwright George Bernard Shaw was a dress reformer and habitually wore "plus fours".

Sportswear influenced women's daytime costumes. The firm of Redferns in London, which had originally specialized in riding habits, developed a modification of riding wear that became the "coat and skirt", or woman's suit. This rapidly became virtually a uniform for women's street wear, both in Europe and in the United States. It created a new kind of sobriety, almost a masculinity, in women's outdoor wear. In the United States the magazine artist Charles Dana Gibson created the epitome of this style in his famous "Gibson Girl", a tall, graceful young woman whose severe white blouse and dark, svelte skirt only enhanced her femininity. A fashion developed for frothy petticoats which peeped from beneath the hems of these sober skirts. It was during this period, when women's ordinary daywear became less feminine, that glamorous lingerie began to be popular.

Before 1800 underwear as we know it hardly existed. A shift was worn to protect the body from the rough material of the clothes, and the clothes from dirt of the body. The advance of hygiene and emphasis on modesty contributed to the popularity of underwear in the 19th century, but until about 1900 it was strictly utilitarian. With the turn of the century women were being more overtly sexual, as the rigid distinctions between the "respectable" and the "fallen" woman began to dissolve, and in the first decade of the 20th century fashionable women revelled in *crêpe de chine* underwear in "sweet pea" colors, covered in lace and ribbons. Unlike outerwear, these confections were still mostly hand-made.

The paradox of reserved outerwear and luxuriously sensual lingerie symbolized the way in which public life and private life had both become more elaborate and more distinct from each other during the industrial period. Social life was now more ritualized for most classes, and this found expression in equally elaborate rituals of dress. The new, lithe beauty of the sportsfield and dance floor, however, was born in the attempt to escape just this elaboration.

The story of Western dress in the 20th century, when for the first time fashionable clothes became widely available, has been one of oscillation between high artifice and studied simplicity, between fashions that glory in their useless glamor and those that are severely functional.

Poiret and Avant-garde Fashion

Paul Poiret was the leading Paris designer from 1908 to World War I. Possibly influenced by the ideas of the German dress reform movement, he designed loose, straight coats cut like kimonos and straight, often high-waisted dresses which hung from the shoulders. He claimed to have made women throw away their corsets, but Vionnet and other designers have also taken credit for the ending of the tight-laced silhouette. (In fact, women continued to wear boned corsets until well after World War II.)

Poiret was influenced by the fashion for oriental colors and styles, and also by the Ballets Russes, Diaghilev's dance company, which took Paris by storm with their exotic productions. These included vibrant backcloth and costume designs by Leon Bakst and Jose Maria Sert, and unfamiliar "modern" music and choreography. Poiret himself minimized the significance of Bakst's influence on his work, but few believed this claim. He achieved his greatest fame with his "hobble skirts" of 1911, which brought public outcry and even Papal denunciation. He used striking, even violent color combinations and his reds, violets, orange, rose and turquoise moved radically away from the pastel prettiness of more conventional *Belle Epoque* tints and equally from the half tones and "off" colors of the Liberty style. Poiret's designs were beautifully illustrated by Paul Iribe and Georges Lepape. He was a great publicist for his designs, and established a training school for young women in which they could learn the art of dressmaking.

▲ An evening coat by Paquin, influenced by Poiret.

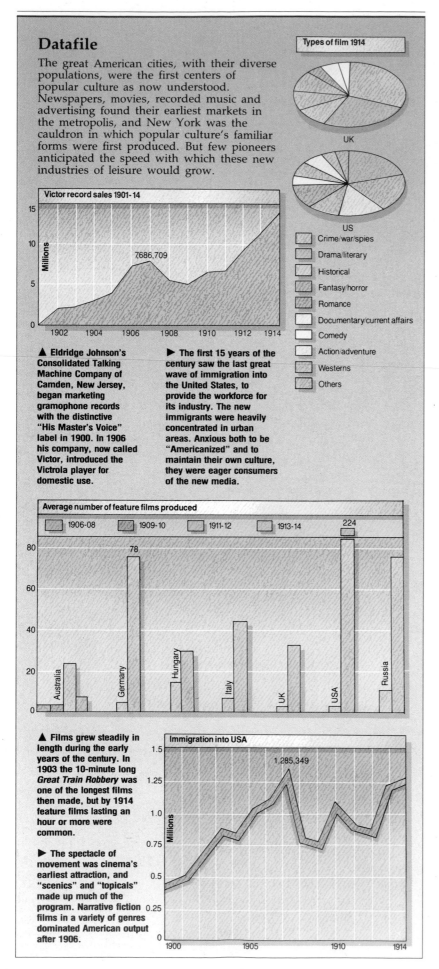

Datafile

The great American cities, with their diverse populations, were the first centers of popular culture as now understood. Newspapers, movies, recorded music and advertising found their earliest markets in the metropolis, and New York was the cauldron in which popular culture's familiar forms were first produced. But few pioneers anticipated the speed with which these new industries of leisure would grow.

Types of film 1914

UK

US

Crime/war/spies
Drama/literary
Historical
Fantasy/horror
Romance
Documentary/current affairs
Comedy
Action/adventure
Westerns
Others

Victor record sales 1901-14

7,686,709

▲ Eldridge Johnson's Consolidated Talking Machine Company of Camden, New Jersey, began marketing gramophone records with the distinctive "His Master's Voice" label in 1900. In 1906 his company, now called Victor, introduced the Victrola player for domestic use.

▶ The first 15 years of the century saw the last great wave of immigration into the United States, to provide the workforce for its industry. The new immigrants were heavily concentrated in urban areas. Anxious both to be "Americanized" and to maintain their own culture, they were eager consumers of the new media.

Average number of feature films produced

1906-08   1909-10   1911-12   1913-14

224

78

Australia   Germany   Hungary   Italy   UK   USA   Russia

▲ Films grew steadily in length during the early years of the century. In 1903 the 10-minute long *Great Train Robbery* was one of the longest films then made, but by 1914 feature films lasting an hour or more were common.

▶ The spectacle of movement was cinema's earliest attraction, and "scenics" and "topicals" made up much of the program. Narrative fiction films in a variety of genres dominated American output after 1906.

Immigration into USA

1,285,349

Millions

1900   1905   1910   1914

The first media moguls of the 20th century were the publishers of large-circulation American and British newspapers. As in so many other aspects of popular culture, British or American examples set precedents that were followed by the rest of Europe, and then by the world. The newspaper as we recognize it today was an invention of the great American cities: a mixture of news, entertainment and advertising, not formally attached to any political party, and financed as much or more by the advertising it carried as by the income from its low sales price. In 1900 half the world's daily papers were sold in the major cities of the United States.

The press and city life

Concentrating large numbers of people into small and tightly defined geographical areas, American cities provided the mass readership that made the distribution of a daily press practical. Many of the new city dwellers had immigrated from small country towns or from other countries or continents, and their sense of dislocation provided a context for the rise of newspaper reading. Through the wire services and news agencies, newspapers provided word from the migrants' homes. At the turn of the century there were more than a thousand foreign-language daily newspapers published in the United States. Immigrants were many times more likely to read a paper in New York than they had been in their native Minsk or Naples, whether that paper was written in their own language or in the English they were learning as part of their process of Americanization.

Even more importantly, newspapers offered their readers explanations of city life. In their exposés of government corruption, their gossip about the metropolitan elite, and in their scandal-mongering pursuit of "human interest" stories – as William Randolph Hearst put it, stories about "crime and underwear" – they gave substance and form to the anxieties of metropolitan existence. The newspapers proclaimed themselves the people's guardians, in small matters as well as large. One Hearst editorial declared, "The force of the newspaper is the greatest force in civilization. Under republican government, newspapers form and express public opinion. They suggest and control legislation. They declare wars. They punish criminals, especially the powerful. They reward with approving publicity the good deeds of citizens everywhere. The newspapers control the nation because they REPRESENT THE PEOPLE."

In many respects the popular press did represent the people, as part of a conscious policy of appealing to their readership. Hearst and his great rival, Joseph Pulitzer of the *New York*

ENTERTAINMENT IN THE CITY

World, campaigned against corrupt city government and the trusts that controlled railroads and other major industries, and declared their support of laborers, small businessmen and "ordinary people". More spectacularly, the American daily press and their British and European imitators were major proponents of the wave of imperialist sentiment at the turn of the century. Hearst and Pulitzer campaigned furiously for the United States to go to war with Spain over Cuba in 1898, and claimed responsibility for both the war and the victory. In Britain Alfred Harmsworth (later Lord Northcliffe), who launched the *Daily Mail* in 1896 in imitation of the New York papers, doubled that paper's circulation during the Boer War, which it charted with maps and columns of impassioned prose. During World War I Northcliffe, owner of *The Times*, was placed in charge of British propaganda.

Although the press barons were very often

politically active as individuals, the popular dailies were not primarily agencies of political opinion. The tycoons were speculators and promoters much more than they were newsmen. Hearst, a millionaire rich enough to indulge even his most extreme fantasies (and the figure on whom Orson Welles' film *Citizen Kane* was based) frequently felt that the news that actually happened had two disadvantages: it was dull, and it was equally available to his rivals. His answer was to invent news, either through straightforward fakery or through self-publicizing reports of "newsworthy" events his papers themselves promoted. *Collier's Magazine*, describing Hearst's tastes in 1906, was exaggerating only slightly when it suggested, "An ideal morning edition to him would have been one in which the Prince of Wales had gone into vaudeville, Queen Victoria had married her cook, the Pope had issued an encyclical favoring free love,...France had declared war on Germany, the

▼ Cities bred newspapers, and made possible the mass distribution of a daily press. From 1906 the residents of London suburbs could have their papers delivered.

▲ Crowded by their poverty into tenement ghettos in New York, immigrants were exhorted by the press to abandon their Old World customs. Simon Lubin and Christina Krysto satirized the idea of the Melting Pot: "Jump into the cauldron and behold! You emerge new creatures, up to date with new customs, habits, traditions, ideals. Immediately you will become like us; the taint will disappear. Your sacks will be exchanged for the latest Fifth Avenue styles. Your old-fogey notions will give way to the most modern and new-fangled ideas. You will be reborn. In short you will become full-fledged Americans. The magic process is certain. Your money back if we fail."

President of the United States had secured a divorce in order to marry the Dowager Empress of China... and the Sultan of Turkey had been converted to Christianity."

The daily press catered for a new market of urban readers, who were not exclusively interested in news. The press adapted an older formula, used by the 18th-century English radical press and 19th-century Sunday papers, of scandal, crime and popular education. The press barons developed the formula to include new features: comics, advice columns, interviews, sport and fashion pages, and photographs. They also devised ever more elaborate promotional schemes (such as free insurance with a subscription), stunts and guessing competitions. Many of these new developments indicated the importance of women readers. One of the earliest uses to which newspaper photographs were put in the United States was as a way of running beauty contests, which, like fashion, gossip and human interest stories, were thought to appeal more to women

than to men. Evening papers such as Hearst's *New York Evening Journal* were aimed quite specifically at women readers, and at the major retail advertisers seeking their custom. Harmsworth launched the *Daily Mirror* in 1903 as a paper for women.

The rise of advertising

The real novelty of the daily press was not so much its content as the scale of its enterprise and its financing. In the last years of the 19th century, as the range of packaged food and drugs and manufactured goods intended for private consumption dramatically increased, advertising became the mechanism by which the distribution of goods within the economy was stimulated, and regulated. In the 1890s advertising agencies no longer simply sold space in newspapers or magazines. They began to advise their clients on the design and appearance of their advertisements, and as they did so they created a crucial instrument, by which a mass public could be educated to desire the pleasures of consumption. Harmsworth and his American counterparts recognized that the new technology of Linotype typesetting machines and the fast rotary printing presses made possible the rapid mass production of millions of copies of a newspaper or magazine. Circulation became crucial because the larger a paper's circulation the more it could charge advertisers for space. Display advertising replaced the uniform columns of classified advertisements. This new source of revenue and the demands of mass circulation meant that the costs of each copy to the reader were cut to a minimum: in Britain the *Daily Mail* sold for a halfpenny, and took nearly half its income from advertising sales.

The press followed the example of other industries in incorporating into larger chains or groups of publications. New owners such as Hearst, Northcliffe and Arthur Pearson (who founded the *Daily Express* in competition with the *Mail* in 1900) came to recognize the advantages of economies of scale. By 1923 Hearst owned 22 daily and 15 Sunday papers, nine magazines, including *Cosmopolitan* and *Harper's Bazaar*, news and syndication services and a Sunday supplement, the *American Weekly*. His publicists claimed that one American family in four read a Hearst publication. He was the biggest user of paper in the world.

In France, the Parisian press operated in a similar way to the American and British dailies, and *Le Petit Journal* even exceeded them in circulation. The French news agency Havas shared the telegraphic distribution of European news with Reuters of London. However, the extreme centralization of the mass-circulation press in Paris led it to depend too heavily on Parisian high culture and government support, and undermined its commercial popularity. In the rest of Europe the press retained its 19th-century organization until well after World War I, with a much larger number of papers, many of them affiliated to a political party, and most having a small local circulation.

◀ The *Ladies Home Journal* had been founded in 1883 as one of the new breed of magazines aimed at a female readership. It was a lively and informative read, and celebrated its mass appeal ("the magazine with a million") rather than its exclusiveness.

◀ Newspaper-reading became an addictive habit of city-dwellers. This French cartoon comments wryly on the alienation brought to personal life by the anonymity of city life. Too engrossed in reports of disaster and scandal, the passers-by ignore the accident before their eyes.

◀ The staff of *Success*, one of several American magazines which emphasized the middle-class virtues of ardent nationalism, the gospel of work, and sincere admiration for the romance of business and the successful businessmen who figured prominently in both its factual articles and its fiction. Other general interest magazines such as *McClure's*, *Everybody's* and *Collier's*, however, also published some of the "muckraking" journalism which exposed the exploitation of the immigrants, the scale of civic corruption and "the Shame of the Cities", during the Progressive era.

▲ E.J. Marey's moving picture camera.

▼ A nickelodeon in 1906: "Last year it was probably a pawnshop or cigar store. Now the counter has been ripped out, there's a ticket-seller's booth where the show-window was, and an automatic musical barker thunders its noise down on the passer-by." Joseph Medill Patterson.

The early film industry

None of cinema's inventors envisaged the vast entertainment industry that would develop from it, for no such industry, and no public for such an industry, had existed before. The motion picture became *the* central commodity of an amusement industry rather than primarily an instrument of science, an educational tool, or a form of family entertainment, more because of the social organization of the modern industrial city than as a result of any properties inherent in the technology itself. Louis Lumière's *cinematographe*, first exhibited in December 1895 in Paris, was regarded as "the crown and the flower of 19th-century magic"; early in the 20th century Hollywood provided the prototype for a new way of life, teaching the United States and the world the fashionable pleasures of conspicuous consumption.

In the earliest years of cinema no one knew quite what they had invented, or to what purposes it could be put. The technology of motion pictures, like that of magazine printing, was the culmination of 19th-century mechanical research. The goal of recording animal and human motion preoccupied inventors such as Marey and Edweard Muybridge during the third quarter of the century. Marey's "photographic gun", designed in 1882, was a prototype of the film-camera mechanism. With the development of celluloid roll film the technological requirements for cinema were complete; they merely awaited assembly. But Marey and Muybridge had little interest in developing their inventions further. Some, including Muybridge himself, thought that one of the principal uses for film would be as mechanical memories, preserving the moving images of individuals for their family and friends after death. Thomas Edison intended to market the Kinetoscope, which he invented with his assistant William K. Dickson in 1893 as home entertainment for wealthy families. It did not project, so the Kinetoscope could be viewed by only one person at a time, and Edison made his profits from sales of the machines rather than of films. Hoping to sell the Kinetoscope in department stores to middle-class customers, Edison was anticipating television rather than movies.

Cinema was a new commodity, unlike anything previously devised, and its early history was preoccupied with defining what that commodity was. Debates over whether the cinema imitated the theater or was itself a new form provided the esthetic aspect of that preoccupation, but there was more concern about how the new commodity should be sold, and to whom. The

Early European Film

For much of the century's first decade, innovation in film production came more from Europe than the United States, where making movies was still seen as an offshoot of the more profitable business of making equipment. In France Georges Méliès exploited the cinema's capacity for illusion in a series of widely-copied science fiction and fantasy films such as *Journey to the Moon* (1902). At the Gaumont studios Max Linder pioneered the character clown achievements of silent cinema. European innovation kept the American market open; until 1908, nearly half the films shown in New York were European imports, and the largest single producer of films shown in America was the French firm Pathé. Using actors from the *Comédie Français*, the *Film d'Art* company introduced a subtler, less extravagant acting style to the screen. The overt appeal to a higher art tradition was also important in the feature films – expensively produced multiple-reel costume dramas and Biblical epics, such as *Cabiria* – which were first produced in Italy.

World War I drastically curtailed European production, and American distributors used this opportunity to secure a monopoly in their home market and expand their share of world

▲ *Journey to the Moon* (Méliès)

business, by selling at prices with which other companies could not compete. From then on through the twenties Hollywood provided not only the overwhelming majority of the world's movies, but also the stylistic model against which all other national cinemas – even those of India and Japan – would define themselves. The French, Italian, German and British industries never regained their pre-war size.

▼ Thomas Alva Edison, "the Wizard of Menlo Park", where his first research laboratory was situated. Einstein called him "the greatest inventor of all time". As much an entrepreneur as a scientist, he was only interested in experiments that had an immediate industrial application. The tickertape machine, the electric light, and the phonograph were among his inventions, as well as the Kinetoscope he devised with William Dickson.

novelty of moving photographic images was at first enough to guarantee its success, and the Lumières and others exploited this by sending their cameramen/projectionists (the *cinematographe* functioned as both camera and projector) around the world to photograph exotica for exhibition in Europe and United States. The earliest films lasted little more than a minute, and typically featured scenic views, topical events, boxing matches, and circus or vaudeville acts. Music hall and vaudeville theaters became the cinema's first permanent home. A dozen films would be presented together as a single turn among the performing animals, singers and comics, and soon managers noticed their popularity, particularly with the more "select" class of patrons.

The sale of films to vaudeville theaters indicated that manufacturers continued to be unsure of what it was they had to sell. The biggest producers were companies such as Edison, Biograph and Vitagraph, who made films – cheaply and with little technical equipment – merely as a necessary adjunct to their primary business of selling projection equipment. Vaudeville provided a convenient outlet as it spared producers the expense of investing in exhibition facilities of their own, but it provided little incentive for the development of the medium beyond its appeal as visual spectacle.

At first prints of films were sold outright, and vaudeville circuits or individual showmen putting on "tent-shows" would exhibit a film until the end of its physical or commercial life. In 1903 came the first film exchanges, middlemen who bought prints from their producers and rented them out to exhibitors. They created a low-cost distribution system that proved vital to the industry's rapid expansion from 1905 onward. Once films were available for rent rather than

purchase, it became possible to show films not as just one attraction among many on a variety bill, but to open theaters devoted to their exhibition, and to sell a movie show more cheaply than other forms of amusement – for no more than the price of a glass of beer. The first "nickelodeons" (the name came from their five-cent admission charge – in Britain they were called "penny gaffs") opened in 1905, and proved immediately and immensely profitable. Five years later there were 10,000 such theaters in the United States alone, attracting 30 million customers a week.

The increased demand for products from the nickelodeons encouraged American producers to revise their strategies. Since 1897 the leading

◀ By 1912 nickelodeons were rapidly being superseded in the United States by larger, purpose-built theaters, some of them seating over a thousand spectators. With their more comfortable and refined decor, they were designed to attract middle-class audiences, and situated in the more affluent parts of cities. Middle-class women on shopping trips were particularly sought-after customers, their presence a guarantee of the theater's respectability.

"Griffith's tender-hearted film morals go no higher than a level of Christian outrage at human injustice." Sergei Eisenstein

INTOLERANCE

I.TEIL

DER UNTERGANG von BABYLON

VERLEIH: FÜR GANZ DEUTSCHLAND WESTFALIA FILM A.G. BERLIN

◄ The huge set for the Babylonian sequences of *Intolerance*, released in 1916, was probably the most lavish yet constructed. The film's complex structure intercut four stories of intolerance in different epochs, but audiences found its multiple plots difficult to follow, and it did not repeat the success of Griffith's spectacular but controversial *Birth of a Nation* (1915).

▼ Griffith (directing with megaphone) saw himself as a reformer, spreading the message of high culture through the movies, but the Victorian view of family and society which his films presented was rapidly being overtaken.

companies had been engaged in endless legal battles over patents, but in 1908 they combined to form the Motion Picture Patents Company to secure a shared monopoly control over the industry. This decision stabilized the American market and restricted the flow of imports.

The increase in demand from nickelodeons caused changes in the pattern of film production, too. From 1907 there was a marked shift towards the production of fictional narratives, rather than the "scenics" and "topicals" that had featured in earlier programming. This was inspired less by audience preference than by the fact that fictional films could take advantage of the economies of scale provided by mass production in a way that other kinds of filmmaking could not. Unlike topical films, a constant supply of story films could be produced from a purpose-built studio at a predictable cost, and released on a regular schedule. With the development of studios employing stock acting companies, the division of labor in production became more elaborate: the single cameraman responsible for everything was replaced by the director system, in which a director would prepare a scenario, supervise the cast and edit the film, while a cameraman handled the lighting, and shot and processed the film. Studios took their actors from provincial and touring companies.

The increased emphasis on narrative encouraged producers to make longer one-reel films, lasting about 15 minutes. This in turn stimulated the development of more complex techniques. By 1911 films derived their narrative mechanisms, and many of their plots, from the popular theater, from novels, and from magazine short stories. The nickelodeon business took over more and more vaudeville theater buildings and occupied more attractive sites in business or shopping districts to provide comfortable and genteel surroundings for their patrons. The Patents Company's acquiescence to a system of film censorship was also evidence of their strong desire to court respectability.

The Patents Company's monopoly was never complete, and their relatively conservative attitude towards production left room for independent exhibitors such as Adolph Zukor and William Fox to offer the public more innovative films from Europe. Their success provoked independent American producers to imitate them, by reproducing Broadway plays and adapting literary classics. By 1915, when D.W. Griffith made <i>The Birth of a Nation</i> from Thomas Dixon's novel <i>The Clansman</i>, the photoplay, a four- or five-reel feature film telling a complete story and carrying a moral lesson, had become the norm for most producers. By then, too, the stylistic techniques for constructing a narrative had been established. A continuous line of action was provided, with events closely linked together to ensure spectator involvement, and the way time and space were used was firmly controlled to ensure that the audience could follow the action.

Hollywood and its stars

Hollywood itself had also come into being. From 1908, production companies sent film units to California to make use both of its reliable climate and of the range of scenery, far wider than that available in New York, Chicago or Florida. Cheap real estate prices and labor costs, together with a cooperative civic administration, made Los Angeles an obvious choice, and production was concentrated there during the 1910s. Hollywood's "commercialized amusement" offered the world something more than mere entertainment; the American film industry was already learning how to teach America, and then the world, how to consume. As early as 1917 "Hollywood" was no longer just a suburb of Los Angeles; it had become an almost mythical place in which work and play were indistinguishable. Young, beautiful, successful movie stars with high incomes provided role models for their audiences and demonstrated the pleasures of the culture of consumption and the enjoyment of leisure. Stars projected a new morality, which demonstrated that leisure, and even sensuality, were no longer sinful.

Nevertheless, the "lower" elements in early American film production have endured more firmly than the feature films – perhaps because they now seem in keeping with the idea of the American cinema as a working-class and immigrant entertainment. The slapstick comedy short

As films became longer and narrative more complex, so techniques and conventions of story-telling were developed – notably intercutting, close-ups, fade-outs and flashbacks. Posters advertised the complexity of their narrative line to draw in the audience.

▼ Mack Sennett took his Keystone comedy troupe to Hollywood in 1912, and by the following year their anarchic mix of clowning and car chases had won a wide audience.

films of Mack Sennett and Charlie Chaplin were criticized for their vulgarity. In their joyous celebration of chaos, knockabout comedies ridiculed some of the most treasured values of contemporary society. Property and the law were treated with an anarchic contempt that in another context might have seemed subversive. Yet, the Sennett characters were never imbued with individual personality. In their hectic collisions with machines, their automobiles might explode or career off cliffs, but the heroes always emerged unscathed. Chaplin's work also revealed a strong streak of sentimentality which made his humor much less threatening even while celebrating the exuberance of a less restrained social order.

► In 1905 Hollywood was little more than a farming village, almost a week's traveling time away from New York. The first movie studios were established in the next three or four years, and the Biograph Company made its first film in the area in 1910. By 1915, when the Universal Studios were opened, Hollywood's climate and convenient access to Los Angeles had encouraged the establishment of all the major American filmmaking companies there.

Ragtime and dance

To one veteran songwriter and publisher the 1910s marked a crucial turning point: "The public of the nineties had asked for tunes to sing," Edward S. Marks remarked nostalgically, "but the public from 1910 demanded tunes to dance to." The tunes in question, provided by the songwriting production lines of New York's Tin Pan Alley, were "rags", snappy, syncopated numbers; the dances were close-contact "animal" dances like the Turkey Trot and the Grizzly Bear. The sources for both of these lay in the black subculture of the late 19th century.

Ragtime had emerged in the United States in the post-Civil War era, rapidly maturing in the hands of pianist-composers such as Scott Joplin (whose "Maple Leaf Rag" was composed in 1899) into a meticulously crafted piano music in which European marching tempos and harmony engaged in a subtle dialog with Afro-American approaches to rhythm. Meanwhile, the cakewalk – a stylized display dance that combined black mockery of white dance steps with the black culture's own approach to movement – had begun to appear in polite white society, where it met with the energetic two-steps of the March King, John Philip Sousa. The establishment of public venues – cabarets, dance halls, restaurants – meant that dancing ceased to be a predominantly private affair. By the 1910s, discovery of the physically emancipating effect of black folk dance had led to a flood of popular new steps.

For the first time styles of music and dance for white America positively encouraged individual expression and suggested that the immediate moment was to be fully savored, even though dancers still had to share in a prescribed pattern. The premier dance couple of the era, Britons Irene and Vernon Castle, led the way.

The Castles managed to combine a trend-setting image as liberalizers of behavior with an air of middle-class moral respectability. This helped to resolve the controversy that developed as custodians of moral and esthetic standards argued over the merits of the new music and dance. Where one critic delighted in the "delicacy of ragtime's inner rhythms", another deplored its "jerk and rattle"; what to some eyes embodied the new "spirit of America" was to others decadent drivel. Underlying the arguments of opponents lay the (by no means always unspoken) fear of racial contamination, not only from the black source of the music and dance, but also from the white ethnic (especially Jewish) groups who dominated Tin Pan Alley's modernized song machine. The marginal status of these groups in American society allowed them readily to identify with the black approach, and also encouraged the use of popular culture as a means of social and economic advancement.

The moral opponents' argument was correct in one respect: more than mere entertainment was at stake. The part of American society that espoused the new styles of music and dance began to absorb, via white ethnic groups, attitudes and practices from the black community. It also raised fundamental questions about the family, about gender and race, and – above all – about the

Sheet Music

The mass production of popular songs in sheet-music form began in the United States in around 1885. Sales reached their zenith in the 1910s, when, with the price as low as 10 cents, stores like Woolworth's helped push annual totals up around 200 million copies. Rags and novelty songs abounded, responding to the demand for songs to be danceable. But the ballad outsold them all, peaking in 1918 with Egan and Whiting's World War I hit, *Till We Meet Again*, said to have sold 3.5 million copies in a matter of months.

A less precisely focused kind of sentimentality distinguished these ballads from their predecessors. But other factors were even more important. Here were songs which, more widely disseminated than any before, were also more capable of being privately owned by each listener. By a strange, often repeated paradox, the better a song was known, the more people seemed able to use it as a way of managing private emotion. This was achieved partly through the lyrics, as songwriters gradually developed the skill of making their words seem relevant to the widest possible audience, but principally through the music – very largely the work of immigrant or second-generation Jewish songwriters. In this music there began to emerge that hard-to-define interplay between subtly shifting rhythms and plaintive harmony which became characteristically American.

Sheet music for cabaret, operetta and music-hall songs was widely available throughout Europe, although the popular-music publishing industry was not so highly developed in Europe as across the Atlantic. In many countries sheet music brought a popularized version of music. Already it was rare for popular-music trends to flow westwards across the Atlantic.

▶ **Sheet music covers of the 1900s.**

► Dances such as the Grizzly Bear, derived from black styles, spread rapidly to Europe. Here, in pre-war Paris, actress Gaby Deslys and her husband demonstrate the potent combination of vigorous movement and bodily contact. While some dancers tempered sexual explicitness, others were less ambiguously sensual.

◄ The wonders of recorded sound are experienced for the first time – for a nickel in the slot – in turn-of-the-century Kansas. Listening to this early juke box, one girl later remembered, was a "magic treat". The sound might have been a Sousa march or an operatic aria – whichever, the potential of recording to offer entertainment was recognized early on by the inventor of the revolving disc, Emile Berliner, whose company soon began marketing the gramophone specifically for the home.

body; for it was to the body's still unexplored capacity for expression that the music and dance most obviously related. The music still had a predictable, march-like meter, the legacy and symbol of a relentless, regularizing value system; what gave it a new, unique character was syncopation, the "offbeat", with the accent placed against the expectations of the pulse. Jazz would soon take this much farther than ragtime, but a crucial point had been made: the control of the regular meter could be challenged – not by outright opposition, but by a change of emphasis.

Black performance style and musicality had interacted with European conventions before, but this was the first time its impact had been so clear. Yet even while appropriating this music, mainstream society neutralized its more expressive qualities. Unsure emotionally, self-conscious in display, at once fascinated and repelled by the implications of the music, the dancing public – taking their cue from leaders like the Castles – attempted to resolve the dilemmas by quickening the rhythms. What had been a subtle music became a display of good-humored impudence and respectable candor, which offered the sexes greater opportunity for intimacy, but froze the hand and eye in order to speed the foot.

The dance craze of the 1910s can be seen as an early example in 20th-century popular culture of the conflict between a liberating force and a conservative tendency. Opposition to developments was to play a part in the story of popular music but the mainstream's capacity for assimilation was to prove even more important.

VAUDEVILLE AND MUSIC HALL

Before ragtime and the new dances captured the public imagination the musical stage was preeminent in the provision of commercial entertainment in both Europe and America. A range of closely related styles had been developed (minstrelsy, vaudeville, music hall, burlesque, revue), presented in a sequence of separate performers. Only revue made an attempt at dramatic cohesion, thereby growing close to comic opera, another popular form. In all except the latter, the transatlantic traffic in people, styles and ideas was two-way. The European variety show, particularly as practiced in British music halls, provided the main model for American vaudeville, while the growth in blackface minstrelsy in Britain had quickly followed its rise to popularity in America.

The origins of British music hall lay in the disparate types of stand-up entertainment common in working-class pubs and supper-rooms. By the 1850s it had coalesced into an identifiable yet heterogeneous form. At first associated with making profits for the drink industry, the halls gradually developed a form of entertainment which was itself marketable, and by 1880 this formula, commercially underwritten and professionally executed, was dominant. Around this time, too, the audience widened to include the middle classes.

Music hall and vaudeville intertwined culture and commerce, setting up the tensions so frequently encountered in 20th-century popular culture. But an equally important legacy was the way in which that tension was undermined through a collaboration between humor and musical eclecticism.

▲ The popularity of minstrelsy – white musicians singing black music with blackened faces – in the United States has been ascribed to a complex of factors involving the social function of racial stereotypes. The same conclusions are harder to draw elsewhere. Curiosity about America and – ironically – abolitionist sympathies were chiefly responsible for its popularity. Minstrel shows were usually staged as family entertainment.

▼ Whoever owned the music halls, nobody could make a London audience feel the culture was theirs better than Marie Lloyd (1870–1922). Appearing in her regal finery, her songs full of street innuendos, she established a "collusive intimacy" with her audience – "one of us", hobnobbing with respectable folk, hinting at subversion. Whether the actual result was subversive or whether it tended to persuade people to accept established society is still a matter of debate.

▼One form of American entertainment never established itself across the Atlantic. The Wild West show, first staged at an open-air arena in New York in 1883 by erstwhile Indian fighter "Buffalo Bill" Cody, marketed its own version of the history of the West to vast audiences for over 20 years. It remained popular, so long as it remained outdoors.

▶The standard format for music-hall entertainment – a succession of unconnected acts – permitted performers to appear at several venues each night. As programs grew longer, dramatic sketches became more ambitious and the number of novelty acts increased. But the comic song retained its popularity, and the comic singer reigned supreme.

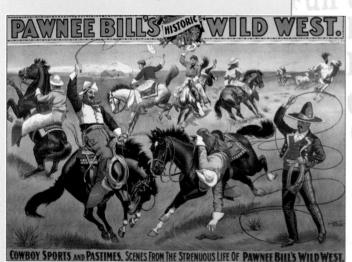

COWBOY SPORTS AND PASTIMES. SCENES FROM THE STRENUOUS LIFE OF PAWNEE BILL'S WILD WEST.

▲ Riotous behaviour was not unknown in music-hall audiences, but when Marie Lloyd sang *Boy in the Gallery* rapt attention was more likely. Walter Sickert's painting of an engrossed gallery audience also reveals that music halls were fairly opulent.

◄ By the turn of the century in Europe the revue had spread from its Parisian base to other centers, most notably in Berlin. In the years before the outbreak of war an international circuit of performers developed, one as open to the British song-and-dance troupe called the "Gala-Girls" as to more established stars.

THE FIRST STARS

Before 1910 the movies had discovered that stars sold cinema tickets; the earliest stars were former stage actors like comic John Bunny or Bronco Billy Anderson, billed in 1912 as "The World's Greatest Photoplay Star". But the greatest stars of Hollywood's formative years were Douglas Fairbanks and Mary Pickford. From 1914 they, with Charlie Chaplin, achieved a celebrity quite unlike anything ever seen before them. More than the scale of their popularity, what made stardom a new phenomenon was that it detached fame from achievement in the strenuous life of work or battle.

Readers of the fan magazines that began to appear in 1912 became as familiar with their idols' off–screen lives as with their movie appearances. Chaplin's "little tramp" first appeared in 1914, and was an immediate success with audiences. But Charles Chaplin the actor behaved quite differently from Charlie the clown. Pickford and Fairbanks projected the same image on screen and off, and between them they offered their audiences new role models.

Fairbanks' comedies ridiculed Victorian restrictions on fun. In newspaper columns and books such as *Laugh and Live* and *Make Life Worth-while*, he advocated sport as a means of regenerating the urban masses. In *His Picture in the Papers*, made in 1916, Fairbanks played the rebellious son of a dour cereal manufacturer. He learned to box, became attractive to women, and rescued a big businessman from criminals. Asked the secret of his strength, he advertised his father's cereal. Sales improved now it was associated with robust fun-lovers.

Mary Pickford embodied the "new woman": healthy, robust, self–reliant, she combined sexual allure with chastity. "Little Mary", "America's Sweetheart", was more popular even than Chaplin. In 1916, she became the first star to be the producer of her own films. In them, she brought out the spontaneity and playfulness which Victorian culture had repressed in women. Emancipated and even a suffragist, in her performances she questioned the female role in the family and at work. When she married Fairbanks in 1920, the Hollywood mansion they built, Pickfair, became famous as a paradise in which high-level consumption was advertised as the basis for a secure and stable family life.

▲▶ Douglas Fairbanks and Mary Pickford, the first King and Queen of Hollywood, taught America that success could best be expressed in the world of leisure. His good-humored athleticism celebrated the male body. She became the "most popular girl in the world" by combining independence and innocence in a "radiant image of girlish beauty" that showed she was "old fashioned but not a prude". After marrying they toured Europe; in Moscow a crowd of 300,000 greeted them.

▶▶ In 1918 Fairbanks, Pickford, Chaplin and Western star William S. Hart traveled the country, raising millions of dollars for Liberty Loans to help the war effort (center image and far right). The next year, together with director D.W. Griffith, they founded United Artists to market and exploit their pictures. One Hollywood wit observed, "So the lunatics have taken charge of the asylum," but in the fast-growing Hollywood of 1920 (main image) it made sound commercial sense to protect their interests.

PICKFORD-FAIRBANKS STUDIOS

Datafile

The years around 1900 saw both a rise in interest in organized sport throughout Europe and the United States, and a tendency for international organization and serious competition. The ethos of much sport was strictly amateur: at the 1912 Olympics, the American athlete Jim Thorpe, winner of the decathlon and pentathlon, was stripped of his medals after admitting to having once accepted $25 for playing baseball in a minor league.

There was widespread concern to improve the physical fitness of the working classes, which led to an interest in gymnastics. The political dimension of this concern meant that, between 1914 and 1918, almost half the volunteers for Britain's armed forces had been recruited at soccer grounds.

The pressure for urban recreational facilities led to increased municipal provision of facilities such as recreation grounds, gymnasia and public swimming pools in many countries.

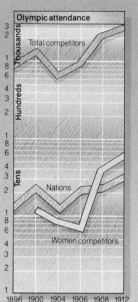

Olympic attendance

◀ The United States established its domination of the modern Olympics at the second meeting, in Paris, but their superiority at St Louis was fairly meaningless as few European countries took an interest in the Games. For the London Games, a large new stadium was built, with a crowd capacity of 66,000.

▲ In the first three modern Olympic Games, at Athens, Paris and St Louis, there was no real national team organization; the Games were treated as a part of the World's Fairs going on at the same time, and some bizarre events (such as barrel-jumping) were included. The 1908 Games were the first organized by sporting bodies.

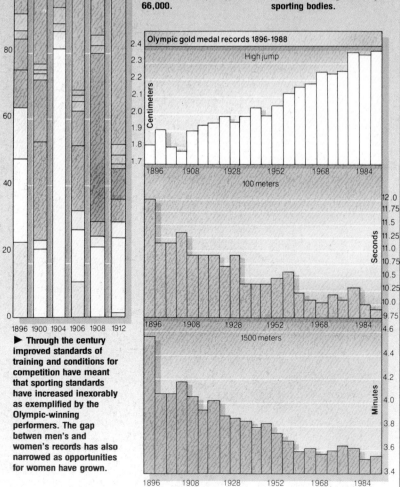

Gold medals 1896-1912

Canada, Germany, Hungary, USA, Denmark, Greece, UK, Others, France

▶ Through the century improved standards of training and conditions for competition have meant that sporting standards have increased inexorably as exemplified by the Olympic-winning performers. The gap between men's and women's records has also narrowed as opportunities for women have grown.

Olympic gold medal records 1896-1988

High jump

100 meters

1500 meters

Before 1900 many sports had developed from local adaptations of traditional folk games into organized activities with uniform rules, special playing kit, cups and trophies, team colors and caps. The most influential setting for the modernization of sports was provided by the British public schools.

British school sports

In the 19th century, football and cricket – the two major British sports – were unrestrained affairs, played in different ways in different schools, not much more than savage battles in which older boys could assert their dominance over younger ones. Their transformation into modern sports resulted largely from the reforming influence of the new industrial middle classes who sent their sons to the public schools to be educated with the gentry; they turned games into a form of discipline. Organized school sports became compulsory instruments of socialization and moral education for the elite young men destined to become leaders of the Empire. Rules limited aggression and ensured "fair play". The games-playing cult, designed to produce disciplined, self-reliant and socially responsible "muscular Christians", had, as its central theme, *Mens sana in corpore sano* (A healthy mind in a healthy body). Games were also seen as channels of sexual sublimation, sufficiently ascetic and exhausting to eliminate "indecent" expressions of sexuality.

Matches between schools became social events watched by huge crowds. The athletic public schoolboy was revered as a hero at school and ex-alted in the press. During the first decade of the 20th century the fiercely amateur cult of athleticism became an obsession in the public schools. But the idea of moral excellence and character training associated with sports did little to inhibit the aggressive display of physical power.

Sports in public schools were never truly virtuous and "civilized" activities. The desire to win was always part of the amateur sporting tradition of the British. The sports cults of the public schools celebrated competitiveness and expressions of brute male power. Violent competitive sport provided a dominant image of sport in Britain and throughout the world.

Organized sport proliferated in universities and independent sports clubs formed by ex-public schoolboys. By 1900 national associations, responsible for codifying rules and administering competitions, existed for football, rugby, cricket, yachting, skating, boxing, rowing, lawn tennis, croquet, hockey, gymnastics, lacrosse (originally a North American game) and badminton. Britain, the world's major sporting nation, exported its sports (and usually their rules) as an element of its

SPORT: THE BRITISH INHERITANCE

cultural imperialism. But while football went to Europe and Latin America in its Association form, in Australia and North America it developed indigenous forms, based on Gaelic football.

International sporting events

The inauguration of international associations, for football in 1904 and lawn tennis in 1913, accelerated international competition. The modern Olympic movement and its organizing body, the International Olympic Committee (IOC), was founded in 1895 by Pierre de Coubertin. It was the exemplar for international amateur sport, in which the contestants participate without being paid. In common with other international bodies, it was controlled by middle- and upper-class men with economic power and elitist ideas. Almost all the athletes who competed in the first Olympics, and the bulk of those who took part in Olympic competition before World War I, were wealthy

► A gold medal from the first modern Olympics, held in Athens in 1896.

▼ Jingoistic Londoners urge on marathon runners in the 1908 Olympics.

Beauty of face and form is one of the chief essentials (for women), but unlimited indulgence in violent, outdoor sports, cricket, bicycling, beagling, otter-hunting, paper-chasing, and – most odious of all games for women – hockey, cannot but have an unwomanly effect on a young girl's mind, no less on her appearance. Let young girls ride, skate, dance and play lawn tennis and other games in moderation, but let them leave field sports to those for whom they are intended – men.

BADMINTON MAGAZINE

▼ Winter sports gained in popularity during the second half of the 19th century, and figure skating was one event open to women at the 1908 Olympics. The first Winter Olympics were held in 1924.

◄ Although gymnastics was accepted as a form of therapeutic exercise for women, competition was deemed unladylike and even unhealthy. The male-dominated organizing body of the modern Olympic movement, the IOC, barred women's gymnastics and track-and-field events until the 1928 Olympics.

▼ During the early 20th century, golf was among the few sports considered acceptable for women of fashion and leisure. Amateur golfing championships for women were first held in Britain in 1893, and in the United States in 1895.

amateur, as opposed to professional, sportsmen, which left an indelible mark on the development of international sport and militated against athletes from less privileged backgrounds. The Olympic movement was inspired by the ideal that the Games would promote harmony between nations, but as early as 1908 there were nationalistic conflicts, commercial interference and disputes over amateur status.

During the 19th century plebian sports such as folk football had virtually been eliminated by legal prohibitions. During the 20th century, new patterns of recreation for the working classes developed. Preoccupied with the moral character of workers' activities inside and outside the factory, churches, schools, local government, industry and the military established clubs to provide them with respectable, organized sports.

Many professional football clubs had religious or industrial origins. Socio-religious organizations such as the Young Men's Christian Association (YMCA) and the Boy Scouts introduced drill, gymnastic exercises and sports that demanded strict control of the body, to promote the "habits of obedience, smartness and order" that were required for work in the factory and action on the field of battle.

There was also growing interest in sport in political circles. The Boer War had shown how few British recruits were physically fit. Success on the playing fields was related to success on the battlefields of the Empire. But the imperialist ideology of "training mind and body for the Empire's need" was applied differently to young men from different social classes: while public schoolboys were being urged to "play up and play the game" to develop their initiative and leadership qualities for military conquest abroad, working-class youths were being encouraged to develop fitness and alertness for following orders. Sport could induce habits of deference as well as dominance.

Many sports clubs had an exclusively middle- and upper-class membership; polo and yachting clubs, for example, restricted membership and charged fees only the rich could afford. Golf was also a predominantly upper- and middle-class game though there were some municipal golf courses. Tennis proliferated in the garden suburbs, and water sports, riding and other field sports were popular with the middle classes. There were sports available for people from all backgrounds, such as cycling, rambling and athletics as well as football, cricket and rugby, but they took place in separate clubs for people with different class backgrounds. There was little mixed-class sport of any sort.

Women and sport
There was a popular idea that women were unsuited to take part in vigorous sports. Only moderate exercise, without overindulgence or risk of strain, was considered suitable for females and their potential to have healthy children. They might enjoy sports such as tennis and gymnastics, which were considered appropriate for women, or remedial and therapeutic forms of exercise, but women faced serious opposition and harsh ridicule if they wanted to participate in traditional male sports, which were supposed to have disabling and de-sexing characteristics.

Nevertheless, the first two decades of the 20th century saw the gradual expansion of a variety of female sports. Croquet, tennis, golf, badminton and skating were all fashionable middle-class sports. Cycling allowed women a new physical independence, and symbolized their revolt against the restrictions of tight-lacing. Women's participation in hockey, netball, lacrosse, rounders, gymnastics, cricket, athletics and swimming was possible only because they were played in "ladylike" fashion. These sports were played separately from the sports of men, in clubs, girls' schools, universities and colleges, and so did not constitute a direct challenge to men. In urban areas many women's sports clubs were attached

to polytechnics and attracted young working women from nearby shops and offices. The "Poly" girls became the pin-ups of the sporting world, providing the impetus for a more general acceptance of female sport and a gradual increase in working-class participation. As sport became increasingly popular, the public image of the new sportswoman was reproduced elsewhere.

The modern Olympics remained a bastion of male sporting privilege and an unambiguous celebration of male supremacy and physical prowess. Prolonged struggle and protest were required before women were officially permitted to take part. In 1908 only 36 women competed, in lawn tennis, archery, figure skating and yachting; there were 2,023 male athletes.

The rise of spectator sports

British football, as it developed in the state school system and clubs, transformed ideas about what modern sport means. By 1910 there were 300,000 football players in 12,000 clubs registered with the Football Association (FA). After 1900, market forces increasingly replaced paternalism, and professional football was promoted by business patrons who saw opportunities to exploit the new mass demand for entertainment. Football led the way toward the general commercialization of sport. Larger, professional clubs were successful commercial ventures, attracting huge crowds and deriving their revenue from gate money and sales of food and drinks. The FA Cup Final attracted enormous numbers of spectators: 120,000 in 1913. Watching professional football became central to the culture of the working classes, and spectators deeply concerned for victory and vociferously partisan, gave it a unique character. The popularity of football developed into a mania. Professional football teams from Britain toured abroad. Players and coaches became emissaries of the game, transmitting skills around the world.

Other spectator sports had also become highly popular and profitable. In 1913 there were 1-kilometer (half-mile) queues on Men's finals day at the Wimbledon Tennis Championships, and touts were selling £1 tickets for £10. The popularity of spectator sport had a knock-on effect, acting as an incentive for people to participate themselves, and for entrepreneurs to profit from sales of sports equipment, clothing and medication. Working-class people avidly followed sports of all kinds: by 1900 there were 25 sporting newspapers in London alone and daily papers were sprouting sports pages. A foreign visitor declared, "All is sport in England.... It is sucked in with the mother's milk."

By World War I sport had become a major industry, and the essential characteristics of professional sport were established. There were separate amateur and professional leagues and competitions, sporting heroes and unruly fan behavior. Sport was increasingly used as a publicity medium by politicians and other public figures. Those who owned sport wielded power: most professional players were working-class, owned and controlled, bought and sold, and subjected to strict disciplinary procedures imposed by wealthy businessmen. There were struggles

The Spread of Boxing

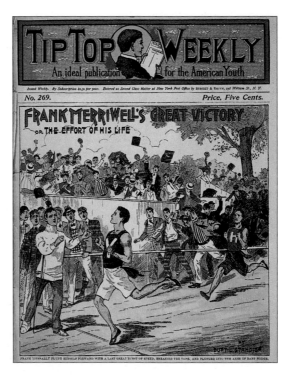

◀ The American magazine *Tip Top Weekly* celebrated the middle-class ethos of the amateur sporting endeavor in this cover illustration. The ideal, that participation and fair play was more important than victory, derived from the British public-school tradition, but even there, winning remained a significant objective.

between players and employers over the minimum wage and the transfer system, and though players' unions were formed, the players nonetheless remained in a weak position.

Popular spectator sport was promoted as an escape from the hardships and poverty of working-class life, and became an extremely effective vehicle of social control. The ruling classes valued it as a socially more acceptable pursuit than political or criminal activities, but working men found football exciting. Its hard physical contact reflected the tough life they were accustomed to. It became an integral part of their lives, and an important setting for male bonding.

▶ The British Soccer club Manchester United in its FA Cup-winning year of 1909. As in most football clubs of this period, the players were professionals, coming from a working-class background, but the club was in the hands of a local brewing magnate. It was unusual for such a club to be controlled by one man: by 1914 most British clubs were limited-liability companies, with a wide range of shareholders.

Boxing was encouraged at amateur level by moralists who argued for the benefits it would bestow on working-class boys: "Like dancing, boxing should be rescued from its evil associations and its educational force put to do moral work. At best, it is indeed a manly art, a separate school for quickness of hand and eye, decision, 'force of will' and self-control. The moment this is lost, stinging punishment follows. Hence it is the surest way of all cures for excessive irascibility and has been found to have a most beneficial effect upon the peevish or unmanly disposition."

The amateur sport was organized and given new rules in Britain in 1880, and in the United States four years later. Professional boxing before 1914 in the United States was dominated by Irish and European immigrants, although Joe Gans and Jack Johnson were black fighters who became world champions in the early 1900s despite encountering strong racial prejudice.

◀ An impromptu boxing match in 1905.

◀ Charlie Murphy, the American bicycle champion, was the first man to cycle one mile (1.6 km) in 60 seconds, and won a brief celebrity for his achievement. The interest in such sporting records as achievements in their own right, distinct from the fact of winning or losing, was developed through the sporting press and became particularly important in the 1920s.

1914 · 1929

THE
MODERNIST
WORLD

Time Chart

	1915	1916	1917	1918	1919	1920	1921	1922
Film	● 8 Feb: Release of DW Griffith's *The Birth of a Nation* (USA)	● Technicolor process first used, in *The Gulf Between* (USA) ● *Intolerance*, by DW Griffith (USA)	● Chaplin signed a contract with First National, worth $1 million annually (USA)	● First Tarzan film, *Tarzan of the Apes*, released (USA) ● 25 Aug: War Industries Board declared moving pictures an essential industry (USA)	● *The Cabinet of Dr Caligari* (Erich Pommer) (Ger) ● 17 Apr: United Artists Corp founded by Chaplin, Pickford, Fairbanks and Griffith (USA) ● 27 Apr: National Association of the Motion Picture Industry agreed to submit films to censorship (USA)	● Marriage of Mary Pickford and Douglas Fairbanks (USA)	● First full-length feature talkie, *Dream Street* (dir DW Griffith) produced by United Artists (USA) ● *The Sheik*, with Rudolph Valentino (USA)	● 5 Mar: Premiere of *Nosferatu* by FW Murnau (Ger) ● 21 Apr: Lee De Forest invented device to record voice and image on the same film (USA)
Media	● 5 Jun: Recital by Dame Nellie Melba broadcast from Chelmsford (UK), heard throughout Europe			● Feb: *New York Times* began home delivery (USA)		● Feb: First public radio station set up by Marconi (USA)		● Sound effects first used on radio ● 5 Feb: *Reader's Digest* magazine first published (USA) ● Oct: Foundation of the British Broadcasting Company (licence given 18 Jan 1923)
Music			● 7 Mar: First jazz record, *Dixieland Jazz Band One-Step*, issued by Victor (USA)		● Rise in popularity of jazz in Europe, after end of the war	● *Whispering/The Japanese Sandman*, by Paul Whiteman, became the first record to sell one million copies (USA) ● Disk autochanger first devised by HMV (UK)	● 2 Aug: Death of Enrico Caruso (It) from pleurisy, at 48 ● Opening of first public record-lending library, in Detroit (USA)	● Dance marathons a craze (USA)
Fashion and Design	● World's first motor scooter, the Auto-Ped, marketed (USA) ● Feb: Opening of San Francisco World's Fair (USA) ● Design and Industries Association founded in UK, modelled on Deutscher Werkbund ● Sharp Co. founded to manufacture propelling pencils (Jap)	● First artificial silk (rayon) knitwear marketed (USA) ● John Redfern (UK) designed the first women's uniform for the Red Cross ● Coco Chanel (Fr) made jersey, then an underwear fabric, chic ● British edition of *Vogue* launched ● Erté (Rus) began drawing covers for *Harper's Bazaar* (USA)	● Gerrit Rietveld (Neth) designed his Red-Blue chair ● US Navy equipped windproof flying jackets with "zippers"	● National Design Organization founded in Norway	● Europe's first mass-produced car, Citröen Type A, launched (Fr) ● Bauhaus design school opened in Germany, with architect Walter Gropius as its first director ● Suzanne Lenglen (Fr) shocked Wimbledon by wearing designer Jean Patou's short sleeveless tennis dresses	● Commercially viable acetate fiber made by British Celanese Ltd (UK) ● First rib-knit elasticized one-piece bathing suit made by the Jantzen Co. (USA) ● French edition of *Vogue* launched ● Avant-garde magazine *L'Esprit Nouveau* founded by architect Le Corbusier (Fr)	● Charles Jourdan (Fr) set up shoe workshop ● Coco Chanel (Fr) introduced her No. 5 perfume	● Discovery of tomb of Pharaoh Tutankhamun, increasing the popularity of Egyptian motifs in design ● *Le Jardin des Modes* fashion magazine first published (Fr) ● V Margueritte's novel *La Garçonne* idealized the androgynous gamine (Fr)
Sport	● Jan: Wimbledon tennis tournament suspended for duration of war (UK) ● Feb: Cancellation of planned 1916 Berlin Olympic Games (Ger)	● Establishment of South American championship in association football		● Invention of orienteering (Swe) ● Foundation of the Budokwai, Europe's first judo club, in London (UK)	● Mechanical hare perfected for greyhound racing (USA) ● Jack Dempsey (USA) won world heavyweight boxing title for first time, with record ticket sales of $1 million	● Jul: Suzanne Lenglen (Fr) became the first player to win all three Wimbledon tennis titles ● Aug: Opening of Antwerp Olympic Games (Belg)		● Aug: Unofficial women's Olympic Games held in Paris (Fr)
Misc.	● May: SS *Lusitania* (USA) sunk by German U-boat		● Apr: USA declared war on Germany ● Nov: Bolshevik Revolution	● Feb: Women over 30 given vote (UK) ● 11 Nov: Armistice on Western Front		● Jan: Beginning of Prohibition (USA) ● Aug: Women given the vote in USA		

1923	1924	1925	1926	1927	1928	1929
• Release of *The Ten Commandments*, by CB de Mille (USA)	• 4 May: Opening of *Men*, with Pola Negri (USA) • May: American Society of Composers, Authors and Publishers (ASCAP) denounced film and radio as "parasitic" (USA)	• *Battleship Potemkin*, directed by Sergei Eisenstein, released (USSR) • Aug: *The Gold Rush*, starring Charlie Chaplin, released (USA)	• Release of *Metropolis*, directed by Fritz Lang (Ger) • Release of *Ben Hur*, directed by Fred Niblo (USA) • 23 Aug: Death of Rudolph Valentino, aged 31 (USA) • Aug: *Don Juan* talkie released by Vitaphone, the film synchronized with phonograph records (USA)	• Clara Bow achieved fame as the It Girl (USA) • *Napoleon*, directed by Abel Gance (Fr) • 5 Jan: Movietone introduced by Fox (USA) • 19 Apr: Mae West imprisoned for indecency in her film *Sex* (USA) • May: *They're Coming to Get Me*, first film with dialog, released (USA) • 6 Oct: Release of *The Jazz Singer* starring Al Jolson, the first widely seen talkie (USA)	• Walt Disney created his first Mickey Mouse cartoon, *Steamboat Willie* (USA) • 21 Jul: Release of the first full-length all-talking movie, with sound on film: *The Lights of New York* (USA)	• Douglas Fairbanks Jnr married Joan Crawford (USA) • Opening of *Pandora's Box*, starring Louise Brooks, directed by GW Pabst (Ger) • First Academy Awards ceremony (USA) • 5 Mar: Opening of *Broadway Melody*, the first film musical (USA)
• Foundation of *Time* magazine (USA) • Mar: Daily weather forecast first broadcast by BBC (UK) • Sep: Foundation of *Radio Times* magazine (UK)	• Feb: Radio used for educational purposes by Columbia University (USA)	• Feb: First issue of *New Yorker* magazine	• 27 Jan: John Logie Baird demonstrated television in London (UK) • 30 Apr: Opening of radio picture service between London and the *New York Times*	• 1 Jan: Incorporation of British Broadcasting Corporation (UK) • 25 Mar: First outside sports broadcast, of the Grand National, by BBC (UK) • Oct: Fox's *Movietone News*, the first sound newsfilm, released (USA)	• 4 Jan: NBC organized a broadcasting hook-up covering 48 states and dozens of well-known entertainers (USA) • 8 Feb: Television pictures broadcast by JL Baird from London to New York	• Color television demonstrated at Bell Laboratories (USA) • Tintin cartoon first appeared in *The 20th Century* newspaper (Belg)
• 12 Feb: Premiere of *Rhapsody in Blue*, by George Gershwin (USA) • Rise in popularity of the Charleston		• Josephine Baker (USA/Fr) danced in *La Revue Nègre* in Paris	• Opening of *Gentlemen Prefer Blondes* on Broadway (USA) • Soundtrack for *Don Juan* produced on the first 33⅓rpm disks (USA)	• 27 Dec: Broadway opening of *Showboat*, directed by Florenz Ziegfeld (USA)	• Opening of *The Threepenny Opera*, by Kurt Weill and Bertolt Brecht (Ger) • Columbia (EMI) took over Pathé (UK)	• *Happy Days are Here Again* popular song (USA) • Jul: Decca launched by Edward Lewis
	• Diaghilev's ballet *Le Train Bleu*, with designs by Chanel, epitomized the fashion for the sporting life (Fr) • Hairdresser Antoine created fashion for dying gray hair blue (UK) • Apr: Opening of British Empire Exhibition in London (UK)	• Opening of Exposition Internationale des Arts Décoratifs et Industriels Modernes in Paris (Fr) • Fashion designer Madeleine Vionnet (Fr) began to use the bias cut, and female curves returned to vogue	• Wide range of synthetic colors for paint launched by Du Pont (USA) • Anthropometric survey results used in Berlei Co's underwear designs (Aus)	• Prototype factory-assembled house, the Dymaxion House, designed by Buckminster Fuller (USA) • Architect Mies van der Rohe organized the first postwar Deutscher Werkbund exhibition, launching the International Style (Ger)	• Ecole de la Chambre Syndicale de la Couture established to teach the craft of fashion (Fr) • Harley Earl (USA) put in charge of General Motors new Art and Color section • Design magazine *Domus* founded, edited by Gio Ponti (It)	• Raymond Loewy designed streamlined duplicator for Gestetner Co. (USA)
• Wembley Stadium, the first national multi-sport center, opened in London (UK) • Yankee Stadium opened in New York (USA) • First speedway race meeting held, in New South Wales (Aus)	• Jan: First Winter Olympic Games held, at Chamonix (Fr) • Jul: Paris Olympics attended by 42 nations (but not Germany) • Jul: American Johnny Weissmuller became the first man to swim 100m in less than 1 minute		• First Central American and Caribbean Games held, in Mexico City (Mex) • Women's Cricket Association formed (UK) • Aug: Gertrude Ederle (USA) became the first woman to swim the English Channel	• 20-21 May: Charles Lindbergh made the first nonstop solo flight across the Atlantic (USA) • First Ryder Cup held in golf (USA) • Sep: Babe Ruth hit his 60th home run of the baseball season, a record that stood for 34 years (USA)	• Feb: Winter Olympics held in St Moritz (Swi) • Aug: Women's athletics included in Olympics for first time, at Amsterdam (Neth)	• 11 Mar: World land speed record set at 223.2 mph (359 km/h) by Henry Segrave at Daytona Beach, Florida, in his streamlined car, Golden Arrow (USA)
					• Women in UK gained equal voting rights with men	• 25 Oct: Wall St Crash ushered in the Depression (USA)

57

Datafile

The 1920s saw the emergence of the United States as the country with an undisputed lead in the economics and business of modernism. Although Paris remained the world artistic center, New York was the city in which the leading advertising agencies were situated, and its rapidly rising skyline exemplified the spirit of the age. The effects of advertising, both economic and cultural, spread throughout the industrial world.

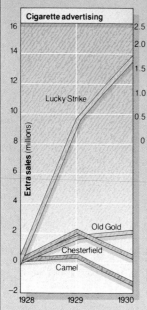

Cigarette advertising

Extra sales (millions)

Lucky Strike

Old Gold

Chesterfield

Camel

1928 — 1929 — 1930

Automobile production

Millions

US, Canada, France, Italy

▲ In 1920 the United States was responsible for about 90 percent of world motor vehicle production, and the car was, thanks to Ford and to installment purchase schemes, in everyday use. The European industry, by comparison, had been affected badly by World War I and motor vehicles remained luxury items.

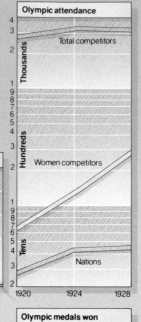

Olympic attendance

Thousands / Hundreds / Tens

Total competitors

Women competitors

Nations

1920 — 1924 — 1928

Olympic medals won

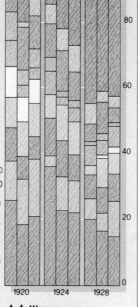

Others, Belgium, Switz, UK, France, Finland, Norway, Sweden, Italy, USA

Gold / Silver / Bronze

1920 — 1924 — 1928

▲ In the last years of the decade, radio began to show its power as a medium for selling products to the public. Products such as Lucky Strike and Old Gold saw significant improvements in their sales following advertising campaigns on US radio linked to popular music shows. Competitors had to follow suit.

▼ The crucial role of advertising in American economic life is shown by the close correlation in overall expenditure in this sector with the nation's economic activity as a whole. Throughout the 1920s and 1930s it remained at a fairly constant 3 percent of national income, falling back in the later 1930s.

▼ By 1930, little more than ten years after the first scheduled broadcasts, radio had become commonplace throughout the world. Unlike television 40 years later, radio was no more popular in the United States than in other industrial countries. European listeners could tune in to stations from many other countries.

Advertising in USA

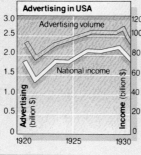

Advertising (billion $) / Income (billion $)

Advertising volume

National income

1920 — 1925 — 1930

▲▲ Women were permitted to take part in Olympic track and field events for the first time at Amsterdam in 1928, when Germany also rejoined the Olympic community. The United States achieved its unchallenged supremacy immediately after the war, in Antwerp, with European countries otherwise dominating the medals.

Number of radio sets per 1000 population, 1930

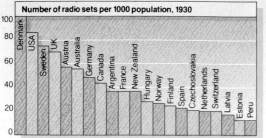

Denmark, USA, Sweden, UK, Austria, Australia, Germany, Canada, Argentina, France, New Zealand, Hungary, Norway, Finland, Spain, Czechoslovakia, Netherlands, Switzerland, Latvia, Estonia, Peru

---

Whatever else called itself "modernist" in the first quarter of the 20th century – painting, architecture, literature – the great popular apostle of modernism was advertising. It spoke not to an elite of connoisseurs and literati, but to the new "mass man" (in reality, a woman). And it spoke not of adaptations of a literary or architectural style for the new age, but of the engine of that age, the new economy of consumption, pleasure and desire.

Advertising men proudly proclaimed themselves missionaries of modernity, champions of the consumerist esthetics of novelty and progress. Advertising provided the images of aspiration, the vision of a better future. It identified the anxieties of metropolitan life as personal problems such as "halitosis" and "clogged pores", rather

CELEBRITY AND MODERN LIFE

than any wider or deeper social malaise. At this, "the dawn of the distribution age", the art of the advertising agencies of New York's Madison Avenue was, in Michael Schudson's memorable phrase, Capitalist Realism.

The advertisement of education

In about 1914, advertisements began to emphasize the benefits that products brought the consumer, rather than just showing the product itself. In stressing the pleasures and benefits of consumption, advertising started to sell not simply goods, but a whole set of beliefs concerning the good life, and a collection of assumptions about what constituted proper satisfactions and rewards for industriousness. Wholeheartedly embracing their own ideology, advertising men saw

themselves engaged in a form of public service, educating their readers in the new way of life. Manufacturers, they argued, merely made products. Advertising manufactured customers, by stimulating desire not just for this thing or that, but for a higher standard of living generally. Properly used, advertising could regulate demand and thus keep the balance between production and consumption. Moreover, advertisers were ambassadors for the consumer to the producer; like the press barons, they saw themselves as representatives of public opinion, and missed the ironies implicit in their claims.

Public opinion, however, was regarded as fickle, flighty, and feminine. Recognizing that women were responsible for 85 percent of consumer spending, advertisers defined their mass

▼ **A grand showroom of Model T Fords in 1927.**

The product of advertising is...public opinion; and in a democracy public opinion is the uncrowned king. It is the advertising agency's business to write the speeches for the throne of that king; to help his subjects decide what they should eat and wear; how they should invest their savings; by what courses they can improve their minds; and even – for so far has advertising advanced – what laws they should make and by what faith they may be saved.

BRUCE BARTON

market as having feminine characteristics. Persistently complaining that it was not possible to sell things rationally to irrational creatures, they acknowledged the "need" to manipulate consumers for their own good through appeals to their emotions. As one argued, "If exaggeration will induce a million people to brush their teeth every morning, who would otherwise neglect that office, then the end justifies the means."

Unlike the movie mogul, advertising men tended to come from the cultural elite. From the middle-class reformers of the previous decades they adopted the idea that they should raise the masses out of their present condition, and they combined this idea with the 1920s image of business as benign and paternal. They identified their function as raising the intellectual and cultural standards of the mass audience, as well as improving its economic well-being. John Benson, President of the American Association of Advertising Agencies, argued in 1927, "It may be necessary to fool people for their own good. Doctors and even preachers know that and practice it. Average intelligence is surprisingly low. It is so much more effectively guided by its subconscious

impulses and instincts than by its reason."

Given such assumptions, it was not surprising that their audience continued to disappoint advertisers' ambitions for them by repeatedly demonstrating a preference, as commentator Leo Rosten put it, for "the frivolous against the serious, 'escape' as against reality … the diverting as against the significant." Newspaper readers preferred tabloid pictures and comics to foreign news, radio listeners chose comedy shows rather than classical music. Reluctantly advertisers decided that their readers bought better when solicited by advertisements that imitated these debased cultural forms. Like tolerant fathers indulging their wilful daughters, advertisers accepted the preferences of the masses, so long as they, the rational elite, could regulate them.

The subordination of woman, the feckless consumer, was central to the new economic and ideological system. By endowing her with irrationality, the advertisers explained and even justified any of the system's foibles – for example, its obliteration of the distinction between needs and luxuries. The subservience of woman was assured by her dependence on men for the means

Cleans everywhere — more easily.

Electrolux will free your home from dust more rapidly, more easily, and more thoroughly than any other cleaning system. It will pry into all awkward corners and under low furniture. It will slip over the windows, across the walls and ceiling, searching out every particle of dust and grit. This most efficient of all labour-saving devices will clean everything within the four corners of your house, even to the extent of purifying and disinfecting the very air you breathe. Think what this would mean to your home. How your rooms would be brightened

and your labours lightened! The drudgery of daily cleaning would be broken. Instead there would be time in your home for the lighter duties and attentions which mean so much to extra happiness and comfort.

Send a postcard for a copy of the new Electrolux Booklet, or ask for a free demonstration in your own home or at our showrooms.

Electrolux
The New Cleanness

ELECTROLUX LIMITED, 153/155 Regent Street, LONDON, W.1 (Gerrard 4947/8)
Branches throughout Great Britain and Ireland

Olivetti

◄◄ Instead of "the drudgery of daily cleaning," new domestic machinery promised more time for leisure and childcare.

◄ At the office, advertisements depicted women decorating office machinery with reverential looks, rather than using it.

▼ Advertising thrived on anxieties; women were told that success in "the beauty contest of life" depended on soap or toothpaste.

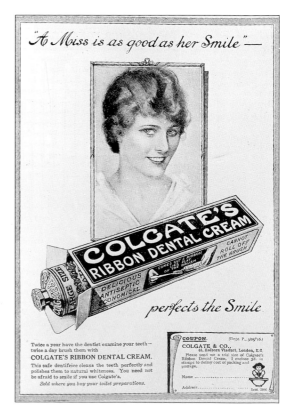

"A Miss is as good as her Smile" —

COLGATE'S RIBBON DENTAL CREAM

DELICIOUS ANTISEPTIC ECONOMICAL

CANNOT ROLL OFF THE BRUSH

perfects the Smile

Twice a year have the dentist examine your teeth — twice a day brush them with COLGATE'S RIBBON DENTAL CREAM. This safe dentifrice cleans the teeth perfectly and polishes them to natural whiteness. You need not be afraid to smile if you use Colgate's.

Sold where you buy your toilet preparations.

COUPON. [Dept. P., 3/25'26.]
COLGATE & CO.,
48, Holborn Viaduct, London, E.C.
Please send me a trial size of Colgate's Ribbon Dental Cream. I enclose 3d. in stamps to defray cost of packing and postage.

Name ....
Address ....

The New Magazines

By 1920 the *Saturday Evening Post* had a circulation of over two million copies a week, and, with its mixture of fiction, current affairs and biographies of public figures, was staple reading for the American middle-class family. A newer, brasher style of magazine appeared in the 1920s. The magazine equivalent of the tabloid dailies, *True Story* and its imitators found a new audience of young, working-class women eager for advice and reassurance. Every story had to be written in the first person in simple, homely language, and preach a strong moral lesson. Perhaps the most enduring stylistic change was inaugurated by *Time*, launched by Henry Luce and Briton Hadden in 1922 on the premise that "People are uninformed because no publication has adapted itself to the time which busy men are able to spend simply keeping informed". Individuals, not governments or mysterious forces, made *Times* news: "Since the personalities of politics make public affairs live...it is important to know what they drink, to what gods they pray and what kinds of fights they love."

▲ ▶ The *Saturday Evening Post* was for all the family. *Time* represented a sharper journalism attuned to the modern business age.

to consume, and her duty was to "keep young and beautiful" through the practice of consumption. Cosmetic advertisements surrounded women in their boudoirs with mirrors, representatives of the judgmental gaze of a male society, and advised their readers, "Watch out you don't disappoint him". Such images emphasized the importance of appearance in the increasingly mobile and anonymous culture of the metropolis. They also endorsed the act of looking at women as objects of desire.

Increasingly, advertising addressed its readers as a friend, advisor or coach, more experienced in the ways of the new world. Companies invented fictitious characters, such as General Mills' Betty Crocker, to personalize their products and advise their use. They adopted a style of presentation that has been compared with radio "crooning", an intimate, conversational tone of voice that belied the nature of mass communications by implying an individual relationship between speaker and listener, advisor and consumer. Advertisements reassured readers that the complexities and fragmentations of modern life could be enjoyed, and that experts in "public service" would provide them with as much advice as they needed in the new techniques and arts of personal presentation, appearance, manipulation and seduction.

Radio, advertising and education

Radio, child of the new technology of electronics, was the first new medium of the 20th century. The Marconi Company had begun communicating with ships at sea in 1897; the military applications of radio speeded its development. Wartime British and American research into the transmission of speech pioneered the close cooperation between government and corporate research in what was later termed the "military–industrial complex". The United States government encouraged the major communication corporations, American Telephone and Telegraph (AT & T) and General Electric (GE), to create the Radio Corporation of America (RCA) as the instrument of American technological preeminence. In Britain, Marconi maintained its dominance of the radio industry.

All this was undertaken with no thought that radio would be used principally for broadcasting. The fact that radio signals could be received by anyone with suitable equipment was considered a major handicap by its military users, and a nuisance by government agencies responsible for supervising the chaotic confusion of signals in early radio. Demand for broadcasting came from amateur enthusiasts who had bought or built receiving sets to listen in to radio signals. In June 1920 the British newspaper the *Daily Mail* sponsored a broadcast recital by the opera star Dame Nellie Melba, which was heard by listeners all over Europe. The publicity this generated showed the new medium's potential public appeal, but further developments in Britain were hindered by official hostility to Marconi and by complaints from the military that an invention ideally suited to be a "servant of mankind" was being treated as "a toy to amuse children".

In the United States Westinghouse, excluded from the RCA–GE–AT&T combine, recognized the commercial potential of broadcasting. It opened its first station, KADA, in Pittsburgh, in the fall of 1920, as part of an aggressive marketing campaign to sell radio sets. Its success was rapidly imitated, and by the end of 1922 there were 570 licensed stations. As with the nickelodeon boom in 1906 (see page 36), radio provided a new means of consuming leisure. The huge demand for entertainment received directly into the home outstripped the manufacturers' capacity to supply equipment. By 1924 two million receivers had been sold.

It was far from clear exactly what this new commodity was, or, indeed, how it should be used.

When the world's first radio play was broadcast by the BBC in Britain in 1923, listeners were encouraged to switch their lights out so they could "more easily imagine the scenes". Programming on early American stations was diverse, mixing live and recorded conservatory music with talks, rudimentary news reports and broadcasts of church services. Almost half the stations that were operating in 1922 were run by radio and electrical manufacturers as a way of merchandising their goods. Others were run by newspapers, department stores and other commercial concerns seeking public goodwill.

These stations were the beginnings of commercial radio, but the first problem they had to solve was how to turn broadcasting into a commercial operation. Once the receiver had been purchased, no further transaction took place between the supplier of home entertainment and its consumer. As John Reith, first Director General of the British Broadcasting Company explained, "The broadcast is as universal as the air ... It does not matter how many thousands there may be listening; there is always enough for others, when they too wish to join in ... It is a reversal of the natural law that the more one takes, the less there is left for others." What, then, could be sold?

The solution devised by commercial radio in effect involved selling nothing to the listeners, but rather selling the listeners themselves to advertisers, who paid for the opportunity to persuade listeners to buy whatever they were selling. The first commercial was broadcast in August 1922, but such a solution to the financing of radio was widely regarded as undesirable, even by advertisers themselves, who saw radio as "the great genteel hope" for the cultural redemption of the masses through the "public service" of business paternalism. In the first years of American radio, one in every eight stations was operated by an educational institution, but by 1925 it was clear that radio was commercially too useful to be left to educationalists. With the passage of the Radio Act in 1927, American airwaves were dominated by three networks supplying local stations with packages of programs: two were fed by the National Broadcasting Company (NBC), a subsidiary of RCA, and the third was the Columbia Broadcasting System (CBS).

To an even greater extent than the movies, radio became both a commodity and an instrument of consumer culture. By 1930 there were 13 million radio sets in use in more than 40 percent of American households, who listened to a mixture of variety shows, based on the format of vaudeville, drama (predominantly comedy, with the blackface duo of Amos 'n Andy, minstrel show characters adapted to radio, the most popular individual program in the late 1920s and early 1930s), news, recorded and live music.

The first priority for any government was to organize the allocation of frequencies. The method used in practice dictated the shape of the national broadcasting system. From the outset, British broadcasters looked aghast at the American experience and insisted that they would learn from and avoid American mistakes. To prevent the chaos of too many competing stations, the British

Post Office proposed that equipment manufacturers should form a consortium, the British Broadcasting Company (BBC), to provide regular transmissions. Advertising was prohibited, and the company was to be financed through an annual licence fee on each receiving set – an entirely different principle from the American system, in that it charged listeners for what they heard. The BBC's monopoly over the airwaves meant that it could adopt a very different attitude toward its audience and programming than that produced through commercial competition in the United States. In 1926 it became the British Broadcasting Corporation, "a Public Commission operating in the National Interest".

The BBC was an organization formed by the British establishment in its own self-image, reflecting the values and beliefs of the professional middle class. Under its first and most influential Director General, John (later Lord) Reith, it became almost a domestic diplomatic service, representing "the best of British" to the British themselves. It fervently rejected American influence: Reith and his class saw the products of American mass culture such as Hollywood movies as childish, vulgar and false – a demonstration of why British broadcasting must avoid "giving the public what it wants". British and American broadcasting evolved into their different forms, and provided the two prototypes for other countries, because of the different attitudes of their culturally dominant upper middle class to the new consumer culture. In the United States the middle class were firmly in its vanguard, defining themselves around its material precepts. In Britain, however, older modes of class definition, which were critical of the materialism of American culture, still operated.

Reith was the architect of the BBC's notion of public service broadcasting, but in expressing it

◀ Dame Nellie Melba's broadcast concert of opera music from eastern England in 1920 reached an audience across Europe. Radio's earliest years were marked by confusion about its purposes, content and audience. For many people the pleasure lay in the skill required in the "DX-ing", getting good reception from the most distant stations possible. But as a columnist of *Wireless Magazine* complained in 1925, "Every woman must have noticed how different her point of view about wireless is from that of her husband or son. To women, wireless is a joy, a distraction, a companion, or an excitement; but it is never what it is to men – a toy. They want to play with it and fiddle with it incessantly, just as they do with their cars."

▶ By mid-decade, the radio was on its way to becoming a center of domestic life in the middle-class households of North America and Europe, as here in Britain.

▲ As "listening-in" became more an everyday activity, radio sets, such as the British design of about 1930, ceased to be just assemblies of electrical components and came to look more like pieces of furniture.

It is occasionally indicated to us that we are apparently setting out to give the public what we think they need – and not what they want – but few know what they want and very few what they need... In any case it is better to overestimate the mentality of the public than to underestimate it.

JOHN REITH 1924

You cannot underestimate the taste of the American public.

ARTHUR BRISBANE

The Radio Times, December 21, 1923

THE CHRISTMAS NUMBER
RADIO TIMES

Registered at the
G.P.O. as a Newspaper

6 D.

"JUST A SONG AT TWILIGHT"

Fads of the Twenties

▲ Atop a flagpole in New Jersey

The 1920s were years in which there were fads more numerous – and in general sillier – than at other times. Fueled by the dare-devil mood of the age and largely sponsored by a tabloid press in search of sensations, some of these fads were both dangerous and shortlived. One of the most unlikely was flagpole sitting – where some individuals managed to survive for 10 days or more living on a tiny platform atop a pole supported by nothing but stirrups. Sitters took short breaks every hour, but otherwise ate, slept and lived on their poles. The most famous, Shipwreck Kelly, claimed to have spent 145 days on various poles during 1929.

Marathon-dancing, in which couples competed for endurance records, was also more entertaining for its spectators than its performers. Couples would dance for days with breaks of only a few minutes each hour, until exhaustion or injury overcame them. One marathon in Chicago lasted 119 days.

A less dramatic but more enduring phenomenon was the sudden craze for crossword puzzles that began in 1924. Roller-skating, yo-yos and parlor games like contract bridge and Mah Jongg were also promoted through newspaper columns.

he acted as a spokesman for the politically powerful, the great and the godly of the nation. When it was established, a dominant version of "national" culture was already firmly in place among the small and cohesive British ruling class, who administered the country through systems of appointment and delegation rather than through centralized state control. The BBC inherited the idea of "public service", defined as the paternalist responsibility of the upper class, as part of the ideological baggage of the British Empire.

The BBC made available the full heritage of English high culture, previously the preserve of a privileged minority, to every member of the nation, at virtually no cost. This *was* a great cultural transformation. However, no-one suggested that the lower classes themselves should be permitted access to the airwaves. Sports, popular music and entertainment were certainly broadcast; by 1934, indeed, the BBC was broadcasting more light music, comedy and vaudeville than any other European station, but the manner in which they were presented, like the voices of the announcers, remained indomitably upper-middle-class.

This attitude of uplift was part of Reith's idea of the BBC as a kind of national church. He argued that it should use the "brute force of monopoly… to instruct and fashion public opinion, to banish ignorance and slavery, to contribute richly and in many ways to the sum total of human well-being." Much of the BBC's effort in its early years went towards achieving respectability among the cultural establishment, by avoiding controversial material as well as by educating its audiences and preserving the proprieties of Sunday by broadcasting only church services and serious music.

While the BBC's success in establishing itself as a national institution led other nations – Japan, for example – to imitate its system of government control, it was nevertheless accused of failing to provide for large sections of society.

In the 1930s as much as half the radio audience in Britain tuned to European commercial stations, Radio Luxembourg and Radio Normandie, on Sundays. Resistance to the BBC was not simply a matter of content. Radio entered peoples' daily lives in an immediate and intimate manner. In its content and financial organization, commercial radio was part of a larger notion, the promotion of a consumer society – giving America's businessmen, as one executive said, "a latchkey to nearly every home in the United States".

The BBC and its government-run imitators in other countries had to enter people's homes not as one instrument in a shared culture of consumption, but in the name of a common national culture, which they, almost alone, were creating. National radio was an agency of cultural centralization at a time when many local communities retained their diversity and a tight-knit resistance to intrusion. The national culture of the BBC reflected the elite culture of southern England; it was inevitable that this culture would meet regional and class-based resistance. Broadcasting would be a powerful instrument in the erosion of the cultural independence and diversity of the regions; not until World War II was there a real need for national unity for the BBC to serve.

"Never before in all the black history of slumland has such a light shone upon the darkness of human ignorance and domestic wretchedness… Imagine what it must mean to East London when the Queen's Hall Orchestra floods its foul courts and dark alleys with the majestic strains of the Fifth Symphony… Imagine, too, what it must mean to the minds of those men and women whose only serious mental effort hitherto has been to grasp the rights and wrongs of their economic condition when a man of science speaks to them of the stars."

RADIO TIMES, UK 1924

Sport and the mass media

Throughout all of Europe and the United States, changes in work patterns and new expectations of leisure in the interwar period fueled a demand for leisure that manifested itself in a growing variety of sporting activities. More people had more time for leisure, which was increasingly viewed as something they had a right to enjoy. Many also experienced a genuine rise in disposable income, and although some sports remained socially exclusive, increasing numbers of people enjoyed spectating and more working-class people found themselves able to participate in a range of sports. As one commentator observed of Britain in the 1920s: "The majority of working people, even those in poor material circumstances, were not entirely powerless in the face of external change to shape their own destiny and to gain a sense of well-being from their own spare-time experiences."

The hedonism that marked the 1920s was accompanied by notions of achievement and challenge, record attendance, and the rapid acceleration of commercialized sport. Between 1919 and 1926 Jack Dempsey, the heavyweight boxing champion of the world, drew crowds totalling over one million. The first luxurious sports areas were built such as London's Wembley Stadium,

◄ One of the earliest uses of radio for entertainment beyond music and news was in the field of sports commentating. In the United States in particular, the new skill of describing a fast-moving sporting event as it happened did much to spread enthusiasm for both sport and radio. This outside broadcast is reporting on a rifle shooting contest.

◄▲ Motor racing was one of the sports popular with the rich in the 1920s. The fascination was technical as much as sporting and the masterpieces of engineering and design produced by the Italian Ettore Bugatti (1881–1947) epitomized the esthetic appeal of the sport. Their handbuilt cars remained luxury items to be enjoyed by those with taste. Bugatti built fewer than ten copies of his classic mid-twenties model, Type 41.

which opened in 1923 and was designed to hold 100,000 spectators. In the 1920s Wembley hosted many types of sporting event, including soccer, tennis, boxing, ice hockey and greyhound racing. Throughout the decade attendance records were broken at professional and elite amateur events. Newspapers and radio brought distant events to a public primed for news, and, for the media, sport had the distinct advantage of taking place, and making news, according to an established calendar of events fixed well in advance. For its spectators, the predictability of sporting events provided a stable element in an unstable world. Sporting events enacted essentially optimistic dramas – there was always a victor (whether as hero or villain), a result, a decision, a definite outcome, and always another game in which wrongs could be righted or triumphs repeated.

Sport as a central interest for many people has sometimes been explained in terms of the backcloth it provided for accommodating the larger and less predictable world beyond. Sport became a celebration of human achievement, constructed around individual sportsmen and sportswomen whose personalities were publicized and manipulated by the media. Although they were not the creation of this period, by the 1920s the notions of sporting records and achievements resonated with the cultural values of capitalism. The statistics, totals and averages of a sport such as American football – the "earned run average", or the "yards gained rushing" – bore marked similiarities to the economic statistics, such as the Gross National Product or the Grade Point Average, that were beginning to enter everyday consciousness at this time.

The obsession with records
In the United States there was particular fascination with records. Two uniquely American games, baseball and football, lent themselves to detailed quantification and established a framework for other sports. Interest was mobilized by the press, but radio broadcasting transformed it into a new home-based entertainment. Matches and results were analyzed and players' techniques discussed long before the press could report on them. Through this process sports personalities emerged, their identities developed and embellished by the media, the celebration of their accomplishments part of the entertainment industry's invention of celebrity. Heroic figures in the culture of industrial capitalism, sportsmen and women were recognized as maximizers of performance and output.

In the 1920s the names of Babe Ruth and Red Grange became familiar because of their prowess in baseball and American football respectively. Babe Ruth was the first modern athlete to be "packaged" and "sold" to the American people, not only for his sporting prowess but also for his character. He became a national celebrity who helped to make professional baseball America's number one pastime. Red Grange has been regarded as one of the greatest college football players of all time. His evasive running earned him the title of "the Galloping Ghost" and when he signed for the Chicago Bears in 1925 not only

did he secure a contract worth $3,000 per game but also, in the eyes of many, conferred respectability on professional football itself. From this time on, it was clear that money could be made in the game by college graduates.

Women in sport
In the interwar period, the sport of lawn tennis proved to be a platform for female achievement. Suzanne Lenglen dominated the game from 1919 to 1926, and redefined what could be achieved by women. One historian said of her: "Her gifts were supreme. Her biting accuracy, coupled with divine balletic grace, dominated the game for so long without real challenge, that her immortality is unquestioned."

Lenglen was unbeaten in seven years of tournament play: she won six Wimbledon Championships, six French Championships and two Olympic gold medals at Antwerp in 1920. The combination of her tennis-playing ability and radically different clothing on court attracted considerable comment. In her last Wimbledon triumph Lenglen won the 1925 Championships, losing only five games in the process. A year later she withdrew from Wimbledon after a disagreement over playing schedules and turned professional, for a reported sum of $100,000.

In the 1920s American players were preeminent in men's tennis. "Big Bill" Tilden treated the

Foremost among the heroes and heroines of the 1920s were the achievers and record breakers of the sporting world. As a growing enthusiasm for sport drew ever larger crowds of spectators, these men and women became increasingly marketable, not simply for their sporting prowess, but also for their personalities. The darlings of the American public were the legendary baseball player Babe Ruth (right center) and footballer Red Grange (right top). Atlanta-born golfer Bobby Jones (below) achieved international fame, as did Frenchwomen Suzanne Lenglen – six times winner of the Wimbledon tennis tournament (left).

game as a science, and developed theories of stroke-play, the power-game, tactics, and the crowd-puller. The enormous public appeal of Lenglen and Tilden helped tennis to develop a mass following.

Tennis was becoming a more active game for women, if only in a form that implicitly accepted that women were physically weaker and therefore played a "ladylike" version of the men's game, though to some extent players like Lenglen threatened such assumptions. In most sports women continued to suffer opposition and discrimination. Women's athletics was one of the last sports to be organized, and throughout the 1920s antagonists of women's sports viewed athletics as indecent, unsuited to women's physiques and in danger of producing "an unnatural race of Amazons". The struggle over the inclusion of women's athletics in the Olympic Games came to a head when the International Olympic Committee (IOC) refused to include them in the Games of 1920 and 1924. In defiance of IOC policy Alice Milliat organized the first Women's Olympics in 1922, which were also held in 1926, 1930 and 1934 under the new title of the Women's World Games. These events were unexpectedly successful, attracting large numbers of competitors and spectators from western Europe, the British Empire and North America, and athletics became a growth sport for women.

THE CHALLENGE OF THE AIR

Flight was the adventure of the interwar years as developing technology briefly made aviation a competitive sport, in search of new speed and endurance records. None captured the popular imagination of the media so much as Charles Lindbergh's nonstop solo flight from New York to Paris in 1927. Competing for a prize of £25,000 which had claimed six lives in the previous year, 24-year-old Lindbergh took off in a Ryan monoplane he called "The Spirit of St Louis" from Roosevelt Field, Long Island on the morning of 20 May. Thirty-three and a half hours later he landed at Le Bourget, Paris.

Lindbergh's flight seemed to have an esthetic purity about it. Unlike his rivals, he flew alone. Although he had financial backing, his plane was built on a shoestring budget. It had no navigational system, and Lindbergh memorized his route. His exploits fed the hunger to discover new objects of attention, new sensations, new people. Christened "Lucky Lindy" and "the Flying Fool" by an already enthusiastic press before he took off, Lindbergh's story sold a record number of newspapers. After the flight, he appeared to confirm his heroic status by remaining aloof from movie offers and requests for testimonials. But in 1932 his baby was kidnapped, and Lindbergh again became front-page news for the weeks of the prolonged hunt for the child and then the trial of the alleged kidnapper Bruno Hauptmann. It offered the press and public another opportunity to gawk at a celebrity's private life; one imposter who claimed to know where the child was, confessed that he had made his story up to "become famous". Later in the 1930s Lindbergh's open support for the Nazis led President Franklin Roosevelt to denounce him as a Fascist.

▲ Charles Lindbergh and "The Spirit of St Louis", the Ryan monoplane in which he made his first nonstop flight across the Atlantic. Stripped to its essentials and with only minimal stores of food and water, the plane carried almost its own weight in fuel, and barely cleared the telegraph wires on take-off. Lindbergh's flying position was so cramped that he could only look out of the front of the cockpit through a periscope. His description of the flight expressed the extreme solitariness of his flight into the unknown.

▼ Barnstorming flyers provided spectacles of all kinds for fairground audiences in the 1920s, including this unlikely game of tennis. They also offered rides to the public – "Your money back if you get killed".

◄ Lindbergh's return to New York in June was a moment of high optimism. The 1800 tonnes of paper in his ticker-tape parade recorded stock prices at record levels. More than a million people cheered.

▼ Lindbergh's achievement was commemorated in every imaginable way. A town in Texas, was named after him. Songs were composed for him, and a new jazz dance was called the "Lindy hop."

LUCKY LINDY!

Words by L. WOLFE GILBERT
Music by ABEL BAER

LEO. FEIST, Inc. NEW YORK

▲ A crowd of 100,000 was waiting to greet the *Spirit of St Louis* when it arrived at Le Bourget airport thirty-three and a half hours after Lindbergh had taken off from Roosevelt Field, Long Island. In just under two days he had become the most famous private citizen in the world.

Datafile

No other decade – except perhaps the sixties – can rival the twenties in its typical image as a "golden age" of popular music.

The first commercially-made electrical recordings appeared in 1925 and set in motion a transformation both in sound quality (therefore also in people's expectations) and in performance style. The most immediate benefits, however, were felt by radio, the successful expansion of which depended very much on its ability to broadcast popular dance music live, from studios or from clubs and ballrooms.

Music proved extremely useful in the commercialization of radio in the twenties, as program sponsors used popular themes or, more often, the sound of individual bands, to give themselves an identity in the public mind. By the middle of the decade, too, the network system was fully operational, permitting the same music to be heard simultaneously across the country – in cars as well as homes.

Phonograph manufacture

21%
Total value 28.2 million $

1914

28%
Total value 158.5 million $

1919

▨ Cost of materials
☐ Value of products

▶ At the start of the decade the record industry seemed to be looking to a future of assured success. Yet by 1921 sales had peaked, and more than 20 years would pass before such levels were reached again. The reason was radio. Sales of radios had more than quadrupled in the first years of the decade.

Record sales in USA

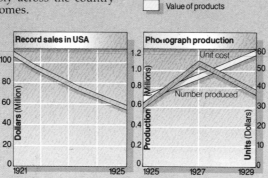

Phonograph production

▲ Phonograph manufacture in the United States, like record sales, expanded dramatically from 1914 to a peak in 1919 (top diagram), but fell back during the 1920s (above). By this time the greatest technical advances in the reproduction of music in the home were found in radio, a fact that hit sales of phonographs.

▶ Among the changes which explain the greater prominence of young people in Jazz Age America, the increase in college education is significant. The doubling of the proportion of those in the 18–24 age-band attending college was important in providing the solid underpinning for more confident self-assertion.

College students in USA

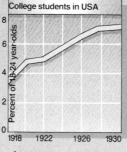

◀ Northward migration of America's black population, so important in the story of popular music, was far from being a mass exodus in the twenties. In 1930 the vast majority of blacks (9.4 million out of 11.9 million) still lived in the South. The black population in the north and north-central regions, however, was almost entirely urban.

▼ The fortunes of one, fairly typical, record company in the twenties show that the peak year of 1921 could be seen as something of an aberration rather than a culmination. By 1930, though, some stability had returned. The merger of Victor with the radio company RCA in 1929 provided a platform for unrivaled power.

US population by race

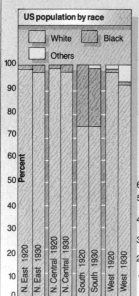

White / Black / Others

Victor record sales

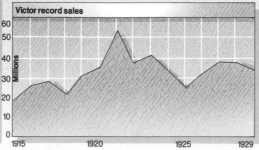

On 9 August 1920 in a New Jersey recording studio, Paul Whiteman, a symphony orchestra musician-turned-dance-band leader from Denver, Colorado, made the first of several attempts to record some newly-minted Tin Pan Alley tunes. The band's first record (*Whispering/Japanese Sandman*), released four months later, rapidly sold two million copies, emphasizing the ascendancy now enjoyed by records over sheet music, and propelling the portly figure of Paul Whiteman to fame and fortune, and to leadership of a new musical dynasty as King of Jazz. In the judgment of posterity he was an imposter; the true royal blood flowed in darker veins. But Whiteman's bland music, with its careful orchestration and its occasional "hot" moments, was real jazz to a large proportion of its listeners who had never been exposed to black music in undiluted form.

Whiteman himself was more opportunist than rebel. He had grown, he said, "listless, dissatisfied, despondent" with the life of a classical musician and had seen the chance of greater rewards in popular culture. The music of which he was a leading exponent was in fact to become the focus of a collision between the old standards of behavior and the new. In the 1920s appropriation and assimilation of black culture continued; the blandness of Whiteman's music seemed more comfortable, staking out a neutral ground amid the furore. There had been collisions between opposing standards before; what took place in the twenties can be seen as a culmination of a long-term process. But new factors had added an undertow of unease to the American scene. The end of the war and the failure of the peace brought a declining interest in world affairs, a shriveling of idealism and a growth in the attraction of pleasure and entertainment. Labor problems, the fear of communism and the rise of the racist Ku Klux Klan each in its own way signified an alliance between a narrow "respectability" and repression.

Prohibition and the Jazz Age

Then there was Prohibition, the policy which made the manufacture, sale and consumption of alcoholic drinks illegal throughout the twenties. F. Scott Fitzgerald's familiar phrase, the Jazz Age, summed up the spirit of the period; Prohibition was the most potent symbol of its lifestyle. A nostalgic view of the period presents jazz and Prohibition as expressions of the triumph of the pleasure principle. Historians on the other hand may see the hedonism of the era as a mask for alienation, and the conservative backlash as a reminder of the power of the establishment. Both jazz and Prohibition make most sense when seen as outstanding examples of the continuing struggle in mainstream American

THE JAZZ AGE

culture between two pronounced tendencies, which have been called the "ecstatic" – celebratory, immediate, implicit – and the "didactic" – controlled, predictable, explicit.

The evidence of the twenties suggests that it was a complex encounter, rarely clear-cut. The Volstead Act, which initiated the era of Prohibition, had more than one ironic consequence. The practices it sought to curb were made more desirable, as behavior hitherto thought of as mildly antisocial now became deliberate revolt. Criminal elements shed some of their marginality and found themselves the center of attention in the tabloid press. The sinister social evil of organized crime was seen to foster and encourage another marginal group - the black subculture, whose music and dance provided the bulk of the entertainment in the gangster-run clubs.

The motives and actions of the predominantly well-to-do urban white Americans enticed by the thrill of "slumming" in Harlem were not unequivocal, either. In part they were reacting against the restrictions of Victorian morality, but there was also a sense in which they felt their wealth required them to consume: something, anything. Often to their intense discomfort, they found that

► Tin Pan Alley, West 28th St, New York, the center of the song-publishing industry in its heyday, was so called because of the cacophony of songpluggers' pianos.

▼ The success of the white Original Dixieland Jazz Band, who took New York by storm in 1917, inspired imitators. Some combined novelty effects with suggestions of southern carnivals.

what was fundamental to the pleasure principle by which they lived at night, was anathema to the principles of personal gain around which their daytime economic world was constructed. As an added twist, the world towards which the pleasure-seekers gravitated was one where pleasures were made available purely as hard-nosed business responses to demand. Organized crime, "the bastard son of corporate capitalism", sold illegal pleasures, providing a perfect metaphor for the contradictions in the businesses of entertainment and leisure.

The argument over jazz, which raged for most of the decade, can be seen as an expression of the conflict between the ecstatic and the didactic. Opposition to the new popular music was mounted, as before, on two fronts: esthetic and moral. The attack was greatly intensified in response to what was perceived as the increasingly rapid spread of degenerative influences. The object of condemnation, collectively known as jazz, included various related styles: the "raggy" music of white New Orleans musicians such as the Original Dixieland Jazz Band and their imitators (music that was itself a limited imitation of the black music most closely associated with the Crescent City), the syncopated dance bands, the Charleston craze, the songs of George Gershwin or Irving Berlin, and the "symphonic" jazz of Paul Whiteman. Equal censure was not applied to them all, but at the start of the decade at least few distinctions were made. Esthetic criticism ranged from the sardonic (Thomas Edison said he preferred jazz records played backwards) to the loftily dismissive. Moral criticism was more strident: jazz, savage, primitive, appealing to the basest instincts, rotted moral fiber, spread a whorehouse culture, polluted children, caused illegitimacy and all manner of unspeakable crimes. A *Ladies Home Journal* article of August 1921 revealed the phobia that lay at the root of the antagonism: "Jazz originally was the accompaniment of the voodoo dancer, stimulating the half-crazed barbarian to the vilest deeds."

There were other reasons for the attack, among them the confusion felt in small-town America over the rapidly changing morality of the big cities. At their core was a perceived threat to white Anglo-Saxon supremacy which found in the sensualism of black America the obverse of all its cherished self-images, and heard in jazz the approaching menace of physical and mental defilement.

Those enticed by the new music reacted in the opposite way to the same perception. Beneath the romantic image of freedom from convention, of individual self-gratification in a return to a more instinctual life, lay stereotypes of black culture as "primitive", sensual and culturally naive. Even among those few members of white society who were familiar with "real" jazz and blues, the fascination of discovery was tinged with paternalism and exoticism.

To these stereotypes of black America were added others; the threat posed by the former slave was complemented by that offered by the more recent immigrant. White ethnic groups had mediated earlier in the popularization of black-

derived dances (see page 42), and they now contributed to the dissemination of jazz. Jewish songwriters such as Irving Berlin and George Gershwin, who had previously been bracketed with ragtime composers, were now included under the new label; the phenomenal success of their music, and in particular of Gershwin's attempt to blend jazz-derived rhythms and sounds with classical techniques in his *Rhapsody in Blue* (1926), caused consternation among some cultural guardians. This was not attributable solely to concern for the *musical* tradition being challenged; the threat was also one of blood, all the more ominous because the music symbolized an alliance between the erstwhile marginal groups of Jews and blacks.

Among songwriters, Gershwin was one of

▲ Floorshows such as this in a 1920s Chicago nightclub reflected the public's ambivalence to black culture. While all gradations of color were permitted in male performers, a policy of employing only light-skinned girls ("high yallers") persisted in the 1930s.

▶ Buyers of sheet music did not want for choice of styles or subjects. Love ballads dominated the market, but songwriters were not slow to incorporate current fashions into their "jazzy" numbers. More significant for the future of the industry was the lure of the movies, which claimed many song-writers by 1930.

▶ For young socialites such as these in Berlin the new fashons in music and dance were experienced at several removes from their roots in black Amerca. The naiveté of the European gaze across the Atlantic has been overlaid by awareness of the momentous political and social developments taking place much closer to home.

▲ One thing at least united all record buyers; the need to change the needle. Access to the world of recorded sound depended entirely on these humble but essential objects. The diamond stylus of Edison's *pièce de resistance*, the Blue Amberol cylinder, was far superior to the steel needle required to play discs; but cylinders had been almost entirely replaced by discs.

those most clearly interested in Afro-American music. Most interesting of the white ethnic performing musicians who gathered around jazz were the Chicago-based players, influenced by both black and white New Orleans musicians. Responding in a way that would be echoed in the fifties by many young whites as they encountered rhythm & blues, Bix Beiderbecke, Mezz Mezzrow, Hoagy Carmichael and others behaved as they did in embracing a new-found way of life that offered an escape from the constraints of their own inherited culture.

Popular music now enjoyed an importance in the debate about culture that was probably without parallel. One has to look back as far as the controversy which raged in 18th-century New England over congregational singing styles to find anything like a precedent. That argument had derived, fundamentally, from the clash of literate and orally based cultures. In the 1920s the players had changed and the plot was more complex, but the underlying antithesis was the same. The gradual "blackening" of white America offered a fundamental challenge to the status quo, and music was in its vanguard. This "blackening" was also taking place in speech, in sport, in dance, but the immediacy of the performance-based black music made it clear that the challenge was not one only of esthetics or morals, or even of racial purity. Jazz was the sound of an orally-based subordinate black culture striking at the basic machinery of control used by the dominant white culture – literacy.

Jazz, blues and the black audience
Within black culture itself music was perceived rather differently. Through the recording industry, the blacks' vernacular culture was made

available to them as a result of mass production becoming part of the popular culture industry. On 10 August 1920 (a day after Paul Whiteman's first studio session), Mamie Smith became the first black singer to record a "blues". *Crazy Blues*, her second record, was actually more of a pop vaudeville song but its commercial success revealed to the record companies the existence of an unsuspected market, and resulted in the so-called "race records" – labels recording and marketing blues, jazz, gospel and other, less readily definable styles for the black audience.

Whatever the particular style – from the guttural dialect of the Mississippi bluesman to the incipient star quality of Louis Armstrong – black music spoke to black society with a confident awareness of its distinctiveness. Immediacy, implicitness and the endless possibilities of the off-beat when removed from the grip of regular rhythm – these features were fundamental, but jazz and blues, in all their wide variety, were principally about emotional and social self-management in American society. As elsewhere in this decade, however, it is a story marked by ambiguity. The music was grounded not in the purity of an oral tradition, but in the interplay between black- and white-derived elements. Black music was based on a dynamic exploration of the tensions between rhythm and harmony, between performer and creator. White popular music's tendency, by contrast, was to assimilate, compromise and thus to neutralize; black music indicated the possibility of a separate co-existence in which there can always be alternatives.

In spite of its distinctiveness, commercially recorded black music of the late 1920s was greeted with reserve by black, as well as by white, society. The greatest hostility came from the black middle class, who most aspired to the level of the white bourgeoisie and detested all manifestations of the subcultural status that might retard their upward progress. Among black intellectuals opinion on jazz and blues was marked by considerable ambivalence. While some writers praised them, others preferred the piety of the spirituals.

An important part of the target audience for this music was now to be found in northern cities close to the mainspring of American society. However, white America's familiarity with styles of black music, as performed for black society, remained very small. Blues singers such as Bessie Smith were known only to a select few, whose influence on popular taste was not great. Only those whites living in some kind of proximity to blacks in the south knew the more rural styles. Among jazz musicians the names of King Oliver, Louis Armstrong and Earl Hines were gradually spread by the enthusiasm of popularizing performers such as Beiderbecke. For most of the decade black bands could be heard in New York's Harlem nightspots (Duke Ellington's stint at the Cotton Club from 1927 to 1932 being the most celebrated example), but this exposure, limited to a small section of society, did not spread the word very far. Those who frequented the clubs seldom bought the bands' records. The prevailing taste in record-buying was for Tin Pan Alley tunes in recordings by Broadway stars such as Al Jolson and Sophie Tucker and white dance bands such as Fred Waring's Pennsylvanians.

White popular music

The white audience was also far from homogeneous. "Hillbilly" music began to be recorded in 1923, and again surprised the record industry by showing that there was a market for the distinctive regional styles of white America. The music of non-English language groups also began to be recorded. The social effects of these developments were complex, but the hostility of the poorer, often fundamentalist rural communities to urban culture was to some extent deflected by this opportunity to become consumers of their own vernacular culture in mass-produced form.

It was through recordings that each social group acquired a public voice, which was both used within the group and also formed part of a larger pattern of cultural communication, of a type not known before. Marketing policies aimed particular products at particular audiences, so wider familiarity with the different musical styles would never have taken place if records had been the only means of communication. It was through radio, broadcasting "music in the night every night, everywhere" and recognizing few barriers, that music of different kinds reached new audiences. The staple fare of radio was provided by the dance orchestras of Vincent Lopez, Guy Lombardo and others who could be relied on to behave respectably in the nation's homes. The studio band system on which radio depended in effect excluded black musicians, but the practice gradually grew of placing "radio wires" in certain New York nightspots. In this way a few black bands were provided with a much wider

The Lost Generation

In the 1920s Paris became the Mecca for every young American who aspired to artistic or literary genius. As the cultural center of the Western world, it popularized a bohemian way of life that was not so much in opposition to bourgeois philistinism as in advance of it. In the past, bohemian or counter-cultural fashions had often been created as a critique of high fashion. In the 1920s high fashion itself expressed the daring of the artistic avant-garde.

Yet the women in these expatriate circles; seemingly free spirits, were often as exploited as any middle-class housewife, their sexual libertarianism often of more benefit to their lovers than to themselves. American author Scott Fitzgerald's own wife, Zelda, suffered repeated mental breakdowns; Nina Hammett, a promising artist in her own right, became an alcoholic. Nancy Cunard, to many the epitome of 1920s womanhood, could not, as a result of botched abortions, have children.

Emblematic of the period's love of the exotic was Nancy Cunard's armful of African ivory bangles. African art influenced Picasso, Diaghilev and many others in the early decades of the century.

▲ Nancy Cunard was a convention-flouting society beauty of the 1920s, with a genuine interest in things African.

▼ The American black dancer Josephine Baker was well aware of the danger of being caught up in white preconceptions about "primitive" art, and brought an irony to her costumes and performances that was often lost on her audiences.

exposure and areas of America were given their first taste of a black jazz band, and something of the accompanying thrill. In areas where "hillbilly" music was popular, radio stations began to broadcast non-networked "barn dance" programs featuring fiddlers and string bands.

The safer experiences offered by the white dance bands and vocalists remained popular. However, before the end of the decade outright opposition to new styles of popular music had modified considerably, principally because bands such as Paul Whiteman's succeeded in convincing the public – if not the various custodians – that with its more "offensive" and "raucous" elements removed the music was no longer a threat. Whiteman had been as irritated as anyone by traditionalist opposition, but his response had been to seek a compromise. By blending techniques derived from classical music (especially in scoring), he sought to show that some of the well-known morally uplifting qualities of that music had been absorbed. He wanted his music to be thought of as "art".

It was to be an art that depended on the successful incorporation of "native" American elements, but the effect, at least superficially, was rather different. Greater rhythmic freedom, individualistic sound, the hint of bodily emancipation – these qualities were still controlled by pre-regulated harmony and rhythm. The question that lurked beneath the surface, however, was whether these new elements could ever be truly assimilated or whether they would refuse to shed their identity or their power to challenge.

▶ The image of the "flapper" and of the "Bright Young Things" is a part of the myth rather than the reality of the 1920s. Only a very few rich young women had the independence, leisure and daring to enjoy love affairs outside marriage. Skirts never rose above the knee, and this suggestive glimpse of suspender would have been an embarrassment to a real-life young woman – though such awkwardnesses did indeed occur.

The new woman and the twenties

Although the fashions gaining ground before World War I prefigured the "modernism" of the 1920s, it was only in the hedonism and boom atmosphere of the Jazz Age that the revolution in women's clothing begun before 1914 was finally accomplished. The wartime experience of young European women from the middle and upper classes in situations where they could no longer constantly be chaperoned, and the casualty toll that devastated a whole generation of young men, meant that with the dawn of the 1920s a new kind of single woman – independent, self-sufficient, adventurous – stepped on to the social stage. World War I had also expanded employment opportunities for women in the affected nations. Women munitions workers, better paid than working-class women had ever been, appeared on the streets wearing makeup and dressed in seal and musquash fur coats. The mutilations caused by the war itself advanced plastic surgery, and indirectly promoted makeup as well.

In the 19th century painters had arranged their female sitters in static poses in gorgeously elaborate plumage; the wives and daughters of rich men almost became luxury objects to be looked at. By the 1920s a more typical fashion image was the photograph, which captured the model as she sprang across a puddle in the street, or disported herself in a bathing suit or at the races. The fashionable woman of the 1920s was associated with speed, daring and travel. Movement was the key to the new fashions. In a few short years, from being enveloped in yards of material that was buttoned, laced and hooked to swaddle and constrain, women's bodies were set free in the simplest of shifts that left arms, legs and necks shockingly bare, while hair was cropped and brilliantined. Faces, by contrast, were openly and brightly painted. Women smoked, drank, swore and made love in a manner that would have ruined their reputations 30 years earlier.

The influence of sportswear on fashion was even more obvious at this period than before World War I; Suzanne Lenglen, the dynamic French tennis star of the twenties, was dressed both on and off the court by Jean Patou, and her ordinary clothes looked hardly different from her on-court outfits (see page 67). Brief pleated skirts, thin stockings, simple strap or laced shoes, a long straight cardigan and plain shirt was one version of the new uniform for women.

Among the fashion designers, more influential even than Patou or Mmes. Vionnet and Lanvin, who revolutionized the cut of clothing (Madame Vionnet invented the bias cut) was Gabrielle "Coco" Chanel. Her designs dominated the fashion esthetic of the decade, but her work also bridged the prewar and postwar epochs, for she had already been experimenting with sports designs and materials before 1914. She, like Redferns (see page 31), had sensed the possibilities of women's riding wear, but she went much farther. She seized upon materials previously used only for male sporting garb and underwear – locknit, jersey and grey flannel – as a revolutionary new medium for her designs. By 1913 she was devising cardigans and sweaters (until then

worn only by fishermen and agricultural laborers) as fashion garments, and by the 1920s she had created an entirely new mode: she replaced the gorgeous colors and yards of silk with beige cashmere, black wool crêpe and men's suitings.

Simple fashions for the wealthy

At this period Chanel's designs were for the leisured rich, the new international set who traveled Europe and the United States in a restless search for seasonal diversions; and the irony of her fashions was that she gave the richest women in the world a look that was indistinguishable from that of a shop girl or office worker. Dressed in this ultra-chic "poor look" – in a simple black dress either with a demure white Peter Pan collar, or, more likely, completely unadorned – the society women who affected it paid everything for a fashion that looked like nothing and reduced women's dress to a minimalist uniform of understatement. Chanel even designed necklaces of uncut diamonds and emeralds that looked as though they were made of common glass.

This, then, was an inversion of values in the so-called democratic century. Dress was no longer a matter of direct display; instead, fashion adopted the language of the streets and of the common man (man, not woman, for both sexes). Chanel flung a trenchcoat around her shoulders and it became the latest thing; jersey, corduroy and tweed, once used to make only workmen's or country clothes, were transformed into high fashion. The concept of casual wear was born.

By this time high fashion was an international movement. Paul Poiret had already toured the United States, where he had been horrified to find his exclusive designs pirated everywhere. By 1930 Seventh Avenue (the New York City garment district) was adapting Chanel's designs for the mass market – and their simplicity meant that they were highly suitable for mass production. In the following year Chanel was invited to Hollywood by Sam Goldwyn. The "poor girl" look that Chanel had made her own was similar to that popularized by Louise Brooks on the screen, where she played ordinary city girls, "good sorts" and tomboys. Goldwyn invited Chanel to dress his stars because she was the most prestigious of all dress designers, but as it turned out her designs were too understated for Hollywood. After designing Gloria Swanson's wardrobe for *Tonight or Never* (1931) she returned to Paris, unenthralled by the celluloid capital, which in turn had no use for her little-or-nothing clothes.

Fashion and modernity

Chanel's collaboration with the Parisian artistic avant garde had been much more successful. As early as 1922 she worked with Jean Cocteau, Picasso and the composer Arthur Honegger on a production of the classical Greek play *Antigone*; and from 1923 to 1927 she worked with Sergei Diaghilev and Cocteau on ballet designs. For the first of their joint works, *Le Train Bleu*, a fantasy about the Riviera, the dancers were costumed in bathing suits, pullovers and tennis or golf shoes, and the leading female role was a tennis player.

So fashion, sport and the artistic avant-garde united to celebrate the modernity of modern life, and Chanel's little black dress (American *Vogue* called it the "Ford of fashion") became the epitome of modernist style. The modernist movement in art transcended both national boundaries and those of artistic form, influencing all the arts from architecture to the novel. Visually, it was the embodiment of the ideal of speed, science and the machine. It was a love affair with a rationalist, utopian future, and in architecture and design this led to an ascetic functionalism that considered houses and flats as machines for living, furniture and household artefacts as items for use, not ornament, and even human beings as machines.

More than almost any other aspect of mass culture, high fashion acted as a conduit for this esthetic, translating it into a popular language of pared-down design and understated chic. In architecture, the Bauhaus movement created buildings that used glass to reveal the inner workings of the design. They stripped away the superfluous ornament that had cluttered 19th-century architecture with what was now regarded as the sentimental idealization of a past recreated in pastiche. In dress, too, the watchword was now functionalism; clothing was simply an envelope for the body, which it impeded as little as possible. If there was to be adornment of any kind, it was to be of the art deco variety. Art deco was so called after the *Exhibition des Arts Décoratifs*, held in Paris in 1925. This exhibition had in a sense inaugurated the idea of a lifestyle, though the expression was not then used. It included a Pavilion of Elegance, in which the fashion designs of Chanel and Poiret, among others, were displayed. They complemented the furniture, ceramics and architecture – throughout, the few ornamental motifs and bright colors permitted were definite, clean-cut and jazzy.

In literature and painting, part of the modernism of modern art had been that the work of art interrogated its own intentions and questioned its own form. Perhaps what Cecil Beaton was to describe as the "nihilism" of the Chanel look was modernist too: it not only mocked the vulgarity of conspicuous consumption but, in inventing a look that was universal, international and reduced to the minimum, it almost sought to abolish fashion itself, creating instead a classic look that defied the one essential of fashion – change. At the same time the geometric, angular design of women's clothing imitated the clean, spare lines of modern abstract art and design. Woman was no longer treated as a voluptuous animal; she had become a futurist machine.

Fashion thus disseminated the new esthetic of the modernist avant garde across two continents, and radically altered the way in which erotic beauty was conceived. Fashion became, superfiicially at least, classless, and the great thing for a woman was no longer to look grand, but simply to look modern.

▼ Swimwear became more streamlined (two-piece costumes came in in the 1930s), and although a holiday abroad was the privilege of the few, lower-middle-class and even some working-class families were beginning to have holidays in their own country. The French Riviera and Venice Lido were the chic spots for the international idle rich.

◀ Skirts were only really short (knee-length) in 1925–27, and these graceful frocks of 1924 show that the more girlish, less garçonne look of the early 1920s was quite romantic. The swirling patterns show the influence of the abstract art of the Delaunays.

▲ Art deco crystallized as a style from 1925. It was modern style for the 20th-century, but drew on many influences; among them Cubism, the Bauhaus and orientalism, and traditional Mexican, Aztec and North American Indian art. These pieces were by Cartier.

For the first time the New World and the Old engaged in a mutual cultural exchange of style and imagery. Although Paris still led the way, the vamps and innocents of Hollywood – Theda Bara, Gloria Swanson, Mary Pickford, Louise Brooks – constructed new tastes in beauty, while the "lost generation" of American expatriates settled in Paris and the south of France. Some of these hoped to create a new art and a literature that would reflect the often excessive and even tragic pleasure-seeking of the postwar generation. Ernest Hemingway, Scott Fitzgerald and many others tried to be as well as to describe a modern breed of sexually free beings, women and men whose minds, hearts and bodies were as untrammeled by traditional notions of morality as their bodies were by constricting clothes. Fitzgerald's characters "discovered" the Riviera in summer – until then it had been only a winter resort – and the suntan became another sign of working-class toil to migrate up the social scale. It became the status symbol of the globetrotter, who need never work and whose wealth permitted this inversion of established tastes. Society ladies took care to become brown as navvies, and Fitzgerald's heroine wore only pearls and a low-backed white bathing suit to set off her iodine-colored skin as she lay on the Mediterranean sands.

Datafile

The 1920s was the decade of the great picture palaces, the grandiose and luxurious movie theaters. It was also a period of consolidation and organization within the American film industry. A trade association was founded to supervise the industry's public relations and its dealings with government. The leading companies expanded into large corporations by buying and building movie theaters in the most profitable city-center sites. The coming of sound in the late 1920s extended the industry's boom period by providing a new novelty to attract audiences, but it also brought unemployment to the musicians of the orchestras which accompanied "silent" movies.

Films released with sound

1928
- 3%
- 22%
- 75%

1929
- 13%
- 30%
- 57%

- ▨ Silent
- ▨ Part sound
- ▨ Talking

▶ Warner Bros. released their first film with a synchronized music accompaniment, *Don Juan*, in 1926, and the part-talkie feature, *The Jazz Singer*, in 1927. The other companies agreed on which sound system to adopt, and negotiated favorable terms with Western Electric. This achieved, the conversion to sound was very rapid.

Types of film 1924

USA

UK

- ▨ Romance
- ▨ Drama/literary
- ▨ Crime/war/spies
- ▨ Westerns
- ▨ Comedy
- ▢ Action/adventure
- ▢ Historical
- ▨ Documentary
- ▨ Fantasy/horror
- ▨ Others

▼ American films earned 20–40 percent of their revenues from foreign sales. By far the most important foreign market was Britain, which accounted for half the European earnings for most films. The Depression, and government regulation of American imports to protect domestic film production, accounted for most of the fall-off in Hollywood's share of films shown abroad (below right)). Until the 1930s Mexico was the only country to attempt to control imports from Hollywood, because of their derogatory representation of Mexicans.

Average weekly attendance in US cinemas

(y-axis: Millions, 0–80)
(x-axis: 1922, 1924, 1926, 1928)

▶ Romance was the staple commodity in almost every film; nine out of ten Hollywood movies featured it as the main plot or an important sub-plot.

◀ Movie attendance figures are notoriously unreliable because of the movie industry's tendency to exaggeration. Some sources claim that 90 percent of the American population went to the movies every week in 1929. These figures are more conservative, but still indicate a weekly attendance equivalent to 60 percent of the population.

Hollywood export revenue

- 35%
- 31%
- 10%

- ▢ UK
- ▨ Others
- ▨ Germany
- ▨ Australia/N. Zealand
- ▨ Scandinavia
- ▢ Argentina
- ▨ Canada

Hollywood feature films as a percentage of all films shown

□ 1925 □ 1928 □ 1937

(Countries shown: UK, Germany, Australia, New Zealand, Scandinavia, Argentina, Canada, France, Japan, Brazil, Aust/Hung/Czech, Italy, Spain/Portugal, Mexico)

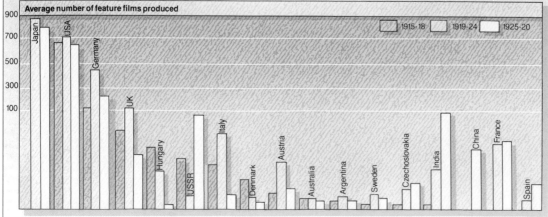

Average number of feature films produced

(y-axis: 100–900)

□ 1915-18 □ 1919-24 □ 1925-20

(Countries shown: Japan, USA, Germany, UK, Hungary, USSR, Italy, Denmark, Austria, Australia, Argentina, Sweden, Czechoslovakia, India, China, France, Spain)

◀ Even in the early 1920s, Hollywood was not the world's largest producer of films. Although Japan's cinema industry was prolific, hardly any of its product was exported even before sound imposed the barrier of language. For most European countries, film production peaked in the early 1920s and then yielded to their domestic audiences' demand for American product. In retaliation, many European governments imposed quota limits on American films. India and China began to develop their industries in the 1920s.

CATHEDRALS OF PLEASURE

As the United States became an increasingly child-centered culture, concern grew about the moral effects of popular culture on the young. This was not simply a matter of its content: many educationalists shared philosopher Charles Horton Cooley's disquiet about its "expressive" function in stimulating emotions. The "rapid and multitudinous flow of personal images, sentiments, and impulses", he feared, produced "an overexcitation which weakens or breaks down character". Such criticisms of the media's failure to fulfil the great educational and cultural mission that reformers had prescribed for them voiced Victorian dissatisfactions with the social developments of the 20th century. This critique is still echoed in contemporary concerns about the effects of television on children.

Hollywood and American taste

Hollywood continued to educate American audiences in the new pleasures of consumption, increasingly justified as a form of therapy for modern life. As psychologist G. Stanley Hall argued, "Everyone, especially those who lead the drab life of the modern toiler, needs and craves an occasional 'good time' ... Indeed, we all need to glow, tingle, and feel life intensely now and then." Intensity and escape were closely bound together. Cecil B. De Mille's films of the early 1920s made it clear that the real escape was from the confines of a personally and sexually unfulfilling marriage. In *Why Change Your Wife?* (1920) and *Forbidden Fruit* (1921), De Mille depicted couples discovering passion as the savior of their marriage. Both might dally with other, often foreign, lovers in the process of discovery, but they were always reunited in a "happy ending" that contained woman's newfound sexuality within the safe boundaries of the private, leisured home.

Later in the decade, Hollywood incarnations of the "flapper girl", most memorably Clara Bow in

▼ Director Cecil B. De Mille (sitting on running board) and his cast in one of the first feature-length Westerns, *The Squaw Man* (1914). Between 1920 and 1960, more than a quarter of all films produced in Hollywood were Westerns.

JESSE L. LASKY FEATURE PLAY Co · HOLLYWOOD ·

The Plastic Age (1925) and *It* (1927), portrayed restless young women escaping from a restrictive home to the city, where short skirts and innocent flirtatiousness represented independence, and the object was to catch a desirable man without losing your virtue. While these movies suggested new attitudes, they did not challenge the proprieties of conventional morality. Instead, they showed how the modernist hedonism of metropolitan life could be contained within the established social order.

These stories attached desire to youth, newness, and the personality that combined them, the star. Young movie heroes and heroines repeatedly broke with the past, experimenting with identities and styles in new stories and the newest clothes and decor. The stars themselves were ephemeral, subject to change for no greater reason than the producers' realization that a commitment to novelty was a commitment to images that came and went, and thus to a kind of planned obsolescence among their star personalities. Hollywood's lesson was that the *frisson* of novelty could be bought, and thus the illusion of freshness, progress, and constant renewal could be acquired without disrupting the status quo.

The projection of overt sexuality was far more difficult for male stars than female. Rudolph Valentino's screen performances were often ridiculed by American men who either accused him of being a gigolo or questioned his masculinity because he consciously made himself appealing to women. His gaudy, stage-managed funeral after his death from peritonitis in 1926 epitomized the public excesses of the decade.

Despite the complaints of moralists, it was an unthreatening rebellion, with its tensions resolved in the cult of youth. Stars encouraged their fans to make the private world of leisure a refuge from somber public concerns. They offered no challenge to economic inequalities, routine work, or the continuing separation of sexual roles in public life. As work came to occupy less of peoples' energies, leisure became an egalitarian arena where imitating the spontaneity of adolescence brought personal fulfillment. The business world was no longer a moral testing ground, but a supply house for new desires. Scandal became an epidemic in Hollywood at this time, as an inevitable part of the process of publicity for the studios and their stars, but it had unfortunate effects on the careers of its victims, notably Roscoe "Fatty" Arbuckle.

The twenties saw some of Hollywood's most exotic epics, including *The Thief of Baghdad* (1924) and *Ben Hur* (1926). Taking a theme that was close to home, in James Cruze's *The Covered Wagon* (1923) and John Ford's *The Iron Horse* (1924) it also produced the first epic enactments of the Western myth. Here the pioneer endeavors of an earlier generation of Americans were seen as laying the heroic foundations of the 20th – the American – century. The worldwide popularity of these films indicated the extent to which the Western was coming to be seen as a myth of origin not just for Americans but for the emerging Western culture of consumption as a whole.

◀ Fritz Lang's *Metropolis*, made in Germany in 1926, was set in the modernistic, mechanical world of AD 2000. Its technological nightmares were combined with a Gothic horror story in a style typical of the German expressionists. Lang went to Hollywood in 1934.

Russian Revolutionary Cinema

"Of all the arts", said Lenin, "for us the cinema is the most important." The energy of the Russian Revolution was closely attached to the impact of rapid industrialization, and nowhere were the effects of that conjunction more firmly felt than in the arts. For a brief period in its early years, the October Revolution produced an atmosphere in which, it seemed, the nature of perception itself had changed. Revolutionary artists endorsed the polemical purposes of new art forms for the people – poster art, popular theater and poetry, but most of all film. Newsreels not only spread the new regime's propaganda message but also revealed the vast diversity and resources of the Soviet Union to its people for the first time.

In their technique, too, Soviet filmmakers enthusiastically adopted the machine esthetic. A chronic shortage of filmstock during the Civil War made necessity the stepmother of Lev Kulushov's inventive theory of montage, but he took the main part of his inspiration from the automobile-factory assembly line. He maintained that two film pieces of any kind, edited together, inevitably combined into a new concept arising out of their juxtaposition. Soviet filmmakers used montage to produce a cinema which rejected Hollywood's conventional construction of space and time and celebrated the fragmentary perception of modern life in the metropolis.

In *Strike* (1924), *Battleship Potemkin* (1925) and *October* (1927), films which mythologized the Revolution for the general public in Soviet Russia, Sergei Eisenstein assembled his images in dynamic collision. He insisted that a film should be constructed in the spectator's imagination, through an association of ideas generated by the clashing of shots.

▶ Still and poster of *Battleship Potemkin*.

I am the cinema eye. I, a machine, can show you the world as only I can see it. From today, I liberate myself for ever from human immobility. I am in perpetual motion, I approach and move away from objects, I creep up to them, I climb on to them, I move alongside the muzzle of a running horse, I tear into the crowd at full speed, ...I ascend with aeroplanes...My way leads to the creation of a fresh perception of the world.

DZIGA VERTOV 1929

▶ Polish film star Pola Negri was one of the first Europeans to be lured to Hollywood, in 1923. Foreign players provided a sense of the exotic for American audiences, but Hollywood's talent-poaching did nothing to strengthen European film.

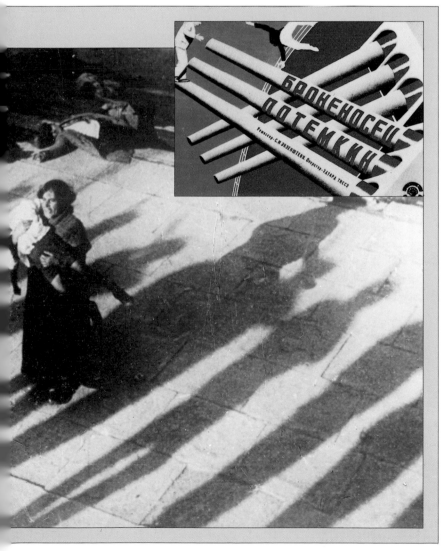

European cinema

The idea that the foreign was exotic was a Middle American assumption to which Hollywood happily pandered. In De Mille's films and in those of Erich von Stroheim, Europe represented a half-admired, yet half-condemned sophistication. Europeans were daring but decadent, sensual but self-destructive, charming but dangerous and even evil. They sought, in other words, to do exactly what Hollywood recognized was not permitted to Americans in the new culture of consumption: to enact their desires rather than to sublimate them. While Parisians and Londoners might not recognize themselves easily in such Hollywood-constructed Babylons, a good deal of European silent cinema enacted aspects of the American fantasy. Toppled from its position of world dominance by the war, the French cinema retreated into the parochial concerns of Parisian high culture. In films like *L'Inhumane* (1924) and *Le Brasier Ardent* (1923) it revealed a concern with self-conscious experiment, often in a Cubist-inspired style.

Many German and Scandinavian films sought to contrast the complacency of bourgeois life with the precarious yet imaginatively richer community of artists, entertainers and prostitutes. The decadence that Hollywood imagined was echoed in many of these films, with their assumption that passion's choice of love-object is arbitrary and often, as in G.W. Pabst's *Pandora's Box* (1928), linked to a wish for self destruction. In other respects German cinema shared with the French a greater concern for technique – the almost constantly mobile camera of F.W. Murnau's *The Last Laugh* (1925), for example – than for character, psychology or politics. Many of the contradictions of European cinema derived from its attempts to define a commercial position for itself, both

within its own culture and in the world market, in the face of the dominance of Hollywood products and styles. But they also resulted from unresolved tensions about the uncertain status of cinema in Europe. Its commercial appeal and its melodramatic plots, frequently derived from pulp fiction, denied it elitist "artistic" value on any quasi-literary grounds of narrative or thematic complexity. Instead, directors like Murnau or Fritz Lang achieved their cultural status as artists in the way that painters did, through displays of technical virtuosity.

For many foreign audiences, the lure of Hollywood movies had much to do with the physical genius of Americans. In Eric Rhode's phrase, "They held the secret of movement, and Europeans went to American movies to learn the secret." In the process, they found themselves seduced into desiring the American things they saw on the screen. Using the maxim, "Trade Follows the Films", the movie industry and the State Department promoted Hollywood as an advertiser of American culture.

For Hollywood the European film industries were a source of talent, a means by which they could import new ideas and faces. Directors such as Murnau and Ernst Lubitsch, and stars such as Pola Negri and Greta Garbo were lured by American money and facilities. There they found that Hollywood's narratives did not have time for the complex characterization of the realist novel or naturalist drama; nor did they draw attention to their techniques. Instead, they focused attention on individual characters and their motivations, and aimed to make the workings of cinematic narration as "invisible" as possible. Typically, a Hollywood narrative would create a problem for characters to solve, show them attempting to solve it, and provide a definite resolution. One action triggered the next in a chain of cause and effect; each scene depicted one event and advanced the narrative one step nearer the climax.

The coming of sound
By 1920 the industry had embarked on a second phase of monopoly control. It was organized not around patents but around the economies of scale permitted within large companies involved in production, distribution and exhibition. Under its president, Adolph Zukor, Paramount developed some of the basic mechanisms of monopoly control such as block booking, by which exhibitors could buy films only in groups, whether they wanted all the films or not. Other companies, including Metro-Goldwyn-Mayer (MGM) and Fox, enlisted Wall Street finance in following Zukor's example. In 1922 they formed a trade association, the Motion Picture Producers and Distributors of America, Inc. (MPPDA). As its president, and "spokesman for the industry", they hired Will H. Hays, then Postmaster-General, and the man who had run Warren Harding's successful presidential campaign in 1920. While the Hays Office, as the MPPDA was popularly known, was most famous for its involvement in film censorship, it was also much less publicly involved in a wide range of political and legal activities on behalf of its members.

◀ Charlie Chaplin's 1920s comedies continued to be immensely successful. But increasingly he placed his tramp in settings removed from the everyday world: a circus, or the Klondike of *The Gold Rush*. Harold Lloyd (seen center in *Safety Last*, 1923) and Buster Keaton belonged to a modern, mechanical age, and accepted its absurdity as a fact of life. Much of their acrobatic comedy arose from their attempts to restore order to a chaotic world. Of all the silent comedians, however, only Stan Laurel and Oliver Hardy (below) really negotiated the change to sound successfully.

▶ Released in October 1927, *The Jazz Singer* was the first "part-talkie"; four of its sequences used the Vitaphone sound system to record vaudeville star Al Jolson's singing.

▼ In 1928 MGM's Leo recorded his roar.

The major companies cooperated with each other on such major issues as censorship, legislation and the introduction of sound. Warner Bros pioneered sound movies as part of a planned program of expansion which included extensive theater purchases. In August 1926 they assembled their first package of sound films, containing six musical performances and the John Barrymore feature *Don Juan*, which had recorded musical accompaniment. Initially uncertain of the long-term profits in sound, the larger companies agreed to spend a year jointly investigating all the available systems. Meanwhile, Warners continued to produce short sound films featuring the biggest stars of vaudeville, including Al Jolson. In 1928 the other companies opted for the Vitaphone system used by Warners. In order to exploit RCA's rival Photophone system which they had rejected, David Sarnoff, head of RCA, organized a series of mergers to create the last of the great Hollywood companies, RKO (Radio Keith Orpheum). A year later, RCA took over the Victor Talking Machine Company, making itself the first entertainment media conglomerate, with interests in broadcasting, recording, movies and vaudeville.

THE PICTURE PALACE

From the early 1910s, going to the movies became an event in itself. As Adolph Zukor explained, middle-class audiences demanded better facilities: "The nickelodeon had to go, theaters replaced shooting galleries, temples replaced theaters, and cathedrals replaced temples". By 1925, the United States had nearly a thousand picture palaces.

The cathedrals of the movies were to be found in the business and shopping centers of large cities. Their elaborate exteriors, featuring exotic motifs from ancient, oriental or European culture, were massive outdoor advertising displays. At night they were lit by multicolored electric signs, sometimes three storeys high. Inside, the foyers were large enough to hold the audience waiting for the next show. There might even be a small orchestra playing to keep them entertained. The two-hour show included a live orchestral overture and stage show, a comedy short and newsreels as well as the feature film.

Despite their grandeur, the American picture palaces were insistently egalitarian, places where the architectural and decorative styles of the wealthiest estates and hotels were made available to all. "Movies", declared William Fox, "breathe the spirit in which the country was founded, freedom and equality. In the motion picture theaters there are no separations of classes ... the rich rub elbows with the poor and that's the way it should be. The motion picture is a distinctly American institution." Indeed, the picture palace was perhaps the only legitimate arena in which the classes and sexes mingled. The "Million Dollar Theaters" sought to convince all their clientèle that, as viewers, they could become part of the glamorous life they watched on the screen. Many cinemas provided free baby-sitting. Mirrors encouraged patrons to recognize themselves amidst the chandeliers and fountains, so they could feel that escaping from the cramped anonymity of the office or the apartment house into these gilded mansions of romance should not be an occasional luxury, but a necessary regular respite from all that was oppressive in metropolitan life.

This idyll proved enormously seductive. Imitating the business strategies of chain stores, the industry looked for ways to present a more standardized product. One of the reasons for introducing sound was that it would reduce the cost of musical entertainment by replacing the theater orchestra and stage shows with recorded music and filmed vaudeville shorts.

▶▶ The 5th Avenue Theater in Seattle, opened in 1926, typified the extravagant decor of the picture palaces based on Chinese motifs.

▶ The theater organ of New York's largest picture palace, the Roxy, which seated 5,889 people. It was named after its manager, Samuel Rothafel, who led many of the trends towards ornate luxury.

▶▲ As well as their luxurious surroundings, cinemas offered voyages into the exotic: the spectacular epics like Ben Hur; the amorous orientalism of Rudolph Valentino, or the rich, flapper world of Clara Bow. As an advertisement for Paramount explained in 1925, "All the adventure, all the romance, all the excitement you lack in your daily life are in — Pictures."

1929 - 1945
THE GLAMOR YEARS

Time Chart

	1930	1931	1932	1933	1934	1935	1936	1937
Film	• Apr: Opening of *The Blue Angel*, (directed by Josef von Sternberg) starring Marlene Dietrich • *L'Age d'Or*, surrealist film, directed by Luis Bunuel (Sp) • 11 Dec: *All Quiet on the Western Front* (directed by Lewis Milestone) banned in Germany	• 6 Feb: Release of *City Lights*, starring Charlie Chaplin (USA)	• 3-color technicolor first used in Walt Disney's *Flowers and Trees* (USA) • Swimming star Johnny Weissmuller starred in his first Tarzan movie (USA) • Release of *42nd Street*, choreography by Busby Berkeley • Film debut of Shirley Temple, at the age of 3 (USA)	• Release of *King Kong* (directed by M Cooper) (USA) • 12 Aug: Release of *The Power and the Glory*, directed by William Howard and starring Spencer Tracy, introducing a new narrative style (USA)	• First use of 3-color technicolor for a live action film, *La Cucharacha* (USA) • 10 Jan: D Fairbanks and M Pickford began divorce proceedings (USA)	• First use of stereo sound in cinema, for *Napoleon Bonaparte* • *Mutiny on the Bounty*, starring Charles Laughton and Clark Gable (USA) • *Anna Karenina*, starring Greta Garbo (dir C Browne)	• Release of *Modern Times*, directed by Charlie Chaplin (USA) • Release of *Things to Come*, directed by Alexander Korda (USA)	• Release of *Snow White* cartoon by Walt Disney (USA) • *A Day at the Races*, starring the Marx brothers (USA) • 7 Jun: Death of Jean Harlow at the age of 26 (USA)
Media	• Baird television, first factory-made set, marketed in UK • 31 Mar: First television program with perfectly synchronized sight and sound broadcast by BBC (UK)	• 23 Dec: First regular television broadcasts began in USA	• 13 Aug: Marconi successfully tested first shortwave radio in Rome (It) • 21 Dec: First Christmas broadcast by a reigning monarch, George VI (UK)	• Frequency modulation (FM) radio transmission perfected by Edwin Armstrong (USA) • 24 Dec: Church bells from Bethlehem broadcast simultaneously throughout world		• Penguin Books published their first ten paperback titles (UK)	• 11 Dec: Abdication of King Edward VIII broadcast (UK)	• First magnetic tape recorder marketed by AEG/Telefunken (Ger)
Music	• *On The Sunny Side of the Street*, written by Fats Waller and sold to Jimmie McHugh	• 3 Mar: *The Star Spangled Banner* adopted as US national anthem • 23 Nov: Bing Crosby recorded *Where the Blue of the Night*, later his signature tune (USA) • Dec: Stereo sound recording patented by A. Blumlein (USA)	• *Brother, Can You Spare a Dime?* written by Jay Gourlay (USA) • *I Got Rhythm*, written by George Gershwin, in Girl Crazy • *Creole Rhapsody* began to win a serious reputation for Duke Ellington (USA)	• Dance craze for "Nira" – in honor of the US National Recovery Administration (NRA) • Stereo 78rpm disks produced by EMI, but not sold	• Opening of *Anything Goes*, a musical with music by Cole Porter (USA)	• Benny Goodman band, with black and white musicians, popularized swing (USA) • *Porgy and Bess*, with music by George Gershwin, featured *Summertime* (USA) • Feb: Meeting of Coleman Hawkins and Django Reinhardt in Paris to mark the founding of *Jazz Hot* journal (USA)	• First popular music chart published by Billboard magazine (USA) • *Pennies from Heaven*, written by Arthur Johnston (USA)	• Death of blues singer Bessie Smith in a car crash (USA)
Fashion and Design	• French architects, decorators and designers formed the Union des Artistes Modernes as an exhibiting society (Fr) • Completion of architect William Van Alen's art deco Chrysler Building in New York (USA) • Noel Coward's wardrobe for *Private Lives* designed by Capt. Edward Molyneux (UK)	• Fashion Group of America founded (USA) • Inauguration of Empire State Building, New York (USA)	• Crease-resistant process for fabric announced by Tootal Broadhurst (UK) • The styles created by fashion designer Adrian for Joan Crawford in *Letty Lynton* were widely copied (USA) • Industrial designer Norman Bel Geddes' illustrated book *Horizons* helped to spread Modernist ideas in design (USA)	• Italian Triennale design exhibitions held in Milan for the first time (It) • Bauhaus design school closed (Ger) • Council for Art and Industry formed (UK) • Fashion designer Elsa Schiaparelli reintroduced broad-shoulders to the female silhouette (Fr) • May: Opening of Chicago World's Fair	• First mass-produced streamlined car, the Chrysler Airflow, launched in USA • Completion of America's first streamlined train, "City of Salina" • Alexey Brodovitch appointed art director of *Harper's Bazaar* magazine (USA) • Apr: First public fashion show in USSR	• Artek furniture company set up by architect Alvar Aalto (Fin) • Two-piece bathing suits modeled in *Vogue* magazine	• Surrealists Elsa Schiaparelli and Salvador Dali created a shoe-shaped hat • Fiat 500, designed by Dante Giacosa, released as Italy's "people's car" • Ferdinand Porsche designed the Volkswagen (Ger)	• Opening of the Paris World's Fair (Fr) • Diana Vreeland became fashion editor of *Harper's Bazaar* magazine (USA)
Sport	• Jul: First Soccer World Cup held • Jul: Cricketer Donald Bradman (Aus) scored a record 309 runs in one day in a Test Match (UK) • Aug: First British Empire (later Commonwealth) Games held (Can)	• Feb: First television coverage of a baseball match (Jap)	• Feb: Winter Olympics held at Lake Placid (USA) • Jul-Aug: Summer Olympic Games held in Los Angeles (USA) • Jul: India competed in its first cricket Test Match	• Jan: Bodyline crisis during MCC cricket tour of Australia • German Jews banned from taking part in 1936 Olympics	• First European athletic championship held, in Turin, for men only (It) • Aug: Fourth Women's World Games held, in London (UK) • US Masters golf tournament first staged (USA)	• 25 May: Jesse Owens (USA) broke five athletic world records in one day • 3 Sep: Malcolm Campbell (UK) became the first man to exceed 300mph (500km/h) in his car Bluebird	• Baseball Hall of Fame opened (USA) • Feb: Winter Olympics held in Garmisch-Partenkirchen (Ger) • Aug: Summer Olympic Games held in Berlin (Ger); Jesse Owens (USA) won four gold medals	
Misc.	• Introduction of sliced bread and packaged frozen foods (USA)		• Aviator Charles Lindbergh's baby son kidnapped and murdered (USA)	• Prohibition ends (USA) • Mar: FD Roosevelt became US president	• Opening of world's first launderette (USA)	• Monopoly game introduced by Parker Bros (USA)	• Dale Carnegie published his bestseller, *How to Win Friends and Influence People* (USA)	

1938	1939	1940	1941	1942	1943	1944	1945
	• Release of *Gone with the Wind*, starring Clark Gable and Vivien Leigh (USA) • 29 Mar: Clark Gable and Carole Lombard wed (USA) • Aug: Release of *The Wizard of Oz*, starring Judy Garland (USA)	• Oct: Release of *The Great Dictator*, directed by and starring Charlie Chaplin (USA) • 13 Nov: Premiere of Disney's *Fantasia*, with stereo sound (USA)	• Oct: Release of *The Maltese Falcon*, starring Humphrey Bogart (directed by John Huston) • Stereophonic system installed by SP Ivanov in Moscow (USSR) • Release of *Citizen Kane*, starring and directed by Orson Welles (USA)	• Release of *Bambi* by Walt Disney (USA)	• Esther Williams achieved stardom in *Bathing Beauty* (USA) • Release of *Casablanca*, starring Humphrey Bogart and Ingrid Bergman, directed by M Curtiz (USA)	• Release of *Frenzy*, directed by Alf Sjöberg (Swe) • Betty Grable starred in *Pin-Up Girl* (USA)	• Release of *Les Enfants du Paradis*, directed by Marcel Carne (Fr)
• 31 May: First television games show broadcast (UK) • 30 Oct: Broadcast of *The War of the Worlds* by Orson Welles convinced US public of a Martian invasion		• Pulse modulation first used to broadcast speech					• Home Service and Light Programme inaugurated by BBC, to broaden the range of broadcast programs (UK)
• Crooner Frank Sinatra's radio debut (USA) • 16 Jan: Benny Goodman gave the first jazz concert at New York's Carnegie Hall (USA)	• Frank Sinatra's second record *All or Nothing at All* sold 1 million copies	• *A Nightingale Sang in Berkeley Square*, by Manning Sherwin • *When You Wish Upon a Star*, by Leigh Harline	• 16 Nov: First publicly recorded jam session, organized by *Melody Maker* magazine (UK)	• First golden disk awarded, to Glenn Miller, by RCA Victor, for *Chattanooga Choo Choo* (USA) • 29 May: *White Christmas* recorded by Bing Crosby, the biggest selling record of all time (USA)	• Frank Sinatra became first music star to be screamed at by young fans, in New York (USA) • Opening of *Oklahoma!* by Rogers and Hammerstein (USA) • Jitterbug dance craze in USA	• 3 Mar: Paris debut by Yves Montand (Fr) • 16 Dec: Bandleader Glenn Miller lost at sea, aged 40 (USA)	• Opening of *Carousel*, by Rogers and Hammerstein (USA) • 15 Mar: First album chart published (USA)
• Neiman-Marcus Awards founded for service to fashion (USA) • Norman Hartnell appointed dressmaker to the British royal family • Edith Head became chief costume designer at Paramount Pictures (USA)	• Nylon first manufactured, by Du Pont (USA) • Apr: Opening of New York World's Fair, the first at which industrial design took prominence over decorative (USA)	• Organic Design in Home Furnishings exhibition at Museum of Modern Art (MoMA), New York (USA) • Packaging for Lucky Strike cigarettes redesigned by Raymond Loewy (USA) • Designers Charles Eames (USA) and Eero Saarinen (Fin) won a MoMA competition with their bent plywood chairs • First Varga girl pin-up calendar issued	• Terylene developed by the Calico Printers Association • May: Clothes rationing introduced in UK	• Feb: Utility design guidelines issued by UK Board of Trade • L85 fabric restrictions introduced in USA • Cosmetics and perfume company Coty founded its American Fashion Critics Award (USA)	• First practical ballpoint pen patented by Laszlo Biro (Hun) in Argentina	• Council of Industrial Design (Later Design Council) established in UK • Society of Industrial Designers founded (USA)	• Fashion houses opened by Hardy Amies in London (UK) and Pierre Balmain in Paris (Fr) • Richard Avedon appointed staff photographer for *Harper's Bazaar* magazine (USA)
• Jul: All Wimbledon tennis titles won by US players	• Little League baseball launched, for boys and girls aged 9-18 (USA) • 29 Jul: Jenny Kammersgaad (Den) became first person to swim the Baltic Sea				• Feb: Baseball star Joe DiMaggio volunteered for the US Army		• Oct: Jackie Roosevelt Robinson became first black player to be signed by a US baseball team
	• Beginning of World War II, as Germany invaded Poland; France and Britain declared war	• Winston Churchill became UK prime minister	• Dec: USA entered war				• 7 May: Surrender of Germany • 6 Aug: Atomic bomb dropped on Hiroshima

Datafile

The 1930s were the golden age of design as an ideal for improving the quality of life for people at every level of society. The art of the industrial designer was taken seriously, and in the United States, at least, design was consciously promoted to encourage the country out of the Depression: the modernistic displays at the World's Fairs of Chicago and New York, in 1934 and 1939 respectively, were emblematic of this.

Elsewhere, the idea of the people's car – the Volkswagen in Germany, designed by Ferdinand Porsche, and its equivalents built by Citroën in France and Fiat in Italy exemplified the desire to bring the benefits of good design to all the people. During the Nazi period, however, German design lost most of the impetus that had been built up under the Bauhaus (which was closed in 1933); whereas other countries were pushing ahead with modernism and streamlining, Germany reverted to neoclassicism until the 1950s.

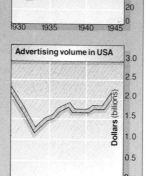

US national income

Advertising volume in USA

▲▲ As in the 1920s, the volume of advertising in the United States had remained generally in line with the overall national income. It fell back somewhat during the later 1930s, and declined appreciably after 1935, when business confidence was lower and advertising budgets more carefully scrutinized. It fell further during the war.

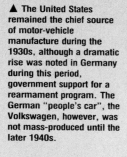

World motor vehicle production 1930 and 1938

▲ The United States remained the chief source of motor-vehicle manufacture during the 1930s, although a dramatic rise was noted in Germany during this period, government support for a rearmament program. The German "people's car", the Volkswagen, however, was not mass-produced until the later 1940s.

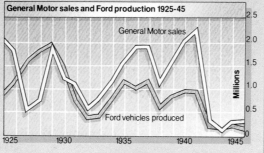

General Motor sales and Ford production 1925-45

▲ During the 1920s General Motors established a sudden lead over their chief rival Ford, as General Motors stressed comfort and style. Both companies were hit by the Depression: Ford's work-force fell from 128,000 in 1929 to 37,000 in 1931. During the war years both companies went over to war work.

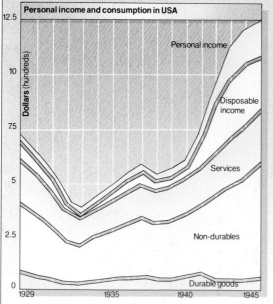

Personal income and consumption in USA

◄ In the early 1930s, average personal income fell in real terms by almost half in the United States; while the amount spent on durable goods held up sales of non-durables and services were squeezed. As disposable income (money available after taxation) rose towards the end of the decade sales of non-durables rose.

During the late 1920s huge changes had taken place in the way new American technological goods, particularly automobiles, were sold and consumed. Since the early years of production at Henry Ford's Highland Park factory – from 1912 until the mid 1920s – the design of his "Model T" had remained fundamentally unchanged. Ford's manufacturing philosophy involved commitment to standardization, achieved through the use of single-purpose machinery and the production line. Ford's aim was to mass-produce a high-quality, low-price car which the American population, particularly the rural sector, could afford. For the first decade of its implementation this formula proved highly successful, but by the 1920s a second-hand automobile market had developed, while more affluent consumers could pay more for goods that were status symbols as well as useful. Standardization preserved economies of scale in production, but its monolithic application to the appearance of the final product became less and less appropriate – the Model T failed increasingly to provide the degree of novelty and fashionability required by the new American consumers of the 1920s.

The annual model change

General Motors, a composite company that had expanded by absorbing smaller firms such as Cadillac, Chevrolet, Pontiac and Buick, was highly sensitive to the new mood of consumption, and in the mid-1920s instigated a program of product variation and stylistic obsolescence in its automobiles. In 1927 Harley Earl became head of the "Art and Color" section at General Motors. He initiated the idea of the annual model change, which quickly became established within the production and marketing habits of the American automobile industry as a whole.

Ford's reaction to the shrinking market for his product and the growing competition from General Motors was highly dramatic. In 1926 Henry Ford closed down his River Rouge plant for a whole year, designing and tooling up for a new automobile, the Model A, which was launched in 1927. Ford's concession to product styling – by 1931 he had introduced yet another model, the "V8" – demonstrated that the era of flexible mass production, allowing for obsolescence and product styling, had begun.

The lesson learned by Ford was soon instilled into the minds of countless other American manufacturers of technological consumer goods. The buying boom and industrial expansion of the early twenties was followed by an economic recession, already beginning to be felt by 1926. The market for domestic electrical appliances, gas-powered goods and many other "consumer machines" that had only recently appeared,

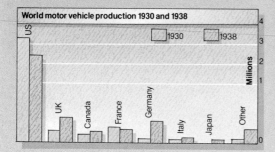

STREAMLINED STYLE

- Industrial design and the high-profile designer
- Annual model change and planned obsolescence
- Plastics and modern design
- The modern movement
- Hollywood and fashion
- German fashions
- Fashion during the war
- Utility style
- The New York World Fair

Airflow

CHRYSLER

Journey's End —
AND YOU'RE READY FOR MORE

◀▼ The *Airflow*, from Chrysler Motors, was the classic 1930s streamlined automobile.

became glutted. Goods competed in the market-place with nothing to distinguish one from another. New means were needed to keep them flowing through the cycle from production to sales. The answer lay in the introduction of a new concept: "industrial design". By introducing the idea of visual differentiation manufacturers began to find ways of individualizing their products and increasing their sales.

Introducing a specialist member of the production team responsible for "product styling" was a logical consequence of the expanding use of advertising. Aggressive marketing was a necessary counterpart of large-scale production, and many of the pioneering American industrial designers – among them men such as Norman Bel Geddes, Walter Dorwin Teague, Henry Dreyfuss, Raymond Loewy, Harold Van Doren, Lurelle

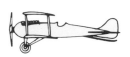

Guild, Donald Deskey and George Sakier – came from the world of "commercial art": notably advertising illustration, store design and window dressing.

From the late twenties countless marriages took place between manufacturers and members of this new profession, many of whom set up small New York offices, offering manufacturing companies the benefits of their specialized skills. Designers charged very high fees: Teague received between $12,000 and $24,000 for each of his consultancy jobs, and Van Doren charged $100 a day for his services. They provided a wide range of work including market research, advice on the costs of retooling, and a survey of the competing products available on the market. While designers earned a public reputation for being "arty", much of their work consisted, in reality, of giving advice of a specifically business nature. They were heralded as national heroes by the popular press, their life stories appearing in magazines such as the *New Yorker* and *Life* in the early 1930s.

The requirement behind the emergence of the industrial designer was founded in the fact that if two competing products were similar in terms of their utility value and price, the one with the more pleasing appearance was more likely to be bought first. Until the early 1920s, the refrigerator was little more than a mechanized ice-box that looked like a wooden safe. The innovations that occurred in the 1920s, through the efforts of General Electric and Frigidaire (a division of General Motors) focused on producing the all-steel electric refrigerator. By the end of the decade this new product was widely available, but sold more on the basis of its technological novelty than on its appearance. Visually it still recalled objects from the past. As with the Model T car, the market for refrigerators quickly became saturated. By the end of the decade the need to make the refrigerator more desirable had grown urgent as competition intensified between the major manufacturers – Frigidaire, General Electric, Sears Roebuck and Westinghouse. The answer lay in employing design.

Streamlining

In 1933 General Electric launched a new, "streamlined" refrigerator, designed by Henry Dreyfuss, which instantly made its competitors look old-fashioned. Westinghouse employed Donald Dohner as an inhouse designer for its whole range of electrical consumer goods. By the middle of the decade Raymond Loewy's design team had provided Sears Roebuck with a number of annual model changes. Its 1935, 1936 and 1937 models were all subtly different from each other, each subsequent design instantly making the previous one obsolescent stylistically. By the mid-1930s nearly all the electrical appliances available on the American market – from the Maytag washing machine to Sunbeam's "Mixmaster" food mixer and Hoover's model 150 vacuum cleaner – had been "styled".

Objects played an increasingly important part in creating and sustaining the social myths of progress, modernity and the beneficence of

technology. Together with the marketing man, the industrial designer became the principal creative force behind their origination, a responsibility that gave him an enormous power in determining the appearance of the consumer society. He provided the main source of imagery in the home, the office and the street. The dominant stylistic idiom was referred to as "streamlining", "streamform" or "streamlined moderne". In architecture and the applied arts, America had developed a popularized version of the faceted, step-formed art deco style that had been in evidence at the 1925 Exhibition of Decorative Arts in Paris. The New York skyscrapers, notably the Chrysler Building and the Empire State Building, proclaimed the style triumphantly to the world. In both automobiles and appliances a style developed that was aggressively "modern" in inspiration and originated in the concept of transport aerodynamics itself, rather than in an abstract notion of design.

Favored by this era's seekers after speed, the "tear-drop" shape, complete with chrome "speed whiskers", epitomized the idea of living with advanced technology, with an eye turned to the future. Before long the style permeated static objects such as irons and gum-dispensers as well as passenger trains and ocean liners. Norman Bel Geddes contributed to the evolution of this dynamic, futuristic style through his models of automobiles, trains, planes and liners of the future – all of which manifested the same curved, bulbous front and tapered rear end. In his design work for the Pennsylvania Railroad Company

▲ The office of the American
industrial designer, Raymond
Loewy, was recreated as a
museum exhibit for an
exhibition held in New York's
Metropolitan Museum of
Art in 1934, entitled
"Contemporary American
Industrial Design". Its
presence signaled the
wide acceptance of the
professional industrial
designer. Loewy's office,
designed by Lee Simpson
and himself, used the
aggressively modern
"streamlined" style promoted
by the designers of America's
new consumer goods, as well
as showing to a wide public a
number of his most recent
designs. His drawings (top
left) of the somewhat fanciful
evolution of the aircraft shape
form part of a set in which
he set out to show the
streamlined style as most
modern and appropriate.

◄ The New York World's Fair
of 1939 represented the high
point of the United States'
infatuation with industrial
design. The Fair stood
for everything that was
"progressive" and modern,
as demonstrated by this
exhibit which showed a
housewife trying out the
many wondrous products for
the home made available
by bakelite.

Raymond Loewy put a number of highly stream-lined designs into production.

The application of streamform to static objects was clearly a stylistic decision, not one based on rational principles or aerodynamics. While historians of streamlining have pointed to its origins in the forms of airships, airplane fuselages, and dolphins, it also clearly owed much to contemporary fine art as well. In their book *Art and the Machine* of 1936, for instance, S. and M. Cheney pointed out its resemblance to forms employed by the French painter Jean Helion and the Romanian sculptor Constantin Brancusi, while Margaret Bourke-White, who used modern machinery as the subject-matter of her photographs, also evolved a similar kind of imagery.

From a manufacturing point of view the curved forms of streamlining were the most appropriate ones for objects made from stamped or pressed metal or from molded plastic. The use of metal and plastic was widespread in the new consumer-goods industries in the 1930s and provided an important justification for the appearance of many of the objects that came off the designers' drawing boards in that decade. Lines of chrome trim were often included for strategic as well as merely decorative purposes, disguising what might otherwise have looked like a concave surface, concealing unattractive joints, or unifying surfaces.

From a theoretical point of view the esthetic embraced by industrial designers in the 1930s in the United States had little in common with the purist, craft-based ideal of "form following function", which inspired the architects and designers associated with the European Modern Movement such as the Bauhaus group in Germany which had flourished in the 1920s. While paying lip-service to this source in their writing, the American designers were really much more conscious of the commercial context of manufacturing than their European counterparts. As a result they adopted a more pragmatic approach towards the esthetic of designed objects.

The all-white "continuous flow" kitchen was as much a product of this period as the bulbous automobile. "Labor-saving" automatic and semi-automatic machines in the kitchen and laundry offered the housewife more free time but the near-obsession with hygiene, also promoted by advertising, required higher standards of house-work and meant that there was more, not less, work to do. Her time was simply spent on a new set of choices. Less time spent on housework meant more time spent on shopping trips; increased consumption meant more time spent making important decisions about purchases – decisions that increasingly had to do with appearance and style, not just content and function. By 1939 the industrial designer, product styling, and object obsolescence were intrinsic elements within modern consumption. Ford's democratic, utilitarian philosophy of the high-quality standardized product available to all was a thing of the past, sacrificed to the merchandizing esthetics of turnover and volume sales.

Hollywood glamor

The fashion image most associated with the 1930s – a decade of Depression, unemployment, fascism and the approach of war – is probably the glamorous Hollywood pale satin evening gown, a bias-cut creation slithering to the floor, low-backed and clinging to the thighs. This ambiguous garment did not look very different from a nightdress, and managed to appear both sultry and languid – chic and upper-class in the pages of *Vogue* or trampishly sexual when worn by Jean Harlow. The slinky lines of the early thirties, and the return to a more waisted, full-skirted and puff-sleeved silhouette later in the decade both emanated from Paris, but it was their interpretation by Hollywood designers such as Adrian and Orry Kelly that ensured their rapid dissemination to a much wider audience. Glamor lingerie, one of the consumer items popularized by the movies in the 1920s, began to be mass produced after the development of synthetic fabrics, notably nylon which was discovered in 1935.

Since the 19th century there had been attempts to manufacture an artificial substitute for silk, the most luxurious fashion fabric. By 1930, rayon was made from pulped wood cellulose; nylon and other synthetics were later developed from chemical products and by 1938 ten percent of apparel fibers in Britain were synthetic. The rich and elegant still wore underwear of real silk, but the availability of artificial substitutes meant that ordinary women could also aspire to a more glamorously attired sexuality and a greater sophistication.

Although sections of the clothing industry remained based in small craft tailoring shops and in the sweatshops of centers such as the Lower East Side in New York City and London's East End there were also major innovations in the mass production of clothes, which further broke down distinctions between skilled tailors, semi-skilled workers in tailoring shops and factory workers and outworkers. Conveyor-belt production was introduced, and the more precise sizing of mass-produced clothes developed. This last was a contradictory development, for the intention was to individualize garments, yet individuals were sorted into groups according to their measurements. It could be seen equally as an index of the expanding possibilities for the expression of a customer's unique personality and as part of the increasing conformity of modern mass society.

Department stores, where clothes could still be altered to fit or were even custom-made, remained the mecca of middle-class customers. The appearance of firms aiming to sell to this market – to men as well as women – was a further development of mass production. Menswear firms with their own factories were able to translate personal measurements into factory-made clothes, while for women "wholesale" or "middle-class couture" firms designed distinctive house styles and took pride in the elegance of their creations. This was the era when it was distinctly possible – but sartorially disastrous – for two identically dressed women to come face to face at a social function.

Women's magazines proliferated during the 1930s and contributed to the greatly increased circulation of fashion images, which could be copied by local dressmakers. Fan magazines and studio publicity also promoted "Hollywood" styles. There was a vogue for movies set in department stores, beauty salons or fashion houses. These films acted as showcases for the latest fashions, which could then be copied *en masse* and retailed through special promotions in the big stores. California developed as a center of the clothing industry, and in particular of sports and casual wear. Backless bathing suits, slacks, halter tops and sweaters – all Parisian couture innovations of the 1920s – were now translated for the beaches and high streets of the whole Western world. Trousers were no longer regarded as eccentric or indecent on women, but were becoming a standard feature of sports and casual wear. In a period when "the career woman" was an acceptable image, women's suits followed the bespoke elegance of those worn by men.

Women's magazines took it upon themselves to instruct and inform women about the latest fashions and changes in style, and also to reinforce ideas about correct wear for different occasions and times of day. This etiquette of dress could now reach virtually all women. The elegant poses of *Vogue* could be subtly adapted for women far down the social scale, and transmitted to women far from metropolitan centers of elegance. This helped to speed up changes of style and break down regional and national stylistic differences. In Germany the Nazis regarded this international style of fashion and glamor as a threat to the purity of Aryan womanhood, and sought to return their womenfolk to a peasant-like style of national dress. Left-wing radicals were also suspicious of the "consumptionism" implied by media fashion promotion, which some saw as drawing women away from a true appreciation of their natural womanly beauty

◄ Marlene Dietrich was one of the great Hollywood icons of beauty in the thirties, representing, with Garbo, the European, more sophisticated and ambiguous (in all senses of the word) side of the celluloid dream.

► Those who could afford to still had their clothes made to measure or bought ready-to-wear fashions at every price level; but home dressmaking also increased in popularity and chic with diffusion of paper patterns via the burgeoning mass market women's magazines.

▼ A fashion show in Berlin in the late 1930s offered a range of international styles.

toward the falsity of the film-star image. "Bohemians", or artistic radicals, of the twenties and thirties endeavored to set themselves apart by disregarding fashion and devising their own uniform of rebellion. The King's Road, Chelsea, in London, was a haunt of artists, whose models and mistresses wore the dirndl skirts and gypsy fashions popularized by "Dorelia", who posed for the British painter Augustus John. These full skirts and sleeves and fitted bodices were soon to become high fashion once more.

As in the 1920s, Parisian *haute couture* had close links with the avant-garde. Chanel now had a rival, Elsa Schiaparelli, who introduced a surrealist element into her designs, with a *trompe l'œil* sweater and a hat made in the shape of a shoe. Fashion began to move away from the speedy modernity of the 1920s; self-conscious

EVAN WILLIAMS (HOLDINGS) LTD

AINTREE ROAD · PERIVALE · GREENFORD

102 NEW BOND STREET · LONDON · W.1

▲ During the war years, rationing of material meant that imagination was lavished on hair and hats. Shampoos and hair dyes ensured that hairstyles remained elegant, while hats, which were not rationed, became more and more extravagant, with bizarre creations perched gaily above sober coats and shirts.

► French models wearing a chic 1940s version of the sober skirt and suit which has remained ever-popular, with minimal changes, through the century. For the most part, elegant clothes were hard to come by in war-ravaged Europe.

femininity was ascendant. In Hollywood, Paris and elsewhere – in the work of the British photographer, Cecil Beaton, for example – one reaction to the Depression and the gathering war clouds was not to adapt dress to sterner political realities, but on the contrary to develop escapist styles and ever more elaborate fantasies of wealth and glamor.

Even Hollywood's big glamor spectaculars, which capitalized on period costume, had an indirect effect on clothing in fads such as the Dolly Varden hat and even panniered evening skirts; while musicals such as Busby Berkeley's *Gold Diggers of 1933* or *42nd Street* popularized the image of the showgirl, with whom millions of

young women now identified as she lost her aura of "easy virtue".

Even more important than Hollywood's influence on clothes was the way in which the movies popularized cosmetics. In the 18th century and earlier, powder and paint had been freely worn, but for most of the 19th century makeup had been taboo for respectable women. In the European capitals and American cities women had started to wear visible makeup again before World War I. In the 1930s cosmetic ranges proliferated for all classes of women, together with the more subtle and wider range of film-star types. The pioneers of the beauty products that grew into huge business empires – Elizabeth

Arden and Helena Rubinstein being two of the best known – certainly did not regard their products as tainted with immorality. Nor were cosmetics any longer seen as hostile to female emancipation; on the contrary, lipstick, like the cigarette, was a badge of liberation. The use of cosmetics even became a symbol of democracy and class equality, evidence that the culture of consumption gave every woman not only a right to good looks but access to the improvement or even the dramatic transformation of her appearance. Along with the powders, lipsticks and increasingly, the eye shadows and mascaras, came creams and lotions that were promoted as preserving youth and beauty, so that the industry latched on to powerful magical fantasies of unconscious origin: a pot of cream from Yardley or Max Factor became the elixir of eternal youth.

These developments were part of a move away from the idea of equality for women, which had lasted through the 1920s; the return of romanticism seemed to signal a retreat for women into more restricted roles. Max Factor, a Hollywood firm, made much of its connections with the film industry, and the use of film stars in promotions pushed further the idea of distinct types of female beauty. It was no longer simply a case of being a blonde, a brunette or a redhead; qualities of character such as passion, class or independence came to be associated with different types of looks, so that the popular consciousness was peopled with stereotypes of dumb blonde, wicked brunette or fiery redhead. "Dress to your type" became a new command to the ordinary woman, and typologies of various kinds were reproduced in magazines, encouraging women to think of themselves as sporty, fluffy, sultry, artistic, and so on.

The increasing romanticism of thirties' fashion was brutally interrupted by the outbreak of war in 1939. For the second time in less than thirty years women were conscripted into the war effort. Their being at risk, like their menfolk at the front, encouraged a renewed belief in women's equality, but the idea that women achieved equality in wartime and were then pushed back into the home afterward is oversimplified. Women did men's jobs "for the duration", but they did not achieve equal pay. Many women with children spent the war in quiet isolation. Rationing, queues, shortages and the constant anxiety about absent lovers, husbands, brothers and fathers – and the real danger to themselves and their families and friends because of air raids – must challenge the popular view of World War II as a period of glamor and freedom for women. Glamor there was, however, despite the hardship. Paradoxically, women's increased participation in the life of the factory, the forces and the office seemed to lead to a greater emphasis on femininity in moments of leisure, even though fashions certainly adapted to the exigencies of the time. In spite of all the difficulties it seemed more important than ever to look nice in order to keep up morale, so there was a greater emphasis than ever before on face and hairstyle.

With occupied Paris no longer the source of new fashions, the war was the American industry's great chance, but in spite of some highly

The Utility Scheme

For a few years during the war the British people seemed willing to forgo the delights of fashion, novelty and status symbols and accept the idea that mass-produced, standardized high-quality products could provide it with all the items of furniture and clothing that it needed. Shortages of timber and cloth, and the need to use labor to produce war materiel rather than consumer goods set the conditions for the National Government's unprecedented experiment in democratizing design. In 1942 an advisory committee produced specifications for furniture "of good, sound construction in simple but agreeable designs for sale at reasonable prices, and ensuring the maximum economy of raw materials and labor."

Britain's situation was unique: it was more embattled than the United States, but not occupied nor a battleground like most of Europe. An advanced and egalitarian rationing system ensured that scarcity was fairly distributed, while under the Utility scheme well-known designers contributed their work so that elegant clothing and furniture could be produced at low cost and with an economical use of materials. Apart from second-hand and home-made articles, Utility furniture and clothing were the only items on the market during the final years of the war and the immediate postwar years.

The twin criteria of simplicity and quality harked back to the ideals of the British Arts and Crafts movement from the end of the 19th century. The furniture was characterized by a stark simplicity, relieved only by the lightly patterned upholstery fabrics, designed in a limited range of colors by Enid Marx. The public and press (less so the trade) responded enthusiastically to the designs. The Utility fashion scheme was less thoroughgoing than the furniture project but it provided, nonetheless, the main source of new clothing in wartime Britain. Strict regulations governed their designs, from the use of a minimal amount of cloth to the elimination of all trimmings and decorations and the use of only three buttons on jackets. Like the furniture designs, the success of Utility clothing depended upon the simplicity of its lines and cut, and it too was at first received with much enthusiasm.

Otherwise, it was "make do and mend". The strongest competition for Utility clothing came from the home-made items that housewives produced for their families.

▲ Utility cotton knit underwear was widely felt to be of better quality than the British prewar equivalent; there was more variation in Utility outerwear, to a considerable extent in quality, less so in design.

original designers they did not achieve stylistic dominance of the market, partly because the fashions of the war years were relatively static. The tight-waisted, full-skirted styles that were on their way back in 1938-39 were modified by rationing and the lack of materials. The influence of uniforms led to the widespread popularity of the tailored suit, with broad padded shoulders, revers, and a short narrow skirt. This fashion, which was popularized in films by Joan Crawford, symbolized the career woman. Sensible country fashions such as tweed coats, boots, ankle socks and headscarves came into vogue, while more casual trousers – often called slacks – finally became acceptable.

THE NEW YORK WORLD'S FAIR

Streamlining spawned visions of the future, nowhere more so than at the Big Fair – the New York World's Fair which opened in April 1939.

International expositions had occured regularly since 1851 – the Eiffel Tower had been built for the Universal Exhibition in Paris in 1899 – but "the People's Fair" proclaimed itself "the mightiest exposition ever conceived and built by man." Its director, Grover Whalen, declared that "By giving a clear and orderly interpretation of our own age, the fair will project the average man into the World of Tomorrow." Its major exhibits were the work of America's leading industrial designers – brilliant displays of their ideas of the rationally planned and re-ordered world of the near future. Behind its façade of education and entertainment, the Fair was a gigantic advertisement for American industrial civilization and what was coming to be called the American Way of Life. *Life* magazine called it "A magnificent monument by and to American business". But most of its 45 million visitors treated it as a amusement park.

There was an irony in the Fair's vision of the future. A pavilion dedicated to "Goodwill and Peace" was planned but never built. The Fair's planners hoped that it would make a "forcible contribution to the cause of peace," but this was little in evidence. Albania and Czechoslovakia flew their national flags at half mast to mark the invasion of their countries by Italy and Germany, and no-one collected the prize for an essay competition: a vacation in "gay, colorful Poland". In exhibits by General Motors and American Telegraph & Telephone, the Fair presented communications as central to its vision of the future, but the Fair's managers decided not to broadcast any news of the war in Europe. In the late 1930s Allied governments expected aerial warfare to cause massive devastation. Americans could only imagine the horrors of Total War, conjured up for them most vividly on Halloween 1938, in the panic caused by Orson Welles' radio broadcast of H.G. Wells' *The War of the Worlds*.

▶ The Avenue of the Flags, leading to the Court of Peace at the New York World's Fair.

▶▶ The Fair's most popular exhibit was General Motors' "Futurama", a model of the American cityscape of 1960 as designer Norman Bel Geddes anticipated it (above). *Things to Come*, based on an H.G. Wells novel, was one of the few 1930s films to anticipate the war (below). Images of catastrophe spoke to an anxious paranoia which lay beneath the decade's surface optimism.

▶▼ The two symbols of the Fair, the 200m-tall Trylon and the 60m globe, the Perisphere (bottom). The Trylon, by one account, symbolized "the infinite aspirations of man," while the Perisphere housed the Fair's theme exhibit, human interdependence in Democracity, the city of 2039.

▶ The term "science fiction" was coined in 1929 by Hugo Gernsback, founder of *Amazing Stories* magazine. Comic-strip heroes of the 1930s were creatures from the future: from 1929 onwards Buck Rogers spent most of the 25th century saving the Solar System from the forces of evil. He rapidly provided inspiration for both toy manufacturers and imitators. Superman appeared to battle for "Truth, Justice and the American Way" from 1938, followed a year later by Batman. Flash Gordon first encountered Ming the Merciless in 1934; Ming's oriental appearance hinted at racial fears of "aliens" closer to home.

A. Hyatt Verrill   Edmond Hamilton   David H. Keller

Datafile

The notion that the audience for popular culture is a passive one – maneuvered into the consumption of useless commodities under an illusion of choice, to provide profits for the few – has been a powerful one. Its roots go back to the 1930s, when evidence of audience manipulation, added to the growth of fascism in Europe, seemed overwhelming. Against this it is possible to discern more independent democratic trends at work in audience responses to popular music. Similarly, it is important to remember the huge variety of individual popular music styles fashioned in the thirties: Billie Holiday, Woody Guthrie, Cole Porter, Lester Young and many others.

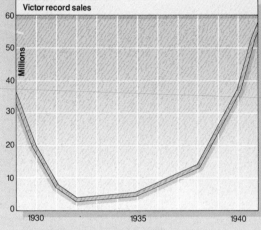

CBS program allocation

- Popular music — 29%
- Symphony/opera/chamber — 26%
- Religious — 22%
- Dramatic — 14%
- Civic — 7%
- Other — 6%
- Instructive

Victor record sales

▲ By 1930 the number of Americans with access to a radio had reached an estimated 60 million, almost half the country's population. And one third of the programs they received consisted of popular dance-band music. These figures, presented by CBS to Congress in 1930, follow a pattern repeated by networks and local stations. The balance between popular and classical music shows radio's desire to live up to its requirements as a public service, while giving the public what they wanted.

▲ The destructive effects of the Depression on record sales are clearly evident in Victor's sales figures. Even back in 1905 the company had sold more records than in 1932 – and sales hit rock bottom in 1933 at $5.5 million, as compared to $105 million in 1921. In Victor's case its new strength in radio saw it through.

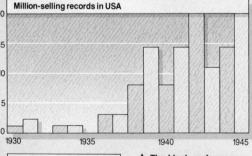

Million-selling records in USA

▲ The bleak performance of the record industry during the Depression is well illustrated by its failure, in 1932 and 1935, to achieve any million-sellers, and only four altogether in the six years 1930–35. The recovery was considerably aided by the introduction of a cheap label by the English-owned Decca company.

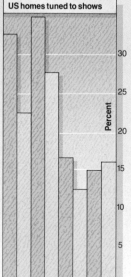

Name band shows

US homes tuned to shows

◄ The left-hand chart shows network radio's heavy reliance on "name" bands, peaking in 1934–35 with no fewer than 26 weekly shows. In that season Guy Lombardo captured an average 23.5 percent of the listening audience (right-hand chart). The year before a larger percentage had opted for rival Paul Whiteman.

On 7 November 1929, nine days after the Wall Street Crash, the song *Happy Days Are Here Again* was registered for copyright. This glaring contrast heralded the escapism of which the music of the next few years is often accused. With a few exceptions (the most famous being *Brother, Can You Spare a Dime?*), the most widely heard music of the 1930s did not relate directly to current problems, and the popular-culture industry seemed insensitive to the problems of its listeners. There was nothing new in this: the music of the 1920s had also celebrated good times, and in that sense thirties' music was a continuation of it. But espousing contemporary music in the twenties had meant taking some kind of stance against established culture; now the onset of the Depression made the music of the time seem to encourage a return to those very values that twenties' music had sought to escape.

For the first half of the decade record sales in the United States dropped steeply, and coast-to-coast radio steadily increased its domination of the entertainment market. Late-night listening became especially popular; tuning in for free to dance bands broadcasting from celebrated night-spots partly compensated for the loss of more costly leisure pursuits. Among the many effects of radio music in the thirties, two stand out: the impact of improved technology on the performance of music, and the creation of a mass audience.

Sweet music

The improvement in the quality of broadcast sound that followed the introduction of the electric microphone in the mid-1920s led to a corresponding rise in the quality of radio receivers. It became possible to discern greater delicacies of instrumental sound and of the singing voice, particularly in the middle range. Songwriters and bandleaders took account of this. It was no longer necessary to limit the size of a band to instruments that could be picked up by the acoustic recording horn, so there was a steady increase in the size of ensembles. Bigger bands, a greater fondness for subtle shades and a higher quality in the middle range meant just one thing: "sweet" music.

Technical changes also had their effect on popular vocal style. The days of declamatory singers such as Al Jolson were all but gone. A whole range of voices previously ruled out for lack of dynamics could now be heard on the air, while the greater clarity of the sung texts increased the importance of lyricists. The microphone's ability to show up not only every flaw in phrasing and enunciation but also each potentially displeasing vocal nuance produced a breed of singers with impeccable diction and with bland, featureless voices. The first singer to respond in full to the microphone's challenge, and to reap its

CROONERS AND SWING

benefits, was one who usually disclaimed having done either: Bing Crosby. So at ease was Crosby with the new technology that he sounded as if he had been "overheard" by it. Crosby's relaxed, intimate style further enhanced the process by which an individual listener could make a private experience out of an ever more widely available musical event. The key elements in this were the characteristic personal timbre – the "grain" – of his voice, his tendency to "talk" a song (coupled with excellent breath control), and his ability to derive effective drama by under-dramatization.

The creation of a mass audience by the networked programs provided the first major opportunity for the manipulation of public taste. In this scheme of things, sweet music had two functions. The first was to create revenue, both for the music industry through its copyright organization, the American Society of Composers, Authors, and Publishers (ASCAP), and for the companies who sponsored the programs. ASCAP had developed an effective system of ensuring that the music of those it represented (Tin Pan Alley) dominated the airwaves. Marketing these songs as standardized products, so they did not attract the critical attention of high-culture opinion-makers, assured large profits.

The second function was less obvious. The peddling of sweet music to a nation whose daily life was often bitter was more than a mere encouragement to escapism. It suited commercial interests for people to soothe the rough edges of their lives with music rather than use it

▼ "Sweet" music, as purveyed by bands such as Glenn Miller Swingers, introduced greater subleties of sound, but its bland unobtrusiveness could meet with ambivalent responses. Critic George Simon cited the reason for his favoring one particular group was that, when it accompanied your dinner, "you could hear a mashed potato drop".

to sharpen their complaints. The music's synchronized control reinforced a shaken sense of order by echoing and embodying that order in its full but conventional harmonies and regular, mechanical rhythm. One day, it suggested, if everyone was compliant, life could be as "full" as these sounds.

Nevertheless, jazz had brought changes in some of the ways that life was perceived. The rhythmic emancipation of ragtime and jazz was built into almost all of the music which followed them, even music that reached a much wider audience than jazz itself. It was most apparent when a number broke into a jazzy section. Then the music's clothing was being shed, and its structural framework revealed. The essential element in the framework was rhythm, in which neither the regular nor the offbeat was dominant; what was important was the suggestion of interplay between the two. Black music itself was developing this to a sophisticated level, but even in "sweet" music it was sufficient to suggest that there were all kinds of alternatives to regular rhythm.

As the United States pulled out of the Depression, a more vigorous style of band music began to be widely heard. Reviving fortunes for the record industry – in particular Decca's introduction of a cheap (35-cent) record – played a part, but radio was preeminently responsible. One crucial element, however, was new: the beginnings of a youth audience. When band leader Benny Goodman won popular acclaim in Los Angeles

▲ With its high levels of energy discharge, the jitterbug provided unprecedented opportunities for inventiveness. Though more abandoned than previous white dances, it still left many blacks unimpressed.

▶ The powerful, highly organized Erskine Hawkins Orchestra was very popular at black dances, especially in New York. Hawkins based his band's sound on the interplay of brass and reeds as pioneered by Fletcher Henderson and Don Redman. In 1938 the arrival of Count Basie's Orchestra from Kansas City revealed the possibilities on offer when a blues-soaked, riff-based sound was fronted by outstanding soloists.

and thus inaugurated the "swing" era in July 1935, his audience were in their teens and early twenties. *Let's Dance*, the show on which Goodman's band appeared, was broadcast too late for the younger audience on the East Coast, but fell right into the mid-evening listening slot of the young West Coast audience, who turned out in force to hear the band live.

Goodman's hugely popular music was not new. It operated on principles borrowed from the Fletcher Henderson band of the late twenties and early thirties. Swing took the form of simplified melodies, using riffs, or short, rhythmically interesting melodic fragments: a propulsive, even meter, call and response between brass and wind sections; and a swinging relationship between rhythm and melody. Swing echoed the familiar pattern: a challenge to the status quo, based on approaches and techniques derived from black music; partial absorption into the white mainstream; conflict with the cultural establishment; eventual compromise. In the case of swing, the conflict took the form not of moral or esthetic condemnation but of a turning by some bands to classically-derived techniques and traditions. This process was clearest in the music of Glenn Miller, whose band led the popularity polls in the early 1940s. Miller's trademark was the sonority of his wind section, achieved by using saxophones topped by a clarinet. The discipline and precision needed to realize his sound were equally important, whether the effect was romantic, up-tempo or even improvised. As a result of these processes, the music did not threaten the mainstream; but for all that, when Glenn Miller's music is compared with that of Paul Whiteman, we can see just how far the black influence on white America had advanced.

Like ragtime and jazz before it, swing was first and foremost a music for dancing; and once again that dancing – "jitterbugging" – was derived from black America. It was also much *closer* to black America. Taken to extremes (as they often were) the physical demands of such dancing confirmed the more youthful fans as the principal

Broadway Musicals

"Give My Regards to Broadway" – George M. Cohan's 1904 song, in the show *Little Johnny Jones*, already reflected the New York theater district's preeminence in the musical stage. Behind it lay a formidable concentration of money. As Tin Pan Alley was the commercial heart of the popular song industry, Broadway was the financial center of the musical – and the closeness of the two ensured the monopoly. Impresarios vied with each other for control – by the mid-twenties the Shubert brothers were said to own half the available seats on the Great White Way. In such a high-risk business quality product was essential, and producers looked to the most sophisticated songwriters of the day for their material, often linking them with professional librettists wise in the necessary stagecraft.

One result of the musical's increasing maturity was the large output of songs which later became "evergreens". The 1930s stage in particular

yielded a rich crop: *Smoke Gets in Your Eyes* (Jerome Kern/Otto Harbach), *Embraceable You* (George and Ira Gershwin), *I Get a Kick Out Of You* (Cole Porter). But many of these songs were well known only to those who were better educated and more affluent than the average radio "fan". Such songs were often judged to lack the necessary immediate appeal to succeed in the aggressive promotion system and received little radio coverage.

This highly accomplished body of song was the product of a convergence of classically-derived harmony, Afro-American concepts of rhythm, the formal structures of earlier popular song and a solo/accompaniment performance convention. The need for effective drama in the musical had enhanced the status of the lyric, and the best lyricists (Lorenz Hart and Oscar Hammerstein among them) drew on the rhythms, cadences and patterns of American speech in ways which themselves *generated* music.

consumers. Radio music in the home, while still the main source of family entertainment, did not satisfy the social and physical requirements of the new dance craze. By the forties, wartime dance halls, throbbing with life as no fantasy nightspot of the Depression had done, became focal points of activity. The reviving record industry, through its new outlet, the jukebox, also encouraged the consumption of music outside the home.

Records and jukeboxes were gradually increasing the familiarity of both whites and blacks with each other's bands, but the mainstream was still not ready to accept black music on its own terms. Perhaps only Duke Ellington was able to "cross over" without sacrificing the essential nature of his music to commercialism. Dances were still largely segregated. Most were for whites only, and featured white bands. It was rare for a white band to play for a black dance – but then, few white bands could have satisfied the black dancers. In the bands themselves, efforts to increase integration had not made much progress. An important gesture was Goodman's inclusion in his band of black musicians Teddy Wilson and Lionel Hampton, on the prompting of impresario John Hammond. Nevertheless, too many black musicians had been exposed to the trauma of racial insult while performing with white bands for this to kindle any enthusiasm.

▲ Bing Crosby provided the anthem for the poor of 1930s America in a song that derived from a musical.

Datafile

The Depression hit Hollywood in 1931. Sound had protected it from the immediate effects of the crash, but attendances and profits dropped sharply in 1932, and took most of the decade to recover. The war years were the industry's most successful. The eight major companies remained in stable control of the industry, and the type of product was standardized and regulated by the Production Code, written in 1930.

▼ Angels with Dirty Faces was a typical late 1930s major studio production, with one big star, James Cagney, and two lesser ones, Pat O'Brien and Humphrey Bogart. The film's budget of $400,000 had $200,000 added to it for overheads and depreciation.

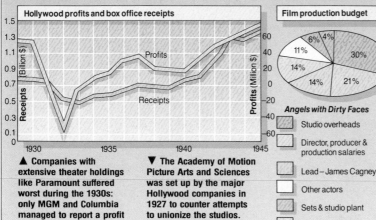

Hollywood profits and box office receipts

Film production budget

Angels with Dirty Faces
- Studio overheads
- Director, producer & production salaries
- Lead – James Cagney
- Other actors
- Sets & studio plant
- Story and writers
- Other costs

▲ Companies with extensive theater holdings like Paramount suffered worst during the 1930s: only MGM and Columbia managed to report a profit every year. War workers had few consumer durables to spend their wages on, and movies were one of the beneficiaries of the wartime boom in the economy.

▼ The Academy of Motion Picture Arts and Sciences was set up by the major Hollywood companies in 1927 to counter attempts to unionize the studios. It became best known, however, for its annual awards, nicknamed Oscars, which became increasingly coveted as badges of success and approval within the industry.

Academy Awards for Best Film of the Year

1928	Wings	Paramount
1929	The Broadway Melody	MGM
1930	All Quiet on the Western Front	Universal
1931	Cimarron	RKO
1932	Grand Hotel	MGM
1933	Cavalcade	Fox
1934	It Happened One Night	Columbia
1935	Mutiny on the Bounty	MGM
1936	The Great Ziegfeld	MGM
1937	The Life of Emile Zola	Warner
1938	You Can't Take it With You	Columbia
1939	Gone With the Wind	MGM
1940	Rebecca	United Artists
1941	How Green Was My Valley	Fox
1942	Mrs Miniver	MGM
1943	Casablanca	Warner
1944	Going My Way	Paramount
1945	The Lost Weekend	Paramount

▼ Sound sharply increased the average movie budget, and brought about a fall in the numbers of films produced. The Depression brought about a change in American exhibition practice: double-bills became the norm, and independent companies appeared to make the cheap B-feature for the second half of the bill. In Britain production was boosted by low-budget movies, made to meet government requirements about the number of British-made films to be shown in British cinemas.

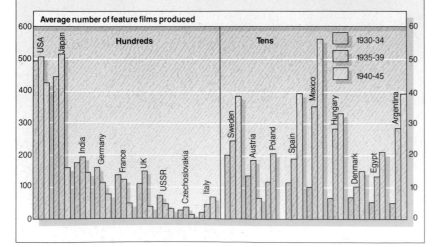

Average number of feature films produced

By the time of the Wall Street Crash in 1929 Hollywood had switched over entirely to "talkies", but even six months later no more than half of the 22,624 movie theaters in the United States had been wired for sound. The conversion cost theaters $300 million, and encouraged a boom mentality that carried the industry over the earliest years of the Depression. The years 1929–31 saw a series of ambitious merger proposals, but the novelty of sound did not have a permanent effect on the box-office and by 1931 the industry was enduring the full rigors of the Depression. Audiences declined. Theaters closed. In 1933, unable to pay their short-term bank debts, RKO and Universal went into receivership, and Paramount was declared bankrupt.

The dominance of the Big Five

These maneuverings of high finance left all the major companies under the control of the largest institutions of American finance capital, but they had relatively little direct effect on the movie-going public. Even during its bankruptcy Paramount promised theater-owners an uninterrupted flow of productions, and underlying the spectacular bids and paper collapses was a gradual process of consolidation. Five companies dominated the industry, maintaining their power by controlling its most profitable sector, first-run exhibition in the cities. As access to this market was vital to the profitability of any but the smallest feature film, this also gave them control of production. Apart from a handful of prestigious independent producers such as Samuel Goldwyn, releasing films through United Artists, the production of big-budget A-features was almost entirely controlled by the "Big Five" – Fox, Paramount, Loew's, RKO and Warner Bros. Smaller firms, including Columbia and Universal, put most of their effort into the production of lower-budget movies, which would play the later-run "neighborhood" theaters as the second or B-feature of a double-bill.

As distributors, the major companies controlled the remainder of the exhibition market by regulating theaters' access to films. By delaying a film's release to cheaper venues and encouraging as many people as possible to see it at a higher-run theater the system maximized distributors' profits. For similar reasons they insisted on selling films in blocks of between five and 50 films; an exhibitor wanting the new Will Rogers or Shirley Temple movie would find himself having to rent half a dozen other less appealing Fox productions in order to get it.

Although the distributors claimed that these arrangements were necessary for them to supply the smaller theaters economically, independent exhibitors continually fought against the majors'

THE STUDIO SYSTEM

control of the movie marketplace. Hollywood publicity concentrated public attention on the glamor of its stars and their purported lifestyles, and on the apparent competition between the studios, but the industry's crucial economic struggles took place between the major companies and the independent exhibitors seeking to break their consolidated power. The Crash, which so publicly discredited big business, gave the independents their best opportunity. The "business of the movies" was conducted very much in the public arena, and their very popularity made the industry particularly vulnerable to criticism of its financial methods as well as its products. For both the film industry's trade association, the Motion Picture Producers and Distributors of America (MPPDA) and its critics in the early years of the Depression, movie morals and the movie business seemed inseparable.

- Hollywood's reaction to the Depression
- The dominance of the Big Five
- Self-censorship
- The style of the studios
- The reassertion of the strong male
- Nationalism and film
- The media and the war effort

▼ First-run theaters in city centers, such as the Fox Theater in St Louis, kept more than half the money spent on cinema attendance.

Morals at the movies

Few Americans understood the economic causes of the Crash, but there was a widespread view that the Depression was a result not so much of the unstable economic expansion of the Jazz Age as of its hedonism. The movies themselves participated in this anxious reexamination of recent history, but often in a way that rendered them more liable to moral condemnation. Many of their stories of gangsters and "fallen women" were set in the twenties. Stern moral conclusions suggested that the wages of sin seldom bought happy endings, reinforcing a lesson broadcast widely elsewhere; but the movies were accused of representing only too graphically the behavior they claimed to condemn.

Accusations that the movies were subverting the young struck a chord among those looking for moral scapegoats for the Depression. Protestant

The Making of a Gangster Movie

January 1938: Warner Bros announced they had bought Roland Brown's story, *Angels with Dirty Faces*, for $12,500, as one of the three movies starring James Cagney that they would make this year. Head of Production Hal Wallis assigned the film to associate producer Sam Bischoff, who would supervise the film's development through scripting and shooting.

February–March: Studio writers John Wexley and Warren Duff prepared a screenplay, knowing Cagney and Pat O'Brien would star.

April: Production Code Administrator Joseph Breen vetted the script and suggested major changes in its treatment of crime. Because of the success of a recent film starring the *Dead End Kids* Hal Wallis told his writers to include them in the script.

May: Breen approved the final script draft. Other major parts were cast from players under contract to the studio. Art director Robert Haas began designing sets, in consultation with director Michael Curtiz and cameraman Sol Polito.

June: Studio Production Manager Tenny Wright budgeted *Angels With Dirty Faces* at $600,000 – about average for a Warner Bros A–feature. Curtiz, the studio's star director of action pictures, began shooting.

August: Curtiz completed shooting, eight days over schedule and slightly over budget. During shooting, editor Owen Marks had assembled a "rough cut" version of the film for Wallis, who supervised the final cut.

September: Max Steiner's musical score was added. The film was copyrighted and its advertising campaign planned. "Sneak previews" were held to test audience reaction and make final adjustments to the editing.

November: *Angels With Dirty Faces* opened in Warner Bros' premier Los Angeles and New York theaters to enthusiastic reviews and the best business of the year.

church leaders and educational groups grew increasingly vocal in their attacks on the majors' monopoly during the early 1930s, demanding stricter film censorship, enforced by the federal government if necessary. Underlying their concern was the anxiety on the part of the white Protestant elite that their cultural authority, particularly over the immigrant working class, was being surrendered to a mass medium that did not reflect their values and, even worse, was apparently largely owned by "aliens" (a euphemism for Jews).

The industry responded to this pressure by introducing a stricter system of self-regulation in the form of the Production Code. Written in 1930, it was brought into operation with increasing strictness during the following four years, but its implementation failed to keep pace with the ever more vehement demands for a wide-ranging reform of the industry. The extreme popularity of gangster movies, Universal's horror films and Mae West's bawdy comedies increased demands for government supervision of so important a social influence, and provoked repeated charges that the moral guidelines of the Hays Code were a sham and Hays himself only a fixer employed to disguise the industry's misdemeanors. Wide-

spread publicity was given in 1933 to the Payne Fund Studies into the influence of motion pictures on the nation's youth, and it became increasingly evident that some more drastic defense than the code against the threat of legislative control was necessary.

The Legion of Decency campaign launched by the Roman Catholic Church in 1934 provided the industry with an opportunity for a suitably public act of atonement and distracted public attention from more drastic proposals to reform the industry's business practices and break the majors' control over exhibition. In fact the stricter enforcement of the Code after 1934 became an instrument for the preservation of their power. As Hays had long argued, once the "organized industry" demonstrated that it could make morally acceptable movies without federal supervision, it could convincingly assert the general benefits resulting from its monopoly on decency.

To some extent each company, or studio, sought to establish a corporate identity in its productions, but only MGM and Warners really succeeded in imposing a consistent style on their output: MGM by the lavishness of its sets, costumes and lighting, Warners by the frenetic pace at which it told its stories. It was not a coincidence

▶ The MPPDA's Production Code stated: "No picture shall be produced which will lower the moral standards of those who see it. Hence the sympathy of the audience shall never be thrown to the side of crime, wrong-doing, evil or sin. Correct standards of life, subject only to the requirements of drama and entertainment, shall be presented." Reformers argued that the blatant sexuality of stars such as Jean Harlow and Marlene Dietrich and the bawdy wisecracking of Mae West, seen here, did little to promote "correct thinking". What they most feared was that girls would imitate the stars' mannerisms and behavior. As one of Will Hays' advisors put it: "The very man who will guffaw at Mae West's performance as a reminder of the ribald days of his past will resent her effect upon the young, when his daughter imitates the Mae West wiggle before her boyfriends and mouths, 'Come up and see me sometime' ".

that these were the only two studios whose management structure and personnel remained constant throughout the decade. At Warner Bros, the flamboyant Jack Warner ran the studio administration, but the Warners' style was dictated by the studio's head of production, Hal Wallis, and his attention to pacing and detail in editing.

With other studios, *aficionados* might notice the *art moderne* emphasis in RKO's set designs (in Van Nest Polglase's sets for the Fred Astaire and Ginger Rogers musicals, for example), or the "European" style of comedy at Paramount, but such consistencies, which came from studios employing particular writing, camera or design teams, were more likely to be observed by industry professionals than by most of the audience, who were drawn to movies above all by their best-known stars.

With each of the major studios producing more

than fifty feature films per year, no company could afford to specialize in any particular genre or type of production. Warners' crime films are remembered for the performances of James Cagney and Edward G. Robinson, but every studio made films about gangsters in the early 1930s, just as each studio had a comedy team spreading harmless anarchy similar to that of the Marx Brothers at Paramount. Musicals and romantic melodramas were also staple products, while most Westerns were B-movies made by small "Poverty Row" companies such as Monogram and Republic.

To provide a comprehensive service to its exhibitors, a studio also needed to keep a stable of stars representing each of the most prominent types. Competition between stars was exaggerated by studio publicity and fan magazines, which delighted as much in inventing feuds between female stars of similar appeal as they did

▼ Watched by some of the production crew, Fred Astaire and Ginger Rogers dance the Piccolino and (below) "Cheek to Cheek" in *Top Hat*. As well as inaugurating new dance crazes, movie musicals showed their audiences the latest fashions in clothes and decor. Fred and Ginger's dancing was as streamlined as their sets; as they glided across RKO's lavish *art moderne* sets, they were filmed by a mobile camera that followed their every move. Between takes, the scratches had to be removed from the high-gloss bakelite floor.

in devising new romantic permutations among Hollywood's leading figures. For dedicated fans, whom the industry presumed were overwhelmingly women, the movie world extended beyond the films themselves into magazines, gossip columns and news stories. Only in Washington were there more reporters than in Hollywood. The studios ensured that their stars stayed as prominently before the public eye as possible, but they were also constantly engaged in private struggles to keep stars powerless to shape their own careers. Actors and actresses were tied to their studio by long-term contracts with harsh penalty clauses, and only the most popular were able to choose their roles or suggest script changes.

Movies told similar stories over and over again, with minor variations on recurring themes. By far the most persistent story element was romantic love – nine out of every ten movies used it either

as the main plot device or in a prominent subplot, while the endless publicity chatter of dalliance among the stars built Hollywood into the "capital of romance". If there was one thing movies traded more energetically than romance, it was "entertainment", a commodity that advertised itself, even during the Depression, as existing outside politics and economics. Movies seldom engaged in direct commentary on current affairs; the commercial failure of films dealing directly with the Depression, such as King Vidor's *Our Daily Bread*, demonstrated industry wisdom that politics was "box-office poison", and even for the pro-Roosevelt Warner Bros overt rhetoric was only rarely included as in the display of the President's face and the New Deal's Blue Eagle symbol in Busby Berkeley's musical finale to *Footlight Parade*. In making films from headline news stories Warners looked more often to the crime and human interest pages of the newspapers for inspiration. The comedies of Frank Capra, the most successful director of the later 1930s, were populist fantasies of goodwill that explicitly recognized the realities of the Depression, but moved rapidly away from them to propose solutions based on a rediscovery of neighborliness, charity and industriousness. If movies rarely depicted the social and economic realities of the Depression, they did offer a series of psychological parallels in their emotionally heightened accounts of the impact of adversity on families and relationships. In the early years of the Depression, when confidence in the businessman as national hero was at its lowest ebb, there was a notable absence of strong father-figures in movies. Without a firm patriarchal presence, it seemed, younger brothers might run riot and become hoboes or gangsters, while wives and daughters could be tempted into worse sins, which might bring on the destruction of the family itself. The chaotic state of movie families reflected the economic chaos and the fears of political chaos in the nation.

The aspect of social instability most closely attended to was, not surprisingly, that implied by Hollywood's representation of women. In 1933 the top box-office star in the nation was Mae West, the most frequent target of movie reformers and the extreme, parodic, embodiment of an independent female sexuality. In 1934 she was replaced by four-year-old Shirley Temple – a shift in public values not accounted for simply by the

▼ Warner Bros musicals were as elaborate but less ethereal than RKO's. Busby Berkeley's troupe of almost identical chorines waving their limbs in synchrony (in *Gold Diggers of 1933*) was among the most dehumanized versions of female sexuality Hollywood produced.

imposition of the Production Code. Temple frequently played an orphan in search of a family, and the discovery or rediscovery of a father was always more important than was the absence of her mother. Temple represented the female as helpless child in need of male protection, and in exchange she offered the boundless resources of love as a form of charity given to the emotionally needy, capable of reuniting or constituting families. The plots of her films conformed to romantic stereotypes in which men were frequently required to prove their emotional or moral worth in order to win her, yet neither producers nor audiences could acknowledge any sexual dimension to Temple's appeal (she and her studio, Twentieth Century–Fox, sued the British novelist Graham Greene for making that suggestion in a review of *Wee Willie Winkie*). Elsewhere, in the "screwball" comedies of Capra and others, women, however beautiful, were always zany, unpredictable, irresponsible and in need of an authoritative man who would bring them under control. Almost always this man advertised his responsibility as a middle-class virtue, and in the movies, as elsewhere in the late 1930s, there was a celebration of the culture of the middle classes as being more truly American than any other. Many of the male stars who had risen to prominence in the early 1930s had tended to be easily identifiable in class terms – aristocrats like William Powell or urban workers like James Cagney or Edward G. Robinson. The new heroic archetypes of the second half of the decade – Henry Fonda, James Stewart – advertised the virtues of the small-town American middle class in their bearing and manners as well as in the stories in which they appeared.

While the early years of the decade tended to look back only at the events of the immediate past, the later 1930s witnessed a much more conscious exploration of history for cultural heroes.

The search for the roots of American virtue looked to a rural past from which great figures might emerge: the later 1930s saw a wave of books and films relating Abraham Lincoln's journey from log cabin to White House; historical biographies sold in large numbers, and historical fiction celebrating the survival of an American spirit through adversity – such as Margaret Mitchell's *Gone With the Wind* and Walter Edmonds' *Drums Along the Mohawk* – sold even better. From the mid-1930s onward both the movie industry and other cultural entrepreneurs – such as the publishers of *Reader's Digest* – were finding new ways of marketing works aimed at a culturally aspirant middle class that wanted "European" sophistication without surrendering their small-town virtues of democracy and industriousness. Adaptations of the less intellectually arduous literary classics such as *Little Women* or *A Midsummer Night's Dream* were part of Hays' campaign to persuade the public of the movies' moral virtue. The success of MGM's series of operettas featuring Nelson Eddy and Jeanette Macdonald and Warners' biographies of 19th-century liberal humanitarians showed that by 1935 such films could be sold to a public looking beyond its immediate concerns less for escape than for confirmation that it had survived the Depression with its social and moral rectitude intact.

Nationalism in the cinema

The United States, the largest consumer economy in the world despite the Depression, remained immune to cultural incursions from abroad, and had no difficulty in following a policy of cultural as well as political isolationism. Elsewhere the commercial power of exported American culture, both of Hollywood and of the consumer goods it celebrated and advertised, was regarded as a threat. In response, governments round the world encouraged cultural nationalism in resistance to

▲ Between 1934 and 1938 Shirley Temple's popularity was phenomenal. An industry developed around the promotion of her image as America's perfect child: dolls, coloring books, dresses, and even child beauty parlors. By 1940 older girl-children – Judy Garland, Deanna Durbin – replaced her as the site of Hollywood's fantasies of sexual innocence.

National Film Traditions

The influence of American culture in other countries was not always welcome. In the 1930s Japan was the most prolific filmmaking country in the world, producing 400 to 600 features a year. Like Hollywood, Japanese cinema had its established genres. The most popular were historical films, swordfight action dramas appealing largely, like Westerns, to male audiences. *Gendai-geki*, films set in modern Japan, included comedies, films about the lower middle class, and home dramas, which dealt with family problems. Like the Japanese, the German and Italian governments restricted the import of foreign films, but they produced their propaganda in newsreels and radio. Their feature films tended instead to express the feeling of their cultures about entertainment, social relationships and individual emotions. Under Mussolini the Italian industry produced far more Italian "pink" films – sentimental comedies and romantic melodramas, – than "black" or truly Fascist films. Similarly, the German film industry produced far more drawing-room comedies and operettas than Nazi propaganda.

◀ The Japanese drama *A Brother and His Sister* (1939).

the invasions of American-dominated international culture.

Nationalist propaganda was latent in the very notion of resistance to American cultural influence, and there was widespread antipathy to Hollywood's "superficiality" – in 1936 Lithuanian censors rejected the Katharine Hepburn movie *Alice Adams* because it was "banal" – among European intellectuals. This did nothing to hinder the emergence of more extreme forms of nationalism. In all the countries of Europe, bourgeois guardians of "traditional national values" linked American and indigenous working-class culture together through their "vulgarity". The appeal of Hollywood to the working classes was taken as evidence of their need for "education" in the superiority of their own traditions. Cultural nationalists throughout the 1930s attempted to restrict the flow of American cultural imports, protested about Hollywood's misrepresentation of their national culture, and sought to create and disseminate a rival cultural idiom. Such attempts were most effective where cultural nationalists exerted most institutional power; in Britain the monopolistic BBC presented its own version of national culture more effectively than the British cinema, which was in economic thrall to Hollywood, while in Japan the film industry, which enjoyed sufficient economic protection as well as cultural distance from American forms, developed genres of its own. Wartime propaganda intensified the cultural nationalism of the previous decade, and for those on all sides whoever their *political* opponent was represented as being, the *cultural* struggle was directed against the American institutions of Hollywood and Madison Avenue.

It is worth notice that when we think of Hollywood we tend to think of its **worst** *movie product, or of the typical. But when we think of books or magazines, plays or paintings, we recall only the distinguished; we have forgotten the malodorous. An audience of the gigantic size of Hollywood's means that, unlike book publishers or magazine editors or play producers, Hollywood must appeal to mentalities ranging from six to sixty, from stevedores to seminary students, from barmaids to dowagers. Hollywood is geared to a mass market, yet it cannot employ the methods of mass production. Each picture is a different picture and presents unique demands; those who say that movies are merely variations of Boy meets Girl, Boy loses Girl, Boy gets Girl would not suggest that symphonies are merely rearrangements of the same notes.*

LEO ROSTEN, 1940

ERROL FLYNN FRED MacMURRAY

DIVE BOMBER

Presented by
WARNER BROS.

IN TECHNICOLOR

▲ The office of War Information wanted movies like *Dive Bomber* (1941) "to arouse the emotions of the apathetic, and direct the energies of the frustrated into the war effort". That challenge was never fully met: in 1944 as many as 40 percent of Americans admitted that they had no "clear idea of what the war is all about". Hollywood's version of the war was criticized for its "escapism" and lack of substance; the majority of movies explicitly about the war were espionage stories, reworking classic crime themes by substituting enemy agents for gangsters. However great the espionage threat in movie after movie, the FBI always got their man in time. One critic complained, "They present the war in absurdly romantic terms and their entertainment value is impaired by the conflict in the mind of the audience between the hard facts of real war and its glamorous embellishments on the screen".

Film and war propaganda

"If it's December 1941 in Casablanca," Humphrey Bogart asks Dooley Wilson, "what time is it in New York? I bet they're asleep in New York. I bet they're asleep all over America." Working with the US government's Office of War Information (OWI), one of Hollywood's wartime roles was to wake the United States up to the end of its period of international isolation. The enduring appeal of *Casablanca* comes from the way it encapsulates the essential qualities of the Hollywood studio production: dialog pushed just the other side of plausibility ("I remember every detail. The Germans wore grey. You wore blue."), delivered by stars enacting their archetypal personas. But in early 1943 *Casablanca*, like many other Hollywood movies, deliberately set out to convince American audiences that World War II required the nation's committed entry into world affairs.

Bogart's character rehearsed a heroic role constantly re-enacted in American culture: the man drawn reluctantly into a conflict he cannot avoid unless he compromises his principles. During the course of the film his cynical isolation is converted into energetic resistance to the Nazis through the resolution of his love affair with the character played by Ingrid Bergman. At the end of the film, he sends her to America with her Resistance leader husband. Bogart's renunciation of her completes the pattern in which characters sacrifice their personal desires for a greater cause.

Hollywood's own sacrifice was a limited affair. Along with every other entertainment business, the film industry enjoyed a boom during the war. This was true in Britain and France, where attendance increased by at least a quarter, as well as in the United States. Compared to the Depression, workers in war-related industries had more money, but fewer durable goods on which to spend it.

There were tensions beneath the surface of Hollywood's "business as usual" attitude. The major companies feared that the government might interfere with their monopolistic control of the industry and even make propaganda films itself. On the other hand, President Roosevelt shared the perception, common in America in the 1930s, that British propaganda had persuaded the United States into World War I, and remembered with discomfort the unfulfilled postwar promises of "the war to end all wars". Like Churchill, Roosevelt wanted his wartime propaganda to say as little as possible about war aims or postwar prospects. Messages about the war were conveyed in the familiar idioms of advertising and movies, and presented predigested information and ideas to a public already familiar with this form of address.

But this was, in Hollywood's limited way, an attempt to address a genuine problem for the American home front: that the "hard facts" of the war were not the pressing reality for Americans that they were for Europeans more immediately involved in the conflict. It was a foreign war, its dangers remote, its sacrifices far less frequent than its temporary inconveniences. As one observer commented, while Europe was occupied, the Soviet Union and China invaded and Britain isolated, only the United States was "fighting this war on imagination alone".

American radio journalist Edward Murrow, famous for his broadcasts of the London Blitz, asked pointedly, "How do you report suffering to people who have not suffered?" Understanding the war was not made easier by the movies' racial

Soviet and Nazi Cinema

Among the combatant nations of World War II, only the Soviets had a cinema which was dedicated completely to the war effort, with all its production geared "to help in the moral, political and military defeat of Fascism". Such unembarrassed propaganda was possible in the Soviet Union, where the media openly operated as instruments of the state. Audiences recognized the appropriateness of Eisenstein's *Alexander Nevsky* – which depicted the peoples of 13th-century Russia repelling the invading Teutonic Knights – being withdrawn after the signing of the Nazi–Soviet Pact in 1939, and reissued after the German invasion of 1941.

The Nazis confined most of their wartime propaganda to *Die Deutsche Wochenschau*, an extended weekly newsreel. During the early war years newsreels emphasized the speed and power of Blitzkrieg to demoralize potential opponents, as well as boosting morale at home. Some wartime fiction films contained overt propaganda messages and, like other belligerents, the Nazis put history to propaganda service. Postwar investigation suggested that only 20 percent of Nazi feature films were directly propagandist, and took this as confirmation of Goebbels' proclaimed strategy of filling cinemas with entertainment features, and carrying propaganda in the newsreels that accompanied them. Subsequent analysis, however, has been less prepared to make such a clear distinction between propaganda and entertainment – even light-hearted items can be seen as reinforcing the political status quo.

▶▶ Riefenstahl's *Triumph of the Will* (1936).

▶ Leni Riefenstahl directing *Olympia* (1936).

stereotyping of the enemy, or by advertisements for War Bonds as a way of both "putting bullets in the bellies of Hitler's hordes" and "systematic saving" for postwar consumer purchasing.

Yet if Hollywood never abandoned its commercial motives, it had patriotic ones, too. In some respects, Hollywood showed a commitment to a liberal postwar agenda that went farther than Roosevelt's did. Dooley Wilson, Bogart's companion in *Casablanca*, was black. His race was neither caricatured nor commented on. One of the *Why We Fight* orientation films produced for the War Department by Frank Capra, Hollywood's highest-paid director, was about *The Negro Soldier*. Such presentations spoke of the OWI's liberal hope that, "By making this a people's war for freedom, we can help clear up the alien problem, the negro problem, the anti-Semitic problem."

In Britain, too, wartime propagandists were liberal or radical in their politics. Documentary filmmakers in particular went much farther in expressing aims for the postwar world than the government wanted. As in America, the initial reluctance to employ propaganda was based on the fear that its manipulative power was so great as to threaten the existence of democratic society. Cinemas were at first closed, but soon reopened. With the experience of Dunkirk and the Blitz, the image of Britain as an island fortress pervaded both fiction and documentary films and the BBC's

radio output. Inside the fortress British stereotypes were revised, as the middle-class image which the BBC had offered as a "national" culture during the 1930s found its niche. The strongest influence on the style of British propaganda came from documentary filmmakers working, from 1940, in the Crown Film Unit. Under the leadership of producer John Grierson, documentary film practice in Britain during the 1930s had acquired a more clearly articulated esthetic than had been the case in the United States, where the dominant force was the *March of Time* newsreels. Grierson, like John Reith a Scots Calvinist critical of "the scarlet women ... and the high falsehood" of Hollywood, saw documentary as an instrument of education.

Documentary filmmakers manned influential posts at the Ministry of Information and produced a steady supply of short films on anything from cooking under rationing to records of campaigns. *London Can Take It*, lauding the endurance and resilience of the population during the Blitz, had a considerable effect on American opinion. Most durable among these films were the evocative documentaries directed by Humphrey Jennings. In *Words for Battle* and *Heart of Britain* he presented images of the English landscape and of ordinary men and women, accompanied by the poetry of William Blake, Robert Browning and Rudyard Kipling, offering his sounds and images as a part of the national heritage.

MICKEY MOUSE

Historian Warren Susman has suggested that "Mickey Mouse may be more important to an understanding of the 1930s than Franklin Roosevelt." His creator, Walt Disney, was a fantasist on a grand scale. Dominating American film animation from 1930, Disney built an empire on the periphery of Hollywood. He then built a magical kingdom, Disneyland, and at the time of his death had begun to build a better world in the wilderness of the Florida swamps. His grandiose schemes survived him, because his fantasies of innocence were rooted in commercial reality: whatever else they might signify, his dreams were saleable commodities.

Disney's career in animation began in 1923 with *Alice in Cartoonland*, a series of films mixing cartoons and live action. His most enduring creation was Mickey (originally Mortimer) Mouse, the leading character in the first sound cartoon, *Steamboat Willie*, in 1928. Disney won every Oscar for cartoon shorts from 1932 to 1939, as well as special Academy Awards for creating Mickey and for *Snow White and the Seven Dwarfs*, released in 1937.

The Disney films created an idealized world, out of time and free from responsibility, where the impossible could happen harmlessly and without consequence. There was, nevertheless, an underlying moral order to this world, which would always assert itself at the end of Disney's narratives. Nevertheless, Disney's world of fun and fantasy also contained images of terror and evil: families are separated, and children seldom have their real mothers.

Increasingly the company's output was aimed at "the child in all of us" – more cynically, at the young families of the postwar baby boom. The Disneyland television series began in 1954, and a year later the world's first theme park opened in Anaheim, California, with Mickey as its host. When *Snow White and the Seven Dwarfs* was re-released in 1987, it took $45 million at the American box-office.

▶ The world's most famous mouse, and perhaps the most widely recognized image in the world, Mickey Mouse has for 60 years been a figure of international signficance. The early Mickey, designed by animator Ub Iwerks, was neither really mouse nor human, but always remorse-lessly cheerful and optimistic. It was a characteristic he shared with all Disney's cartoon creations except the irascible Donald Duck. As the thirties progressed, Mickey acquired a wider emotional repertoire, but became respectable, even bland. The studio needed Donald to provide the anarchy Mickey could no longer supply.

▼ Disneyland, the world's first theme park, might equally have been called Waltopia. Disney said of it, "I don't want the public to see the world they live in while they're in Disneyland, I want them to feel they're in another world."

▶ Mickey in a variety of the guises he had appeared in by the time of his 50th birthday including his first sound role as *Steamboat Willie*, and his costume for the *Sorcerer's Apprentice* sequence of *Fantasia*, Disney's second full-length animated feature.

Datafile

During the 1930s the major spectator sports – soccer, baseball, cricket – won some of their largest audiences. Even the outbreak of war did little to avert enthusiasm for spectator sports in belligerent countries. Sport offered its participants a way out of poverty, gave the spectators an escape from the daily grind, and, through gambling, held out the hope of instant riches for little effort.

The popularity of mass sport, and enthusiasm for international competition, meant that political conflicts could easily spill over into the sporting arena, and the metaphors of sport provided a comprehensible expression of national ideology – whether it be the Aryan myth in Nazi Germany, the British ideal of gentlemanly fair play, or the American vision of equality or opportunity. Even Soviet Russia gave an important role to sport, reorganizing it within trade-union-based sporting societies.

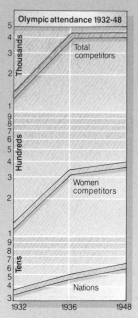

Olympic attendance 1932-48

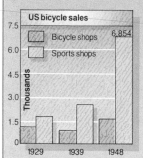

US bicycle sales

◀ **The Depression hit sport less severely than most other industries in the United States. The emphasis on war production, which cut the numbers of cars being built, may have served to promote the sale of bicycles. Similarly, in Britain, sales of bicycles rose sharply during the Depression.**

▲ **The 1936 Berlin Olympics were more successful, in terms of athletes participating, than those held four years previously in Los Angeles. The Los Angeles Games were a lavish extravaganza that made a profit of more than $1 million. The outbreak of war meant that no further Games were held until 1948, in London.**

World Cup winners 1930-86

Year	Winners	Runners-up	Venue
1930	Uruguay	Argentina	Uruguay
1934	Italy	Czechoslovakia	Italy
1938	Italy	Hungary	France
1950	Uruguay	Brazil	Brazil
1954	West Germany	Hungary	Switzerland
1958	Brazil	Sweden	Sweden
1962	Brazil	Czechoslovakia	Chile
1966	England	West Germany	England
1970	Brazil	Italy	Mexico
1974	West Germany	Holland	West Germany
1978	Argentina	Holland	Argentina
1982	Italy	West Germany	Spain
1986	Argentina	West Germany	Mexico

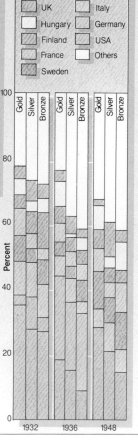

Olympic medals

▲ **The World Cup became Association Football's showpiece competition between the world's top national professional teams. The trophy was named for Jules Rimet, the president of the international football association (FIFA) from 1921. Only 13 countries took part in the first competition, deterred by the difficulty of traveling to Uruguay during the Depression years. The second World Cup, held in Italy, was used by Mussolini as an instrument of Fascist propaganda.**

▶ **The striking success of United States athletes at the Los Angeles Games, and of German athletes at the Berlin Games four years later, initiated the tendency for the host country to achieve disproportionately good results. Games were planned to be held in Finland in 1940, but these were cancelled owing to the outbreak of war. The 1948 Games were held under difficult conditions in war-ravaged London, with minimal preparation time and rationing of many vital materials.**

The Depression left an uneven pattern of poverty and prosperity. Like the rest of the service sector and the mass entertainment industry, spectator sports expanded during the Depression, as those who could afford it grasped the alternative vision of fun and the "good life" that sport provided. In Britain it was the "golden age" of soccer and cricket attendances, and in the United States baseball, football and basketball were flourishing businesses.

Professional football was still organized for the working class rather than by them. Like baseball and other sports, soccer (Association football) provided working-class men and boys with the fantasy of escape from hardship and poverty. By the 1930s it was played almost exclusively by men with working-class origins. Soccer was also used by entrepreneurs to cultivate legalized gambling, institutionalized in the football pools. By the mid-1930s more than sixteen times as many people gambled on football in Britain as watched it, attracted by the potential jackpot win. As early as 1931 there was one pools win of £345,000. By 1938 the annual turnover was close to £40 million.

The football pools' jackpot was one of the dreamlike scenarios sport provided for working-class people in the 1930s. The poverty of the Depression induced people to look to sport to transport them from the ghetto: poor people under capitalism believed that sport, like other forms of popular culture, might change their rags to riches.

In the United States boxing became a route out of poverty for some blacks. Inspired by the supremacy of Joe Louis, world heavyweight champion from 1937 to 1949, blacks began to dominate professional boxing, though prizewinners' purses remained relatively small until after 1945.

Throughout Europe and in North America participation sports remained rigidly class-specific: skiing, climbing, tennis, sailing, yachting and motor-racing remained middle- and upper-class sports. New working-class hobbies and recreations developed as a direct result of unemployment and enforced leisure. An open-air and fitness movement developed, symptomatic attempts to escape from the industrial environment. Working-class people took to cycling, camping, hiking and rambling. The fear of Fascism provoked concern about national fitness and unity through sport, and governments actively encouraged young working-class people to take up sport and exercise. In France the *auberges de jeunesse* expanded under the Popular Front government

SPORT AND NATIONALISM

(1936–39), which encouraged outdoor activities through the Office of Sport and Leisure Time. One historian has even suggested that the most enduring legacy of the French Popular Front "was probably the paid holiday to the sea".

The expansion of women's sport was still slow, but there was some relaxation of attitudes about women's physical abilities and an increasing interest in, and demand for, opportunities to participate. Girls were playing sports in schools, thanks to the development of the women's physical education professions in Europe and North America. In 1930 the Women's League of Health and Beauty was founded in London with 16 members – by 1939 there were 166,000 members, centers in Canada, Australia and New Zealand, and representatives in Hong Kong, Denmark and the United States.

Alternatives to conventional sport

There was still opposition, on both moral and biological grounds, to women competing in vigorous sports. Sports heroines such as the Americans Mildred "Babe" Diedrikson and "the world's fastest woman", Helen Stevens, who disavowed conventional images of femininity, were exploited and ridiculed by the press, who treated them as freaks. Female athletes began to match the attainments of their male counterparts, yet sought to preserve the feminine qualities of their style. There was however, no stigma attached to women's participation in the Workers' Sports

Association, which maintained a philosophy of democracy and openly encouraged female athletes. By 1930 Workers' Sports Associations were flourishing in most parts of Europe and many areas of North and South America and Asia, with a total membership of over four million. Opposed to both national and sexual chauvinism and to elitism in sport, the Workers' Sports Movement was a massive internationalist working-class organization. In 1932 it organized the second Workers' Olympics, which took place in Vienna with over 100,000 competitors from 26 countries. The third Workers' Olympics was scheduled to take place in Barcelona in 1936, in opposition to the Nazi Olympics in Berlin, but the Spanish Civil War began on the morning of the opening ceremony. When they returned home, however, many worker athletes were banned from their national associations, whereas those who took part in the Nazi Olympics were hailed as national heroes.

The Nazi Olympics

The 1936 Olympics were the first Games to be televised, although only to 160,000 people in and around Berlin. They became a stage for the incitement of nationalism and ritualistic struggle of one nation against another. In August 1936, *The Times* editorialized on the "failure" of the British team and the relative success of other countries: only three years after the Berlin Games Britain and Germany were at war again.

▼ Governments were quick to encourage the passion for health and fitness that arose during the 1930s, in response to the enforced leisure of the Depression years. United by sport into huge national teams, men and women could be fit and ready when the struggle over Fascism broke into war. Here a group of hardy swimmers enjoy a midwinter dip in London's Serpentine.

"To the spectators at Berlin, Owens was not only a great athlete – he was athletics."

► "Babe" Diedrikson was one of the most versatile female athletes in the history of sport. She broke the world javelin record at the age of sixteen. Two years later, in 1932, she competed in eight events in two and a half hours at the US Championships, winning five of them. At the Los Angeles Olympics she won two gold medals and one silver. In 1934 she took up golf; from 1940 to 1954 she was one of the foremost amateur and professional golfers on the women's circuit. She was voted Athlete of the Year five times in a career that included not only athletics and golf but also baseball, basketball, tennis, swimming, diving and billiards.

"Heroic" performance and achievement in sport has fuelled the notion that individual merit is more important than national affiliation. The case of the black American athlete Jesse Owens, seen as the perfect counterbalance to Nazi propaganda, argues against this.

The conspicuous success of a black athlete dealt a serious blow to Hitler's philosophy of the natural supremacy of the Aryan race. Outside Nazi Germany, Owens' victories were celebrated as evidence that sport provided a setting for equality of opportunity and an avenue for social mobility. Owens was heralded as symbolic proof of the openness of American culture, in which ability, not color, was the sole criterion for success.

For many people the 1936 Berlin Olympics are regarded, mistakenly, as the first example of the serious intrusion of politics into sport. The Olympic Games of the modern era have consistently offered a platform for national political gesturing in various guises. The Nazi doctrines enshrined

◄► The rhetoric that greeted Owens' Berlin success embodied nationalist sentiments and notions of cultural supremacy. Germany and Japan used sport as a means of national expression and political propaganda with unprecedented success. Germany had a long tradition of state intervention in sport with national scheme of physical fitness designed to promote German unity. In Nazi Germany sport was again contrived to promote and reinforce communal solidarity. The pageants, rallies and festivals of the 1930s were massive extravaganzas, including marching, gymnastics and eurythmics, carefully planned so that the emotional involvement had an intoxicating effect, barely different to the ceremonial of the Olympics. And the Olympic posters reflected Nazi ideas of the super-race.

in the 1936 Games merely presented an extreme version of the Eurocentric roots of most modern sport. Despite international concern about the Games, the official British Olympic Association report on Berlin suggested that there was only one real incident to mar the Games: the withdrawal of the whole Peruvian team following a dispute in the soccer tournament. The writers of the report concluded that the Berlin Olympiad "Was surely one of the greatest sports festivals of all time, having made its magnificent contribution towards a fitter youth and more peaceful international relations."

The diplomatic language of the British report and the optimism of these sentiments presented a familiar paradox: idealist sentiments were being expressed that sport could rise above politics, at a time when sport was undeniably politicized.

International conflict expressed in sport was not limited to the quadrennial Olympic Games. The soccer matches played between England and

Germany in 1935 and 1938 became propaganda events for both sides; the British ambassador to Berlin saw England's victory in 1938 as a triumph for British prestige, not least, apparently, because the England team gave the Nazi salute before the game began. The 1932–33 cricket tour of Australia by the British national team, the Marylebone Cricket Club (MCC) produced its own diplomatic controversy: the so-called "bodyline" series seemed to challenge the essence of the game of cricket. During the Test Match series, the MCC team adopted a particular bowling strategy – one that threatened physical injury – to minimize the effectiveness of the Australian batsman Donald Bradman. The series was almost halted when the strategy was labeled "unsportsmanlike" by the governing body of cricket in Australia, the Australian Board of Control. The MCC captain, Douglas Jardine, and one of the bowlers, Harold Larwood, were castigated for "dangerous" bowling. After diplomatic talks between the two countries, the tour continued but with "undiminished bitterness" and the conflict between the ideals of fair play and the search for effective tactics remained unresolved.

Throughout World War II, cricket at the highest level was encouraged by the British government to boost national morale, although international contacts – as in most other sports – ceased until the return of peace. Similarly, professional football continued, although subject to restrictions on traveling and on the size of the crowds, and occasionally endangered by air raids. In all sports, teams were weakened by players entering the armed forces, but spectator enthusiasm was undiminished.

▲ After his success at the Berlin Olympics, winning gold in the 100m, the 200m, the long jump (seen here) and the 4x1000m relay, black American athlete Jesse Owens' extraordinary talents were exploited for profit: he became a sideshow attraction, racing for money against horses and motorcycles in sleazy hippodromes in Mexico and Reno.

The only things that will produce the class performers is numbers, time and extreme specialization ... But would the production of one 25ft long jumper, one 52ft weight putter, or one 230ft javelin thrower really demonstrate anything of national importance?... The criterion of an Olympic victory must not be exaggerated.

HAROLD ABRAHAMS, 1936

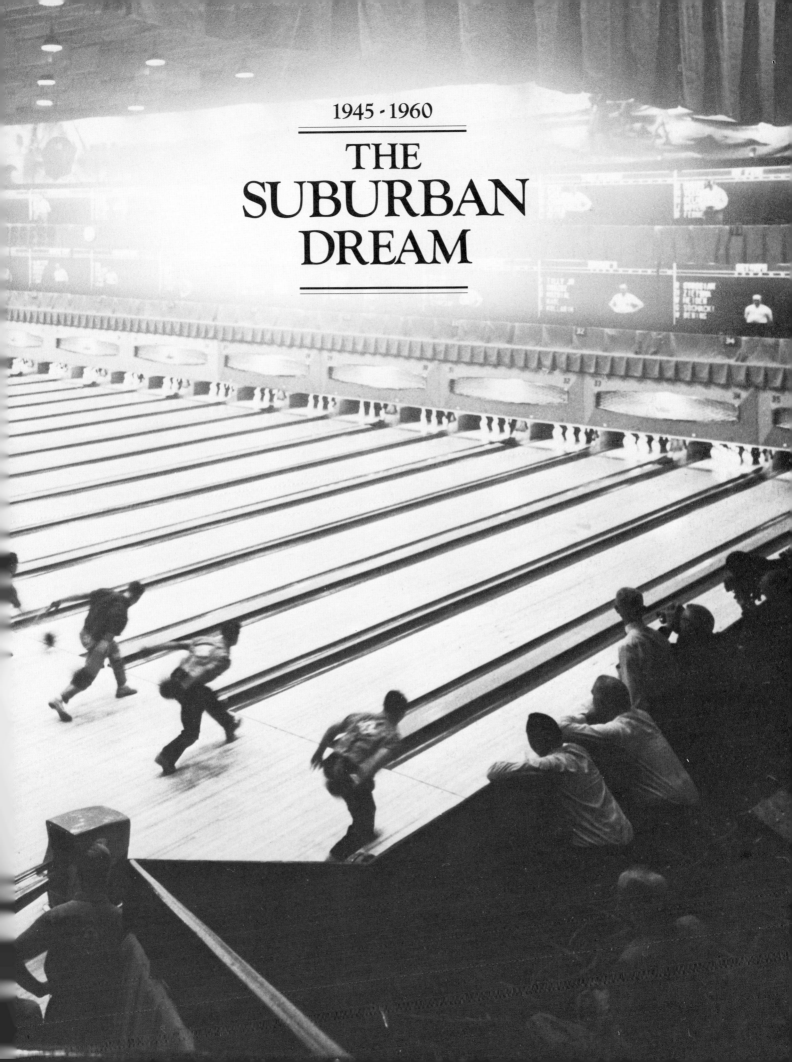

1945 · 1960

THE SUBURBAN DREAM

Time Chart

	1946	1947	1948	1949	1950	1951	1952	1953
Film	• Release of *Beauty and the Beast*, directed by Jean Cocteau (Fr) • 20 Sep: First Cannes Film Festival held (Fr)	• 20 Oct: Joseph McCarthy's House Un-American Activities Committee (HUAC) began anti-communist "witch-hunt" of the film industry (USA)	• Release of *Hamlet*, directed by and starring Laurence Olivier (UK) • Release of *Bicycle Thieves*, directed by Vittorio de Sica (It)	• Release of Jean Cocteau's *Orpheus* (Fr) • *The Third Man* released (director Carol Reed) (UK)		• *Rashomon*, directed by Akira Kurosawa, released (Jap) • British Board of Film Censors established (UK)	• Feb: Gene Kelly starred in and co-directed *Singin' in the Rain* (USA) • 19 Sep: UK-born Charles Chaplin's US entry visa withheld pending a disloyalty inquiry (USA) • 23 Oct: *Limelight* released, with Chaplin directing (USA)	• 20th-Century Fox announced conversion to Cinemascope, a system including a wide curved screen and stereophonic sound (USA) • Premiere of Walt Disney's *Peter Pan* (USA)
Media	• 29 Sep: BBC's Third Programme started, broadcasting classical music and theater (UK)	• First transistor produced, by Bell Laboratories (USA)	• NBC's *Hopalong Cassidy*, the first TV Western series (USA) • First LP, micro-groove and 33⅓rpm, produced (USA) • Victor introduced 45rpm singles (USA)	• 25 Aug: RCA produced a color television system (USA)	• The first regular color TV transmissions began (USA)	• 28 May: *The Goon Show* first broadcast (UK) • 12 Jun: Study launched by the Ford Foundation to raise the cultural level of television (USA)		• The coronation of Queen Elizabeth II televised worldwide • First recording of television on tape, by RCA (USA)
Music	• Jukebox boom began (USA & UK) • Irving Berlin's musical *Annie Get Your Gun* opened (USA)		• Fats Domino prefigured rock'n'roll with his million-seller *The Fat Man* (USA) • *Alexander's Ragtime Band* recorded by Bing Crosby and Al Jolson (USA)	• BB King made his first recording, *The Blues Boy* (USA) • Opening of *South Pacific*, by Rodgers and Hammerstein (USA)	• Emergence of "cool" jazz Premiere of *Guys and Dolls* by Loesser and Burrows (USA) • The samba became very popular (USA)	• Bill Haley and the Comets released *Rock the Joint* (USA) • Opening of Rodgers and Hammerstein's *The King and I* (USA)	• Disk jockey Alan Freed called his show "Moondog's Rock'n'Roll Party" after a slang term for sex later applied to rhythm & blues • The first UK singles' chart appeared, in the *New Musical Express* magazine	• Apr: Elvis Presley paid Sun Records $4 to cut a record, "My Happiness", for his mother (USA)
Fashion and Design	• Lurex, a metallic yarn, produced by the Dow Chemical Co. (USA) • Conference entitled "Industrial design as a new profession" held at New York's Museum of Modern Art (MoMA) • C d'Ascanio designed the Vespa motorscooter for the Piaggio co. (It) • The bikini swimsuit launched (Fr)	• The first tubeless car tire made by the Goodrich co. (USA) • Feb: Dubbed the New Look, Christian Dior's first collection cast off wartime austerity, bringing back long full skirts (Fr) • Elsa Schiaparelli was one of the first fashion designers to license her name	• Utility clothing restrictions lifted in the UK • Marcello Nizzoli (It) designed the streamlined Lexicon 80 typewriter for the Olivetti co. • Photographer Norman Parkinson joined the staff of *Vogue* magazine (UK) • German fashion magazine *Neue Mode* first published	• Designer Harley Earl (USA) added tailfins to the Cadillac car's rear bumper	• First Japanese tape recorder made, by TTK (Sony) • Inaugural Good Design show at MoMA, New York (USA) • Institut de l'Esthétique Industrielle was established (Fr) • Sixten Sason designed the aerodynamic body of the Saab 92 (Swe) • *Design* magazine launched in the UK	• 4 May: Festival of Britain opened (UK) • The first International Design Conference held in Aspen (USA) • Rat für Formgebung (Council for Design) established (W Ger) • First Lunning prize awarded, for excellence in Scandinavian design	• MoMA, New York, devoted an exhibition to the Italian co. Olivetti's products (USA) • Aug: Inventor Buckminster Fuller's Geodesic Dome house displayed at MoMA (USA) • Japanese Industrial Designers Association (JIDA) established	• Mainichi Press sponsored Japan's first industrial design competition • Bonnie Cashin opened her fashion studio in New York • Canon Camera Co. established a design department (Jap) • Founding of Italian magazine *Stile Industria*
Sport	• UK Jockey Club decided to install photo-finish cameras on all racecourses • Aug: UK footballers demanded a £7 minimum weekly wage	• UK Football Writers Association formed • 14 Oct: US test pilot Chuck Yeager became the first human to travel faster than sound	• Feb: Winter Olympics held at St Moritz (Swi) • 29 Jul: Opening of the London Olympics, the first games for 12 years (UK) • Donald Bradman (Aus) retired from first-class cricket	• May: Italy's national football team killed in an air crash • Baseball player Joe DiMaggio paid $90,000 for a one-year contract (USA)	• May: First world championship Grand Prix motor race held, at Silverstone (UK) • May: American Bowling Congress lifted its color bar (USA) • First men's world basketball championships held	• 4 Mar: Opening of the first Asian Games, in New Delhi (Ind); ten nations took part • First Pan-American Games held, in Buenos Aires (Arg) • Citation became the first horse to win US $1 million • International Judo Federation formed	• 14 Feb: Winter Olympics opened in Oslo (Nor) • 19 Jul: Opening of Helsinki Olympics (Fin); USSR competed for the first time since the 1917 Revolution • Aug: The first automatic pinsetter was installed in a New York bowling centre (USA)	• May: Jacqueline Cochran became the first woman to fly faster than sound (USA) • May: Hillary (NZ) and Tenzing Norkay (Nep) reached the summit of Everest • Jun: Len Hutton became the first professional cricket player to captain the English team
Misc.	• UNESCO founded		• 30 Jan: Gandhi assassinated (Ind)		• McCarthy accused 205 of communism in the State Department (USA)		• *Scrabble* produced; it rivaled *Monopoly* as a best-selling boardgame	

1954	1955	1956	1957	1958	1959	1960
● Release of *The Seven Samurai*, directed by Akira Kurosawa (Jap) ● *On the Waterfront* released, directed by Elia Kazan and starring Marlon Brando (USA)	● Jun: *Release of The Seven-Year Itch*, directed by Billy Wilder and starring Marilyn Monroe (USA) ● *Rebel Without a Cause* released, starring James Dean and directed by Nicholas Ray (USA) ● 30 Sep: James Dean died in a car crash, aged 24 (USA)	● 19 Apr: Grace Kelly married Prince Rainier of Monaco ● *And God Created Woman*, directed by Roger Vadim, introduced Brigitte Bardot (Fr)	● *The Bridge on the River Kwai* (director, David Lean) won eight Academy Awards (UK) ● Release of *The Three Faces of Eve*, starring Joanne Woodward and directed by Nunnally Johnson (USA)	● Elizabeth Taylor starred in *Cat on a Hot Tin Roof*, directed by Richard Brooks (USA) ● Release of *Gigi*, directed by Vincente Minnelli and starring Leslie Caron and Maurice Chevalier (USA)	● *Ben Hur* released, starring Charlton Heston (director, William Wyler) (USA) ● Release of *Hiroshima Mon Amour*, directed by Alain Resnais (Fr) ● Release of *Some Like It Hot*, starring Marilyn Monroe and directed by Billy Wilder (USA)	● Otto Preminger's *Exodus* released (USA) ● Release of *Psycho*, with Tony Perkins and Janet Leigh, directed by Alfred Hitchcock (USA)
● Jun: Victor marketed the first pre-recorded tapes (USA) ● 6 Jun: The Pope opened the Eurovision network, in Rome	● Aug: The world's first mass-produced transistor radio launched by Sony (Jap)	● 14 Apr: Ampex displayed a device for recording television shows (USA) ● 24 May: Eurovision Song Contest first televised	● 4 May: First prime time rock music TV network special (USA)	● The BBC began experimental stereo radio transmission (UK)	● The first portable transistorized television, TV-8-301, launched by Sony (Jap) ● 28 Sep: The USA's Explorer VI spacecraft took the first television pictures of Earth	
● 12 Apr: *Rock Around the Clock* recorded, by Bill Haley and the Comets (USA) ● 18 Jul: First Newport Jazz Festival held (USA) ● The Crew-Cuts' *Sh-Boom* was the first rock'n'roll hit (USA)	● 12 Mar: Jazz saxophonist Charlie Parker, originator of bebop, died aged 34 (USA) ● Elvis Presley signed with Victor	● 15 Mar: *My Fair Lady* opened on Broadway (USA) ● Release of *Rock Island Line*, sung by Lonnie Donegan (USA) ● Sep: Five months after *Heartbreak Hotel* topped the charts, Elvis Presley emerged as a TV teen idol (USA)	● *West Side Story* (by Leonard Bernstein) opened (USA) ● Buddy Holly and the Crickets' first single, *That'll Be the Day*, released (USA) ● The first stereo disks marketed (USA)	● 24 Mar: Elvis Presley entered the army for two years (USA) ● Release of *Move It*, by Cliff Richard (UK)	● *It Doesn't matter Anymore* was Buddy Holly's first solo release (USA) ● 3 Feb: Buddy Holly and Richie Valens died in a plane crash (USA) ● 17 Jul: Billie Holiday died, aged 44 (USA)	● 17 Apr: Eddie Cochran died in a car crash, aged 21 (USA) ● Aug: Elvis Presley was declared Public Enemy No. 1 after riots (W Ger) ● 18 Aug: The Beatles' first public performance, in Hamburg (W Ger)
● May: Prototype 707 plane shown by Boeing Co. (USA) ● "Design in Scandinavia" exhibition began touring the USA ● Italy launched its Compasso d'Oro awards for product design ● Marlon Brando wore denim jeans and a leather jacket in *The Wild One* (USA) ● *Industrial Design* magazine launched in the USA ● Coco Chanel's first collection since 1939	● Hochschule fur Gestaltung (College for Design) founded in Ulm (W Ger) ● US furniture co. Knoll International began returning classic pre-war Modernist designs to production ● Fashion designer Mary Quant opened her shop Bazaar on London's King's Road (UK) ● Japanese fashion designer Hanae Mori's first shop opened, on Tokyo's Ginza street	● The Design Centre building opened in London (UK) ● Associazione per il Disegno Industriale founded in Milan (It) ● Belgium launched its Signe d'Or design awards ● Couturier Cristobal Balenciaga created his loose chemise dress, the "Sac" (Fr)	● Britain launched its first Design Centre award scheme ● Japan's inaugural Good Design awards, the G-Mark ● Furniture designer Eero Saarinen (Fin/USA) created his elegant plastic and aluminium tulip chair ● Fashion designer John Stephen opened his first menswear shop in London's Carnaby Street (UK)	● Lycra elastic fiber was introduced by Du Pont (USA) ● Apr: Opening of the Brussels World's Fair (Bel) ● The Beat generation's look was epitomized by the black outfits of folksinger Juliette Greco (Fr) ● Rockers cruised on motorbikes, Mods on motorscooters (UK)	● Aug: Alec Issigonis' Mini car first shown (UK) ● Orry-Kelly (Aus) designed Marilyn Monroe's costumes for *Some Like It Hot* (USA) ● Fashion designer Pierre Cardin showed his first pret-a-porter collection (Fr) ● *The Teenage Consumer* published a report commissioned by a UK advertising agency ● Australian *Vogue* first published	● The world's first felt-tip pen, the Pentel, sold (Jap) ● Japan Design House created, as a permanent exhibition centre ● Yves Saint Laurent's Beat Look collection made street fashion haute couture (Fr) ● The mini-skirt born on the streets of London (UK)
● First World Cup (later International Championship) held, in rugby league ● 6 May: Roger Bannister (UK) became the first man to run the mile in under four minutes	● Nov: The BBC obtained exlusive rights to the television coverage of Test cricket (UK) ● Nov: First floodlit international football match played, at Wembley (UK)	● 16 Jan: Winter Olympics opened at Cortina d'Ampezzo (It) ● Apr: World heavyweight boxing champion Rocky Marciano (USA) retired, having won all 49 bouts of his career ● 22 Nov: Opening of the Melbourne Olympics (Aus)	● First Admiral's Cup held, in yachting (UK) ● 6 Jul: Althea Gibson (USA) became the first black player to win a Wimbledon tennis title	● 6 Feb: Most of the Manchester United football team killed in an air crash (UK) ● Jun: Brazilian soccer player Pele became a star after his team won the World Cup for the first time ● Aug: Herb Elliott (Aus) broke two world running records in one month	● First National Finals Rodeo held (USA) ● Jun: Ingemaar Johansson became Sweden's first world heavyweight boxing champion	● 18 Feb: Winter Olympics opened at Squaw Valley (USA) ● 21 Jul: Francis Chichester (UK) won the first single-handed transatlantic yacht race ● 25 Aug: Opening of the Rome Olympics (It); Abebe Bikila (Eth) won black Africa's first gold medal
		● USSR launched Sputnik I, the Earth's first satellite			● Craze for hula-hoops	● 9 Nov: John F. Kennedy elected US president

Datafile

The 1950s saw the establishment of great prosperity in the United States. Its overwhelming dominance, politically and economically, meant that its fashions, its objects and its music pervaded the rest of the world as never before: the age of cultural imperialism by the United States had begun. In design, however, it was in Europe that the new pioneers of tasteful design were to be found.

▼ The automobile was the consumer product *par excellence* of the United States in the 1950s. Gasoline prices remained virtually static throughout the decade, effectively falling in real terms. This made gas-guzzling limousines acceptable throughout the social scale.

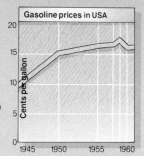

Automobile production

◀▼ The 1950s saw the start of the erosion of American domination of automobile manufacture, as the European industry was placed on a firmer footing. The fifties' American car was often attacked as vulgar and ostentatious, a sign that the United States had lost sight of the principles of good design of the 1930s.

Gasoline prices in USA

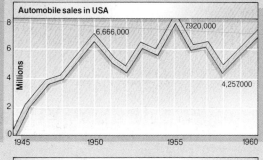

Automobile sales in USA

6,666,000   7,920,000

4,257,000

Legend:
- USA
- Britain
- Other
- France
- Canada
- FRG
- Italy
- Japan

▼▶ The 1950s saw a steady rise in personal disposable income (shown here in current prices) for the majority of people in the United States, and this was reflected in the increase in spending on consumer products below. The emphasis on items for the kitchen reflected the domesticity of the suburban ideal.

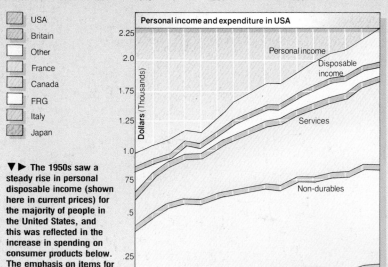

Personal income and expenditure in USA

Personal income
Disposable income
Services
Non-durables
Durables

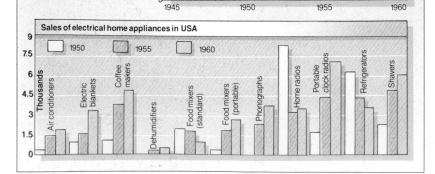

Sales of electrical home appliances in USA

1950   1955   1960

Air conditioners · Electric blankets · Coffee makers · Dehumidifiers · Food mixers (standard) · Food mixers (portable) · Phonographs · Home radios · Portable clock radios · Refrigerators · Shavers

With the war over, for women some things changed while others remained all too much the same. It is an oversimplification to see the war as a period of outright liberation for women, but nor is it true that they were just pushed back into the home after the cessation of hostilities. In Britain at least, there were serious labor shortages and women were encouraged to remain in the workforce. They were, however, ejected from many of the well-paid skilled jobs traditionally reserved for men, and were re-assigned to low-paid "women's" work, in the professions as well as in factories and offices.

At the same time popular culture – in films, magazines and in fashion – moved away from prewar and wartime images of women on an equal footing with men, back into a nostalgic fantasy world in which women were either romantic period heroines or ambivalent *femmes fatales*. Meanwhile, there was a conscious ideological emphasis on the overriding importance of family life.

The Nazi occupation of France had temporarily closed the Paris *haute couture* houses. Initially their wholesale removal to Berlin had been canvassed, but eventually they remained on French soil. Some of the top designers refused to work under the Nazis, but many worked on through the war with the aim of preserving the industry in French hands. Both French and German fashions during this period became more fussy, romantic and extravagant, and in fact laid the basis for the postwar "New Look". At the end of the war Paris pulled out all the stops to regain worldwide domination over the fashion industry. Its success had much to do with a massive injection of funds into the industry by leading cloth industrialists – notably Marcel Boussac, the silk magnate, who put up the money for the new house of Christian Dior. In 1947 Dior took the Western world by storm with his ultra-feminine "New Look", which was almost early Victorian: a tight-waisted, full-skirted romantic look.

There was an immense longing for this new extravagance in dressing. The New Look came to symbolize glamor, fun and luxury for women, who were tired of their drab wartime lives. Despite the Labour Government in Britain, which fulminated against this anti-egalitarian "caged bird" style, and feminists in the United States who saw it as an attack on the independence of American women, women flocked to the New Look. Dior's first great success laid the basis for the triumphant return of French *haute couture*. France fought off the American attempt to become the world leader of fashion, and for the next 20 years was to continue to lead the field. The great French couture houses learned from the advanced methods of American ready-to-wear

STYLE AND THE HOME

▼ In the New Look of 1947, sleeked-back ballerina chignons replaced the cascades of film star curls, and skirts made from yards of material swirled round the ankles of hour-glass-shaped mannequins.

merchandising, while maintaining their exacting standards of hand craftsmanship and exclusivity, as they still kept their private clients and dressed the richest, most aristocratic and famous women in the world. Although Dior pioneered new links with the mass market and franchised his designs, Paris designers still regarded themselves as true artists endowed with "genius", and a clear distinction was made between their exquisite individual creations and the general run of department-store fashion. In most of Europe, middle-class women still preferred to seek the services of a "little" dressmaker, who could copy the new lines from the grand houses – for the illusion of exclusivity was still a necessary part of the mystique of fashion, however widely styles might be copied, however popular they might become.

At the same time as Christian Dior was creating a nostalgic fashion and the French film industry was revitalizing itself, with period romances in which the stars appeared in dresses

that seemed only slightly more exaggerated than the evening crinolines of the modern couture salons, Hollywood *film noir* was in its heyday. These ambiguous movies portrayed women whose independence and sexuality was linked with betrayal, destruction and even murder. In *Mildred Pierce* (1946) Joan Crawford, the "clothes horse" star, was seen deserting virtuous domesticity for the dubious independence of her own business, with disastrous results (though she was retrieved for the traditional feminine role in the last reel).

In these films the costumes of the stars reinforced their ambiguity, their *femme fatale* quality. In *Gilda* (1946), for example, the high point of Rita Hayworth's performance is her rendering of the famous *Put the blame on Mame*. She sang the song in a classic "temptress" gown – floor-length, tight, black and strapless – and also wore long black gloves which she stripped off during the number as she used her abundant, wavy hair as a

▲ Although the New Look was associated with full, sometimes almost crinoline-width skirts, the "pencil slim" skirt – often pinned back in fashion photographs so that it almost resembled a hobble skirt – was also an essential feature of the New Look, as was the long furled umbrella. Either way, the Look, at the couture level at least, was very formal, very groomed, and it was a fashion which made women look sophisticated and mature.

suggestive torch singer's accessory, flinging it back or letting it hang forward over her face in a performance that approached, but never became, parody; yet the words of the song themselves commented ironically on this performance and their – overtly feminist – complaint was that when anything goes wrong men always "put the blame on Mame" – blame women. Rita Hayworth's role in *Gilda* is simultaneously a treacherous two-timer and a victim whose heart is lost to the man who spurns her. She appeared in this latter aspect in a demure, coolly cut 1940s suit, while in a third (fancy-dress) persona she acted the dominatrix with whip and boots.

Film noir heroines all had this double aspect expressing the inability of the American nation to deal with the freedoms that wartime had offered its women. For Hollywood, neither the period romanticism of French cinema nor the British return to class consciousness could have expressed adequately the mood of a pioneering but deeply conservative nation trying to impose cultural cohesion on a land of enormous diversity, suddenly burdened with world dominance in the threatening climate of the atomic bomb and the paranoia of the "Communist menace". *Films noirs* expressed some of the resulting unease. They were male fantasies, in which stars such as Humphrey Bogart or Robert Mitchum investigated a terrifying hole in their knowledge of the past. These investigative heroes were often thinly disguised war veterans, anxious about what either they had done, or their women had done, during the war, during the Absence that the war had been. Themes of personal betrayal, of sterility within marriage and sexual terror without, displaced anxieties such as national treachery and

Fashion Illustration

Poiret had commissioned leading avant-garde photographers to photograph his work in the early 1920s; however, until after World War II fashion magazines and store catalogs most often used line drawings in illustrations. Illustrators such as Patou and Erté produced highly stylized work; Benito, Christian Bérard and the American artist Eric provided an image of the clothes themselves, and their designers' intended style, elegantly and economically. In the twenties and thirties, however, black-and-white photography was becoming an important art form and photo portraits of famous personalities of the day highlighted their clothes as well as their looks (for example, Cecil Beaton's photographs of Nancy Cunard wearing an armful of ivory and ebony bracelets, see page 77). The Hollywood portrait publicity still in the 1930s added to the association between photography and glamor. From the 1940s, photography came completely to dominate the fashion magazine although illustration was still common into the 1960s. Initially prized for its "truthfulness", it is often less informative than line drawing, and can be just as mannered. Irving Penn in the United States, and Anthony Armstrong-Jones in Britain moved fashion photography towards a new informality and movement in the 1950s.

◄ Fashion portrait by Cecil Beaton.

▲◀▼ The romantic look for evening had reappeared in the late 1930s – for example, Norman Hartnell had designed crinolines in 19th-century style for Queen Elizabeth of England. In the early fifties this was the full evening-dress style in the upper reaches of society – although the short, "cocktail dress" version was just as popular. Accessories including handbags and long gloves completed the look.

symbolized the spiritual wasteland of a culture in which personal advancement seemed to be the only god.

In the 1950s reconstruction in Europe and the boom brought about by the Korean war boosted the fashion industries of the capitalist world. Cheap, mass-produced clothes that closely followed prevailing fashions were more widely available than ever before. For the first time in this early postwar period all classes had access to clothes in up-to-date styles. Until the 1930s the poor and the old had tended to wear clothes in styles long out of fashion, either from choice or by necessity, but now even they were incorporated into the language of style.

Italy, Britain and the United States had their own *haute couture*, but even the Italian designers,

despite their innovations in leisurewear and their use of vivid and at that time unusual color combinations – shocking pink with orange, emerald with cobalt blue – could not compete with the French. The huge success of the New Look, and the stringent attempts of Dior and his contemporaries to limit the pirating of their fashion designs and take advantage of worldwide licensed copying and the adaptation of their creations for the mass market, led to an awareness of the news value of fashion. The evolution of styles was now dramatized so that each season was to have its own "look" or "line". It had been possible to present the New Look as a revolution because of the hiatus of the war; henceforward dress designers sought to repeat this miracle in the molding of popular taste.

129

In the 1950s every season's new line was front-page news and most newsworthy of all was the length of the hemline. The height of the hemline was almost bound to be an easily changed variant of fashion when neither full-length skirts nor trousers were a serious option. Couturiers emphasized variations in cut and length and sought to encourage the association of fashion with exclusivity. Parisian fashion in particular was promoted on the basis that it sold to the French aristocracy, to international royalty (women such as Queen Soraya of Iran) and pseudo-royalty (Jackie Kennedy was a great fan of Pierre Cardin and Chanel). These clients were even more prestigious than internationally famous actresses and film stars, though they too used to publicize their favored couturiers – Audrey Hepburn, for example, whose slender figure and waif-like face fixed the *gamine* look for the decade, was often dressed by Givenchy. Her appearance in his clothes in popular movies such as *Funny Face* (1957) gave them even more powerful publicity than they received from *Vogue* and other magazines.

The reappearance of youth fashions

Even as the established couture houses tightened their hold, a new spirit was abroad, and their dominance came under attack. The New Look had been a sensational and ostentatious fashion, and fashion continued to be associated with an international aristocracy of birth and talent, but the 1920s' ideal of understated chic had never entirely vanished. In the 1950s it took new forms – the chic of having a Burberry raincoat lined with mink, for example, or the throwaway gesture of wearing your mink with jeans. The appearance of jeans can be seen as the first intrusion of youth culture into the world of fashion.

By the mid-fifties there was a new generation in Britain, France and the United States who, still in their mid-teens, had more money to spend than their age group had ever had before. Full employment had created a mass of low-paid but regular work even for the unskilled young. Even if the individual wage-packet was not large, collectively their spending power was huge, as for many teenagers virtually the whole of their income was instantly disposable. Smart clothes, increasingly associated with music cults, were major items of expenditure, but they did not want the aging, formal fashions that filtered down from Paris to the high-street chains. From the early fifties the department stores introduced "young idea" departments, where more youthful versions of couture-inspired styles could be purchased for middle-class youngsters. But the working-class teenager – and, increasingly, the children of the middle classes as well – wanted something altogether less prim. At first inspiration for youth styles came largely from the United States. The distinctive British Teddy Boy style began, in part, as a parody of upper-class British Jermyn Street tailoring, but it was influenced by motifs from the American West. The youth cult in the United States had been under way between the wars, when an expanding student market and the casual and sports fashions particularly associated with the West Coast had given birth to the notion

The Beatniks

In the United States the Beats, or Beatniks, were originally a West Coast phenomenon. Like the Parisian Existentialists of the late 1940s they were an esthetic/radical movement of dissent whose rebellion took a cultural rather than a directly political form. These movements were born in smoke-filled cafés rather than smoke-filled meetings, and the Beats aimed to shock and innovate in art and literature and in the way they lived. In fact, the Beats practised a form of bohemianism accompanied by jazz. Whereas Teddy Boys, Mods, bikers and *blousons noirs* were mainly working-class rebels, these were intellectuals who hung out at the poetry readings at the Hungry I Café and other venues of the North Beach area of San Francisco, where there were links both with the homosexual subculture and with the radical tradition from the 1930s. Allen Ginsberg might recite his poetry, and Okey bands from the Oklahoma Dustbowl might be playing.

◀ Beats in a San Francisco café.

◀ Although the New Look was sophisticated, French couture and Hollywood combined to present an alternative ideal – the *gamine* look, of which Audrey Hepburn was the embodiment. Barbara Hulanicki, who created Biba in the 1960s, (see page 164) has said that Hepburn was her fashion ideal when she was a young fashion student.

▲ Marlon Brando in *The Wild One* epitomized the rebellious youth of the 1950s; from then till now the sub-cultural uniform of black leather jacket and blue jeans has never lost its frisson of deviancy.

◀ The Teddy Boys – British, mostly working-class and rebellious – developed a street fashion by parodying upper-class styles; but the boys in this picture look much more "genuine" than the girls, who seem to be posing artificially. High-street stores were later to retail cheap fashions based on street styles and teddy girls did have their distinctive way of dress; but the Teddy Boy style was essentially a male style.

of youth fashions. By the 1950s these had incorporated the nearest thing that America had to a folk costume: blue jeans. Blue jeans were (and are) the prime example of workman's garb turned high fashion, and in the 1950s they symbolized a generation in revolt against the stuffiness of the times. Suburban domesticity and the nuclear family in the nuclear age generated the rebellion of teenagers trapped within its conformity, and blue jeans symbolized this rebellion. Worn with a black leather jacket they became the sign of instant untamed masculinity (Marlon Brando in *The Wild One* was the most threatening version of this rebel on a motorbike), but with their extraordinary versatility they also came to represent a simple youthfulness and a free and easy, casual lifestyle on the one hand, and female youthful sexiness on the other. No other garment has achieved the seemingly impossible feat of representing at the same time both ultra-feminity and ultra-masculinity, the careless innocence of youth and the deviance of the outlaw, the traditional frontier values of the West and the jazz and music culture of the metropolis.

Design for the nuclear family

In the America of the 1950s, it has been said, "each householder was able to have his own little Versailles along a cul-de-sac". For the first time, many middle-class American families could afford to buy their own house, set in its own plot of land with an integrated garage. The growth of suburban living brought with it a new lifestyle, in which leisure took on a new significance. A wide range of new domestic artefacts appeared as symbols of this "affluent society".

Desire for the new lifestyle goods was created and communicated by the mass media in magazine and television advertisements. As well as the readily available mass-produced additions to the household, there was a growing tendency in interior decoration for householders to "do-it-yourself" to achieve a luxurious "modern" interior at a fraction of the price which it would cost to bring in an interior decorator.

The suburban "dream house" had its roots in late 19th-century America: Frank Lloyd Wright's turn-of-the-century "Prairie" houses provided a model for later developers to emulate. By the early postwar years the "dream" had been made available to a new sector of the American population, through improved methods of building cheap, standardized, pre-fabricated houses and mortgage schemes provided for former members of the armed forces. A major justification for suburbia was the fact that it was safe for the children of the postwar baby boom. Increased automobile ownership also helped to make suburban living a practical proposition.

The kitchen was the most important room in the suburban home of the 1950s, as appliances began to take over from the automobile as the prime symbols of living in the modern age. The automatic washing-machine, the deep-freeze and the dishwasher were essentially products of the postwar era. They facilitated living in the new setting, provided consumers with the latest technology in their own homes and filled the ever expanding space that constituted the kitchen area in the new suburban house.

The kitchen became a living space for the whole family – a place for entertainment as well as a practical working environment. It no longer resembled the all-white "laboratory" of the interwar period. Color and decoration were introduced to the postwar "live-in" kitchen. This dramatic change coincided with, and indeed helped form, the new role for the suburban housewife as "glamorous hostess" rather than mere servant substitute. By 1950 Frigidaire were manufacturing a refrigerator and an electric range, created by Raymond Loewy, boasting details owing their origins to the world of automotive styling. The refrigerator handle operated on a press-button principle which had first been introduced in automobile design and the control panel on the back of the range had much in common with the complex, chrome-finished console of a highly styled automobile.

This evocative, transportation and technology-linked imagery disappeared at the end of the

▶ The *Britain Can Make It* exhibition, masterminded by the designer James Gardner, provided an opportunity for the British public, starved of new goods during the war, to get a taste – sometimes lighthearted – for the new postwar products represented here by a range of labor-saving kitchen devices.

▼ In the United States in the 1950s, the surburban dream dominated the lives of a vast majority of the population. Inspired by the need for safety for the children of the post-war consumer boom, it represented an idyllic existence in which every man had a house, an automobile, and a garden of his own. In this picture a husband returns from work, greeted by his wife and children.

▼ For the American housewife of the 1950s the 'fridge' constituted an important status symbol. This advertisement produced by the Frigidaire company, depicts a proud "hostess" housewife showing off her bulging refrigerator.

▲ This American advertisement from the mid-1950s serves to pinpoint the objects of consumer desire in this decade. The dreams of the newly wedded housewife of these years were fulfilled by the possession of a range of domestic electrical goods – irons, kettles, vacuum cleaners, electric fires, food mixers – which would bestow upon her the status symbolism required by a suburban housewife. Possession of these goods was a prerequisite for becoming a part of the "suburban dream".

decade, when a more minimal, angled "sheer look" was introduced, allowing appliances a much more integrated and anonymous role within the general kitchen environment. Appliances ceased to be free-standing monoliths dominating the space around them and became instead elements within the new, increasingly efficient, modern kitchen.

One explanation for the move towards color and decoration in the mid-fifties, American kitchen was the need for personalization within what were standardized suburban environments. Property developers attempted to inject a degree of variation into these pre-fabricated homes, but inevitably there was a high degree of similarity among them, and the inclusion of colour and pattern – albeit within the limited range of those suggested by such magazines as *Ladies' Home Journal* or *Good Housekeeping*, and those supplied by the appliance and plastic laminate manufacturers – went some way towards providing a necessary degree of individualization.

In their attempts to promote the goods manufactured by the mass production industries of the day, advertisers went to great lengths to project a complete lifestyle around the product. For the most part this was characterized by the concepts of efficiency and modernity and the idea of the happy, unified family featured strongly in all their efforts. The mother was invariably depicted as suburban housewife first and foremost, never a wage-earner, and appliances were promoted less as time-savers – the main selling point used in the 1920s and 1930s – than as a means of raising standards of housework.

If the suburban kitchen represented the high point of modernity and efficiency, the living-room in the same house was more ambivalent in its ideology. Although the terms "modern" and "contemporary" were often used to describe furniture and interior design, frequent references were also made to "Colonial" and other traditional American styles in an attempt to link the environment of the "newly arrived" population of suburbia with that of past generations of affluent, middle-class Americans.

The modern interior look was heavily promoted, and gradually the avant-garde designs of Charles Eames and George Nelson for Herman Miller, and of Eero Saarinen, Isamu Noguchi and Harry Bertoia for Knoll filtered, through repeated emulation, into the suburban living-room with the growing preponderance of plastic chair shells, metal rod legs, and upholstered forms in boomerang and kidney shapes. Nelson described the popular modern look in interior decor as the "plywood and rubber plant school", decrying the tastelessness with which avant-garde ideas were transplanted into products for the mass market.

The promotion of lifestyle

The suburban consumer of the 1950s clearly had more money to spend on goods, and more goods from which to choose, than ever before, and consumption responded less and less to basic utilitarian needs and more and more to the exigencies of status and comfort. A firm emphasis was placed on the family as the main unit of consumption, with the mother/housewife making all the consumption choices. Household goods played, increasingly, the most important role in establishing social status. In this orgy of consumption, objects became intricately linked with the concept of lifestyle. Their strictly utilitarian value was far outstripped by the way in which they provided a means of making the suburban family part of the community. As the home became, increasingly, the focus for a way of living and consuming, the objects consumed became "marks of belonging".

In Britain, although rationing and the Utility schemes were not declared officially defunct until the early 1950s, it was clear by then that the brief interlude during which it had seemed that a form of design control, which took as its starting point "the greatest good of the greatest number" was at an end. Utility goods seemed to represent all that was dull, uniform and uninspiring by comparison to the new consumer goods, from furniture to fashion to electrical appliances on display at the *Britain Can Make It* exhibition of 1946. Although many of these were merely prototypes or for export only, the British population, starved of such novelties for a number of years and bored with the "common sense" of Utility items, yearned for the color, decoration and expressive forms of the new goods.

The emerging Contemporary style for the domestic interior was characterized by a new use of materials, particularly aluminum and plastics, a love of color and pattern, an overall lightness and humanism and a delight in variation. Manufacturing companies and retail outlets, such as Ernest Race Limited, Hille, Heals, and Dunns of Bromley, capitalized on the new optimistic spirit, commissioning items from the new postwar generation of designers – among them Clive Latimer and Robin and Lucienne Day – who could clearly see that the only way ahead was to create a new, modern, expressive esthetic to herald the "new age".

In the United States, two distinct, indeed opposing, ideologies were communicated through the goods that earned it its greatest international reputation for design in the 1950s. On the one hand, the rapid growth of mass consumption, and the overt materialism of that decade, gave rise to a sudden proliferation of popular symbolism in the environment, expressed most strongly in that status symbol to beat all status symbols – the American automobile. On the other, the design establishment in the United States sought to show that it was as capable of understanding "good design" and "good taste" as the European modern design movements. Two clear design cultures emerged in the USA at this time, one firmly entrenched within the context of the commercial world and expressed most dramatically through the practices of object obsolescence and product styling, the other considerably more elitist, highminded, resistant to the popular appeal of commercial values, and finding its chief outlets in

the more traditional areas of furniture and the applied arts.

Dream machines

The idea of planned object obsolescence had been a given in American design since the mid 1920s, when the highly secretive and competitive process of designing the "annual model change" became common practice for all three of the large automobile companies – General Motors, Ford and Chrysler. American automobile styling represented the most advanced example of designing goods to fulfil consumers' dream and aspirations. Raymond Loewy's "MAYA" principle – his belief in designing objects which were the "most advanced yet acceptable" – characterized the products of American industry, resulting in some

► The radio, complete with its all-plastic body-shell, survived the war and moved into the immediate postwar period as a major status symbol. It was superseded soon after, however, by the television set.

► Charles Eames' armchair and ottoman of 1956, made of black leather and rosewood, and manufactured by the Herman Miller company, represented one end of the American "contemporary" furniture spectrum in the 1950s. It was, inevitably, an expensive chair and was seen, therefore, only in the most luxurious of modern interiors. It also became a familiar sight adorning the covers of hugely popular glossy interior magazines of the decade.

► This illustration depicts a typically "modern" living room of the 1950s. Like so many others of its kind it boasted such seminal furniture items such as an "organically" sculpted chair; tables with splayed, spindly legs; wallpaper adorned with angular, abstract motifs. The whole interior is dominated by the vibrant colors typical of the decade and it exudes an atmosphere of hypermodernity. The love of the "modern" extended beyond the sophisticated urban dweller to the occupants of the new suburban developments who culled most of their ideas from fashion-conscious interior magazines.

Japanese Design in the 1950s

Among the new countries to embrace the concept of design in the 1950s was Japan. Inevitably, due to the presence of American troops on Japanese soil at that time, the model of design it adopted originated in the United States. Thus many of the new technological goods – among them radios, tape-recorders, hi-fi equipment and cameras – that poured off Japanese assembly lines in these years bore the traces of the "Detroit" styling familiar to American markets.

Although styling was apparent in the new goods that Japan began to produce in these years it was not yet as important as the technological wizardry and low pricing which marked out Japanese products from their competitors'. For the most part companies such as Sharp, National Panasonic, Canon, Pentax, Toyota and others considered "design" as an afterthought rather than an essential component of the manufacturing and marketing processes. However, the Sony Corporation saw the benefits of "good design", and engaged an in-house design team which worked closely with its engineers on the forms of its products – tape-recorders, transistor radios, and television sets among them. From the start, though, the Japanese industrial designer was seen as an anonymous team member rather than the "super-star" that he had become in America.

In the area of automotive production the Honda company stood out as a firm which laid emphasis upon the role of design. Towards the end of the decade it launched its "Super-Cub" motorbike, a small specimen of two-wheeled transport intended to penetrate the American market-place and exist as a shopper alongside the larger bikes associated with film idols such as Marlon Brando.

▼ The 1950s was a decade which loved to apply pattern to as many surfaces as possible. Thus walls, floors and kitchen surfaces became an easel for the pattern-maker. The preferred patterns, as demonstrated by these Formica samples, incorporated many of the angular and organic shapes which were widespread in the abstract fine art of this decade.

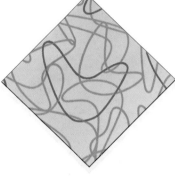

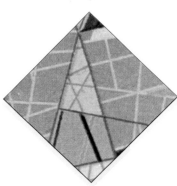

▲ Electronic and motor transport innovation in 1960.

of the century's most fantastic and extravagant design exercises.

By the early 1950s, brightly polished chrome on bumpers, door handles, headlight surrounds and body trim had become the main means through which automobiles expressed more than their mere utility functions. Their bulbous pressed steel bodies provided a canvas upon which all sorts of imaginative delights could be portrayed. While it was a highly capital-intensive exercise to modify the shell itself, it was relatively cheap to vary the amount of chrome detailing in order to provide a range of differently priced models. The fact that General Motors sold automobiles under a range of different brand names – Cadillac, Pontiac, Buick, Chevrolet and Oldsmobile, each aimed at a different sector of the market – meant that it could simultaneously standardize the production of major components and provide different models through varied body decoration.

The main development in American automobile styling of the 1950s was the influence of jet fighter-plane styling and the emergence, by the middle of the decade, of tail fins as expressions of the power, speed, and image of the future that so many consumers clearly felt played an important role in suburban lifestyles. The 1948 Cadillac, designed by Harley Earl, was the first model to move beyond the curved aerodynamic streamlined look – a heritage from the prewar period – and adopt a suggestion of tail-fins.

In 1954 sleek, powerful, finned, low-priced cars were introduced to the mass market for the first time. The seller's market of the previous years had begun to disappear, and the industry had to concentrate on persuading customers to change their models or on awakening new consumption desires. Earl's 1955 Chevrolet, modeled once again on the airplane – this time the needle-nosed jet-engined Douglas F-4D Skyray – introduced a new visual vocabulary into the automobile which was within reach of almost everyone's pocket. Almost instantaneously the other two large automobile corporations, Chrysler and Ford, joined General Motors in styling their models in the same highly evocative, sharp-angled, tail-finned idiom. With the employment of jet- and rocket-inspired features, twin-toning, the use of light, bright colours, and wraparound windscreens in imitation of the glass-domed airplane cockpit, came a highly aggressive and essentially masculine image for the American automobile. The style's overt references to power and sex were underlined in the advertising and publicity campaigns which constituted the "hard sell" techniques of the large automobile corporations.

The heroic period of American automobile styling fell between the years 1955 and 1960, when the tail-fin took on increasingly dramatic proportions, often incorporating tail lights within it, and the side profile of the automobile became lower and lower. This last characteristic was offset by the heavy styling of the front, which emphasized weight, a necessary quality of the new luxury status symbol. These frankly commercial symbols of achievement looked luxurious but they were available to everybody and they quickly became essential appendages of the American suburban

Advertising for Men

◀ This ad for Viceroy cigarettes contains many of the recurrent icons of the era – among them the rugged, clean-shaven male, the automobile, and the all-important cigarette.

While, in the interwar years, most consumer goods had been aimed at a female market (even if it didn't earn the money to pay for them), by the 1950s men had become, increasingly, the target for the ad-men of Madison Avenue. A wide range of supremely "masculine" goods – from cars to electric shavers to cigarettes – showed that the male species was as susceptible as women to the none-too-subtle tactics of the advertisers. The ads stressed the importance of self-reliance, strength and, above all, sophistication. Many of the masculine role models of the decade, visible in the ads, originated in the cinema. Whereas cigarette ads tended to focus on the enjoyment of leisure hours, advertising for men located its image increasingly in the world of work, with the male shown to be in control of his office or workshop environment.

▲ One of the most familiar masculine ideals to which the 1950s American male aspired was that of the Charles Atlas figure. His rippling muscles spelt out overt virility, conveying a he-man image which was widely reproduced in this decade. Advertisers inevitably made frequent reference to it in their attempts to sell consumer goods to the male sector of the population.

lifestyle, representing the aspirations of a mass market which valued, in this area of its life at least, the twin concepts of dynamism and modernity. Price was ultimately less important than status symbolism and consumers were prepared to accept and enjoy stylistic obsolescence as an inevitable feature of mid-20th-century living. 1958 saw a recession of the American automobile industry, however, and it looked as if years of excess were beginning to draw to a close. By 1960 the "big three" companies had each produced a compact car, indicating a reverse trend which, by the 1970s, had become the norm.

The era of the rise of the tail-fin and the general expansion of the fantasy element within the American automobile had represented a special relationship between production and consumption in which large corporations had been forced to sharpen their sales pitches in an all-out attempt to reach new customers. These consumers had few preconceived ideas about the nature of modern design or any pre-established taste-values in this area of consumption. Their primary motivation was to demonstrate their newly found wealth and level of material achievements in a tangible form, and automobile designers of these years like Earl and Virgil Exner showed themselves to be virtual magicians in their ability to turn, through the use of visual metaphors, public fantasy and aspiration into finite form.

In sharp contrast to this upsurge of popular styling more establishment American design values were still under the sway of European Modernism, interpreted in a strict, rather ascetic way. Modernism's transference across the Atlantic in the 1930s began the official promotion of "good design" in the United States, when the Museum of Modern Art in New York (MoMA) began a collection of mass-produced artefacts, selected on grounds of "quality" and "historical significance".

In the late 1940s, when the slogan "good design is good business" began to be discussed by the museum world, there were still no references made to the commercial achievements of the American consultant design profession which operated in a different cultural realm. In 1940 Eliot

Noyes, curator of design at MoMA, organized an exhibition and competition called "Organic Design in Home Furnishing" at which the furniture designers Charles Eames and Eero Saarinen presented their experiments in bent plywood; the pieces' strong Scandinavian links placed them firmly within the scope of the Museum's interests. With their European heritage, craft affiliations and minimal esthetic, their products came to typify "good modern design".

MoMA played a crucial role in defining "Good Design", as the single stylistic idiom of European Modernism, and with a strong emphasis on the contribution of the Scandinavian countries. It was an exclusive concept not related to sales potential. Social exclusiveness remained at the heart of "good design" as it evolved through the postwar period in the USA, a design language that appealed only to the educated, discriminating consumer. With its emphasis upon visual refinement and sophistication, it was diametrically opposed, both ideologically and stylistically, to the concept of "popular taste".

The co-existence of two distinct design cultures in the United States in the 1950s – the mass cultural commercial version, and the high cultural establishment model – established a division which has continued to characterize American design since that decade.

▲▼ American automobiles such as the Oldsmobile (above) represented the ultimate in style and sexuality for the youth of the 1950s. Teenage boys demonstrated their masculinity by associating themselves as closely as possible with "automobile culture".

COCA-COLA: THE REAL THING

In the vortex of the 20th century's constant change it has been a source of reassurance to find a few points of stability, a few commodities not subject to the whims of fashion and planned obsolescence. The red and white Coca-Cola logo is instantly recognizable, a guarantee of standardization and an emblem of the American Way of Life, as potent as the Stars and Stripes itself. Coca-Cola was the most widely distributed mass-produced item in America when World War II began, and the war provided an opportunity to spread the product into Europe and Asia. Its standardization of experience is both what we admire about its production, and what we occasionally dread about its effects. When European conservatives inveighed against the incursions of crass American values into their ancient cultures, the Coca-Cola logo epitomized all that they resented, and for the young the very act of drinking Coke became a minor form of rebellion against stifling tradition.

Coke's advertising tells us that this carbonated syrup "Is It," although we have not been told what "It" is. The formula is a long-held, well-guarded secret, and so it should be, because the foaming dark brown liquid is an elixir: Coke "Adds Life". Things, whatever things are, "Go Better" with it. They always did: a 1905 ad declared it to be "a delightful palatable healthful beverage. It relieves fatigue and is indispensable for business and professional men, students, wheelmen and athletes." Such claims might be disputed, but not for the drink's supreme claim, the perfect ad-line for the perfect product, that Coca-Cola is "the Real Thing". This is a triumph of the American corporation and advertising industry. If Coke is the Real Thing, what can we possibly call artificial or fake?

◀ A 1920s Coca-Cola advertising campaign gave the world Father Christmas as we all now recognise him, in his red and white costume; before that he was as often dressed in blue or yellow or green. World War II gave the world Coca-Cola. Persuading the US military that it was an essential product for troop morale, Coca-Cola followed the flag wherever American forces went. By the end of the war a worldwide distribution system, complete with bottling and production plants, had been established, along with a worldwide enthusiasm for an identifiably American taste.

▼ In Third World countries, people who have seen standards of American material life in the movies or through shop windows may feel that they can buy a small part of that prosperity by choosing the drink.

◀ Unloading Coca-Cola in the Philippines. There was nothing more American than Coke, and no easier way to display your cultural affiliation than by drinking it.

▲ Originally a mixture of nut-oil and sugar, Coca-Cola was invented in 1886 by a chemist from Atlanta, Georgia, and sold as a "brain tonic." It lost its traces of cocaine in 1903, and first appeared in its immediately recognizable bottle in 1915. The width of the bottle's curves changed with fashion through the century; in 1955 designer Raymond Loewy "slenderized" it to the shape we are most familiar with.

◄ Throughout the century, Coca-Cola has projected an image of what it is to be young, free, well-off and comfortable. Coca-Cola was a major sponsor of the 1984 Los Angeles Olympic Games, as well as being the Games' "Official Drink".

▲ Sun, sand and Coke: a 1950s Coca-Cola ad contained a barely concealed hint of sexual promise in the girl's assent to the gift of the bottle.

Datafile

The 1950s was a period of unprecedented richness in popular music. The dramatic arrival of rock 'n' roll and the emergence of the teenage consumer market were major events, but in musical terms rock 'n' roll was one area of innovation among many.

Jazz, for example, traveled a course from the highly-strung, inventive bebop of Charlie Parker, Dizzy Gillespie and others, via the "cool" reaction, to a complex situation in which John Coltrane's virtuosity and Davis's own renewed lyricism were both heard. Country music, meanwhile, had found itself with a nationwide audience for the first time, and this had a marked impact on the development of styles such as Hank Williams' which drew on southern (white and black) and mainstream popular idioms to speak to a contemporary state of mind. At the same time a different approach (by Bill Monroe) to the reworking of tradition in a new environment produced the fresh sound of bluegrass.

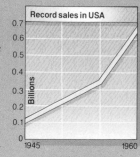

▲ The steady commercial progress made by the record industry in the decade after the war seemed decidedly unspectacular by 1960. That was because the advent of rock 'n' roll had helped to double the industry's selling power in the space of five years. Some 60 percent of all units sold were singles.

► Big bands found life more difficult in the late 1940s but their basic support remained. The significant change in mainstream popular music was that the popularity of solo singers increased dramatically. In terms of broad appeal, therefore, this was the age of Frank Sinatra, Perry Como and Patti Page.

► The teenage and young adult population in 1955 contained more than 2.5 million students in higher education. Historians usually describe this group as middle-class, likely to prefer Pat Boone while Elvis Presley appealed to youngsters in manual work. The high proportion of college students suggests this may be too simple.

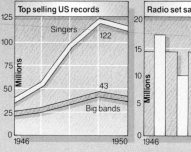

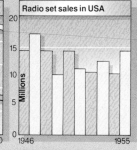

▲ The erratic sales performance by radio-set manufacturers in America in 1944–55 conceals the fact that in other respects the industry was growing fast. Independent radio stations increased rapidly in number after the postwar changes in legislation, outnumbering the network stations by more than two to one by 1950.

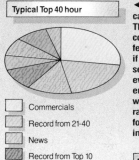

◄ A Top 40 show was a carefully calculated affair. The proportion of music to commercials and other features was controlled as if by formula. In the actual sequence of items everything was done to ensure any hint of boredom was kept at bay, and it was rare for one record to follow another immediately.

▼ The sharp rise in million-sellers discloses that it was not only the volume of record sales that increased in the 1950s. More individual recordings emerged from the pack. That meant a new kind of stardom, sometimes sustained (Elvis Presley logged over 30 million-sellers in 1956–58), sometimes capricious.

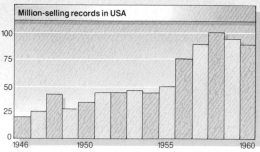

There had been teenagers before the 1950s. The word "teenage" had first appeared in the popular press in the 1920s, but the idea that there was a time of life between childhood and adulthood that could be isolated, and that had its own peculiar characteristics, belongs largely to the 1950s. The long-established belief had been that people remained children until they suddenly became adults; this conviction lost its hold partly because of social changes, partly as a result of the flourishing postwar consumer economy.

What has been called the "self-conscious subculture" of the young developed during the 1920s and 1930s as a largely urban white middle-class response to the increasing leisure opportunities afforded by changing social attitudes. After World War II the extra years spent in education both broadened the base of the group and gave it a clearer sense of identity. At the same time, teenagers in work (many of them working-class) found that increases in spending power and in leisure time enabled them to move to a position where they could both assert their independence and be courted by leading representatives of entrepreneurial America. Ironically, while teenagers were more open than ever before to market influences, they were frequently hostile to the adult culture of which the market was a part.

The identification of teenage culture with popular music, which was to become so pervasive (and so profitable), was not immediately apparent. Most popular music was still felt to be by adults and for adults. Significant changes occurred in radio and the record industry in the 1940s to make music the principal point of convergence between the young in search of identity and business in search of consumers.

Putting the popularity into pop music

In 1940 ASCAP (the American Society of Composers, Authors and Publishers), in league with the broadcasting networks, still exercised control over what most people heard in the United States (see page 103). A relatively small number of songs received a disproportionately high number of broadcast performances. Bribery was by no means uncommon (*Variety* magazine had coined the term "payola" for it in 1938). Union opposition still prevented the networks from using records on the air (though smaller, independent, stations relied heavily on them). However, when ASCAP demanded large increases in fees the networks responded by forming a rival organization, Broadcast Music Inc. (BMI), which sought to create an alternative music catalog for the broadcasters. As part of its efforts it turned to minority areas of the business, in particular to "hillbilly" and "race" music (black music generally). It also began a system of paying copyright holders a fee

THE EMERGENCE OF THE TEENAGER

Pop-music, broadcasting
and disk jockeys
Rhythm & blues and
rock 'n' roll
The Top 40
Elvis Presley
Bebop

for each recorded performance. Without anyone realizing it, the ground was being prepared for these kinds of music to play a more significant part, both financially and culturally.

In a second development, which prepared the way for a prodigious rise in the importance of records for radio programming, an appeals court found that stations were not obliged to pay record companies for broadcasting their records. The major record companies were slow to seize this opportunity; the running was made by the growing number of smaller independent companies. One in particular, Capitol, saw the chance to promote its products by providing the newly important figure, the disk jockey, with free copies. The results were spectacular.

The increasing number of local independent stations, some of them set up exclusively for the black community, showed more awareness of changing audience requirements. Without the need to think in terms of national taste they included more black and country music in their programs. In this climate of transition, and helped by the arrival of the reel-to-reel tape recorder, independent record companies sprang up, many of them founded by members of white ethnic groups. A relationship rapidly developed in the postwar years between audiences, independent stations, new record companies, new publishers – and BMI.

Rhythm & blues

In the wider social arena the war had emphasized the hypocrisy of participating in a crusade in the name of democracy and anti-racism, while at home blacks were the victims of systematic discrimination. Race riots in Detroit and elsewhere demonstrated the depths of black disaffection, but in the aftermath of the war blacks found that most of what little they had gained was transient. Black music was being more widely heard, but it was still produced and marketed principally for a black audience. Segregation not only remained an acceptable marketing strategy, it also enabled most of the companies to maintain a system of exploitation (tested by others in earlier years), under which the companies themselves assumed the rights, for a token fee, of the music recorded by black musicians. Nevertheless, in the 1950s black music once again provided the catalyst for change. In the century's recurrent musical cycle of challenge and compromise, the challenge was now stronger than ever and the eventual compromise involved an irreversible shift in the balance of the musical culture, and the society that supported it.

Swing had appropriated elements of black jazz, but it had paid little heed to the blues. The blues tradition, meanwhile, had continued to develop a

▼ Of the white jockeys who promoted r&b none was more influential than Alan Freed. Persuaded in 1952 to turn his Cleveland radio program over to black music, he regularly accompanied the records with a "moondog" howl. Controversy over his effect on teenagers was heightened by his organization of concerts for mixed audiences. None of this was forgotten when, in 1960, he was indicted in the Congressional payola investigation.

variety of styles growing up to express the experience of a switch to urban life. Searching for a new catch-all term with which to sum up the various styles of contemporary black music in its now inappropriately named "race" chart, the magazine *Billboard* introduced the description "rhythm & blues" on 25 June 1949. This happy choice of phrase covered many varieties of music, from big band shouters and Chicago's updated Mississippi style to the "sepia Sinatras" of the West Coast's racially integrated bars. Two styles began to predominate in the early 1950s. "Jump bands" played small combo dance music derived from blues, with a boogie-woogie bass, rhythmically infectious and with an obligatory saxophone "break" halfway through. Vocal groups mixed strong gospel influences with a discernible pop song input. This music had a ghetto street-corner association, both for its musicians and for its audience of black urban youth. Its lyric content mixed adolescent emotion, often humorously treated, with sexual themes heavy with *'double entendre'*.

The growing number of radio stations catering to a black audience (270 by 1953) meant that rhythm & blues became the first undiluted black music to be readily available to those who were prepared to look for it. Those exploring the radio dials were very often teenagers. Their elders were

by now listening to the radio less. The growing lure of television shared responsibility for this with the fact that network radio, with its reliance on safe mainstream white taste, was rapidly surrendering the airwaves to the independent stations, whose musical output was often beyond the understanding of many older listeners. Adult white musical tastes were increasingly being catered for by the newly arrived long-playing record or LP (originally developed by CBS in 1948); the equally new-fangled seven-inch 45rpm single (produced as a rival by RCA) seemed tailor-made to give the younger market its identity badge.

The ending of the war brought a decline in the

following of the big bands; this was partly because their music was associated with a pre-war world which had gone, but an important contributory factor was a change in the laws requiring licences for public dancing.

Black radio stations attracted considerable white teenage audiences, particularly in the South and on the West Coast. In 1952 one Los Angeles record store reported that 40 percent of its black music sales were to white audiences. The West Coast's tradition of mixed audiences allowed teenagers there to go beyond the first excitement of discovery into a region of experience that was often (as had been the case with jazz) spoken of in terms echoing religious conversion. But wherever

▲ Over a glass of milk in Karl-Marx-Allee two young East Berliners keep up with the latest dance records. The controlled environment is not a café, but a state-provided young people's sport and leisure club.

▶ Records and 7-Up give the fizz to a middle-class teenage pyjama party. The ability of teenagers to claim and construct their own domestic space was thought of more in social terms in the United States than elsewhere. In countries where private consumption was more the domestic norm, the search for space was more likely to be centered on public venues such as the local youth club or dance hall.

white, particularly working-class, teenagers identified with rhythm & blues, a lifestyle rapidly grew up centered on some kind of outlaw or deviant status.

The birth of rock 'n' roll

Radio and the record industry responded to these changes. From 1952, white disk jockeys began including black music in their programs. The most celebrated, Alan Freed, called his Cleveland broadcasts "Moondog's Rock 'n' Roll Party", introducing into common currency a term that had long been familiar in black music circles (with sexual rather than musical nuances). Soon black records appeared regularly on the white charts.

At this point some of the major record companies, whose interest in black music – especially if it belonged to the blues family – had dwindled almost to nothing since the war, began to wake up to the market opportunities offered by the teenage consumer and the unprecedented degree of stylistic "cross-over" between black and white culture. The tactic that they (and one or two independent companies) used was the "cover version": a modified recording of a song that had already been recorded.

Cover versions, like teenagers themselves, were not a new phenomenon, but this was the first time that the process was based on cultural appropriation: taking black music and adapting it for a white audience. As with earlier instances of borrowing in popular music, the original was often watered down both musically and lyrically and the now more socially acceptable product successfully marketed. The record that marks the start of this particular era, the Crew Cuts' 1954 cover of the Chords' *Sh-Boom*, made changes in rhythm and harmony to make the song follow the conventions of pop song. While the original only ever reached Number Nine in the charts, the cover held the Number One place for 20 weeks.

Alan Freed and others only played original black rhythm & blues/rock 'n' roll, but most disk jockeys gave the cover version far more exposure, usually omitting to mention the original. Covers by leading white performers such as Pat Boone consistently outsold the originals over the country as a whole. To some people only the original black music had the necessary connotations of non-conformity, but for many middle-class teenagers clean-living Pat Boone's perfectly enunciated version of Little Richard's *Long Tall Sally* offered enough assertiveness without too much risk of overstepping the social and moral mark.

The lyrics of *Sh-Boom* were unaltered in the Crew Cuts' cover version, but that was an exception; in many cases wholesale changes were made to cope with lyrics of unaccustomed frankness and innuendo. The music of the covers was also often toned down. These changes, undertaken partly to avoid incurring society's wrath, partly to ensure good sales, could not disguise the fact that penetration of the mainstream by black and black-derived approaches was taking another, decisive step. The interplay between the offbeat and heavy, insistent rhythm were different from anything the white popular music scene had heard before. In introducing new

▲ Muddy Waters electrified version of the Mississippi blues suited the mood in postwar Chicago. Of the various strands of black music collectively known as "rhythm & blues", the Chicago blues bands with their raw, impassioned sound had least interest in reaching an audience beyond the urban black adult community. But their impact on the wider scene was just as great. The difference was that while a style such as Louis Jordan's contagious jump blues, with its knowing lyrics, directly influenced rock 'n' roll, Chicago blues entered white consciousness via the interpretations of British r&b groups such as the Rolling Stones. Ironically, by this time the black audience for the music was largely lost.

Bebop

The tensions felt by blacks in the United States – musically, between the need to maintain a separate culture and doubt about the entertainment industry; socially, between the pressure to protest injustices and the knowledge that action in so doing might further stigmatize the community – were fundamental to the emergence of the "radical new jazz" of the forties known onomatopeically as bebop.

The musicians involved came from a cross-section of urban and small-town America: Charlie Christian from Oklahoma, Dizzy Gillespie from South Carolina, Charlie Parker from Kansas City, Thelonious Monk and Bud Powell from New York. But it was particularly in New York, in after-hours jam sessions at clubs like Minton's and Monroe's Uptown House, that the music came together.

The distinguishing features of bebop were greater rhythmic complexity, expanded harmonic vocabulary, increased instrumental virtuosity; these developed out of the course black jazz was taking in the thirties, but that the younger generation of musicians for swing had attenuated the music. In seeking to move to a level where commercial music would find it hard to follow, musicians dug deeper into improvisational black culture. Meanwhile their determination to escape the stereotype of the black entertainer resulted in bebop musicians pointedly ignoring their audiences.

elements, mostly derived from the blues, cover versions unwittingly helped to prepare a wider audience for the music that followed.

Had there been no life beyond Pat Boone, the later 1950s would hardly have come to mark the beginning of a new era for white popular music. The main reasons why they did so can be found in the emergence of a distinctive style of white rhythm & blues among musicians with a country-music background, and in the marketing of these performers to the now recognized teenage audience as its own first individual stars. The cover version remained the basis of the white rock 'n' roll of Bill Haley, Elvis Presley and others, but a different approach can be detected between these and the version of the Pat Boone school. In place of the attempt to divert rhythm & blues into more broadly acceptable channels of sound, the country-bred musicians and their producers sought to develop a new style, based on a dynamic encounter between black and white. Having more allegiance to country music than to Tin Pan Alley conventions, the musicians were also part of the longstanding Southern tradition of familiarity with black music, a tradition that per-

sisted regardless of political and social considerations. Instead of pale imitation, their musical approach favored a process of adaptation and re-creation not very different from that behind much black music. It allowed self-expression and independence, where other styles had seemed to amount, in the end, to a kind of voyeurism. Elvis Presley's powerful impact was one result.

Such encounters had taken place many times before, especially in the South, quite separately from the context of domination in which mainstream metropolitan white America had continually borrowed – or more often stolen – from blacks. Linked to the new teenage consumer market, this time the resulting, much sought-after product owed its identity to two of the socio-cultural groups middle America cared for least.

It did not follow, any more than it had before, that black musicians themselves reaped many benefits, but in the wake of rock 'n' roll some were able to gain widespread exposure and popularity on an almost equal footing, and without compromising their style. Significantly, those who did so, such as Chuck Berry, pitched their appeal unambiguously at the teenage audience. One effect of this was to encourage changes within black music itself. The music of black vocal groups of the early fifties already contained less racially specific material; now this was taken further, and the way opened for mass-appeal black music.

In the aftermath of Elvis Presley's arrival on the national scene in 1956, rock 'n' roll reawoke radical changes in popular music culture from earlier eras. Ironically, representatives of the musical idioms that had been denounced in the past were often in the forefront of the attack. Benny Goodman, though, was an exception.

Rock: revolt or revolting?

The radical fear that had been a feature of earlier hostility to popular music was again present, as before only partly cloaked in general descriptions of rock 'n' roll as "barbaric" and "primitive". But there were also important differences. While much of the language used echoed past struggles, there was a new tendency to draw on psychological terminology. Science – "objective", energetic, modern – was summoned in support of battered morality. But what psychology most clearly revealed – and it was fairly obvious without it – was that the crux of the latest cultural collision was not in mental or emotional deficiencies, but in something much more normal, the so-called "generation gap". The development of a separate teenage identity had resulted, among other things, in the perception by the adult world that its authority was being eroded. Rock 'n' roll was being castigated as the most powerful symbol of the teenage attempt to tilt the balance in the parent-child relationship. But, as in previous collisions, the attitude of the group that feared for its control was profoundly ambiguous. Inseparable from the older generation's hostility to the teenage culture was its envy of the freedom and independence which that culture seemed to have been achieved – in contrast to the life, past and present, that the old had known.

▼ The first indignant response of the British popular music press to rock 'n' roll ("one of the most terrifying things to have happened to popular music") was addressed to its adult audience of jazz and dance-band musicians and fans. As the commercial possibilities of a teenage readership became apparent, magazines such as *Melody Maker* began addressing a younger audience directly, offering a disturbed paternalism alongside the Top 20.

▶ In the limping but explosive frame of Gene Vincent Capitol Records thought they had found an alternative to Presley. But when the cleancut image took hold of the American scene in the late 1950s it was Britain that idolized the now all-leather figure. Vincent's hugely popular act also gave the lie to stateside rumors that the rasp in his voice was a studio fabrication.

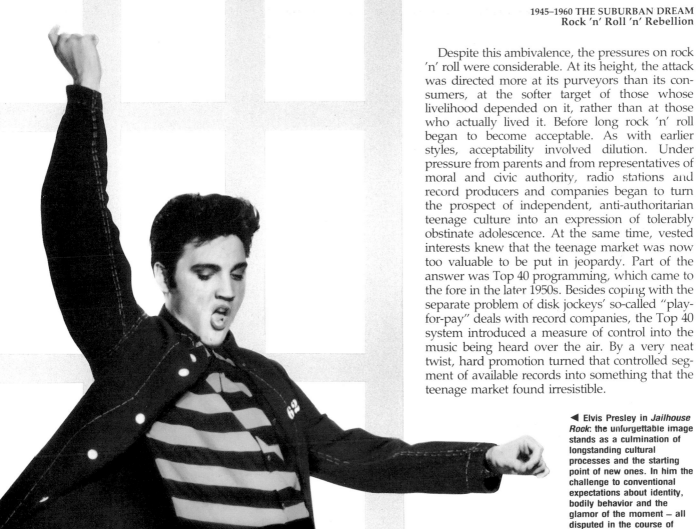

Despite this ambivalence, the pressures on rock 'n' roll were considerable. At its height, the attack was directed more at its purveyors than its consumers, at the softer target of those whose livelihood depended on it, rather than at those who actually lived it. Before long rock 'n' roll began to become acceptable. As with earlier styles, acceptability involved dilution. Under pressure from parents and from representatives of moral and civic authority, radio stations and record producers and companies began to turn the prospect of independent, anti-authoritarian teenage culture into an expression of tolerably obstinate adolescence. At the same time, vested interests knew that the teenage market was now too valuable to be put in jeopardy. Part of the answer was Top 40 programming, which came to the fore in the later 1950s. Besides coping with the separate problem of disk jockeys' so-called "play-for-pay" deals with record companies, the Top 40 system introduced a measure of control into the music being heard over the air. By a very neat twist, hard promotion turned that controlled segment of available records into something that the teenage market found irresistible.

◄ **Elvis Presley in *Jailhouse Rock*: the unforgettable image stands as a culmination of longstanding cultural processes and the starting point of new ones. In him the challenge to conventional expectations about identity, bodily behavior and the glamor of the moment – all disputed in the course of 20th-century popular culture – achieved its clearest statement yet from a white American source. Musically, the electric charge Elvis obtained from his own way of crossing black and white performance styles was arguably the most exciting result of that recurrent encounter. With Elvis the teenage audience realised that it could now express its own identity, even within the world of consumer culture.**

Datafile

Television sold faster than any other consumer durable ever had. It was the perfect commodity for the suburban 1950s: a piece of furniture that did something – and what it did was to bring entertainment into the home. Inevitably this affected cinema attendances, but not directly. The movie-going audience became increasingly concentrated in a narrow age-band of teenagers and young adults. The Supreme Court decision which forced the major companies to split their production and distribution companies from their theaters brought about major changes in the number and nature of the films Hollywood produced. Studios concentrated their resources on fewer, and more expensive, movies.

Academy Awards for Best Film of the Year		
1946	*The Best Years of Our Lives*	RKO
1947	*Gentleman's Agreement*	Fox
1948	*Hamlet*	Columbia
1949	*All the King's Men*	Universal
1950	*All About Eve*	Fox
1951	*An American in Paris*	MGM
1952	*The Greatest Show on Earth*	Paramount
1953	*From Here to Eternity*	Columbia
1954	*On the Waterfront*	Columbia
1955	*Marty*	United Artists
1956	*Around the World in Eighty Days*	United Artists
1957	*The Bridge on the River Kwai*	Columbia
1958	*Gigi*	MGM
1959	*Ben Hur*	MGM
1960	*The Apartment*	United Artists

Legend:
- USA
- Local
- UK
- France
- USSR
- Mexico
- India
- Other

► Only the Eastern bloc and India resisted Hollywood's penetration. Apart from a few cinemas in university cities, Americans had no opportunities to see foreign films.

◄ Oscars for Best Picture invariably went to prestige productions of one kind or another: either large-budget extravaganzas or "social consciousness" films like *Gentleman's Agreement*, *On the Waterfront*, or *Marty* which indicated that Hollywood was at least capable of taking itself seriously. In 1957 the Academy at least recognized the existence of a movie world outside Hollywood, when it instituted a new category for Best Foreign Language Film, which was first won by Federico Fellini's *La Strada*..

The origin of feature films 1948
(India, Czechoslovakia, Austria, Egypt, Algeria, France, Burma, Norway, Colombia, Israel, Costa Rica, Italy, Spain, United Kingdom, Bolivia, Canada, United States) — Percent 0, 20, 40, 60, 80, 100

US television sales (Millions) 1946–1955

◄ Rather than saying that the decline in cinema attendance was *caused* by television, it is more accurate to say that the decline resulted from the same factors that produced the rise in television sales: a rise in real wages, more comfortable homes, and the emergence into working-class life of the nuclear family.

Wide screen processes (Films) 1953–1960

◄ Hollywood countered television by turning to fewer but larger-scale films. Studios experimented with 3-D and widescreen processes, of which the most successful was CinemaScope, because it required the least costly alterations to existing movie theaters. Widescreen processes were used throughout the 1960s.

▼ In 1954 television had reached over half the households in the United States, but was far less advanced elsewhere. The countries with the greatest market penetration were those where American influence was strongest. No country other than those shown had more than five televisions per thousand people at this date.

UK TV licences (Thousands) 1945–1960

◄▼ In Britain, as television ownership rose, cinema attendance fell by 9 percent between 1946 and 1954, and then plummeted drastically by 1959. Even at its height, British cinema-going was a habit of young working-class people. This audience declined as the emerging youth culture of the 1950s offered a wider range of leisure choices.

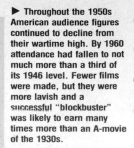
UK cinema admissions (Thousands) 1945–1960

► Throughout the 1950s American audience figures continued to decline from their wartime high. By 1960 attendance had fallen to not much more than a third of its 1946 level. Fewer films were made, but they were more lavish and a successful "blockbuster" was likely to earn many times more than an A-movie of the 1930s.

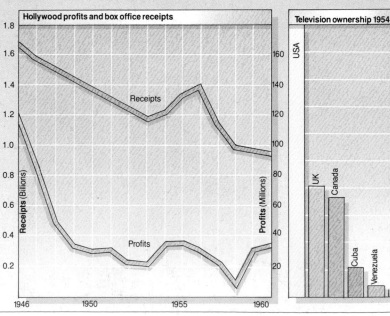
Hollywood profits and box office receipts — Receipts (Billions), Profits (Millions), 1946–1960

Television ownership 1954 — Sets per thousand population (USA, UK, Canada, Cuba, Venezuela, Belgium)

146

SCREENS LARGE AND SMALL

Although 1946 was the most successful year ever at the box-office, Hollywood entered the Cold War era in a climate of unease. Considering that they were made in a period so commonly remembered for its placid, affluent certainties, the movies of the 1950s displayed unexpected anxieties, suggesting that, in Hollywood's representation of American culture at least, stability was only on the surface, and the desperate monsters of the undercurrent could at any moment emerge from beneath the dark waters. If movies showed more concern with the insecurities of American life, one reason was that television had come to take over their role of celebrator of American virtues. As television relocated family entertainment inside the nuclear family's bunker, the suburban home, the movies found that their primary audience was becoming younger and more restless; so they responded quickly to its darker demands.

▼ As television found its way into living rooms all over the world, the furniture was re-arranged to make the set the focus of attention.

Hollywood and the Cold War
In the late 1940s Hollywood had its own industrial and ideological anxieties. In 1947 the House Committee on Un-American Activities (HUAC) chose to investigate "Communist Infiltration of the Motion Picture Industry". Its accusations were without substance, but gained it publicity when its "unfriendly witnesses" were christened the "Hollywood Ten" by the press. HUAC redirected the Hollywood fantasy into its own paranoid vision, and inaugurated a Cold War climate in the United States, in which attacks were launched on individuals on the flimsiest evidence by Red-baiting groups with no credentials beyond a belief in a "Communist menace" under their beds and a list of people they thought "controversial". Industry personnel without studio protection who had past "controversial" allegiances – having married someone who signed the wrong petition once in the 1930s might be more than

"CBS – the world's greatest cigarette vending machine" – newspaper ad, late 1950s

enough – found it increasingly difficult, and finally impossible, to work.

Blacklisting destroyed the careers of individuals on little more than a hysterical whim or the timidity of a television program sponsor concerned about the political purity of his consumer products. At the same time, the US Supreme Court dismantled the system under which the American film industry had made its movies and its money for the previous twenty years. In 1948 it found in favor of the Department of Justice in an anti-trust suit against the major film companies. They were obliged to divorce their theater holdings from their production and distribution operations, breaking up a crucial component in their system of control over the industry.

No longer guaranteed a market for all their products, producers and distributors alike were forced to sell each film on its individual merits. Production values and costs rose to ensure sales, with an ever-increasing emphasis on the prestige production, and the concentration of profits on a shrinking number of "blockbuster" films. A-feature budgets of over one million dollars, rare in the 1940s, became the norm after 1953 as talent and finance were concentrated on a smaller number of productions intended to play for long spells on early-run theaters. Prior to 1950, only 100 films had ever grossed more than $5 million worldwide. In 1953–54, 30 films did. Nevertheless, box-office receipts dropped in 1947, and continued to drop steadily for the next decade, leveling off at half the level of the early 1940s.

Switching on to television

Suburban development and the rapidly booming postwar economy boosted all forms of home entertainment and domestic hobbies, but no new consumer commodity has ever sold so fast or penetrated the available market so thoroughly as television did in the US in the 1950s. In 1947 there were fewer television sets in use in the United States than there were movie theaters. By 1954 there were 32 million receivers. It was the perfect commodity for the moment. The arrangement of furniture in living rooms across America and increasingly throughout western Europe changed to accommodate the television set as the focus of attention. Like the recliner chair, it was a consumer durable that "did" something; better than radio, it brought entertainment into the home, and so reinforced the value that suburbanites put on the nuclear home as the center of their existence.

Suburbia relocated American isolationism; the skies over Texas and Alaska might always be marked with the vapor trails of Strategic Air Command's eternally vigilant B-52s, but the nuclear family had taken ideological refuge in what David O. Selznick had called "that other unconquerable fortress, the American home". Television brought families together to share their entertainment with a huge disembodied audience they need never encounter. The communal experience of cinema-going was being replaced by an ever more abstract sense of homogeneity that came from watching the same TV shows in the similar but separate environments of suburban living rooms.

◀ Like radio before it, television in the 1950s borrowed many of its most successful forms from vaudeville. Sometimes, though, it showed its ingenuity by combining journalism and the variety show to produce what the BBC called "light entertainment." If audiences ever felt like throwing knives at commentators, reporter Bob Danvers-Walker told them what it felt like to be on the receiving end.

▼ In 1930 the BBC had insisted that its radio announcers wear dinner suits to read the news, and remain anonymous. Television required its presenters to be personalities, but until the appearance of a rival channel in 1955, the BBC presenters, like Mary Malcolm and Sylvia Peters, remained very formal in their dress, their manners, and their speech. Nevertheless, television made them celebrities.

The accidents of technology placed control of television in the hands of the radio networks. As radio had borrowed its essential forms from earlier entertainment modes, television borrowed extensively from the media whose cultural role it replaced: movies and radio. The earliest television successes were variety shows – hosted by Ed Sullivan, Milton Berle, Sid Caesar – based, like radio's Rudy Vallee's Varieties, on the traditional acts seen in vaudeville. Television adapted the forms of radio comedy and drama to make its own genres: sitcoms, soap operas and series. Like radio, it had a "Golden Age" of New York-based drama production. Between 1953 and 1955, anthology series such as Philco Television Playhouse and Kraft Television Theater employed rising Broadway performers and directors including Paul Newman, Sidney Poitier and Arthur Penn, in single plays like *Days of Wine and Roses* and *Requiem For a Heavyweight*. Writer Paddy Chayevsky described their social realist themes as aiming to present "the marvelous world of the ordinary" on television.

Despite their consistently high ratings, advertisers objected to the challenge such plays presented to the fantasy world of fulfilment through consumption which they viewed the medium as existing to sell. Live drama was prestigious, but it was also expensive, difficult to schedule, and could only be screened once. It had neither the permanence nor the resale value of film. The most successful programs in terms of audience ratings in 1951 – *I Love Lucy* and *Dragnet* – were both filmed in Los Angeles. Sponsors and talent moved to Hollywood as the film production industry slowly abandoned its initial attempts to ignore or deride television and sought ways to live with it.

As television production moved from East Coast to West Coast, its dominant influences changed. The traditions of naturalist theatre, presenting action within an enclosed set, were replaced by cinematic conventions and genres. In 1956 the majors began selling their film libraries to programming syndicates, and films shown on TV became a staple of prime-time viewing. Warner Bros, initially so hostile to television that they had banned any mention of it in their films, began producing filmed series for television screening. Television Westerns such as *Cheyenne* or *Gunsmoke* came to substitute for B-film production in industry economics. Following Hollywood's example in the 1910s, the filmed series were sold abroad at cut-rate prices, far more cheaply than comparable material could be produced. America's Coca-Colonization of the world's media and systems of representation took its next step forward.

As the first choice for a television genre, Westerns were both safely uncontentious and economically advantageous, since they could use stock B-movie settings, scripts and shots. The Western series were pietistic homilies to the American male virtues and certainties, endlessly renewing the adolescent fantasy of the Righteous Man with a Gun restoring Order to a troubled frontier, but never himself having to endure the settled blessings of the civilization he brought into being. Sitcoms presented the domestic aspect of patriarchy in their patterning of family life with Father as the stoic centre of a world constantly disrupted by the zany behavior of women and children. The homogenized suburban middle-America of *Father Knows Best* and *Leave It To Beaver* may never have actually existed outside the world of television, but television brought it into the living rooms of a suburban middle-America which instantly recognized the scenarios it enacted. Television's favourite characters were either children or, like Lucille Ball's Lucy or Jackie Gleason's Ralph Kramden in *The Honeymooners*, childlike; a simple device to permit a level of

▼ Sport was important to television's capturing a male as well as a female audience. It created a new kind of spectator, the armchair expert who watched in the comfort of his own home. Television provided him with the best view of the game, and later, instant replays of the highlights; the perfect viewpoint from which to criticize the players or the referee.

Pabst Blue Ribbon
"IT'S BLENDED...IT'S SPLENDID!"

◄ Fred and Wilma Flintstone and their neighbors, Betty and Barney Rubble, were Stone-Age suburbanites in the first cartoon series broadcast on prime-time television. Despite their costumes, their lifestyle resembled that of their American audiences. Cartoons using similarly limited animation formed a large part of the programming that the American networks directed at children. Elsewhere, where government regulation of television was more strict, greater emphasis was put on using television for education; in 1957 Japan opened a channel devoted to educational broadcasting exaggeration and unpredictability in the essentially settled domestic world their shows presented.

Unpredictability was a commodity television rationed carefully, as became apparent in 1959 when contestants confessed that, in competing for the big money prizes on quiz shows such as *The $64,000 Question*, they had frequently been given the answers by the shows' producers to engineer exciting results. The quiz show scandals revealed the extraordinary level of audience manipulation regarded as normal television behavior by the networks. The subsequent public outcry obliged them to polish their tarnished image by abandoning direct sponsoring of programs and improving their current-affairs coverage. From then on, game shows concentrated on trivia rather than the taxing questions asked on *The $64,000 Question*, but high-value prizes, and the fantasy they presented of easily acquired wealth, remained central components of television's creation of its own version of the American dream.

If advertising pressure prevented television from offering explicit cultural criticism, Hollywood found not only a new source of talent in emigrés from television, but also a new cultural function in providing its younger, more mobile and better-educated audiences with mild forms of social criticism. The studios' initial response was to concentrate on offering the public what television did not give them: color, the big screen, extravagant sets and lavish production values. CinemaScope proved more successful than 3-D or Cinerama because of the comparative cheapness of the modifications to existing projection facilities that it required. Even so, it was not widely adopted until Fox announced that all their future product would be in in CinemaScope, and that they had persuaded MGM, Columbia and Universal to adopt it, too.

More films were produced by smaller independent production companies, with the majors increasingly acting as financial backers and distributors. Between them, they produced only 116 movies in 1956, less than half the number they had made a decade before. With its heavy investment in the overheads of studio plant and contract lists, the studio system became an economic liability. RKO had its assets stripped by Howard Hughes, and was closed down in 1955.

Despite the roar and bluster of the HUAC hearings, and the more permanent humiliations and injustices wrought by blacklisting, a liberal consensus secured for itself the conventional structures of American cinematic narrative, recast them in its own image, and celebrated its ideological daring by awarding its Oscars to self-consciously "serious" and "committed" films. Hollywood's output reflected a plethora of Cold War liberal anxieties: the Bomb, if seldom mentioned explicitly, was never very far away. Robert Aldrich's *Kiss Me Deadly*, almost the last and most extreme *film noir*, ended with the apocalypse. Science-fiction stories of alien invasions, in which large parts of the planet were regularly devastated, were thinly disguised allegories of what to fear from the Russians.

The cinema's heroes and families were much less secure than television's. Westerns and epics alike defined the hero as someone to whom violence is done; loser, martyr or victim, the liberal hero was passive, defensive, unwilling or unable to take the initiative himself. There was an inescapable taint of masochism in the inevitability with which James Stewart, Charlton Heston, Kirk Douglas, even Gary Cooper, were deliberately maimed and humiliated. Heston seldom survived an epic without being stripped and mutilated at least once. Younger male stars, trained in the neurotic mannerisms of the Method school of acting, took the performance of physical and

▲ James Dean became the icon of the 1950s teenage angst, a cult perfectly reflected in the title of his second film, *Rebel Without a Cause*.

▼ The postwar decade produced the most elaborate and colorful of Hollywood's musicals. By the mid-1950s, however, companies increasingly played safe by adapting already successful Broadway shows such as *South Pacific* and *Gigi*.

Drive-in Cinemas

While many movie theaters in small American towns closed in the 1950s, an equal number of a new kind of theater, which recognized the supremacy of the automobile in American life, opened up. In the 1920s concerned parents had been anxious about the effects of automobiles and movies on their children's morals; their grandchildren could now combine these menaces to their moral welfare at the drive-in. The first drive-in movie theater opened in 1933, but they mushroomed in the decade after World War II. By 1956 there were 4,200 drive-ins, earning nearly a quarter of total box-office receipts. They were promoted as "the answer to the family's night out"; a way for married couples to avoid the expense of baby-sitters, but their real attraction was to the youth market, where teenagers could escape parental supervision.

The drive-in market encouraged a new kind of filmmaking, pioneered by Columbia producer Sam Katzman and American International Pictures (AIP). Discarding conventional formulae such as the Western, they geared their films solely for the teenage market, hooking a story on to any gimmick they could think of.

The success of *Rock Around the Clock* in 1956, and the cycle of rock 'n' roll movies that followed made it clear that "teenpics" could reap huge profits even if they pointedly excluded an older audience. These mainstream productions spawned imitations, such as *Teenage Crime Wave* (1955) and *Hot Rod Rumble* (1957). The other major "teenpic" genre was the horror film: low-budget "exploitation" movies (so-called because their publicity budgets were higher than their production costs), with titles like *I Married a Monster from Outer Space* (1958) were pumped out to provide the material for the double- and triple-bills at the drive-ins.

Teenagers liked double-bills for the simple reason that they lasted longer – especially when offered on "midnite matinées". Few of these movies shared classical Hollywood's concern with tightly constructed narrative. Instead, their emphasis on spectacle implicitly recognized that the audience might have other things to do than just watch the film.

By 1960 the established industry had learnt at least some of the lessons of exploitation producers, and were successfully producing material for the teenage market.

▲ Drive-in theaters were an important part of teenage culture from the 1950s. Teenagers became the most frequent movie attenders, and drive-ins catered to them with double- and triple-bills of movies targeted at teenage audiences. Some theater owners attempted to ease parental concern by providing "flashlight patrols" to check that the audience in the back rows – the "passion pit" – was actually watching the movie. Drive-ins made their profits at the concession stands, where patrons bought soft drinks, candy and fast food. Most operators expected to take a dollar at the concession stand for every dollar admission.

▶ The teasing publicity campaign for *Psycho* (1960) announced that viewers would not be admitted once the movie had started – to conceal its twist that the film's star, Janet Leigh, was murdered half an hour into the film. Most earlier American horror films were set in Europe or in the Gothic past. In a move that was enormously influential on later films in the genre, *Psycho* brought horror home to small-town America, to the family, and to the bathroom.

▶ In *North By Northwest* (1959) Cary Grant played an advertising executive plunged into a world of espionage and double agents where a crop-dusting aircraft tries to kill him and he has to climb down the monumental faces of the Presidents on Mount Rushmore. One of the few Hollywood directors whose name on a poster could sell tickets, Alfred Hitchcock guaranteed his audiences suspense and a plot constructed of utterly impossible coincidences. His films also suggested that he took a sadistic delight in manipulating his viewers' emotions and propelling them, like the almost ordinary people who were his central characters, into a world of chaos and absurdity. In these twisted and disturbing entertainments, madness, guilt and sexual obsession lurked beneath the surface of 1950s' normality.

emotional vulnerability even further. What often seemed to be being celebrated was their capacity to soak up punishment, and no-one responded better to this treatment than the sulky and indecipherable Marlon Brando, whose mumbling was always most justified after a beating. Even John Wayne, the great icon of conservative male stability, did not escape without having repression and neurosis attached to his character in John Ford's *The Searchers*.

Domestic film comedies were constructed around broken marriages or displaced families, while family melodramas directed by Douglas Sirk, Vincente Minnelli and Nicholas Ray explored the murkier psychological depths of a

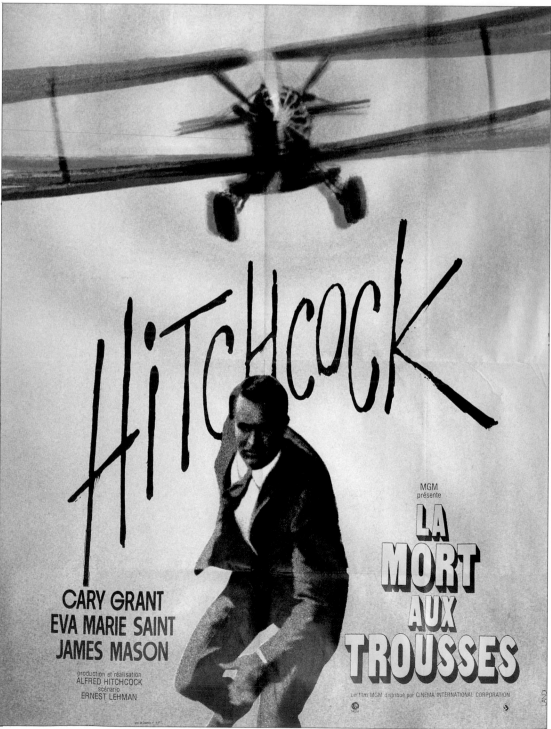

HITCHCOCK

MGM
présente

LA
MORT
AUX
TROUSSES

CARY GRANT
EVA MARIE SAINT
JAMES MASON

production et réalisation
ALFRED HITCHCOCK
scénario
ERNEST LEHMAN

un film MGM distribué par CINEMA INTERNATIONAL CORPORATION

recognizably suburban world in tales of intense disquiet. Ray's *Rebel Without A Cause* immortalized James Dean as the image of what middle-class adolescents wanted their parents to worry that they might become. The gratification of the mammary fixations of American males, which was represented by Jane Russell, Jayne Mansfield and Marilyn Monroe, rarely passed without some barb directed at the childish fatuity of the version of male desire they embodied. The success of Alfred Hitchcock's films, premised on the inexplicable, intolerable disruption of bourgeois normality which plunged its leading characters into an absurd chasm of madness, guilt and adventure, implied an audience excessively interested in exploring its anxieties. The hero of *North By Northwest* (1959), played by Cary Grant, is an advertising executive called Roger O. Thornhill. The O., he explained, "stands for nothing", suggesting a hollowness at the centre of American materialist culture which permitted the abyss to open. Hitchcock's next film, *Psycho*, toyed obscenely with even more intimate terrors, of murder in Mother's bedroom and compulsive behavior in the toilet.

The export market was becoming increasingly important for Hollywood, and its operations were aided by the State Department, which had long recognized the usefulness of movies as advertisements for the American way of life.

But the harder motive, as ever, was economic. With the decline in American revenues after 1946 and the sharp rise in production costs, foreign sales became increasingly important. By 1955 the stability of the international market was as vital to the major distributors as the stability of the home market had been in the 1930s. Expanding foreign interests was less difficult than finding ways of maintaining home audiences. The industry's failure to resist the encroachments of television in part provoked, and was in part permitted by, the exploitation of an undeveloped market elsewhere. However much the masses stayed at home, film was now definitely mass entertainment, and was increasingly designed for an internationally undifferentiated audience.

Film Outside Hollywood

The renaissance of Italian neo-realist cinema in the immediate postwar period excited American critics as much as Europeans, and stimulated the appearance in several American cities of small theaters showing European films to at least a small audience anxious to take the cinema seriously as art. While never seriously challenging the industrial dominance of American production, the art-house circuit in America and Europe was large enough to sustain a largely European cinema that, in its themes and avant-garde esthetics, was substantially independent of Hollywood. Italy and Sweden, in particular, developed a notion of "national cinema" reflecting specific cultural traits in a mode in which they could be successfully exported. In France, Japan and Eastern Europe a similar process was under way, but in these countries the economic viability of "national" production was less dependent on the export trade.

▶ Produced in 1957, Ingmar Bergman's *The Seventh Seal* epitomized the European art film. Somber in mood, it told a despairing, allegorical tale of a medieval knight's encounter with Death during an outbreak of plague, and his loss of faith. Unlike the workers in Hollywood's factories, Bergman was seen as an artist of comparable stature to a novelist or playwright.

▼ Kurosawa's *The Seven Samurai* (1954) was the first major Japanese commercial success in the West, where it was compared to the Hollywood Westerns which had influenced Kurosawa.

Japanese films were hardly seen abroad until 1951, when Akira Kurosawa's *Rashomon* won the Golden Lion at the Venice Film Festival. The distribution of Eastern films in America and Europe did not necessarily mean that they were fully understood by Western critics and audiences. The few Japanese films that did reach Western screens, such as those of Kurosawa, were often those that could be most easily incorporated into European traditions of filmmaking. *The Seven Samurai* became *The Magnificent Seven*, and another of Kurosawa's samurai films, *Yojimbo* (1961), was the basis for the first spaghetti Western, *A Fistful of Dollars*, directed by Sergio Leone in 1964.

MARILYN: THE DREAM WOMAN

Walk down any shopping street anywhere in the Western world and there will be Marilyn Monroe – on posters and greetings cards, T-shirts, dresses and ads of all kinds. After her death at least as much as during her life, the image of Marilyn Monroe has fueled prurient fantasy. An industry devoted to the exploitation of the enigma has invaded every aspect of her life in search, not of answers, but of new images. The hot-lipped girl in the plunging gold lamé dress is also Norma Jean the illegitimate, abused, girl-child and the Marilyn of the Last Sittings, worn out by satisfying all that desire aimed at an object which shared her body. Marilyn was Woman-as-Madonna, child, whore and victim, all in one.

For at least one generation of Americans, she was woman as the perfect physical object. But her sexual lushness went hand-in-hand with vulnerability; the star was also the poignant victim of a million male desires.

Reviews at the time consistently described her as a thing, her body some kind of object of nature divorced from a personality. Inside "The Body" an actress wished to escape and aspired to serious roles. But the struggle against stereotyping defeated her, propelling her into non-appearances on the set, hospitalizations, and the drug overdose that killed her. The public mourning which followed was a guilty grief: by now everyone knew that Marilyn had needed loving protection; that they might have offered it, but, somehow, they had failed her.

▶ Marilyn Monroe offered men the fantasy of sex without guilt, responsibility or threat, always on offer, with no sexual needs of her own beyond the gratification of men.

▶▶ Born Norma Jean Mortenson, raised by foster parents and orphanages, first married at 14: her insecure childhood has given psychologists ample material to explain her career on and off screen, and her embodiment of the death of an American Dream.

▶ Andy Warhol's image of Monroe, produced in 1964 two years after her death, turned her into an icon of the vacuous blonde, an empty and incomplete figure for any man to shape as he pleased.

▶▼ When she married Arthur Miller in 1956 one headline read "Egghead marries Hourglass." As time passes her image became increasingly able to carry any meaning the writer chose. Alive, she was a figure women felt threatened by rather than identified with; after her death she became the martyr-heroine to masculine exploitation.

▼ Marilyn, alone, shortly before her death in 1962.

Star's Life in Photos, Stories

Los Angeles Times

FINAL!

MARILYN MONROE FOUND DEAD

Sleeping Pill Overdose Blamed

Red Super Bomb Kicks Off Series

Nixon Team at Helm of State GOP

Unclad Body of Star Discovered on Bed; Empty Bottle Near

Junta Pledges to Seat Victor in Peru Election

Help She Needed to Find Self Eluded Marilyn All Her Life

1960 · 1973
THE
REVOLUTION
OF YOUTH

Time Chart

	1961	1962	1963	1964	1965	1966	1967
Film	• Release of Walt Disney's *101 Dalmatians* (USA) • *Judgment at Nuremberg* released, directed by Stanley Kramer (USA) • Release of *Last Year at Marienbad*, directed by Alain Resnais (Fr) • *West Side Story* released, directed by Robert Wise and Jerome Robbins; Natalie Wood starred (USA)	• *Lawrence of Arabia* (director, David Lean) brought Peter O'Toole to stardom (UK) • Release of *Dr No*, directed by Terence Young – the first James Bond movie starring Sean Connery (UK) • *Jules et Jim* released, directed by François Truffaut (Fr) • 5 Aug: Marilyn Monroe found dead of a drugs overdose (USA)	• *Cleopatra* (director, Joseph Mankiewicz) brought Richard Burton and Elizabeth Taylor together (USA) • Release of *8½*, directed by Federico Fellini (It) • *Tom Jones* released, directed by Tony Richardson and starring Albert Finney (UK) • Release of *Dr Strangelove*, starring Peter Sellers and directed by Stanley Kubrick (UK)	• Release of the Beatles' first movie, *A Hard Day's Night*, directed by Richard Lester (UK) • Release of *Zorba the Greek* (director Michael Cacoyannis) starring Anthony Quinn (Gr) • *My Fair Lady* released, directed by George Cukor and starring Audrey Hepburn and Rex Harrison (USA) • Sidney Poitier became the first black actor to win the Oscar for Best Actor (USA)	• Release of *Dr Zhivago*, directed by David Lean, with Julie Christie and Omar Sharif (UK) • *The Knack* released, directed by Richard Lester and starring Rita Tushingham and Michael Crawford (UK) • Release of *The Sound of Music*, directed by Robert Wise and starring Julie Andrews, with a score by Rodgers and Hammerstein (USA)	• Release of *Un Homme et une Femme*, directed by Claude Lelouch (Fr) • Paul Scofield starred in *A Man for All Seasons*, directed by Fred Zinneman (USA) • *Torn Curtain* was Hitchcock's 50th movie (USA) • Release of *Who's Afraid of Virginia Woolf*, directed by Mike Nichols and starring Elizabeth Taylor and Richard Burton (USA)	• Catherine Deneuve starred in Luis Bunuel's *Belle de Jour* (Fr/It) • Release of *Bonnie and Clyde*, directed by Arthur Penn and starring Warren Beatty and Faye Dunaway (USA) • *Elvira Madigan* released, directed by Bo Widerberg (Swe) • *The Graduate*, directed by Mike Nichols, starring Dustin Hoffman (USA) • 8 Jul: Death of Vivien Leigh, from TB (UK)
Media	• Production of the satirical revue *Beyond the Fringe* (UK)	• Feb: *The Sunday Times* introduced Britain's first newspaper color supplement • 11 Jul: Live TV transmitted from Europe to the USA by Telstar	• 22 Nov: President Kennedy's assassination was televised (USA) • 23 Nov: The first episode of BBC TV science fiction series *Dr Who* broadcast (UK)	• 28 Mar: Radio Caroline, the first pirate radio station operating from the North Sea, began to broadcast • Jun: Comedian Lenny Bruce arrested (USA)	• 8 Feb: Cigarette advertising banned on British TV	• Premiere of science fiction serial *Star Trek* (USA) • 15 Aug: Closure of the *New York Herald Tribune* announced (USA)	
Music	• 28 Sep: Bob Dylan caused a stir, playing in Greenwich Village (USA) • Sep: Chubby Checker's *The Twist* started a dance craze (USA) • Dec: Clarinettist Acker Bilk's *Stranger on the Shore* reached no 1 (UK)	• 30 May: Benny Goodman played in Moscow (USSR) • The Beatles signed with EMI, and released *Love Me Do* (UK) • Release of Bob Dylan's *Blowin' In The Wind* (USA)	• Fans screamed at the Beatles in a huge London Palladium concert (UK) • The Beatles' *I Want To Hold Your Hand* sold 1 million copies before release (UK) • Rolling Stones' first record, *Come On* (UK) • 11 Oct: Edith Piaf died aged 47 (Fr)	• 15 Jan: The world's first discotheque, *Whisky-a-Go-Go*, opened in Los Angeles (USA) • Aug: Death of country star Jim Reeves (USA) • 10 Oct: Ravi Shankar played at New York's Town Hall (USA)	• 11 Jun: The Beatles received MBE awards from the Queen (UK) • Release of *The Sound of Silence* by Simon and Garfunkel (USA)	• Mar: *Uptight* was Stevie Wonder's first hit (USA) • May: The Beach Boys' *Sloop John B* entered the charts (USA) • Van Morrison left R&B group Them to pursue a solo career (UK)	• May: *Purple Haze*, by Jimi Hendrix, at no 3 (USA) • 18 Jun: The first large pop festival was held at Monterey, featuring Hendrix, Janis Joplin, The Who (USA)
Fashion and Design	• IBM Selectric typewriter produced by designer Eliot Noyes (USA) • Oleg Cassini was appointed Jackie Kennedy's official dress designer (USA) • First couture minis presented by Marc Bohan at Dior and André Courrèges (Fr)	• Apr: Opening of the Seattle World's Fair, the Century 21 Exposition (USA) • Council of Fashion Designers of America founded • Camera Nazionale della Moda Italiana founded (It) • Mary Quant won the first Bath Museum of Costume "Dress of the Year" award (UK) • Yves Saint Laurent opened his fashion house (Fr)	• Issey Miyake showed his first fashion collection in Tokyo (Jap) • Pierre Cardin produced his first ready-to-wear collection (Fr) • London fashion taken to America by chainstore JC Penney	• Apr: New York World's Fair opened (USA) • Terence Conran opened his first Habitat home furnishing store (UK) • Barbara Hulanicki's Biba boutique opened in Kensington (UK) • Vidal Sassoon created his geometric "five-point cut" (UK) • André Courrèges and Pierre Cardin produced "Space Age" fashions (Fr)	• Former architect Paco Rabanne created a plastic dress (Fr) • Nov: Model Jean Shrimpton's miniskirt shocked racegoers at the Melbourne Cup (Aus) • America's first Mod store, Paraphernalia, opened in New York	• Fashion designer Jean Muir formed her own company (UK) • Experimental design studios Archizoom and Superstudio founded in Florence (It) • Twiggy was the Face of '66 (UK) • Hemlines dropped, as the midi was shown in London and Paris	• A totally inflatable plastic chair was designed for Zanotta Co. (It) • Apr: Expo '67 opened in Montreal (Can) • First injection-moulded plastic chair designed by Joe Colombo (It) • Laura Ashley opened her first London shop (UK) • Beatle John Lennon's Rolls Royce was given a psychedelic "coat of many colors" (UK)
Sport	• 6 May: Tottenham Hotspur won the FA Cup and the League title, the first team to do so this century (UK)	• Jul: Dawn Fraser (Aus) became the first woman to swim 100m in under 1 minute • Sep: Rod Laver (Aus) became the first man since 1938 to win the tennis Grand Slam	• Sir Adetoklunbo Ademole became the first black African IOC member • Feb: René Lacoste patented a metal tennis racket (Fr)	• 29 Jan: Opening of ninth Winter Olympics, at Innsbruck (Aust) • Aug: South Africa banned from Olympics because of apartheid • 10 Oct: Opening of the first Olympics to be held in Asia, in Tokyo (Jap)	• 1 Jan: Stanley Matthews was the first professional footballer to be knighted (UK) • 1 Feb: Ron Clarke (Aus) broke 5000m world record twice in three weeks • East and West Germany decided to compete separately in the 1968 Olympics	• 4 Sep: Racing driver Jack Brabham (Aus) won the world championship in a car he had built, the first man to achieve this • Dec: Francis Chichester completed the world's longest nonstop solo sea voyage, from Plymouth, UK, to Sydney, Aus, in 107 days	• 4 Jan: Donald Campbell died in an attempt on world water speed record (UK) • 15 Jan: Inaugural Super Bowl match between Football League champions (USA) • 30 Apr: Muhammad Ali (Cassius Clay) was stripped of his world boxing title
Misc.	• Yuri Gagarin was the first man to go into space and back (USSR)	• 22 Oct: President Kennedy ordered the Cuban missile blockade	• Martin Luther King's "I have a dream" speech, in Washington (USA)	• The first US pilot was shot down and captured in Vietnam	• Jan: Skateboards became a craze	• Aug: The Chinese Cultural Revolution announced	• 150,000 marched in protest against the Vietnam war (USA)

158

1968	1969	1970	1971	1972	1973
• Release of *If*, directed by Lindsay Anderson (UK) • *Funny Girl* (director, William Wyler) gave Barbra Streisand her first starring role (USA) • Paul Newman directed his wife, Joanne Woodward, in *Rachel, Rachel* (USA) • Release of *2001 – a Space Odyssey*, directed by Stanley Kubrick (USA)	• John Wayne won his only Oscar, for *True Grit*, directed by Henry Hathaway (USA) • Release of Federico Fellini's *Satyricon* (It) • Paul Newman and Robert Redford starred in *Butch Cassidy and the Sundance Kid*, directed by George Roy Hill (USA) • Release of *Romeo and Juliet*, directed by Franco Zeffirelli (It) • *Easy Rider*, directed by and starring Dennis Hopper, also with Peter Fonda, epitomized the "acid culture" (USA)	• Release of *Days and Nights in the Forest*, directed by Satyajit Ray (Ind) • Release of *Patton* (director Franklin Schaffner) (USA)	• Release of Stanley Kubrick's *A Clockwork Orange* (UK) • Dirk Bogarde starred in *Death in Venice*, directed by Luchino Visconti (It) • Release of *The French Connection*, directed by William Friedkin (USA)	• Liza Minelli and Joel Gray starred in *Cabaret*, directed by Bob Fosse (USA) • Release of Tarkovsky's *Solaris* (USSR) • *Last Tango in Paris* (director, Bernardo Bertolucci) released; Marlon Brando starred (USA) • Release of *The Discreet Charm of the Bourgoisie*, directed by Luis Bunuel (Sp) • Release of Francis Ford Coppola's *The Godfather*, starring Marlon Brando (USA)	• Release of *Day for Night*, directed by François Truffaut (Fr) • *The Exorcist* released (director, William Friedkin) (USA) • Release of *Fear Eats the Soul*, directed by Rainer Werner Fassbinder (Ger)
• *Hawaii Five-0* pilot program shown (USA) • ABC news special "How Life Began" showed *in utero* pictures, and film of a birth (USA)	• Premiere of *Monty Python's Flying Circus*, on BBC TV (UK) • 10 Jan: *New York Saturday Evening Post* closed • 18 May: Apollo 10 sent the first live color TV pictures of the Earth	• Amateur radio stations helped with communications in the Peruvian earthquake disaster • 9 Nov: David Frost's LWT program disrupted by Jerry Rubin and Yippies sprinkling Frost with flower petals (USA)	• Soviet TV broadcast the BBC costume drama series *The Forsyte Saga* • The editors of the underground magazine *Oz* on trial for obscenity (UK)	• Dec: The last issue of *Life* magazine (USA) • *Cosmopolitan* launched in the UK • Two feminist magazines launched, *MS* in America, and *Spare Rib* in the UK	• BBC presented *War and Peace* (UK) • 500 million worldwide watched the wedding of Princess Anne and Mark Phillips (UK)
• 22 Jun: Judy Garland died, aged 47 (USA) • 7 Jul: Rolling Stone Brian Jones died aged 25 (UK) • Joni Mitchell's first album *Song for a Seagull* (USA) • Premiere of hit hippy musical *Hair* (USA) • The Beatles formed Apple Co. (UK)	• 15 Aug: 400,000 attended the Woodstock pop festival (USA) • Sep: The Isle of Wight festival was Britain's biggest • Nov: Hells Angels stabbed a fan to death while the Rolling Stones played at the Altamont festival (USA)	• 10 Apr: Paul McCartney quit the Beatles (UK) • 18 Sep: Jimi Hendrix died of a drug overdose aged 27 (USA) • 4 Oct: Janis Joplin died of a drug overdose aged 27 (USA) • Release of Simon & Garfunkel's *Bridge Over Troubled Water* (USA)	• 3 Jul: The Doors' Jim Morrison died aged 28 • 1 Aug: A concert to raise money for victims of flood and civil war in Bangladesh was organized by George Harrison and friends	• 17 Jun: *Fiddler on the Roof* hit a record 3225 straight performances (USA) • 30 Aug: John Lennon and Yoko Ono played Madison Square Gardens (USA) • Premiere of *Jesus Christ Superstar*, by Tim Rice and Andrew Lloyd Webber (UK) • The Moog synthesizer patented	• 26 May: Carole King played to 70,000 in Central Park (USA) • Release of *Killing Me Softly With his Song*, by Roberta Flack (USA)
• Shoji Hamada awarded the Order of Culture medal for reviving the art of ceramics (Jap) • The Beatles' Apple boutique was psychedelically decorated by the Dutch group Fool (UK) • Zandra Rhodes formed her own fashion house (UK) • Calvin Klein started his own fashion business (USA) • Balenciaga retired from couture (Sp)	• Mar: Concorde 001, the supersonic airliner, made its maiden flight (UK/Fr) • Japan Industrial Design Promotion Organization established • Fashion designer Rei Kawakubo (Jap) founded Comme des Garçons • The musical *Hair* popularized Afro hairstyles	• Mar: Expo '70 opened in Osaka (Jap) • Fiorucci launched his designer jeans (It) • Kenzo (Jap) opened his fashion shop, Jungle Jap, in London (UK) • Ergonomi design group founded (Scan) • *Women's Wear Daily* coined the term "hot-pants" (USA) • *Harpers & Queen* magazine launched (UK)	• Intel Co introduced the microprocessor (USA) • The Crafts Council set up (UK) • Publication of *Design for the Real World*, the book by Victor Papanek which inspired design for the handicapped and the "third world"	• New York's MoMA presented an exhibition in recognition of the contribution of Italian avant-garde designers (USA) • Frei Otto designed a lightweight tent-like roof for the Munich Olympic stadium (Ger) • Fashion retailer Joseph Ettedgui (Mor) opened a London store (UK)	• IBM's Selectric self-correcting typewriters featured an ergonomically designed keyboard (USA) • Nov: Le Grand Divertissement, Versailles, was a showcase for the collections of five leading French and five US fashion designers (Fr)
• Feb: Winter Olympics held in Grenoble (Fr) • Sep: South Africa cancelled MCC winter tour because Basil D'Oliveira was on the team • Oct: Mexico City Olympics: altitude was a problem for many athletes; two US athletes sent home after giving the Black Power salute during the 200m award ceremony	• May: Graham Hill (UK) won the Monaco Grand Prix for a record 5th time • Jun: Brazilian soccer star Pele scored his 1000th goal • Nov: Anti-apartheid demonstrators disrupted the South African Springbok rugby team's British tour	• May: South African cricket tour of the UK cancelled, and SA banned by the IOC from the 1972 Olympics • Jun: Tony Jacklin was first British golfer for 50 years to win the US Open • Jun: Brazil was permanently awarded the soccer World Cup trophy, after winning it for the third time	• 26 Dec: Rod Laver (Aus) became the first tennis millionaire • Princess Anne named Sportswoman of the Year (UK)	• 2 Feb: Winter Olympics opened in Tokyo (Jap) • 26 Aug: Opening of Munich Olympic Games, at which US swimmer Mark Spitz won seven gold medals (Ger) • 5 Sep: Arab guerrillas attacked Israeli building at the Olympic village; 17 killed (Ger) • Sep: Bobby Fischer became first US world chess champion	• 31 Mar: Red Rum won the Grand National in record time (UK) • Aug: 180 arrested for soccer violence (UK) • Jackie Stewart, champion racing driver, retired on the eve of his 100th Grand Prix (UK)
• 4 Apr: Martin Luther King assassinated (USA) • 6 Jun: Assassination of Senator Robert Kennedy (USA)	• 20 Jul: Neil Armstrong was first man on the Moon • First *in vitro* fertilization of human egg cells, (UK)		• Idi Amin seized power in Uganda	• 30 Jan: "Bloody Sunday" in Belfast (UK) • 17 Jun: Watergate break-in (USA)	• US troops quit Vietnam

159

Datafile

The affluence of the 1960s and early 1970s brought a renewed confidence in modernity and technology, this time coupled with an emphasis on the young, and an impatience with tradition. In fashion, this brought a revolution that threatened to sweep away the established systems for the creation and dissemination of fashion; in design the sense that everything would soon be replaced by something newer led to a celebration of impermanence itself. Furniture was made of plastic and paper; and the idea of built-in obsolescence became widespread for most consumer durables. Fashion and design, together with music, seemed ready to revolutionize the world.

Advertising expenditure

- USA & Canada
- Europe
- Asia
- Latin America
- Others

◀ The Western Hemisphere and Europe dominated the advertising business in the 1960s, reflecting the fact that the Third World was still a long way from joining the consumer society: it remained a region to be exploited for its raw materials, rather than for its markets.

▼ The mid-1960s represented the swansong of the dominance of the American automobile industry: never again was it to achieve 40 percent or more of world production.

World motor vehicle production

11,137,830
- 1960
- 1965
- 1970

USA   UK   France   Other   Italy   Japan

Worldwide possession of TV receivers

- 1970
- 1976

USA, Canada, Denmark, UK, FRG, Netherlands, France, Belgium, Japan, Italy, Irish Republic, Hong Kong

Rate per 1000 population

Leisure activities in UK, 1968

- Physical recreation
- Other activities
- Television
- Excursions/parks/etc
- Crafts and hobbies
- Drinking/social
- Gardening/decorating

Males / Females (repeated across age groups)

Percent

Age group: 15-18   19-22   23-30   31+

▲ In the 1960s the lifestyle of the young became of overriding importance, as many industries, from the movies to fashion to retailing, saw the emergence of a new market. The younger generation was perceived as living in an independent, unrestricted manner, paying little attention to the patterns of life of their elders. This freedom was more myth than reality, and analysis of the leisure activities of British young people in 1968 showed a fairly unchallenging pattern of behavior.

◀ The television was the cultural object of the 1960s and 1970s, and in these years spread throughout the world. The United States remained the pioneer of the multi-television household, with more than one television for every two people in the country by 1976. Although attempts were made to introduce modern styling – notably in the white televisions of Bang & Olufsen, and in the growing popularity of portables – the television was relatively unaffected by the new design ideas of the period.

The music and youth subcultures of the 1950s and early 1960s generated a number of dress styles, especially in Britain. That of the teddy boys never lost its outlaw status, but the mod fashions of a slightly later period, which originated among art students, fertilized mainstream fashion and created a new cheap instant high fashion. It was designed from the beginning to be mass-produced and to be worn by the young, yet still the product of individual artists; inspired by the teenager, it was not yet "street fashion" as such.

This style was popularized, first in Britain, later in the United States, by television pop-music shows, later still by new women's magazines catering to specific sections of the market, and especially to the under-25s. In catering for this new clientèle, younger than the previous fashion market, manufacturers were almost bound to produce youthful styles; but the new youth styles were taken up everywhere, by fashion writers in *Vogue* and in the more staid newspapers as well as in the trendier magazines. At the beginning of the 1960s the youthful – and soon the positively infantile – styles seemed to express the optimism of the "affluent society", the joy of consumerism, and even a kind of innocence, as the old, rigid hierarchies of deference and the stifling sexual puritanism of Western culture after World War II began to dissolve. Simple shift dresses, sometimes with childish raised waistlines, flat shoes with cream or black stockings, tight ribbed sweaters, pinafore dresses and long or short straight hair and "Christopher Robin" fringes replaced the over-sculptured cuts of the fifties. All these expressed not just a rebellion of youth, but a general reaction to the hierarchic modes of the previous decades. Subsequently associated with the "permissive society" or the breakdown of sexual restraint and family values, short skirts initially seemed to express the innocence of a new generation growing up with the hope of a thaw in the Cold War.

The new fashions testified that the New Look and its aftermath had never been adequate for the lives that women – and not just young women – were leading in the 1950s and 1960s. Although the new youth fashions are often said to have been the brainchild of British designer Mary Quant, there is a sense in which they originated from within Paris, the heartland of French *haute couture* itself.

Paris and London

After World War II Chanel had been in eclipse, (owing in part to her wartime association with a Nazi officer), but in 1953 she decided to re-open the doors of her salon. Her first collection seemed to be a disaster – the simple little dresses and suits were quite out of tune with the carapace-like

THE SWINGING SIXTIES

Fashion for the young

Miniskirts and modern style

Fashion and the counter-culture

Fashion photography

The good design movement

Italian design in the 1960s

creations of Dior, Balenciaga and Pierre Balmain, and the show was panned. Yet within a year the American ready-to-wear manufacturers had seen the potential of the Chanel suit, and the design went into mass production. Chanel claimed she was no longer interested in designing for the few, but for the woman in the street. With its simple jacket and skirt and its signature of braid trim and gold chain necklaces, an off-the-face hat and bag with a chain handle, the Chanel suit became the uniform of the smart American business or career woman. Jackie Kennedy was wearing such a suit when her husband was assassinated, and the Chanel mode of simplicity was the inspiration for the mainstream fashions of the early sixties.

Another Parisian, André Courrèges, introduced the two most revolutionary fashions of the 1960s: the miniskirt and the trouser suit. His futuristic designs expressed the optimism of the space age. But it was Mary Quant who did more than anyone else to bring this youthful style of fashion to the mass market. Her designs displayed an amalgam of influences: the Mods, the London art-school scene of the fifties – already

bohemian and avant-garde – and French *haute couture*. She described her fashions as "mod" and classless, "pop" fashions in a time of pop songs and pop art. But although she herself was an original artist, with her husband she married her talent for design to an awareness of the latest American mass-production and merchandising techniques. Improved sizing was one innovation; another was her original presentation, first in her own shop Bazaar, in the King's Road, Chelsea, where the displays were young and zany instead of still and lifeless, and in her use of pop music during the showings of her collections; another was in her use of original materials. In the space-age sixties, synthetic materials could be translated into high fashion. The use of shiny PVC for raincoats and hats was her most successful experiment, but she later used "old-fashioned" synthetic crêpes and satins in the "off" colors of the 1930s and 1940s – maroon, burnt orange, eau de nil and salmon pink – for droopy blouses and minidresses that began to have a "retro" feel about them, rather than invoke pure modernism.

As she successfully launched into cosmetics in

▼ **In 1967 the fashion esthetic changed – from the bright Mary Quant image to a hippy or ethnic style with hallucinatory overtones. Style became – for both sexes – soft, droopy and "feminine": long hair, full sleeves, flared trousers. Boutiques such as this one in London were drenched in color and music.**

the second half of the sixties – and as she and her models wore the geometric hairstyles created by Vidal Sassoon – she, like Chanel before her, initiated a total look. Significantly, one of her most successful products, a foundation cream called "Starkers", was advertised as looking so "natural" that it was as if you were wearing nothing (ie your face was stark naked), but by this time the cult of the natural – in reality, no more natural than any other fashion – was in full swing. The name "Starkers" was a typical use of the upper-class slang of an earlier period. This language – "super", "smashing" – united with the language of the criminal fringe – "dolly-bird", "my old man" – is revealing not so much of any classlessness of the period as of a knowingness about class and a new kind of snobbery, "trendiness", which rejected the middle-class and "square" in favor of the glamor of both the upper and the lower classes. It was also a childish language, of the school playground and the 1930s schoolgirl story.

By the mid-1960s the British designers had snatched the fashion initiative from Paris, but it was not immediately clear that this was the beginning of a waning in the dominance of the Paris "system". That system had presupposed that women formed one homogeneous group, all equally receptive to the same fashion styles, and divided only by whether they purchased original models, expensive copies or cheap adaptations.

The advent of youth fashions, which had begun, tentatively at first, in the 1950s but escalated in the 1960s, indicated that there was instead a variety of consumer groups, each aspiring to something different and distinctive.

Fashion and the counter-culture

Various specific fashion styles developed within counter-cultural groups, often organized around pop-music styles and bands, and these became a growing influence on *haute couture*. The hippy look of flowing scarves, loose, flowery robes and flowing sleeves and trousers was widely copied. But "hippy" dressing was a critique of the very fashion system it both plundered and influenced. The counter-culture of the late sixties also loved second-hand clothes. Quite apart from cheapness, recycling clothes was part of a tactic of bricolage and of self-sufficient living on the margins of capitalism, which demonstrated their opposition to the wastefulness of the consumer society. They snapped up old "frocks" from the thirties and forties, tailored men's and women's jackets and suits, and antique hats and shoes. A Chelsea dress shop called "Granny Takes a Trip" epitomized the late sixties esthetic, with punning reference to hallucinogenic drugs as well as to the rifling of the past for "old-fashioned" styles. In addition, the political concerns of the student movement of the period brought various forms of

▶ The British model Twiggy, (Leslie Hornsby) who began the trend for very young models, was nominated the *"Daily Express"* face of the year" in 1966. She was then a sixteen-year-old weighing 90lb (41kg) and perfectly suited the clothes of the period. With her androgynous haircut, she epitomized the waiflike, childish look which miniskirts, high waists, very short or very long hair and as here, schoolgirlish fashions gave women in the mid-sixties.

▼ The Mods were a British subculture of super-cool boys (and girls) on Italian scooters. Their hair was short and neat, their jackets were short, Italian style, and some of them even wore makeup. They were reputed to swallow "purple hearts" (amphetamines) and to lead a lifestyle centered round London's West End music venues.

◀ Male fashions in the 1960s became highly feminine, with long, often carefully cut hair, richly colored shirts, ruffs, frills, and flared trousers which reached an extreme form in velvet "loons". Pop bands such as the Equals became clothes horses for the latest styles.

dress from exotic cultures into Western fashion, in an attempt – perhaps contradictory – to celebrate rather than exploit the Third World.

Instead of a Paris-dictated line of artistic evolution imitating the manner in which other art forms developed, fashion became knowingly self-conscious. Designers seemed to acknowledge more openly that fashion is all about novelty and change for the sake of change. Although pastiche and the rifling of history for decorative and fashion motifs has been part of fashion at least since the early 19th century, the scale of the borrowing was intensified in the esthetics of "retro-chic".

One of its early innovators was Biba of London. Biba's creator, Barbara Hulanicki, started in 1964 with a mail-order service selling dolly dresses at rock-bottom prices to the newly fashionable teenagers of the period. By the late sixties she had branched out into art nouveau/art deco fantasy shops where you could buy feather boas, sleazy thirties' pyjama suits in cream or flesh-colored

Fashion Photographers

Between the wars, and even more in the 1950s, the love affair of black-and-white photography with high fashion gave birth to the frozen perfection of the fashion image. The sharp lines, dark shadow and white light dramatized the angular, exaggerated creations of the New Look period particularly well. American photographer Richard Avedon captured the self-dramatization, the confidence, sophistication and self-mockery of *haute couture* in his work for *Harper's Bazaar* in the early fifties. Avedon and others loved to place their glacial or cavorting models in bizarre or incongruous situations.

By 1960 a new generation of photographers was seeking inspiration from the grainy images of the new cinematic realism of British films such as *Saturday Night and Sunday Morning* or *Room at the Top*. Their work displaced line drawing as the main medium for fashion illustration, but was at times even more mannered, while the search for novelty could lead to downright eccentricity in choice of angles or location. At times the fashion photograph seemed less to attempt to convey information about the latest styles than to capture the mood of an ensemble, or even to suggest a whole lifestyle. The fashion photographs of the 1960s made of high fashion a performance, a street event, a triumph of the will. They also transformed photographic models into celebrities and stars, while the photographers themselves – David Bailey, Lord Snowdon, John French – became household names, heroes of the swinging sixties. Michelangelo Antonioni's film *Blow Up* – often taken to epitomize "Swinging London" – involved just such a fashion photographer as its main character. In the 1970s, the imagery became even more mannered and eccentric, or else banal. Black models appeared more frequently, but models tended to become ever more precocious, while some photographers, notably the German Helmut Newton, flirted with an imagery drawn from soft pornography.

▶ **The Rolling Stones, photographed by John French.**

▲ ▼ **The Biba look that flourished in London in the 1960s provided a total design environment that repackaged Hollywood art-deco and art-nouveau imagery for sixties' youth. The vast store itself opened in 1973 but was not viable. Biba's distinctive styling included packaging, the actual store (including, especially, the showcases for the goods on sale), mail-order material and the clothes themselves.**

satin, wide-shouldered, dumpy forties' dresses, and endless period accessories, all available in a range of "dirty" shades from old rose to chocolate. Her final gamble was to fill the whole of an old department store – which retained its original art-deco carpets and fittings – with clothes, accessories, furniture and even food in the Biba style. She over-reached herself, and her magic emporium was gutted, to be replaced by chain-store predictability.

All this was part of a wish to replace the products of the consumer society with objects and artefacts that had a craft rather than a commodity relationship with the owner. Although, for example, the fashion for crocheted garments was initiated by the fashion industry in Britain in 1963, this was often introduced in popular women's magazines as an opportunity to make your own. Waistcoats and shawls made from crocheted multi-colored squares, fairisle and other patterned sweaters, hats, macramé belts and other do-it-yourself alternatives to consumerism were featured in new magazines such as *Honey*, aimed at the young, trendy mass market of relatively affluent women in their early twenties.

The use of exotic motifs in alternative fashion

was highly eclectic. One such fashion was a band tied round the head in the manner of American Indians - much later to become a fashion for gay men in San Francisco. Another was the kaftan, which matched a fashion for long skirts on women. Despite the hippy trail to the Indian subcontinent, Indian fashions never really caught on; men would wear African-style shirts and students the PLO-type Arab head scarf, but the adoption of Third World styles was gestural rather than serious. For some young women the early 1970s was a period of fashion refusal, in an attempt to find an alternative mode of dress that moved away from obvious self-objectification as much as from *haute-couture* discomfort. In the United States this was more likely to be achieved by styles based on sportswear; in Britain a kind of dusty picturesqueness was achieved with the combination of home-knits with jeans, dungarees and long skirts in Laura Ashley old-fashioned prints.

Soon *haute couture* was introducing ethnic borrowings into its twice-yearly shows. The appetite of the mass clothing market for new styles was so intense that rebel fashions were quickly taken up, but without their political content.

Perhaps it was inevitable that the adoption of clothing from cultures in which garments were relatively unchanging was superficial, since after all, these alternatives were all about style. The styles themselves signaled rebellion or disaffection from the dominant culture; since, however, that culture was highly organized around styles and their changes, to adopt a stylistic alternative was still to remain part of the culture which expressed change, dissidence and difference in these symbolic terms.

Design and ephemerality

The democratization of design became a reality for the first time in the economic boom years of the 1960s, as goods with a strong visual content reached a more youthful audience. Through increased consumption young people in Europe and the United States began to manifest their newly acquired wealth and to assert their "alternative" values. From the motor-bikes, motor-scooters, transistor radios and record-players of the early youth sub-cultures through to the fashion items, graphics, furniture and other lifestyle accessories of the pop sixties, they demanded artefacts which provided them with a means of identifying themselves with each other. Many designers responded to the challenge: in Britain, Mary Quant, Foale and Tuffin, Ossie Clark, John Stephens and others provided clothing for the new youth market. Graphics designers Martin Sharp and Michael English produced posters and other pieces of two-dimensional ephemera to accompany the pop music now so central to the new culture. Even furniture designers responded to the new values of expendibility, producing, by the middle of the decade, pieces of furniture which were knock-down, throw-away or blow-up.

More importantly, perhaps, where consumption itself was concerned, the pop revolution brought with it a dramatic change in retailing patterns. New boutiques sprang up aiming their goods – from fashion to ephemera – at the youth market specifically. In doing so, they emphasized the role that the visual and lifestyle aspects of their products play in consumption, stressed individualism rather than anonymous mass production, and focused as much on the visual context of the goods as on the goods themselves. Boutiques relied on peoples' buying products for reasons other than those of utility and low price.

This new approach to retailing moved, quickly, beyond the area of fashion into other lifestyle goods. In 1964 the British designer/retailer Terence Conran opened his first Habitat store, its furnishings and household goods appealing to young, educated, fashion-conscious consumers. Selling objects ranging from brightly colored enamel trays and mugs to French Provençal crockery to items of pine furniture, Habitat concentrated less on the individual product than on the total environmental effect of putting together, in a single space, a wide range of objects which expressed the same "taste" values. A careful selection of goods which together created a visually unified ensemble proved a clever way of selling customers a complete lifestyle even if they left the

▲ The Habitat catalog, offered a lifestyle "improved" by good design, relying on brightly colored domestic fittings and goods such as tableware imported from France or Italy.

▼ The geodesic dome was the most spectacular achievement of the alternative design movement of the 1960s in which Victor Papanek and Buckminster Fuller argued for appropriate use of materials and energy.

shop with only a single item. Habitat was the first store to sell goods on the basis of "good taste" to a mass market, and in so doing it set an important precedent which was to become increasingly influential.

The "good design" movement
By the mid 1960s the concept of design as a commodity "added" to consumer objects to increase their value had become economically and culturally integrated into all the capitalist countries of the industrialized world. Design differentiated products in competition with each other, or else served as a form of national self-identification on the world market.

During the 1950s the reconstructed economies of Germany, Italy and Japan, had sought to restore themselves in international trading through identifying their goods with a particular product esthetic. For the most part, only goods aimed at

a fairly exclusive, wealthy international market were overtly described as incorporating "design", often with the name of a well-known designer attached to them. Only those companies which aimed their goods at the top end of the market made sure that they were seen by the media as being design-conscious. Others, with a mass market in mind, concentrated more on minimizing the price of their products than on their esthetic content.

The "good design" movement of these years became a clearly defined cultural phenomenon, supported by museum collections, exhibitions such as the Milan Triennales, and conferences, competitions, awards and glossy magazines. A very tightly delineated design culture grew out of this network, and as long as it remained in the hands of an international elite it was easy to identify its ideological function and cultural effects. Synonymous with the concept of good taste, it preferred minimalism to ostentation and elegance to vulgarity. Well designed products became increasingly identified with a cosmopolitan, middle-class, well-educated lifestyle. Some furniture and electronic equipment manufacturers – Olivetti and Cassinini in Italy; Hille in Britain; Bang & Olufsen in Denmark; Braun in Germany; Sony in Japan; and IBM in the United States – established their identities through their commitment to design and largely depended upon it for their commercial success.

The national styles of these goods varied one from another, however, and the modern design movement in Italy had the greatest international impact. Industrial and cultural reconstruction in the years since 1945 had encouraged close collaboration between consumer-goods manufacturers and a group of highly creative architect-designers. The economic boom of the years 1958–63, combined with a forward-looking attitude towards new materials and a commitment to an aggressively modern esthetic with its roots in sculpture, resulted in the proliferation of goods for home and office which were associated with a sophisticated, cosmopolitan lifestyle.

Italy's ability to compete favorably in international markets stemmed primarily from its policy of paying low wages to its workforce rather than from investing in advanced technology. Italian design was limited to those goods which depended on low technology – furniture, household appliances – rather than the more complex electrical and electronic products to which Japan was dedicating its energies. Forbidden by the terms of the postwar settlement to develop an armaments industry, Japan had come to dominate the consumer electronics market, in part because of American industry's preoccupation with military contracts.

"Italian design" became linked, in the minds of many, with glossy plastic tables and chairs, sumptuous leather armchairs and sofas, sculptural lamps in steel and marble, and other items of household and office equipment which appealed more on the basis of their elegant forms than their technological sophistication.

The exclusivity of Italian design gave rise to an alternative design movement in that country, to challenge the glossy, status-ridden image of mainstream fashion. Linked to social and economic factors such as the students' revolution of 1968, the anti- or counter-design movement sought to reunite design in Italy with the cultural base which had inspired it in the early postwar years. Kitsch, stylistic revivalism and irony were used in an attempt to take design out of the hands of industry and to reposition it within the mass culture. Radical architectural groups based in Florence presented Utopian visions of the future which were destined for the art gallery rather than the factory floor.

The alternative design movement

In the early 1970s a growing consciousness of the distance between Western conspicous consumption and underdevelopment in the Third World encouraged a number of designers to rethink the social and moral functions of design.

◀ Rosenthal's "Drop" tea-service, designed by Luigi Colani in 1971 represented that company's firm commitment to avant-garde design. Its rounded, "organic" forms were typical of that particular designer's work, visible in a wide range of other products, from cars to cameras.

Perceptions of the world as a global village gave designers a different idea of their role than as the adjuncts of manufacturing industry. Victor Papanek's 1971 book *Design for the Real World* was one stimulus behind this movement to re-direct design into the service of the underprivileged, whether the impoverished of the Third World or the old and infirm in the West.

Papanek argued that for too long designers had been concerned with little more than creating "toys for adults". He proposed a number of areas in which designers could contribute to relieving hardship in underdeveloped countries, among them "communication systems, simple educational devices, water filtration, and immunization and inoculation equipment."

By the mid 1970s a number of Third World design schools had taken responsibility for working not only on goods aimed at western export markets but also on projects which directly helped their own population. At the National Institute of Design at Ahmedabad in India, students worked on a symbol system for contraceptive education; an artificial limb which allowed disabled people to pursue their accustomed lifestyle, and on a range of other goods designed specifically for an Indian market. However, such work remained marginal to mainstream design and failed to undermine the main economic function of design in the century, as the guarantor of added value for goods aimed at a mass society.

▼ The Danish company Bang and Olufsen's "Beogram 4000" record player was among the most minimal and sophisticated examples of its kind to emerge in the 1970s. In sharp contrast with the complex, high-tech, value-for-money machines with which Japaneese manufacturers were flooding world markets, Bang and Olufsen opted for a more up-market look which appealed to a smaller, more discriminating group of consumers. This was reflected, inevitably, in the price of the product.

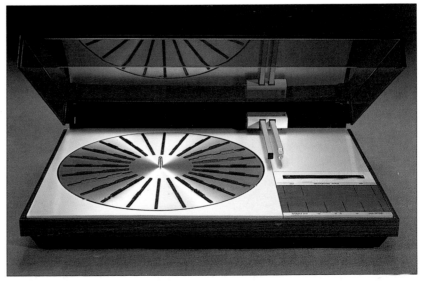

Datafile

Even though Hollywood spent the 1960s floundering without much sense of what its domestic audience would pay to see, it maintained its hold over foreign markets, and American television followed its example, offering developed and Third World countries programming at a much lower cost than their own television industries could provide. If the new technologies of communication were turning the world into a "Global Village," it was one in which only some would speak, and those who did were likely to have an American accent. In 1968 the American film industry abandoned its Production Code, ushering in a wave of "realism" that looked to critics like explicit sex and violence.

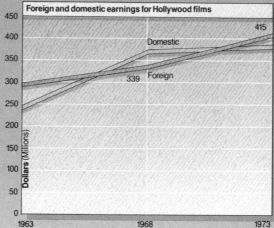

Foreign and domestic earnings for Hollywood films

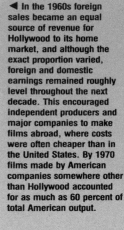

◄ In the 1960s foreign sales became an equal source of revenue for Hollywood to its home market, and although the exact proportion varied, foreign and domestic earnings remained roughly level throughout the next decade. This encouraged independent producers and major companies to make films abroad, where costs were often cheaper than in the United States. By 1970 films made by American companies somewhere other than Hollywood accounted for as much as 60 percent of total American output.

Academy Awards for Best Film of the Year

1961	West Side Story	United Artists
1962	Lawrence of Arabia	Columbia
1963	Tom Jones	United Artists
1964	My Fair Lady	Warner
1965	The Sound of Music	Fox
1966	A Man for All Seasons	Columbia
1967	In the Heat of The Night	United Artists
1968	Oliver!	Columbia
1969	Midnight Cowboy	United Artists
1970	Patton	Fox
1971	The French Connection	Fox
1972	The Godfather	Paramount
1973	The Sting	Universal

◄ The Oscar winners of the 1960s reflected Hollywood's stagnant imagination; only one was not based on a book or musical. There was a sharp change in 1969 as the Academy caught up with Hollywood's pursuit of the youth market. *Midnight Cowboy* was directed by an Englishman, John Schlesinger, but its sleazy tale of New York street-life was a sharp departure from the kinds of movies previously rewarded by the Academy. *The French Connection* was the first crime movie to be voted Best Picture.

US cinema attendance

◄ Cinema attendance continued to fall steadily during the 1960s in the United States. The studios remained uncertain about what would attract audiences, and as the blockbuster phenomenon developed, they lurched headlong from one expensive project to another. Many of their difficulties were caused by the studios' continuing reluctance to accept that the family audience had been permanently lost, and that they now had to gear production exclusively to a younger market.

Feature film imports

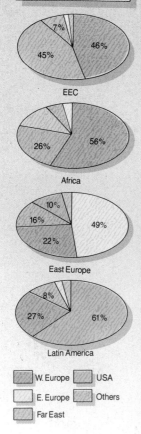

EEC — 7%, 46%, 45%

Africa — 26%, 56%

East Europe — 10%, 16%, 22%, 49%

Latin America — 8%, 27%, 61%

Legend:
- W. Europe
- E. Europe
- Far East
- USA
- Others

Hollywood's largest foreign markets

1963
1974

Rank: Canada, Italy, Australia, Japan, UK, FRG, France, Spain, South Africa, Brazil, Mexico, Sweden, Argentina, Venezuela, Netherlands

◄ American films recovered 40 percent of their production costs in Europe, while European films recovered only 10 percent of theirs in the United States. The Middle East and Asia showed a preponderance of American product only a little less than that in Latin America, while the Australian market was still dominated by Hollywood until the mid-1970s, when its government promoted a new national film industry. Only the Eastern bloc remained effectively closed to Hollywood's influence.

► American television repeated Hollywood's conquest of the world. At times it was almost total: in 1969, in the event billed as "the greatest show in the history of television", 723 million people watched Neil Armstrong take the first steps on the Moon. To some extent, Europe immunized itself from transatlantic pollution by quotas to limit the amount of American programs which could be screened, but such luxuries were not available to Third World countries, whose native industries were undermined.

◄ In 1974, 15 countries accounted for 74 percent of all Hollywood's foreign earnings. The American film industry was dependent on foreign markets; however, American pictures kept half the world's movie theaters open. In addition, all the major international distribution companies were American; even when distributing British of French films in other foreign markets, they were taking their share of the profits, and American companies were also frequently the financial backers of French, Italian or British films.

Imported programs on television

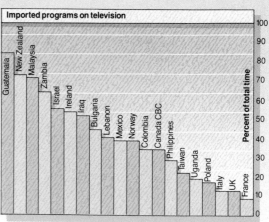

Guatemala, New Zealand, Malaysia, Zambia, Israel, Ireland, Iraq, Bulgaria, Lebanon, Mexico, Norway, Colombia, Canada CBC, Philippines, Taiwan, Uganda, Poland, Italy, UK, France

Percent of total time

THE NETWORKS AND THE NEW WAVE

By 1960 television had "liberated" cinema by taking over its function as mass entertainment. Without a clear idea of what its post-television role should be or how to satisfy its increasingly disparate audience, Hollywood was in limbo for much of the next decade. The old studio moguls were either dead, in retirement, or battling to maintain a tenuous control over their companies. With them had gone confidence about production. The strategy of high-budget costume epics that had sustained Hollywood through the 1950s came crashing down with the extravagant failure of *Cleopatra* (1963), at $40 million the most expensive film ever made. The film's colossal losses nearly bankrupted Twentieth Century–Fox; the lesson both it and the rest of the industry chose to learn came from the movie that restored the studio's fortunes, *The Sound of Music* (1965). Made for $8 million, it grossed $78 million in the United States and Canada alone.

The industry was lured by the prospect of such returns into ever greater recklessness, spending extravagantly on visible production values in the hope that the "money on the screen" would draw in audiences. Sometimes it worked spectacularly well. Together with the re-release of *Gone with the Wind*, *Doctor Zhivago* (1965) kept MGM solvent for the second half of the decade. But in 1969 only one film in ten showed a profit. In the second half of the 1960s the studios resembled gambling addicts in the terminal stages of their illness, locked into a pattern of borrowing heavily from banks to finance another blockbuster that they hoped would defy the rules of movie profitability and solve the company's financial problems at a stroke. With the successive failures of lavish musicals such as *Star!*, *Hello Dolly* and *Dr. Doolittle*, Fox lost $78 million in 1970, and nearly bankrupted itself again.

Hollywood now derived more than half its income from abroad, with the European market supplying 80 percent of that total. Economically dependent on their international appeal, American films became more cosmopolitan, or mid-Atlantic, in their appearance. Thrillers developed convoluted plots that toured the landmarks of European capitals and pushed aging American male leads – Gregory Peck, Cary Grant – into affairs with younger European women such as Sophia Loren. "Runaway" productions made in Europe had the advantages of government subsidies and lower production costs. Epics such as David Lean's *Lawrence of Arabia* (1962) were given international casts to enhance their appeal to European distributors.

These meanderings were signs of Hollywood's uncertainty. The industry's lack of financial self-confidence led to the studios being bought by major American conglomerates for well under their market value. Universal was bought by MCA, a former talent agency, Paramount by Gulf and Western (steel, mining, plastics), United Artists by Transamerica Inc. (insurance), Warners by the Kinney Corporation (car rentals, building maintenance, funeral parlors), and MGM by Kirk Kerkorian, a Las Vegas hotel magnate. Bought for their real estate and undervalued film libraries, and for the possibility of windfall profits in good years, the companies became small elements in much larger corporations. In 1974 Paramount's film rentals amounted to only 3.5 percent of Gulf and Western's revenues.

As the studio system disintegrated in a morass of agents, deals and "packaging", the machinery which had once regulated Hollywood production crumbled. The Production Code had survived more or less intact through the 1950s, but became increasingly untenable against the industry's need to cater to a more permissive audience hostile to anything it could label "censorship". The Code was finally abandoned in favor of a ratings system in 1968.

The year 1967 was a pivotal one in Hollywood's development. Audience figures increased for the first time since 1946, partly because of the massive success of *The Graduate* and *Bonnie and Clyde*, each made for $3 million and returning more than ten times its cost. The significant increase in

▼ Many producers blamed *The Sound of Music* (1965) for nearly destroying Hollywood in the mid-1960s. It was such a huge hit that every studio tried to copy it, investing in big-budget musicals that failed disastrously at the box-office.

attendance was among 18- to 25-year-olds, and the studios began to search for new product to cater to this young audience. *Easy Rider*, made in 1969 for $400,000, grossed $25 million, bringing into being a new genre, the youth film, and a new system of low-budget independent production, based on the model pioneered by Roger Corman, who had specialized in "schlock" movies for the drive-in market.

Films for the young

The Hollywood "Renaissance" of the early 1970s followed an influx of a new generation of managerial talent – Richard Zanuck, Robert Evans, Alan Ladd, David Picker. The success of *Easy Rider* sent them scurrying in search of untried directors who could turn a low-budget "personal" film into both artistic masterpiece and commercial success. Production companies such as BBS and Pressman-Williams emerged to provide the brief

▲▶ In the late 1960s Hollywood tried to capture the youth audience. *The Graduate* (1967) was one of the first films to succeed, wrapping Dustin Hoffman's aimless adolescent rebellion in selfconscious stylishness. Three years later, after the police violence at the 1968 Democratic Convention in Chicago, *The Strawberry Statement* (above) took the radicalism of youth revolt and student protest more seriously. A more acceptable form of rebellion brought Robert Redford stardom in the early 1970s. In *Butch Cassidy and the Sundance Kid*, (above right) Redford and Paul Newman presented their anti-social activity as a form of comic play for them and the audience.

Art Cinema and the New Wave

In France, a New Wave of filmmakers, many of them former critics, emerged in 1959 when Francois Truffaut's *400 Blows* won the Best Direction prize at the Cannes film festival. As critics on the magazine *Cahiers du Cinéma*, Truffaut, Claude Chabrol, Jacques Rivette and Jean-Luc Godard had attacked the dominant tradition in French film of respectful adaptations of "quality" novels, and asserted that the true creators of cinema were its directors. As directors, they experimented with subject matter and technique, producing films dealing with more complex and daring themes than the conventional sentimentalities of Hollywood.

This experimentation would not have been possible without an audience prepared to regard cinema as an art form comparable in esthetic merit to the theater. This new audience – young, middle-class, educated and internationally minded – welcomed a cinema that provided the stylistic innovation and thematic substance of literary modernism, for evening entertainment. Critics in the press and specialized film journals now championed the director as author, and this individualization of creativity made "cinema" critically respectable, something the bourgeois

delusion that in the Hollywood renaissance anything might be possible. Movies made for the youth market – *Medium Cool, The Revolutionary, The Strawberry Statement* – even suggested that Hollywood might be capable of an explicit political radicalism as well as an increasingly explicit depiction of sex and bloodshed.

Those moral guardians who feared that the Code's collapse would usher in the demise of decency were not far wrong. As Hollywood grew increasingly explicit in its treatment of sexuality, so the pornography industry grew less peripheral. In 1972 *Deep Throat* became the first piece of hardcore "porno-chic" to play in regular movie theaters as well as in those that showed only "adult" rated films.

By 1973 the Hollywood Renaissance had collapsed. It had become possible, however, to take American cinema seriously. In the early 1970s courses in film began to be available at American universities, and to use the words "film" and "art" in the same sentence was no longer the mark of an oddball or a film publicist.

Television in the sixties

It would be some time before anyone tried to make the same case for American television, which had changed little from the way Newton Minow, chairman of the Federal Communications Commission, had described it to its producers in 1961, as "a vast wasteland".

Minow had just been appointed to his post by John F. Kennedy, and many in his audience might have expected gentler treatment from a president who had been elected, they believed, on the strength of his appeal on television.

Television obliged politicians to become performers in a way radio never had. Kennedy, youthful, authoritative and almost handsome enough to play the lead in a TV doctor series,

seemed perfectly cast. Pursuing a policy of accessibility to the camera, he held live press conferences, delivered an ultimatum to Khrushchev via television during the Cuban missile crisis, and encouraged his wife to take the nation on a *Tour of the White House*. The impact of his assassination was intensified by the fact that he was not just the President, but a television celebrity whom the viewing public had been encouraged to feel they knew through the intimacy of the medium. For the four days between the assassination and the funeral all three networks suspended their regular schedules and carried no advertising.

By 1960 half the population of the United States depended on television as its prime source of news. Network prime time had settled into a mixture of half-hour comedy shows and hour-long action/drama series. Drama, like comedy, was constructed around a repeatable situation, usually provided by a professional activity. Lawyer- and doctor-shows provided an ideal format for hour-long stories featuring guest stars as clients or patients, but the same formula was used for series on teachers and social workers.

The formula had its limitations. The central characters had to remain unchanged by the episode's events, in order to be in their proper places by the following week's episode. The serial form provided the programming stability necessary to deliver viewers to advertisers on a regular basis. Networks tried to carry their audiences from one show to the next, employing the principle of Least Objectionable Programming. This meant that the majority of viewers who simply watched television, rather than selecting specific programs, would watch whichever show they disliked least. The unit of television viewing was not the individual program but the daytime or evening schedule as a whole. As a result, television placed little emphasis on the

You will see on US television a procession of game shows, violence, audience participation shows, formula comedies about totally unbelievable families, blood and thunder, mayhem, violence, sadism, murder, western badmen, western goodmen, private eyes, gangsters, more violence and cartoons and, endlessly, commercials – many screaming, cajoling, and offending ... Gentlemen, your trust accounting with your beneficiaries is overdue. Never have so few owed so much to so many.

NEWTON MINOW 1961

audience could care about. After 1960, enough people cared about cinema to constitute a market sufficiently large to support a personalized cinema that delighted in idiosyncratic stylistic touches, particularly if they were used to embellish sexual or psychological content.

The development of a general market for the cinematic form of self-conscious modernism established by Ingmar Bergman, Federico Fellini and the French New Wave gave room to further experimentation. In such films as Alain Resnais' *Last Year at Marienbad* (1961) and *Je T'Aime, Je T'Aime* (1968), orthodox chronology was abandoned in favor of stylized meditations on the uncertainties of time. It also opened up a Western market for East European films for the first time since the 1920s. The Hungarian director Miklos Jancso and the filmmakers of the Czechoslovak New Wave formed part of the European art film movement, until the Russian invasion of Czechoslovakia brought the "Prague Spring" to an end in 1968.

▶ Federico Fellini's *Satyricon* (1964).

distinction between fact and fiction. In sports and game shows it offered its audience an engagement with an endless dramatic experience, in which consequences and conclusions mattered less than the exuberance of competition, choice and performance. Television had a peculiar capacity to dissolve distinctions between comedy, drama, news and commercials.

Television's other typical form, the talk show, perfected its formula in the early 1960s with *The Tonight Show*, hosted by Johnny Carson. Talk shows packaged personality as a commodity, but all television employed it; even newsreaders became celebrities.

Vietnam, the first rock 'n' roll war, was also the first television war, with combat footage on the nightly news. Johnson tried assiduously to manage television coverage of the war, pundits debated endlessly about whether television had "brought the war home" or had trivialized it as just another interruption in the stream of commercials, and whether the scenes of carnage and the reports of American atrocities had numbed its audience or had increased anti-war sentiment or street violence. Television reporting was brutally attracted to scenes of violence and dissent – they made good pictures. By the end of the 1960s political groups denied conventional access to the media had recognized the staged act of violence as an effective means of gaining attention. Terrorism happened for the television camera.

Johnson's successor, Richard Nixon, saw the media as his enemy. Although his 1968 campaign was an object-lesson in the packaging of a candidate's image, his attitude had been indelibly marked by his failure in the televised debates with Kennedy in 1960. Even before the Watergate Senate hearings topped the ratings in 1974, Nixon and his staff regularly denounced television's "nattering nabobs of negativism."

In common with most Western television systems, the Federal Communications Commissions Fairness Doctrine enforced the provision of equal time for the expression of opposing views on any given issue. Its effect was to secure the middle ground for television itself, and to make its presenters the arbiters of political dispute. Television's credibility relied on its apparent neutrality, something that marked it out from the partisan allegiances of newspapers.

By the late 1960s television news was expected to be profitable as well as prestigious. *CBS Evening News* cost $7 million to produce in 1969, and made a profit of $13 million. The need for pictorial content meant that television took to "managing" the production of news in ways reminiscent of the "yellow press" at the beginning of the century (see page 34). Needing to deliver stories with both drama and immediacy, journalists passed from gathering news to creating it, in the form of predictable and manageable events such as press conferences and publicity stunts.

Television news stimulated an ever-growing cynicism and disaffection with politics by its emphasis on dissent and disagreement. At the same time the medium itself became the vehicle for the

▲ Richard Chamberlain as *Dr Kildare*, which premièred in 1961. Lawyer- and doctor-shows provided an ideal format for stories featuring guest stars, but they had their limitations. *Dr Kildare* could never marry, just as the *Rawhide* cattle drive could never end.

▶ Vietnam was the first television war. Some commentators believed that Lyndon Johnson decided not to run for re-election after Walter Cronkite, anchorman of *CBS News* and "the most trusted man in America", declared in March 1968 that the United States might not be able to win the war. But the presence of television had not deterred South Vietnam's police chief from shooting a bound Vietcong suspect in the head on camera during the Tet offensive the month before. Neither, later that year, were the student protestors at the Chicago Democratic convention protected from the nightsticks and billyclubs of Mayor Daley's rioting police force by their chants of "The whole world is watching".

normal. It existed to sell viewers to advertisers, and advertisers were little interested in showing their wares to black ghetto-dwellers, for example, who might want the proffered consumer goods but lacked the wherewithal to purchase them. Television's largest advertisers – the manufacturers of automobiles, cosmetics, food, drugs, household goods and, until 1971, tobacco – wanted the networks to supply them with a middle-class audience for their sales pitch.

In the late 1960s the American networks discovered that a detailed study of the audience provided them with a way of selling advertising time at higher prices by selecting programs aimed at a wealthier, educated audience. Fewer shows were aimed at middle-aged, middle-class viewers in large towns and rural areas. More programming was directed at a younger, urban audience with more money to spend. The controlled irreverence of *Rowan and Martin's Laugh-In*, launched in 1967, was one gesture toward this audience.

American television and the wider world

In the early 1970s there was a renaissance of comedy on American television, much of it coming from Americanized versions of British programs. *All in the Family* (1970–77) took its formula and characters from the BBC's *Till Death Do Us Part*, first screened in 1964. *The Mary Tyler Moore Show*, the first sitcom to feature an independent woman as its main character, also began in 1970.

In 1969 the Public Broadcasting System (PBS) was established as a network of mainly educational stations funded partially by the federal government and partially by subscription. PBS imported much British television: the BBC's adaptation of *The Forsyte Saga* was a major ratings success in 1970, outstripped in 1974 by the surreal comedy of *Monty Python's Flying Circus*.

The main flow of television business went the other way. Before 1960, as part of an aggressive marketing strategy, American television was dumping entertainment product in Europe, Australia and the Third World at rock-bottom prices. In 1970 the BBC could buy American drama at less than one-tenth the cost per viewer-hour of producing it themselves. To some extent, European television protected itself from transatlantic pollution by quota systems, which limited the amount of American programming that could be screened. German broadcasting had been strongly influenced by the BBC model after World War II, and a national television had begun service in 1953. From the early 1960s German television supported filmmakers in producing plays and films which ventured outside the American-dominated conventions of the international film and television industries. While they produced an impressive body of work, they failed to raise the technical level of production and limited their foreign sales, which kept their cultural production marginalized.

President de Gaulle saw state domination of French television as a necessary counter-measure to the opposition expressed towards him in the French provincial press. Despite reorganization in the wake of the demonstrations of May 1968, the *Office de la Radio et Télévision Française* (ORTF) re-

▲ *Monty Python's Flying Circus* was the most successful British television export to the United States. With its catchphrase "and now for something completely different", it constantly parodied other television forms.

◀ In the early 1960s Johnny Carson's *The Tonight Show* perfected the talk-show formula, inviting the audience to spend time in the company of the celebrated (like Cassius Clay) while they discussed themselves.

mained firmly and openly in support of the conservative political status quo. Television in France and in Italy, where *Radio Televisione Italiano* (RAI) had a programming monopoly similar to that of ORTF, transmitted more informational and cultural programming than Germany or Britain.

Britain preserved its reputation for the "least worst television in the world" by actively promoting minority programming and "quality television". The BBC established its second channel in 1964 to maintain the ethos of public service broadcasting while allowing BBC1 to move downmarket into more direct competition with the commercial ITV. The adaptations, documentaries and one-off television plays that gave British television its envied reputation for quality all upheld the tradition of things English and literary. Documentaries sponsored the dissemination of knowledge, while literary adaptations of the classics and semi-classics of English literature reproduced the "worthiest" remnants of British culture. One consequence was that, as in Germany, television absorbed writing and directorial talent that might have contributed to a cinematic renaissance. The vapid British cinema of the later 1960s was evidence of the effectiveness of this.

Datafile

After 1960, international competitive sport developed a contradiction between the ideals of free competition between individual sportsmen and women representing their countries, and the reality of sport as an adjunct to international politics. Sport was never free of politics, and it became increasingly absurd to claim that it should be. Nevertheless, many of those who continued to argue for keeping sport free of politics were themselves administrators of international sport.

Many Third World countries found that success in sport could provide them with international prestige, and the sporting boycott was developed, particularly by opponents of apartheid in South Africa. It proved effective as a means of bringing the issue to public attention around the world. Those who argued that sport and politics should not mix also tended to claim that sporting contacts were generally beneficial in resolving conflict.

▶ **The European and South American Cup was** effectively the competition for the world's leading club, played between the winners of the competition for each continent's championship the previous year. The game was played less physically in Latin America than in Europe, which led to controversy during the 1960s.

▶ **Sport was used to encourage people to participate in community life in many socialist countries.** In Cuba the sports industry increased dramatically after Castro's revolution, with factories producing sports goods springing up everywhere. The Cuban baseball became the internationally accepted standard.

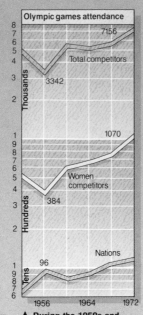

▲ **During the 1950s and 1960s the Olympic games were more widely sited than ever before, visiting Melbourne in 1956, Tokyo in 1964 and Mexico in 1968; and more nations competed.** The altitude of Mexico City (2300m above sea level) led to the criticism that it was an unsuitable site for middle- and long-distance running.

World Club Championship	
1960	Real Madrid (Spa)
1961	Penarol (Uru)
1962/3	Santos (Bra)
1964/5	Intermilan (It)
1966	Penarol (Uru)
1967	Racing Club (Arg)
1968	Estudiantes (Arg)
1969	AC Milan (It)
1970	Feyenoord (Hol)
1971	Nacional (Uru)
1972	Ajax (Hol)
1973	Independiente (Arg)

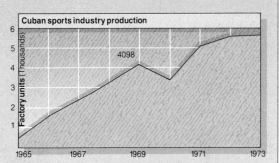

Cuban sports industry production

◀ **In China, sports facilities were prioritized under the Communist government.** Sport had traditionally played an important role in Chinese life, but while the country was isolated from international contact, facilities were geared to social needs, following the slogan "friendship first, competition second."

▼ **The German Democratic Republic (East Germany) emerged as a sporting superstar within 12 years of joining the Olympic community.** The nations' political leaders saw sport as a means to international prestige, and encouraged a policy of sport for all. A high proportion of the champions trained with the armed forces sports club.

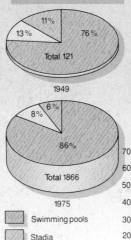

Sports facilities in China

1949 — Total 121: 11%, 13%, 76%

1975 — Total 1866: 6%, 8%, 86%

Swimming pools
Stadia
Gymnasia

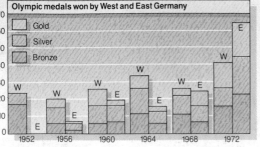

Olympic medals won by West and East Germany

Gold
Silver
Bronze

Russia was a founder member of the modern Olympic movement, but after the Russian Revolution of October 1917, no Soviet team took part in the Olympics until 1952. Initially, there was an explicit rejection of "bourgeois" sports: the Soviets boycotted important Western competitions. Instead, a centrally organized government program of national fitness, "physical culture" and sport for the masses, free of charge, was designed to create in every citizen a sense of emotional identity with the aims of the Soviet state, as a way of uniting the diverse nationalities and cultures of so vast a country.

After World War II, sport assumed a focal position in Soviet foreign policy, as a way of injecting a spirit of nationalism at home and gaining international prestige abroad. The Soviet Union emerged as a world sporting power after the 1952 Olympics, the last year in which the United States won more gold medals than the Soviet Union.

Sport and the Cold War

The Soviet presence, and their unequivocal acknowledgement of the political nature of sport, exposed the contradictions between the idealist philosophy of the Olympic Charter and the post-war actuality of intense sports competition being used as a weapon of international propaganda. The Olympics, in particular, embodied the Cold-War ideological struggle between the Eastern and Western blocs. By the late 1950s, a number of writers were lamenting the way sport had become "war without weapons".

The Soviets used sport explicitly as a vehicle to nurture solidarity with Third World nations, providing sports buildings and equipment, free of charge, and sending experts to train gifted athletes and arrange tours, displays and teaching. The Soviet Union provided sport aid to Eastern Europe and Cuba, developing a system of mutual assistance, with friendly sports meetings, athletic scholarships, and exchanges of coaches, advisors and specialized knowledge. By comparison, Western countries persisted in a haphazard and more traditionally amateur approach to sport, Western athletes had to negotiate for opportunities and compete for finance.

The conspicuous achievements of Eastern-bloc athletes fueled controversy about the pursuit of excellence and the degree to which socialist sports systems embodied the political interests of their governments or the individual interests of the citizens who comprise those societies. The 1950s started a process of re-appraisal of Western sports policies, moving towards an increase in state intervention, with the recognition that efficient mass systems of sport must be established to maximize available talent. The Soviet insistence on free access for all to sport as the basis of a

SPORT AND THE THIRD WORLD

The Cold War

Sport behind the Iron Curtain

The challenge to the sporting establishment

Boycotts – the Olympics and other major events

Sport and television

Ali and Pelé

fundamentally non-elitist system was, however, much less rigorously followed. In 1953 evidence about the fitness levels of American schoolchildren provoked Cold War anxieties about the physical condition of young people. In a 1960 article "The Soft American" in *Sports Illustrated* President-elect Kennedy proposed a national fitness system to invigorate the American nation in order to meet the Soviet challenge.

The USSR's success in using sport as a vehicle for social progress was particularly attractive to Third World countries, although lack of facilities prevented them providing comprehensive sports systems. With indigenous games traditions eroded by colonial contact, Third World nations struggling for self-identity saw modern sport as an excellent opportunity to foster patriotism through the celebration of national heroes. After the emergence into international sport of Asian and African countries, sport became a global idiom, uniting people from disparate cultures. Associations and competitions specifically for Third World countries were inaugurated to extend opportunities to Third World athletes, but all new moves – the Asian Games, the Pan American Games, the Mediterranean Games – engendered political controversy. Ironically, the more obviously politicized sport became, the more vehement were the refusals of Olympic purists to acknowledge this. In 1956, six nations withdrew

▼ Massed pageantry at the 1957 Moscow Festival. The USSR ended its boycott of major Western sports competitions by attending the 1952 Olympic Games in Helsinki, and used sport as a means of developing international friendship throughout the period.

from the Melbourne Olympics, for reasons connected either to the conflict in Suez or the invasion of Hungary earlier in the year.

The politicization of sport

With the nation state the primary unit of international sport, nationalism provided the most conspicuous form of political interference. Sophisticated ceremonial, ritual displays of nationalism, pageantry, medals and tables of results became intrinsic to all big international competitions, and the media exploited the volatile nature of sport to promote feelings of patriotism and rivalry, often carrying racist overtones. Competition was treated as a drama of national emotions, survival, and political and ideological superiority.

The Olympics were the most political event; propaganda, protests, boycotts and terrorism became commonplace. Western powerbrokers in international sports federations such as the International Olympic Committee (IOC) sought to maintain their control over the definitions under which sport and politics interact, as socialist and Third World countries, with little reason to accept the ideology of competitive individualism that Western nations attached to the forms of modern sport, increasingly participated and constantly challenged the bland assertions of Western terms of reference. The patronizing praise bestowed by European and American commentators on

athletes such as Kipjoge Keino for gaining Kenya's first Olympic gold medal in 1972, served to reinforce the neo-colonialist attitude of the West toward Third World countries. At the same time it served as evidence that sport is meritocratic, that individuals with supreme ability will surface, regardless of obstacles.

Countries with limited economic resources copied many of the characteristics of sport that evolved in the developed world. Controversy arose about the morality of nations burdened with poverty and debt investing in a sporting elite, or even in a sports policy and program. Western cultural influence, whether in media, food, music or sport, tended to benefit Third World elites, and at the same time the promotion of imported sport from the developed world turned people away from their own traditional sports and games.

When countries other than those Western industrial powers that had been in charge of international sport since the early years of the 20th century sought to redefine the relationship between sport, ideology and power, the contradictions became inescapable. A "socialist-inspired" answer, based on the philosophy that sport in the developing world should be an expression of new-found independence and "an instrument of emancipation from imperialist fetters", was symbolized by the first and only Games of the New Emerging Forces (GANEFO) in 1963. This competition stimulated more conflict with the sporting establishment: GANEFO records were not recognized and GANEFO athletes were banned from Olympic competition. From that time, the Eastern bloc and Third World countries sought more representation in existing international organizations. In 1963 Sir Adetoklunbo Ademola of Nigeria became the first black African member of the IOC. By voting with members of developing countries, the Eastern bloc started to threaten the grip of the Western world on international sport.

The suggestion that, since sport is self-evidently political, the political terms of engagement must be acceptable before agreeing to the rules of competition emerged most strongly in the 1960s over the issue of apartheid and southern Africa. The anti-apartheid sports movement, which sought to prevent all sporting contact with South Africa, gained momentum after African countries founded the Supreme Council for Sport in Africa (SCSA) in 1966. In the same year Afro-American athletes and civil-rights activists pressured the US Olympic Committee to oppose South African participation in the Olympics. By 1968 the boycott movement created widespread opposition to sporting links with South Africa: the new nations of black Africa, the Caribbean, Islamic and Communist countries threatened to boycott the Games.

In 1970 South Africa was banned from the Olympic movement. Avery Brundage, president of the IOC, reluctantly acknowledged, "We have to face the facts of life – political powers have more to say than we do." He believed that conceding to one demand that breached the fiction of sport's separation from politics would only lead

◀ Kenyan athlete Kipjoge Keino won his country's first Olympic gold medal at the 1972 Games in Munich, for the steeplechase. Black Africa's increasing participation in international sport was accompanied by mixed feelings. It was feared that indigenous games were being neglected at the expense of modern sport, with its emphasis on competition and individual achievement.

▼ When US 200m medallists Tommie Smith and John Carlos lowered their eyes and raised their black-gloved fists in silent protest on the victory rostrum at the 1968 Mexico Olympics, media coverage enabled them to focus the eyes of the world on the Black Power movement in the United States.

to increasing politicization. His fear was realized four days before the opening ceremony of the 1972 Olympics, when 27 African nations, some other countries outside Africa and some American black athletes threatened to pull out of the Games if Rhodesia, with a similar racial policy to that of South Africa, was allowed to compete. Brundage described this pressure as "naked political blackmail", but in 1975 Rhodesia was expelled from the Olympic movement, and Zimbabwe was accepted after independence. In 1976 Tanzania, and then a further 19 African countries along with Guyana and Iraq pulled out of the Games because the IOC refused to ban New Zealand athletes. The New Zealand All Blacks Rugby team had toured South Africa at the time of the Soweto riots, and the New Zealand government had ignored an appeal from SCSA to cancel the tour. This "third party boycott" introduced a new dimension: it was in opposition to a country collaborating with apartheid sport.

More than once, a different interpretation of politics has tragically intruded into Olympic sport. At Munich in 1972 17 people, 11 of them Israeli athletes, were killed when Palestinian Black September guerrillas took hostages at the Olympic village. Linking this with the boycotts, Brundage insisted, "The Games must go on...The IOC has suffered two savage attacks within the past few days – one on the Rhodesian situation, in which political blackmail was used, and now this."

Sport and the media

As an increasing number of countries came to participate in international competition, sport became a global phenomenon in another sense. Satellite television, new developments in electronic technology and rapid and relatively inexpensive travel made televised sport as a form of popular entertainment accessible throughout the world. As late as 1960 American network television was not yet providing full weekend sports coverage, and CBS bought the American television rights to the Rome Olympics for a mere $500,000. Network interest had, however, already improved the fortunes of American football, turning it from baseball's poor relation into the dominant American media sport.

In Europe, as in America, established national sports and large-scale international competitions were the first beneficiaries of television, but rivalry between television networks increased the variety of broadcast events. Sports organizations that had initially resisted television coverage out of fears of lost ticket sales came to recognize the potential revenue in television rights. By the mid 1960s CBS was paying the National Football League $14 million a year for exclusive television coverage, and was pioneering a further development of television's relations with sport by buying its own baseball team, the New York Yankees.

Television came increasingly to select people's experiences of local, national and international competitions. The development of video technology facilitated the presentation of sport as entertainment by the selection of key moments to be replayed. This also made possible the instant "action replay" and allowing studio experts to analyze the play and criticize the judges, superseding the old style of commentary which had attempted only to inform about the run of play and to convey some the the excitement of the event. In 1964 color cameras were used to transmit live pictures of the Olympic Games in Tokyo via satellite to audiences around the world. People in Europe, North and South America, Asia and Africa saw the imaginative flair and efficiency of the first Olympic Games to be held in Asia. Champions from other countries became household names. Sport became a prime subject for the world communications of McLuhan's "global village" to watch, to witness, and to argue over.

▲ Millions of television viewers saw Yoshinori Sakai, born on the day of the Hiroshima atom bomb, carrying the Olympic flame for the 1964 Tokyo Games.

◀ Soviet gymnast Olga Korbut captivated the world with her performance at the 1972 Munich Olympics. Although individual sporting heroines have long been highly visible, few of the countries entering the competition since the early 1950s have fielded female athletes – for religious, historical and cultural reasons. Of the 121 nations taking part in the 1972 Olympics, only 61 entered female competitors. Asian and African women were almost totally absent.

SPORTING SUPERSTARS

In the 1960s there emerged two sportsmen – both black men from unpromising backgrounds – who each won vast fortunes and became amongst the best known faces and names in the world. The two of them challenged many conventional assumptions about the place of the sportsman in modern society.

Born in 1940 in the small town of Três Corações in the state of Minas Gerais in Brazil, Edson Arantes do Nascimento (Pelé) began playing professional soccer for the Santos club at the age of 16. Two years later he attended his first World Cup Finals in Sweden.

In a career spanning 20 years and over 1300 games, Pelé established unparalleled scoring records. Late in a career which had witnessed three World Cup Final victories for his native Brazil, he became the focus for the expansion of the game in North America. His pre-eminence as a sporting legend made him a powerful symbol of the possibilities of sport as an avenue to social mobility in the 1970s. He was the highest- salaried team athlete in history and probably the richest.

Pelé's success attracted attention to Brazil itself, and his team. He showed that a Third World country could compete against and challenge economically "advanced" nations.

In 1960, two years after Pelé had appeared in his first World Cup Final, Muhammad Ali (then Cassius Marcellus Clay Jr.) won the Olympic light heavyweight boxing gold medal at Rome, at the age of 18.

In twenty years, Ali rose from the obscurity of Louisville, Kentucky, to global prominence. As a sporting role model for young blacks he explicitly confronted racial stereotypes.

His audacity in promoting his own ability, his successful challenge for the world heavyweight championship in 1964, his conversion to Islam, his stand against the Vietnam War and the regaining of "his" world title all thrust him into the center of world sport.

In the 20th century American boxers have monopolized the world heavyweight champion-ship. The pre-eminence of black champions since 1956 has fueled racist sentiments. Ali himself saw boxing as "the fastest way for a black person to make it in this country". As his career developed, many people were prepared to pay vast sums to see him beaten.

In 1966, Ali claimed conscientious objector status because of his Black Muslim beliefs. He was convicted of draft evasion, stripped of his world titles and had his boxing licence revoked. In 1970, the United States Supreme Court unanimously reversed the conviction and Ali was allowed to fight again. In 1971 he fought Joe Frazier for the world heavyweight title and lost in 15 rounds. Three years later he defeated George Forman in Kinshasa, Zaire, to regain the world title and in the process earned $5,450,000. In the six years after his return to boxing, Ali earned an estimated $26 million; but shortly after his retirement he was diagnosed as having suffered brain damage from his boxing career.

▶▲ Brazilian soccer genius Pelé, photographed right in 1970 after his team's third World Cup win, was remarkable for the power and accuracy of his kick and his uncanny skill in anticipating other players' moves. His soccer prowess brought Pelé international fame – his face was everywhere in 1970, even on stamps.

▼ Early days in the career that proved "rags to riches" could be achieved outside Hollywood – the camera froze Cassius Marcellus Clay Jr in this sparring pose in 1954, when he was just 12 years old. Six years later, Clay won Amateur Athletic Union, Golden Gloves, and Olympic Games championships. He turned professional the same year, adopting his Muslim name of Muhammad Ali in 1966. The change of name signified a change in the way in which he was seen: he now appeared a genuine threat to white America.

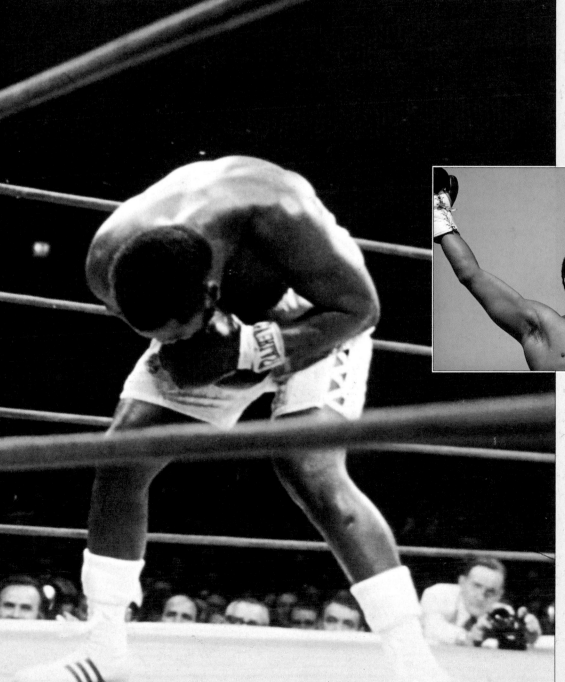

▲ One of the boxing world's loudest and most efficient self-promoters, Ali was also among its most controversial champions, challenging conventional wisdom about the sport through his statements on politics, personal and international. He himself claimed that "until now boxers could not even speak; now they can think."

◀ Seen in action with fellow world champion Joe Frazier, Ali was unusually light on his feet for a heavyweight. In a pop song commemorating his 1974 World title bout in Zaire, he was said to "float like a butterfly, sting like a bee". At his peak Ali was probably the fastest and most skillful heavyweight of all time.

179

Datafile

In the 1950s popular music had played, as one of its key functions, its part in the self-assertion of the young; in the 1960s this developed until it was central to the lives and even the politics of many people. Some viewed this as grafting extraneous elements on to music, but the ability of popular music to articulate personal, cultural and political experience had been developing throughout the century.

▼ The rise in record sales in the United States, during the 1960s reflected the growing vitality and importance of popular music across the entire social spectrum, as well as the increasingly large disposable income available to the young.

▼ Rock is often thought to have had it all its own way in the late sixties, but the number of full-time country music radio stations in the same period points to a high level of activity elsewhere on the American music scene. Radio, which gave the initial impetus to country music in the twenties, was now sustaining it once again.

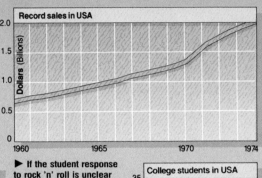
Record sales in USA

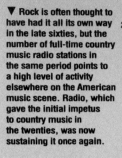
Country stations in USA

▶ If the student response to rock 'n' roll is unclear there has never been much doubt as to their interest in the music of the sixties. By 1967 students formed almost one third of the 18–24 audience. A connection would not be hard to find between this and the growing "seriousness" of the music.

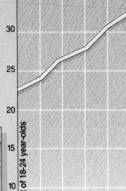
College students in USA

▶ With provincial touring largely ended, Broadway success was critical for musicals, and increased costs meant success had to be sustained to break even. Capturing the public's imagination, giving it tunes to whistle, and adhering to the contemporary liking for "concept" shows was a stern challenge.

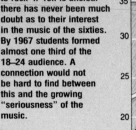
Longest-running musicals

Radio sets in use in USA

◀ The acceleration in the popularity of the radio which began in the mid-sixties had two linked causes. The first was stereo. Its first successful use in commercial recording came in the wake of the LP in the late 1950s. Radio followed in the early 1960s, and the improved sound quality boosted sales.

▶ The second cause of radio's improved fortunes was FM (frequency modulation). The old system, AM (amplitude modulation), could not carry stereo so FM took more music broadcasting, while AM stations specialized in spoken words. By the mid-1980s the two systems stood in parity.

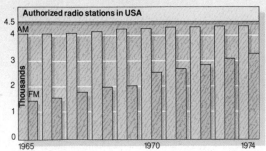
Authorized radio stations in USA

The sixties were to see American popular music receive an unprecedented degree of attention. They began inauspiciously enough, dominated by the inoffensive sounds of "Philadelphia schlock". This was a neutralized, watered-down version of rock 'n' roll. This music accepted the emancipating changes wrought by Elvis and others in the fifties, but, unlike theirs, remained transparently artificial and commercial in intent. The music was predictable and unambitious, and, in reaction, many people began to seek something "authentic", untainted by commerce.

The folk revival

Throughout the postwar period a small nucleus of musicians had followed a path that ran counter to the prevailing tastes of young and adult markets alike. They sustained and developed the part of the rural folk tradition (white and black) that had made a point of articulating its social grievances. This urban musical left wing was a mixture of an educated white middle class (Protestant and Jewish) and a "genuine" ex-rural proletariat. Combining a fundamentalist approach to folk music with a form of political radicalism that drew heavily on the bitter experiences of the unions in the interwar period, their songs expressed two basic needs – the need for roots, and the need for change – in one form. The music of Pete Seeger, Woody Guthrie, the Almanac Singers and others demonstrated the stark contrasts between the phoneyness of contemporary popular music and the honesty of the traditional sounds, between the duplicity of current politics and an idealistic vision of justice. This radical and libertarian thrust of the folk revival found political form in the association between the music and the civil rights movement in the United States, as well as the anti-nuclear movement in Europe in the early sixties.

A major contribution to popular music of the ensuing "folk revival" lay in the increased importance of the lyrics, and the fact that the folk singer usually wrote his own material. Here one particular figure embodies both the achievements and the paradoxes of the genre. Bob Dylan's songs, delivered in tones more nasal even than those used by earlier rural singers, specialized in a "shimmering collage of literary metaphor, alliteration and imagery" which musicians of an earlier age would have found incomprehensible. In the context of early sixties' pop, though, this music opened immense possibilities for the use of language, and gave a sense of cultural tradition.

Dylan's lyrics and his delivery also had the effect of moving the music firmly away from dance and providing the basis for the more intellectual reception of popular music characteristic of the later sixties. Once again, therefore, a tension

MUSIC CAN CHANGE THE WORLD

The folk revival and the protest movement

The decline of rock 'n' roll

British beat conquers the world

Californian music

Rock and art

Soul music

Rock festivals

became apparent, between music as supporting the domination of the explicit, literate tradition, and music as expressive of alternative, implicit ideas. Now, however, the poetry seemed to come "from within", as if it were a companion the music had long sought; it was also frequently identified, if not always unequivocally, with politically radical sentiments, and this considerably broadened the range of subject matter. Furthermore, Dylan's complex lyrics were so lacking in the traditional qualities of popular music that they proved virtually unusable by the vested interests of the music industry.

The sense of possessing qualities equal to but set apart from those of established culture was an important element in the counter-culture of the later 1960s. But as increasing store was set by poetic texts, however radically they might be interpreted, the music was in danger of being cut off from its source of inspiration. As singers

▼ The link between music and radical politics, as renewed by Dylan and Joan Baez was fundamental to activists such as these in Washington D.C. in 1968.

became prized for originality, and originality led to complexity, complexity negated the political point (just as it negated the symbolic simplicity of the singer-and-his-guitar).

A second major contribution of the folk revival was the creation of an audience whose members identified themselves as a community. Until now, even the most committed notions of audience solidarity had centered on sharing the status of being deviants from the social norm; milder forms of teenage commonality had been limited largely to tastes in entertainment. The audience for Dylan, Joan Baez and Phil Ochs began to see their music as the first, essential step in the forging of a whole way of life.

A basic tenet of this lifestyle was antipathy to "commercialism" and the trappings of mass consumerism. Here the political contradictions soon became apparent – contradictions that dogged the fully-fledged counter-culture later in the decade.

Many adherents found themselves torn between the desire to spread a cultural and political message, via folk music, and the fear that the channel used to do so – the communications market-place – would taint the musical tradition through commercial exploitation. Successful dissemination brought with it the risk of betrayal: "Folk music," wrote *Sing Out* editor Irwin Silber in 1964, "is the voice and expression of generations of ordinary folk who were on familiar terms with hard work. Success is the 'American Dream', the middle-class confusion of illusion and reality."

Dismayed by the appearance of the personality cult, that most hated aspect of "rat-race culture", diehards saw no gains in the coming together of folk and commerce: "The fundamentally healthy content of the folk music tradition (is) lost in the caverns of Tin Pan Alley". From the perspective of popular music, rather than folk, however, the encounter was significant: it marked the beginning of a "creative space" or division between art and image, or between the artist's authentic voice and the product that reached the market-place. Later musicians would find this space a fruitful area in which to explore and dispute meanings.

To younger folk-revival musicians – and perhaps to Dylan especially – by 1964 the limitations of the idiom, of its audience, of its saleability, had become too clear to overlook. Wholly unexpectedly, the impetus to switch direction and absorb the sounds of rock (as rock 'n' roll had now come to be known) came from a country that, according to critic Charlie Gillett, "had made no previous significant contribution to popular music in the 20th century".

Popular culture in Britain

In the early 1960s British popular culture emerged from the long winter of postwar austerity, rejuvenated by the assertive claims to attention of the young working class. Responding to prime minister Harold Macmillan's 1958 election message, "You've never had it so good", previously unregarded groups began to demand consumer cultural goods designed specifically for them. Just as rock 'n' roll had provided a commodity around which the American teenage market could be defined in the 1950s, the Mersey Beat – a raucous and driving form of rock that emerged from Liverpool in 1962–63 – signaled the arrival of the young British consumer as a commercial cultural force. But, as so often in Britain, their arrival was touched with class division. To be young, affluent and rebellious was not enough. As John Lennon later put it, "A working-class hero is something to be". Unexpectedly, this new kind of British cultural artefact proved highly exportable, and provided a major stimulus to popular culture all over the world.

Superficially at least, the radicalizing effects of rock 'n' roll seemed to have worn thin by 1960. Bland American "high school" sounds predominated. Britain's own Elvis clones, such as Cliff Richard, had turned into entertainers for all the family, while its imitation Sinatras continued to prosper both on records and on the airwaves. Though this apparent decline was due in part to a moral and/or cultural backlash, it had much to

do with ingrained aspects of national life and character. One of these was a readiness to live with maiden "Auntie" BBC's paternalism. British record companies were content – if not enthusiastic – to sell rock 'n' roll, but BBC resistance severely restricted airplay. The only alternative – the commercial radio station Radio Luxembourg, broadcast from mainland Europe – was very popular with teenagers (especially at 11 pm on a Sunday night for the Top 20), but that popularity did not translate itself into wholesale dissatisfaction with the BBC's music policy until 1964, when a rash of "pirate stations" broke out, broadcasting unlicensed from ships moored just outside territorial waters. The pirates introduced an American style of disk jockey to an enthusiastic British audience.

Beneath the surface there was an unprecedented amount of popular musical activity. The steadily increasing popularity of the dance-hall as a venue for "sweet Saturday night" created a demand for bands at a local level. The existence of such bands was in large measure the product of a short-lived skiffle boom. This hybrid of American blues and folk music and British music hall was an offshoot of the fashion for traditional jazz ("trad") of the mid- and late fifties. It had three important consequences: it gave a considerable push to the evolving process of musical

▲ "Beatlemania" entered the language after the crowd scenes that followed the group's *Palladium* show in October 1963. These unprecedented displays of hysteria were greeted by a widespread incomprehension, but expressed a special sense of belonging. The appearance of badges and other fan club symbols confirmed this underlying message. A whole sub-industry of miniatures and similar icons began to appear. American standoffishness to the Beatles' music and its attendant paraphernalia melted with their arrival on American soil in February 1964, an occasion which marked a decisive shift in the fortunes of British popular culture abroad (opposite above).

"democratization"; it raised the guitar to pre-eminence; and it introduced a direct link to the roots of black American music.

One further reason for rock 'n' roll's fading into entertainment had been that British listeners had no means of recognizing, let alone comprehending, the context within American culture from which it sprang, and therefore heard it in a vacuum. By the early sixties, however, skiffle had led many to an interest in black rhythm & blues, often via records brought over by sailors and American servicemen. From this they began to form a sense of the depth, significance and vitality of Afro-American musical culture, and of the unexplored potential within rock 'n' roll.

The surge of British "beat" music which followed the meteoric rise of the Beatles (from number 19 in the charts in December 1962 to unchallenged supremacy by the late summer of 1963) was greeted with much national wonderment on all sides; the grassroots activity which lay behind it had passed unobserved. This outbreak of energy and creativity from overlooked people in ignored regions – notably Liverpool and Newcastle – suggested that the country might still be alive after all.

The new music overwhelmed the British teenagers. As well as transforming the British Top 20, it engendered a spate of hysterical enthusiasm from the public – musicians such as the Beatles were greeted by screaming teenage girls every time they were seen in public. "Beatlemania" may, in part, have been generated by the popular press. But its chief importance lies in the fact that for the first time girls took a leading role in the formation of popular culture. British girls had not enjoyed the same opportunities as their American counterparts to participate in creating and enjoying the stardom of their heroes. For them, "the sounds of pop were deeply associated with a largely 'bedroom culture' of pin-ups and a Dansette record-player". Beatlemania not only permitted this adulation to come into the open, it also provided girls with the chance to impose themselves in some way upon events around them.

In the wake of the Beatles, pop music held center stage in fashionable culture for the first time. But as it did so other groups were emerging from deeper explorations of rhythm & blues with a more profoundly unsettling music. The Rolling Stones, the Animals and others appealed to a wide section of the youth audience who felt that society's cuddly adoption of the Beatles and "beat" had undermined the element of opposition which was fundamental to the music. On the other side, sentinels ever on watch for moral degeneration began to clear their throats at the

▲ Society's trick of adopting what threatens it could not be repeated with the Rolling Stones. The arrogant sexuality of Mick Jagger and the erotic message of a song like *Satisfaction* (1965) went beyond ready assimilation. Even when held in check for television audiences, it could cause a riot in the studio.

► The brilliance of Jimi Hendrix's guitar would have set him apart even within the context of black music. By moving into rock, he opened up a unique opportunity: to integrate his innovative, blues-derived, technique with the possibilities offered by rock technology. The results were astonishing. But for Hendrix himself the tensions of being a black superstar were tragically destructive: he died of a drugs overdose in 1970.

Stones' way of mixing middle-class bohemianism with a troubling and arrogant display of very un-British eroticism.

Britain and California conquer the world

The Beatles-led British invasion of American airwaves and record stores in the 1960s influenced all aspects of the American popular music scene. In Britain and the United States, few towns were without their amateur groups, almost all of whom attempted to write some of their own material. Self-penned songs were unusual for the mainstream of popular music, but held no fears for folk revivalists; what struck them most forcibly was the immense, unsuspected capacity of this new form of rock 'n' roll for personal expression.

The greatest impact of British music may not have been on "creative artists", however, but on the music industry. The industry had grown bored with the popular-music scene in the early 1960s. The Beatles in particular reawakened its interest. The reinvigoration of popular music recording brought with it a search for new ways of marketing, and a scramble for new performers to meet the demand. The Beatles pioneered the idea that the long-playing record (LP) should be more than a discrete collection of unrelated songs. This encouraged the industry to move much of its popular music production into that area – a shift

▼ However much rock might attract ideas of revolution, put on a California beach it seemed merely part of a fun 'n' health program. Even the exiled London bus, a hostage to the demand for "authentic" British culture, helped surfers to ride the waves, not make them.

made permanent a little later in the decade by the arrival of the "concept album" (usually attributed to *Sergeant Pepper's Lonely Hearts Club Band* – 1967). And the simple but effective notion of reducing the traditional number of tracks (and hence the royalties) meant that LPs could be sold at the same price but bring in more revenue for the music industry.

To an audience that took its music with a growing seriousness, the LP was confirmation of the status of that music. It also proved particularly attractive to the ever-increasing number of FM (frequency modulation) radio stations in the United States. This system of broadcasting, conceived in 1933, was based on a fuller range of frequency than AM (amplitude modulation), and was characterized by its ability to filter out intruding noises. Finally taking hold in the 1960s, FM stations steadily grew in number, helped by several related factors such as the introduction of stereo sound in about 1960 (stereo systems soon came complete with FM); the consequent improvement in LP quality; and the adoption of the LP for rock records. Beginning in San Francisco, FM stations became closely associated with "progressive" rock.

California dreamin'

It was to California that the focus of musical attention shifted in the middle of the decade. The state had a laid-back image, at a time when ex-Harvard professor Timothy Leary was extolling the virtues of turning on, tuning in, and dropping out with the aid of hallucinogenic drugs, but this was only partly responsible. The tradition of racially integrated audiences on the West Coast had produced a rich undercurrent of musical culture, out of which emerged the only "indigenous" music that could rival British beat in its ability to inject new life into popular music.

The relaxed, celebratory nature of "surf music", as purveyed by bands such as the Beach Boys, seemed deplorably hedonistic beside the tense concern of the "folkies" in New York's Greenwich Village, but surf music, like British beat, demonstrated the vitality of the country's musical traditions, and the rich possibilities still within them for the development of distinctive styles. One important feature of the West Coast scene was the role of the record producer. The work of Phil Spector in particular gave the producer unprecedented significance, and created a core of session musicians with a wealth of hard-earned experience. These factors, and the West Coast's film and entertainment industry (and its dollars) all encouraged the westward migration of American musicians.

The emergence and fate of the counter-culture in California's two major cities, Los Angeles and San Francisco, and its spread across much of the nation, has been much discussed. Music was consistently to the forefront of this complex of esthetic, political and social aspirations, where mysticism rubbed shoulders with revolution, where a sharply focused anti-materialism was allied with a much fuzzier, drug-induced belief in the ease of "self-discovery". And although the counter-culture asserted its dislike of commerce, the

◄ Girl groups such as the Ronettes were often seen later in the decade as being merely a pop representation of black femininity. But they showed again how blacks could take on an aspect of the mainstream "game" – in this case an artless teenage glamor – and simply do it better.

▲ With the appearance of Janis Joplin a remarkable reversal had taken place: black girls now had command of showbiz glamor, and a white girl sang the blues. Part of Joplin's achievement was in countering stereotypes of femininity, claiming sexuality as a common denominator, not the exclusive right of the beautiful. Nonetheless her music relived the familiar blues singer's paradox of assertiveness and suffering.

Soul and Tamla Motown

"Soul" – by the late fifties the word had a rich resonance in black society. As the fervent optimism and vocal intensity of gospel was joined with the secular energy of r & b, a powerful idiom emerged in which individual expression and the social activity of dance combined. Songs like Otis Redding's *Respect* – especially as performed by Aretha Franklin – or James Brown's *Say It Loud* took the music into a more political area.

Commercial confidence was vital, too, and no-one showed this better than Berry Gordy, Jr. His Motown company, formed in 1960 and based in Detroit, not only pioneered black ownership in the music business, but operated a system of in-house production which ensured that all stages of a record's life remained within the company's control. The Tamla Motown "sound", epitomized by the Supremes and the Four Tops, was patronizingly described as "pop-soul"; Motown was too inventive, however, to be constrained as a mere hybrid of black music and white commerce.

involvement of music, musicians and record companies soon compromised this stance.

Los Angeles provided the first venue for the familiar encounter between music and business in its new guise. Though a little slow to begin, the city's record companies soon recognized the market potential of "folk rock", following the success in 1965 of the Byrds' distinctive studio-sound version of Dylan's *Mr Tambourine Man*. In late 1965 *Variety* magazine coined a celebrated headline, "Folk + Rock + Protest = Dollars". The trend was epitomized by the contrived "protest" of the chart-topping single *Eve of Destruction* by Barry MacGuire in 1965. Record companies eagerly followed such successes and musicians could begin to look for what they had admired in the Beatles, that combination of creative independence and financial reward. But Los Angeles moguls had other strings to their bows: before long they marketed the Monkees – a family version of the Beatles for television consumption. Concurrent with rock's growing sense of maturity and independence, the Monkees' fame was a reminder of the continuing importance of the teenage pop market.

Farther up the coast, meanwhile, San Francisco maintained a certain disdain for the material culture that so exercised Los Angeles. The absence of record-company involvement in the music scene there permitted San Francisco's music to develop along its own, less market-conscious lines. Crucially, in the words of critic Dave Laing: "The San Francisco musicians worked from a sense that they were part of something more significant than an entertainment industry." In dances and, especially, in multi-media light shows, music's sense of community was joined to psychedelia, the visual and aural experiences paralleling those obtained from the newly popular (and still legal, until 1967) drug, LSD.

By early 1967, with no small contribution from the news media, the San Francisco area was being celebrated as the center of the new lifestyle. "Flower-power", that intoxicating antithesis to all that was conventional, attracted would-be hippies from all over, and also had a sweet smell of dollars to a record industry not averse to striking an anti-Establishment stance. There was a price to pay on both sides. Never before had record companies granted their performers such latitude; never had they laid their own principles open to mockery. Yet for the performer there was no escaping the fact that, try as the companies might to seem streetwise and create the illusion of shining revolutionary ideals, to sign up with a record company was fundamentally to join the "system".

It was nevertheless intriguing that the major companies went as far as they did. The counter-culture was essentially a movement of and for the middle-class male. Its ideas of liberation, especially when crudely understood as "from work, for sex", struck resonant chords across a broad spectrum of American male society, whose members sought to take advantage of the freedoms being won by the counter-culture.

The middle-class nature of the movement is also evident in the development of two closely related ideas and practices: rock music as art, and

rock criticism. As musicians' solos grew more ambitious, and their lyrics more involved, it became obvious that there was a role for the interpreter, outside the existing trade and fan magazines. Rock criticism grew out of the "underground press", which had developed a profound mistrust of the commercial and had singled out rock as expressing most clearly the ideals of the youth movement. As practised in the newly founded journals such as *Rolling Stone* and *Creem*, it operated at least partly on a circular argument: rock's growing seriousness made criticism necessary, and criticism's existence proved rock's seriousness. The step from "serious" to "art" was a small one, especially when aided by the well-known parallel between the esthetics of modern bohemianism and those of the 19th-century Romantics, whose revolutionary achievements in art, politics and life criticism had been enshrined sky-high.

The academic study of popular music, while often bedeviled by the contradictions implied in much sixties' rock criticism, owes it many debts. Not least is that of having articulated the links between culture and politics. On the public level, this connection was made most clearly by the responses of the counter-culture to the Vietnam War (and especially to police intimidation of demonstrators) and to the continuing racial unrest. Short-

▲ Indian classical musician Ravi Shankar's first impact on Western music was on jazz rather than rock. But it was through his involvement with rock that he and the sitar became well known, and this marked an important early stage in the opening up of Western ears to "world" music. Rock's first attempts to incorporate Indian music, as evidenced by the Beatles' *Norwegian Wood* (1965) were made without any direct contact with Indian musicians or understanding of the music's meaning. Shankar taught Beatle George Harrison, and brought a greater proficiency to his subsequent use of Indian music, but the approach remained superficial and made Shankar and other Indian musicians uneasy.

lived though these responses were, they pointed to a breakdown of the barrier that had traditionally separated politics from life. "The personal had become political", and this was a profound achievement for the counter-culture of the 1960s.

Rocking round the world

The counter-culture was not confined to California; and many of the most dramatic political moments of the radical politics were seen in Europe. Rock music played its role in this movement, though its position was still rarely clear cut. One unifying factor, however, behind the protests of students around the world was their hostility to the United States' involvement in the war in Vietnam, and the young in Europe looked primarily to America to supply the images and music of the alternative politics.

As British music continued to develop a status equivalent to that of America, the sixties saw the domination of the English language as the *lingua franca* of the the youth culture. French and German bands sang in English as often as in their own languages, and adopted the model of Anglo-American rock in preference to indigenous popular music. The rock festival, developed in the United States as an experiment in alternative living centered around rock music, was likewise imported wholesale into Europe.

◄▲ By 1967 "rock" had consciously distanced itself from "pop". It even mounted an invasion of Broadway, the nudity of the musical *Hair* signaling rock's confidence in its "inner" qualities. That confidence, visible also in the ascendancy of the LP, was founded in large part on the increasing representation of recording-studio technology (though the effects on *Sergeant Pepper* itself were achieved by producer George Martin's prizing of nine tracks out of a four-track machine). The other source of confidence was the musicians' growing ability to develop and sustain more grandiose ideas. In the blues-based improvizations of Cream and the "space rock" of Pink Floyd (concert image) the late sixties saw this tendency at its most effective.

ROCK FESTIVALS

For a few years, the large, outdoor rock festival – an idea borrowed from the tradition of folk and jazz festivals begun in the 1950s and from San Francisco's "human be-in" gatherings or "happenings" – became a symbolic expression of the counter-culture. The Monterey Festival of June 1967, usually seen as the first, set both the musical and the idealistic tone. The effect of so much good music, from Jefferson Airplane to Jimi Hendrix, was confirmation of rock's stature: fees were kept low and profits were donated to charity, thus giving musicians, audiences and organizers a sense of common cause.

But from the start the festivals were asked to carry the ideals of fraternal community while in part their actual effect worked against that concept. The very act of exposing San Francisco's most idealistic musicians to wider audiences planted the seeds for the break-up of that musical community. And each succeeding festival witnessed to some degree the uneasy co-existence of distant visions, anticipated political upheaval and immediate marketing hard-sell.

In the mind of the general public the festivals provided clear evidence of the threat posed by a radical youth movement. It was not just their political rhetoric, nor the widespread use of drugs; it was the sheer weight of numbers.

The sixties' largest festival took place at Woodstock in upstate New York on 15–17 August 1969, with an estimated attendance of 450,000. Despite all predictions of catastrophe the occasion provided an overwhelming display of camaraderie, and in doing so gave its name to a generation. It was also an enormous financial undertaking, with substantial payments to the performers setting them apart from their "brothers and sisters" in the audience. The organizers claimed Woodstock made them bankrupt, but after all the assets were counted, including film and record rights, it seems likely to have yielded a handsome profit.

Woodstock raised hopes of a new beginning. But by the end of the year, the "dream" seemed over. Widespread violence occurred at the Altamont Festival in December, and a youth was knifed to death during a Rolling Stones performance. This was taken as an assault on the very spirit of the counter-culture itself.

But in the course of time idealism re-surfaced. Wedded to political causes with wider popular support it shaped a festival where, with the benefit of global communications hook-ups, frustration with the prevailing ideology of self-interest could find positive expression. In this sense Live Aid, the 1985 trans-world concert to raise money to combat famine in Ethiopia, seemed to many the true inheritor of the spirit of Woodstock. To others it seemed to have inherited the paradoxes of the festivals, and added new ones. In this view the implausibility of rock stars and the music business displaying genuine altruism was compounded by the belief that rock and pop's very existence as a capitalist phenomenon made it part of the reason for the famine in the first place.

▲ The natural imagery beloved of festival-goers was taken to represent peace and love. Linked with magic, it provided another metaphor. Summoning up a witchdoctor, if not intentionally, invoked one of rationalism's oldest adversaries.

► Given fair weather, open-air venues provided ideal settings for the growth of a sense of community. Outside the constraints of the concert hall, too, one could believe that both the music and the new spirit knew no boundaries.

▼ The counter-culture's links with the "Beat" generation was evident in the presence of poets such as Allen Ginsberg at San Francisco "human be-ins" in 1967. Ginsberg's aim "to let my imagination go, open secrecy and scribble magic lines from my real mind" found a sympathetic response.

GM RECORDS AND TAPES *The Home...*

▲ Technology could never quite capture the feeling of "what it was like" to attend a festival, but it could, and did, help spread the word about them. To festival organizers the camera's presence sometimes had more to do with money than messages.

▲ One month before Woodstock, in July 1969, the Rolling Stones played a free concert in London's Hyde Park, featuring Ginger Johnson's African Drummers (left). The spirit of the event was encapsulated in the release of hundreds of butterflies, in memory of former Stone Brian Jones. Less than six months later the Stones gave another free concert, but this time in response to allegations of greed and overpricing during their US tour. The notorious event, at Altamont Raceway in California in December 1969, was marked by violence and, finally, the murder by Hell's Angels (nominally in charge of security) of a young black man in the audience, Meredith Hunter (above).

THE GLOBAL VILLAGE?

Time Chart

	1974	1975	1976	1977	1978	1979	1980
Film	• Release of *Blazing Saddles*, directed by Mel Brooks • *Chinatown* released, directed by Roman Polanski and starring Jack Nicholson and Faye Dunaway (USA) • *Phantom of Liberty* released, directed by Luis Bunuel (Sp)	• Audiences screamed at *Jaws*, Steven Spielberg's shark blockbuster (USA) • Release of *One Flew Over the Cuckoo's Nest*, directed by Milos Forman and starring Jack Nicholson (USA) • Release of *Picnic At Hanging Rock*, directed by Peter Weir (Aus)	• Release of *Rocky*, the first vehicle for Sylvester Stallone (USA) • Robert de Niro and Jodie Foster starred in *Taxi Driver*, directed by Martin Scorsese (USA)	• Release of Woody Allen's *Annie Hall*, starring Diane Keaton (USA) • *Close Encounters of the Third Kind* released, directed by Steven Spielberg (USA) • Release of the blockbuster *Star Wars*, directed by George Lucas (USA)	• Release of *Grease* (director, Randal Kleiser) starring John Travolta • Release of two films about the Vietnam war, *Coming Home*, directed by Hal Ashby, and *The Deer Hunter*, directed by Michael Cimino (USA) • *Superman* released, directed by Clive Donner (USA)	• Release of Woody Allen's *Manhattan* (USA) • *Nosferatu the Vampyre* released, directed by Werner Herzog (Ger) • Release of *Apocalypse Now*, directed by Francis Ford Coppola (USA) • First *Mad Max* film released, directed by George Miller (Aus)	• Release of *Kagemusha*, directed by Akira Kurosawa (Jap) • *The Elephant Man* released, directed by David Lynch and starring John Hurt (UK) • Nov: Steve McQueen died of cancer
Media		• *Barney Miller* began on ABC TV (USA) • *Fawlty Towers* first shown (UK)	• Derek Jacobi and Sian Phillips starred in the TV serial *I, Claudius* (UK) • *Dynasty* premiere (USA)	• CB radio had become a craze (USA) • Jan: Rupert Murdoch (Aus) bought New York Magazine Co. (including *Village Voice*) and *New York Post* • 1 Feb: Audience of 80 million watched the last episode of *Roots* (USA)	• *Holocaust* drew a massive TV audience (USA) • Sep: *Dallas* TV soap opera premiere (USA)		• NBC mini-series *Shogun* shown (USA) • *Dallas* episode revealing who shot JR broke viewing records (USA) • ITV feature *Death of a Princess*, concerning Saudi Arabia, provoked a political storm (UK)
Music	• Swedish group Abba shot to international stardom after winning the Eurovision Song Contest	• Reggae star Bob Marley came to fame with his *Natty Dread* album (Jam) • Bruce Springsteen emerged as a star with *Born to Run* (USA) • Disco music became popular (USA)	• Dec: Release of the first punk rock single (UK)	• 16 Aug: Elvis Presley died aged 42 (USA) • The Sex Pistols' concerts banned from TV (UK) • *Saturday Night Fever*, sound-track album from the movie starring John Travolta, a worldwide bestseller	• Police's first album released (UK) • *Wuthering Heights* brought fame to Kate Bush (UK) • Opening of *Evita*, a musical about Eva Peron, by Tim Rice and Andrew Lloyd-Webber (UK)	• 1 Jan: The first digital recording in the UK • 2 Feb: Sex Pistols member Sid Vicious died of a heroin overdose (UK) • Elvis Costello became internationally famous with his third album • Release of Dire Straits' first single (UK)	• Electronic music popular, with Gary Numan its best-known exponent • 8 Dec: John Lennon shot outside his hotel by a deranged fan; hundreds gathered there in a candlelight vigil (USA)
Fashion and Design	• The Volkswagen Golf created by designer Giorgio Giugiaro (It) • Vivienne Westwood and Malcolm McLaren renamed their Kings Road shop, selling fetish fantasy rubberwear, Sex (UK) • Jeff Banks established the Warehouse Utility clothing chain (UK)	• Bic's disposable razor was marketed in the UK • LCDs for calculators and timepieces marketed for first time by BDH (UK) • London Designer Collections founded to promote young UK designers • Japanese fashion designer Kansai Yamamoto's Paris debut (Fr)	• The Canon AE-1 was the first camera with micro-processor-controlled exposure (Jap) • The Apple computer was created in a Californian garage (USA) • Summer: Punk emerged on the streets of London (UK) • 22,000 saw the Fly With Issey Miyake fashion show (Jap)	• Westwood and McLaren's shop renamed Seditionaries; it was the first to sell punk clothes (UK) • Ralph Lauren created casual layered chic with his costumes for Diane Keaton in *Annie Hall* (USA)	• Designer Jasper Conran launched his own label (UK)	• Sony Walkman launched (Jap) • Braun's ET55 calculator designed, in white, by Dieter Rams (Ger) • The term "Sloane Ranger" first used, in *Harpers & Queen* magazine (UK)	• Street style magazine *The Face* first published (UK) • New York women began to wear training shoes with their business suits (USA) • Azzedine Alaïa's body-hugging camp designs for women first seen in Paris (Fr)
Sport	• 6 Jan: Power cuts led to the first ever Sunday professional football match (UK) • Triathlon (swimming, cycling, and running) created in the USA	• 21 Jun: First World Cup cricket tournament, at Lords, won by the West Indies (UK) • Jun: Soccer star Pele (Bra) signed a three-year $7-million contract with the New York Cosmos (USA) • 9 Sep: Martina Navratilova (Cze) requested political asylum in the USA	• Feb: Innsbruck Winter Olympics, where British skater John Curry won gold with his innovative balletic style (Aut) • 17 Jul: Montreal Olympics opened (Can); most African athletes boycotted them because the IOC refused to discipline New Zealand for its sporting links with South Africa	• 2 Apr: Women allowed to ride in the Grand National; Red Rum became the first horse to win it three times (UK)	• 15 Feb: Leon Spinks (USA) was the first boxer to take the world heavyweight title from Muhammad Ali (Cassius Clay) • May: Ryder Cup competition now included European golfers as well as US, UK and Irish • Aug: First balloon crossing of the Atlantic made by three Americans	• 9 Feb: Soccer player Trevor Francis signed with Nottingham Forest in the first million-pound transfer (UK) • 17 Aug: Sebastian Coe became the first man to hold the 800m, 1500m, and mile world records simultaneously (UK) • 21 Oct: Grete Waitz (Nor) became the first woman to run the New York Marathon in under 2½ hours (USA)	• 12 Feb: Lake Placid Winter Olympics opened (USA) • 5 Jul: Bjorn Borg (Swe) became the first man to win five successive Wimbledon titles (UK) • 19 Jul: Moscow Olympics opened, boycotted by Kenya, W Germany and USA over the Soviet invasion of Afghanistan (USSR)
Misc.	• 9 Aug: Richard Nixon became the first US president to resign		• The town of Seveso was evacuated after an accident at a chemical plant (It)		• Birth of the first "test-tube" baby (UK) • John Paul II became the first non-Italian pope for 455 years	• 3 May: Margaret Thatcher became the first female prime minister in Europe	• The World Health Organization announced the eradication of smallpox

1981	1982	1983	1984	1985	1986	1987	1988
• *Chariots of Fire*, directed by Hugh Hudson, heralded a boom in the British film industry • Release of *Raiders of the Lost Ark*, directed by Steven Spielberg and starring Harrison Ford (USA) • Release of *Reds*; Warren Beatty directed and starred (USA)	• Release of *ET*, directed by Steven Spielberg (USA) • *Gandhi* released, directed by Richard Attenborough; Ben Kingsley starred (UK) • 10 Sep: Princess Grace of Monaco (Grace Kelly) died after a car crash	• Release of *The Year of Living Dangerously*, directed by Peter Weir (Aus) • *Terms of Endearment* released, directed by Richard Brooks and starring Shirley MacLaine and Jack Nicholson (USA)	• *A Passage to India* released (director, David Lean) (UK) • Release of *The Killing Fields*, directed by Roland Joffe (UK) • *1984*, directed by Michael Radford, was Richard Burton's last film (UK)	• Release of *Out of Africa*, starring Meryl Streep and Robert Redford (USA) • Release of John Boorman's Brazilian rainforest movie, *The Emerald Forest* (USA)	• Release of Woody Allen's *Hannah and Her Sisters*, starring Barbara Hershey, Mia Farrow and Michael Caine (USA) • Tarkovsky's *The Sacrifice* released (USSR) • 8 Apr: Clint Eastwood elected Mayor of Carmel (USA)	• Jack Nicholson played the Devil in *The Witches of Eastwick*, directed by George Miller (USA) • *Crocodile Dundee* released (director Peter Faiman) bringing international fame to Paul Hogan (Aus)	• Release of Wim Wenders' *Wings of Desire*, with Bruno Ganz (Ger) • Animation and live actors mixed in *Who Framed Roger Rabbit?*, starring Bob Hoskins (USA)
• *Hill Street Blues* won the Emmy for outstanding drama series (USA) • Philips introduced the first compact disc player (Neth)	• *Barney Miller* won the Emmy for outstanding comedy series (USA)	• A record 125 million watched the last episode of *M*A*S*H* (USA) • 20 Nov: TV film *The Day After*, on the effects of nuclear attack (USA)	• *The Cosby Show* entered the TV ratings at no. 6 (USA) • 12 Aug: President Reagan joked about "nuking" Russia in a microphone test, unaware that he was being broadcast (USA)	• 13 Jul: 1.5 billion worldwide watched the Live Aid concert to raise money for famine victims in Ethiopia (USA, UK) • 12 Dec: General Electric announced they would buy RCA (USA)			
• Bruce Springsteen emerged as a major star with his UK tour • Opening of *Cats*, by Tim Rice and Andrew Lloyd-Webber (UK) • 11 May: Bob Marley (Jam) died aged 36, of a brain tumor (USA)	• "Rap" became popular and increased in sophistication (USA, UK)		• Michael Jackson's *Thriller* album sold over 37 million (USA) • Prince's album *Purple Rain* was a bestseller (USA) • 1 Apr: Marvin Gaye shot dead by his father (USA)	• 13 Jul: Live Aid raised £40 million • 31 Dec: Ricky Nelson died in a plane crash aged 45 (USA)	• Paul Simon used black South African musicians on his album *Graceland* (USA)	• Popularity of Youssou n'Dour and others marked an upsurge of interest in pure African music	• Jul: Many world-famous rock stars played in a concert for Nelson Mandela's 70th birthday (UK)
• Memphis design studio started by Ettore Sottsass Jnr (It) • Japan Design Foundation's first annual international festival held in Osaka (Jap) • David and Elizabeth Emmanuel designed Lady Diana Spencer's wedding dress (UK)	• Innovative fashion designer Gianni Versace used lasers to seam rubber and leather (It) • The XA Olympus camera was given Japan's G-mark award	• Chanel's new design director Karl Lagerfeld began to modernize her style (Fr) • Former architect Rifat Ozbek (Tur) showed his first fashion collection in London (UK) • Singer Madonna showed her navel and wore underwear as outerwear (USA)	• Katherine Hamnett's collection was inspired by women's anti-nuclear protests at Greenham Common (UK) • Body Map put male models in skirts (UK) • John Galliano's Les Incroyables fashion degree show brought him instant success (UK)	• Sharp's QT50 pastel-colored radio cassette player was the first Japanese "lifestyle" product to reach the West • Interior designer Eva Jiricna (Cze/UK) gave Harrods' Way-In boutique industrial chic (UK)	• London's "young fogies" bought secondhand classics from Hacketts (UK)		
	• 19 Mar: 15 UK cricket players who made a "rebel" South African tour were banned from international cricket for 3 years • May: Footballer Diego Maradona (Arg) bought by Barcelona for £5 million (Sp) • Jun: Cocaine usage threatened US professional football, warned the National Football League	• Aug: First world athletic championships held in Helsinki (Fin) • 26 Sep: Australia II (skipper, John Bertrand) became the first boat to take the Americas Cup from the New York Yacht Club (USA)	• 7 Feb: Opening of Winter Olympics in Sarajevo (Yug) • Apr: South African runner Zola Budd joined the British Olympic team • 28 Jul-8 Aug: Los Angeles Olympics, boycotted by most of the Eastern Bloc; Carl Lewis (USA) won four gold medals	• 29 May: 41 people died at Heysel Stadium, Brussels, as a result of British soccer hooliganism (Bel) • Jun: UEFA (United European Football Associations) banned British soccer clubs from Europe indefinitely	• Jul: South Africans Zola Budd and Annette Cowley were banned from the Commonwealth Games (UK)	• Jun: New Zealand All Blacks won the first Rugby Union World Cup • Aug: Canadian Ben Johnson broke the 100m world record • Dec: English cricket tour of Pakistan threatened after a row between captain Mike Gatting and Pakistani umpire Shakoor Rana	• Jan: Winter Olympics held in Edmonton (Can) • 20 Sep: Seoul Olympics were the largest yet; athletics overshadowed by drug scandal surrounding Canadian sprinter Ben Johnson (Kor)
• 29 Jul: Wedding of the Prince of Wales and Lady Diana Spencer (UK)	• Argentina invaded the Falklands, and Britain declared war	• Lech Walesa was awarded the Nobel Peace Prize (Pol)	• 31 Oct: Prime Minister Indira Gandhi was assassinated by two Sikhs from her security guard (Ind)	• 11 Mar: Mikhail Gorbachev elected Soviet prime minister • Sep: The World Health Organization declared AIDS an epidemic	• 28 Jan: Challenger space shuttle exploded on take-off (USA) • Apr: Nuclear accident at Chernobyl (USSR)		• 50,000 killed and more made homeless by an earthquake in Armenia

Datafile

Diversification and conglomeration dominated the media after 1974. As broadcasting became internationalized, ownership of the media became concentrated in fewer hands. In 1983 one analyst identified "the 50 corporations that control what America sees, hears and reads." Four years later, that number had fallen to 22. Complex multimedia empires, observing neither national boundaries nor distinctions between the media, grew up. By the mid-1970s television viewing in the West had reached something close to saturation level; there simply was no more time available for people to do it. In response, producers began to target programs more closely at particular segments of the audience.

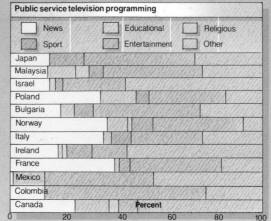

Public service television programming

Legend: News, Sport, Educational, Entertainment, Religious, Other

Japan, Malaysia, Israel, Poland, Bulgaria, Norway, Italy, Ireland, France, Mexico, Colombia, Canada

Percent — 0, 20, 40, 60, 80, 100

◄ Public service television is defined very differently around the world. Public service television came under attack in the 1980s from Western governments enthusiastic to deregulate the airwaves. In part this enthusiasm was ideological, but it also had to do with the economics of broadcasting. Satellite and cable greatly increased the hardware costs of television, forcing program-makers to keep costs down. Public service broadcasters had to follow suit, and programs for minority interests became early victims of ratings wars.

Academy Awards for Best Film of the Year

1974	*The Godfather Part II*	Paramount
1975	*One Flew Over the Cuckoo's Nest*	United Artists
1976	*Rocky*	United Artists
1977	*Annie Hall*	United Artists
1978	*The Deerhunter*	Universal
1979	*Kramer vs. Kramer*	Columbia
1980	*Ordinary People*	Paramount
1981	*Chariots of Fire*	Columbia
1982	*Gandhi*	Columbia
1983	*Terms of Endearment*	Paramount
1984	*Amadeus*	Orion
1985	*Out of Africa*	Universal
1986	*Platoon*	Rank
1987	*The Last Emperor*	Columbia

► In 1981, 137 countries had television services. The price American companies charged a foreign television service for its programs was indicative of how widespread television was in that country. Western Europe and Japan were prize markets, but selling cheaply to the small markets in the Third World created demand for American work that would grow.

▼ India still produced more than double the films of any other nations in the years around 1980, and Asia in general accounted for half the world's film output.

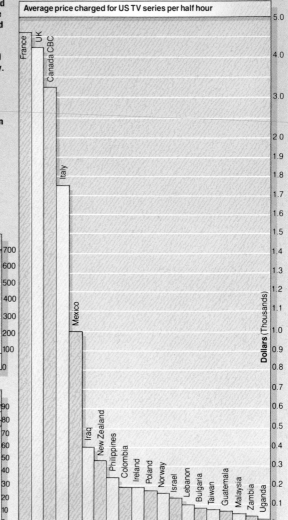

Average price charged for US TV series per half hour

Dollars (Thousands): 5.0, 4.0, 3.0, 2.0, 1.9, 1.8, 1.7, 1.6, 1.5, 1.4, 1.3, 1.2, 1.1, 1.0, 0.9, 0.8, 0.7, 0.6, 0.5, 0.4, 0.3, 0.2, 0.1, 0

France, UK, Canada CBC, Italy, Mexico, Iraq, New Zealand, Philippines, Colombia, Ireland, Poland, Norway, Israel, Lebanon, Bulgaria, Taiwan, Guatemala, Malaysia, Zambia, Uganda

▲ The Academy Award-winning films in the second half of the 1970s and 1980s showed more dissimilarities than similarities. The two most successful filmmakers of the period, George Lucas and Steven Spielberg, remained unrecognized by the Academy, which looked to reward films which would enhance the status of American cinema rather than pack more 12-year-olds into the box office. Most of the Oscar-winning films were shaped around one or two central dramatic performances and it became the norm for the year's Best Picture to also win two or three of the other major awards — best director, best actor or actress. The awards came to represent the Hollywood establishment's best opinion of itself.

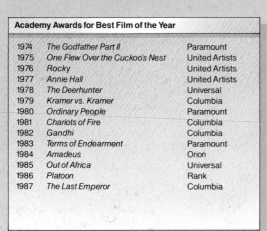

Annual feature film production 1975-85

Films: 700, 600, 500, 400, 300, 200, 100, 0

India, Japan, France, USA, Taiwan, Turkey, Philippines, USSR, Italy, Thailand, Hong Kong, Spain

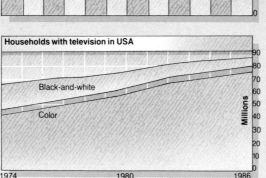

Households with television in USA

Black-and-white, Color

Millions: 90, 80, 70, 60, 50, 40, 30, 20, 10, 0

1974, 1980, 1986

► Cable television and home video recorders offered more viewing choice. Cable usually meant channels devoted to children's programs, news, sports or pornography. Video freed the viewer from the tyranny of the schedule: it was used for showing rented or bought movies, or for recording broadcast programs to be watched at a more convenient time.

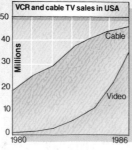

VCR and cable TV sales in USA

Cable, Video

Millions: 50, 40, 30, 20, 10, 0

1980, 1986

▲ ► In 1983 there were 790 television sets per thousand viewers in the United States, and two radios for every American. The richer and more developed the country, the more widespread was the reception of media, and, with a few exceptions such as Britain, the greater the number of channels. The more TV sets there were, the longer people spent viewing.

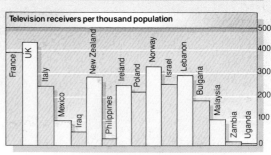

Television receivers per thousand population

500, 400, 300, 200, 100, 0

France, UK, Italy, Mexico, Iraq, New Zealand, Philippines, Ireland, Poland, Norway, Israel, Lebanon, Bulgaria, Malaysia, Zambia, Uganda

MEDIA IMPERIALISM

The later 1970s and 1980s saw a revolution in the technology of broadcasting and the distribution of the visual media. This revolution – involving video-cassette recording, satellite television and high-definition television – remained fixed firmly within the world of consumption rather than enlarging the possibilities of more democratic media production. The vast majority of affordable video equipment is used either to replace 8mm film for home movies, or for watching pre-recorded video cassettes; few took advantage of the simplicity of making videos to get their message to a wider audience than before. The paradox of media development during the 1970s and 1980s is that while the choices of what, how and when to consume have increased greatly, media ownership has been increasingly concentrated into the hands of a small group, and profitability has been similarly concentrated. Nowhere demonstrates this more clearly than Hollywood, where the blockbuster phenomenon has grown ever more exaggerated.

Stability through blockbusting

Throughout the 1970s the six major American distributors reduced the number of movies made and concentrated their earnings on ever fewer

films. The share of the total film audience taken by the ten highest-grossing films increased by 250 percent during the decade. Publicity budgets rapidly expanded, often exceeding the production cost. More prints were made, but of fewer films, so that attendance was concentrated on those few films. Despite the enormous cash-flow figures of individual films and the occasional expensive miscalculation (such as Michael Cimino's *Heaven's Gate* in 1980), the blockbuster approach was designed to guarantee commercial stability. In the mid-1970s the major companies began to recognize the value of markets other than conventional distribution through cinemas, to the point where television sales in particular were often negotiated in advance of production, and their revenues

▼ *Star Wars* (1977), the most financially successful movie of all time, spawned an enormously profitable toy industry. By the time its sequel, *The Empire Strikes Back*, was released in 1980, the toy stores were already well stocked. Big-budget movies became part of "packages" which included books, toys, games and soundtrack albums.

WOODY ALLEN
DIANE KEATON
TONY ROBERTS
CAROL KANE
PAUL SIMON
JANET MARGOLIN
SHELLEY DUVALL
CHRISTOPHER WALKEN
COLLEEN DEWHURST

IO E LE DONNE
di WOODY ALLEN
"ANNIE HALL"

taken into account in calculating budgets. As the distribution companies developed into multi-media conglomerates, contemporary Hollywood came to deal in packaged "concepts" rather than films. Movies no longer exist as autonomous products, but are increasingly manufactured as one item in a multimedia package of paperback books, records, toys, and bubble gum. The status of the movie has been diminished by a need to compromise with the demands of other products. Producers have been obliged to consider the possibilities for exploitation as a series of linked but separate commodities, and assembling a production entails constructing a package of elements – stars, spectacle, sometimes directors – but seldom plot or theme – that seem likely to sell.

In the mid-1970s this tendency enhanced the influence of stars over production. As the studios disintegrated as production centers, the stars' independence and economic value correspondingly rose. In the industry's terminology, stars such as Paul Newman and Robert Redford, for instance, were "bankable", their presence critical to the raising of funds for a new project. Some of the more politically radical films of the 1970s were made through the involvement of a bankable star, notably in the collaboration of Newman with Robert Altman in *Buffalo Bill and the Indians* (1976). Hollywood seemed to be reexamining its cultural role, moving, in work such as Altman's, closer to the practices and ambiguities of style and content common in the European art cinema. Many of the commercial successes of the mid-1970s, such as *The Godfather*, were "revisionist" versions of staple cinematic genres, looking at traditional themes from a more critical viewpoint and adopting a cinematic language new to Hollywood for the purpose. The careers of film directors

Altman, Francis Ford Coppola, Martin Scorsese, and Sam Peckinpah suggested that this revisionism might produce a more radical American cinema, but consistent financial success eluded them, and the industry returned to conservatism again later in the decade.

In general, the failures of political radicalism and the disillusionment in the aftermath of Watergate contributed to a widespread abandonment of clear social objectives and encouraged the retreat into the self that is the most readily observable trait of American culture since 1974. For much of the seventies, films were obsessed with questions of identity. The obsessive concern with the self which has preoccupied American culture during the last two decades has replaced the sexual neuroses of orthodox Freudian psychology as the central cultural uncertainty, a fact reflected in Hollywood. Woody Allen's games with his persona – as in *Annie Hall* – left audiences persistently uncertain not only how they felt about the schlemiel with the dialog above his station, but how Allen himself felt about this character.

In the age of media saturation, film advertising could blur the boundaries of fiction and reality. The *Jaws* campaign orchestrated hysterical stories about shark sightings around the American coast in 1975 and the film's release led to increased hysteria about sharks that summer. When the Three Mile Island nuclear power-station alarm occured within days of the release of *The China Syndrome*, in 1979, many people (at least in California) initially took it to be a promotional stunt for the movie. This was just one example of an interplay between movie and reality: *Dog Day Afternoon*, based on an actual bank robbery, led to at least one imitation. *Taxi Driver* (1976) was in part based on the diaries of Arthur Bremer, who shot

▲▶ As Hollywood made fewer Westerns, the production of science-fiction films expanded. In the 1950s creatures from other worlds had been thinly disguised communists intent on world domination, but in Steven Spielberg's *Close Encounters of the Third Kind* (1977 and, in 1980, a re-edited "special edition") and *E.T.* (1982) the aliens were benign and even cuddly. The childish mysticism of these movies occasionally inspired fans to seek "close encounters" of their own – without any reported success.

◀▲ Woody Allen's wry, self-deprecating humor in films such as *Annie Hall* (1977) seemed to match the narcissism of the 1970s. The films starred Allen as an insecure neurotic making despondent jokes about the impossibility of sex and the inevitability of death; audiences were unsure whether they were autobiography or parody.

▶ Werner Herzog's *Fitzcarraldo* (1982), in which Klaus Kinski dragged a boat across the Peruvian Andes from one river to another, was one of the more exotic European films of the 1980s. German filmmakers were initially most successful in finding ways to live with television by making co-production deals.

Governor George Wallace in 1968; it provided the source of John Hinckley's infatuation with its star Jodie Foster – and in imitation of the film's central character, Hinckley shot United States' president Ronald Reagan.

The movie brats

From the mid-1970s the new bureacratic and corporate style of Hollywood combined with the enhancement of the status of the "director as superstar". In the work of Coppola, Scorsese, Steven Spielberg, George Lucas, Brian de Palma, William Friedkin and John Milius there appeared a body of films which demonstrated a "personal cinema" through their mannerisms yet also fueled the entertainment machine. Storytelling no longer mattered. Disaster movies demonstrated the packaging possibilities of incident without narrative – the plot of *The Towering Inferno* (1974) was summarized by one critic as, "A building catches fire, some people die, some people don't" – while the movie was sold on its spectacle and the array of stars who appeared in cameo roles. Later variants of the package took the phenomenon to even greater extremes. As the technology of special effects proliferated, the films that employed it did so at the expense of narrative complexity. One critic accused *Star Wars* of reducing "the rich philosophical possibilities of science fiction to a galactic pinball game," and the Disney Studios actually located its science fiction fantasy adventure *Tron* (1982) inside a computer video game.

The most successful of the new wave of "Movie Brat" directors, Spielberg and Lucas, were particularly attracted to fantasy forms, expressing a naive faith in space as the new frontier. In an increasingly conservative world, the *Star Wars* saga of a group of rebels restoring an old patriarchal order seemed appropriate. The late 1970s and 1980s saw several large-budget juvenile male fantasies such as *Superman – the Movie* (1978) and *Flash Gordon* (1980), which disguised their patriarchal attitudes with a veneer of knowing self-reflection. Other science-fiction films, such as *Alien* (1979), *Blade Runner* (1982) and *The Thing* (1982) owed their appeal more directly to the horror films of the early 1970s. Some critics argued that, in their brutal assault on their audience's sensibilities, films such as *The Texas Chainsaw Massacre* (1974) offered a critique of the patriarchal family as the monster in the American home, but few found much to defend in the "slasher" movies, which drew their prototype from *Friday the 13th* (1980), and alternated bouts of teenage sexual activity with the brutal destruction of those who engage in it. It was to teenagers themselves that these movies played most successfully.

The ironic, self-aware element in all these films, their willingness to step outside their fictions and disarm their spectators with a self-deprecating acknowledgement that no one is really supposed to take this seriously, has remained a persistent feature of Hollywood in the 1980s. The counterculture of the early 1970s was contained by the second half of the decade within a form of comedy that Hollywood took from television. The frenetic comic formula of many of the most

successful Hollywood films of the 1980s was inherited from the television of *Saturday Night Live* and *SCTV*, as were some of the most successful 1980s stars: John Belushi, Dan Ackroyd, Chevy Chase, Eddie Murphy. Their movies catered to the dominant American movie audience: young and mobile, preferring to find their entertainment in the smaller cinemas built in large numbers in suburban shopping malls.

Other critics saw in the horror cycle a response to the Vietnam War, which Hollywood was, at least for the war's duration, unable to address directly. Hollywood could not manufacture fictions about defeat on such a scale, any more than other areas of American life could easily accommodate the failure of the liberal technological dream in southeast Asia. Nevertheless, the trauma of Vietnam was reflected in the pervasive uncertainties of every aspect of film production in the decade, and more overtly in the recurrent appearance of heroic psychopaths who offered the simple solution of successful American violence to urban disorder. However ambivalent these heroic figures, such as Clint Eastwood's *Dirty Harry* Callaghan, appeared to be, their movies always showed the violent repression of disorder as successful.

When, at the end of the 1970s, Hollywood began to consider Vietnam nore directly, it was still ambivalent. Michael Cimino's *The Deerhunter* (1978) and Coppola's *Apocalypse Now* (1979) seemed to argue that anything undertaken in the name of survival was justified. During the 1980s it became possible almost to pretend that the war had not been lost. Sylvester Stallone emerged as the archetypal representative of the American white working class in the *Rocky* movies. His *Rambo* character directed the psychopathic individualism of the Clint Eastwood–Charles Bronson vigilante cop movies at the Vietnamese, who had demonstrated the inferiority of American technological heroism. Muscle-bound and loaded with military hardware, he went back to fight the war single-handed until he came out with the right result.

Amid the ironic and knowing films of the 1980s, *Rambo* was one of the few to take itself seriously, innocently proclaiming that might must be right. *Rambo* encouraged a second wave of movies about Vietnam, which, unlike the first, found ways to incorporate the war within something very close to the conventional rhetoric of the war-movie genre. *Platoon* (1986) and *Full Metal Jacket* (1987) resembled earlier war movies in telling stories of the sentimental education of young men under duress. The politics of the war itself, like the Vietnamese, were nowhere in sight.

After Vietnam real wars were treated differently in the media. Western democracies had learned significantly from the media coverage of Vietnam: whatever its effects were on the home population, no-one suggested that this coverage enhanced support for the war. When the British Task Force invaded the Falkland/Malvinas Islands in 1982, they did so without benefit of live television coverage. Preventing television journalists from reporting on the sinking of HMS Sheffield, an officer explained, "Don't you realize that you are

◄▲ After Vietnam, it was difficult to depict American heroes. Clint Eastwood's cop *Dirty Harry* (1971) looked like a hero but behaved like a psychopath (left). In *Taxi Driver*, (1976) Robert De Niro was a psychopath taken for a hero (above).

with us to do a 1940 propaganda job?" Such attitudes were by no means confined to the British military: German television, superior to the British system in terms of its accountability to the public and its representation of community interests, also came under increasing attack from Christian Democrats, long hostile to the concept of public service broadcasting.

Television and everyday life
Media analyst Marshall McLuhan once described television as lacking in intensity as a medium. Because television has become central to our domestic environment, it does not appear a very "heroic" medium; its most appreciated personalities celebrate their "normality". It is in its domesticity that it reveals its difference from the cinema, the appeal of whose stars always contained an element of the exotic. Television characters

seem most capable of generating audience identification when they are at their most mundane
and vulnerable, caught up in the predicaments
of everyday life. Whether nominally fictional or
not, television characters have become familiar
figures, inhabitants of our domestic environment,
and often more readily tolerated than those with
whom we actually share our lives. They rehearse
our recurrent emotional encounters, and acquire
substance through our acceptance of them into
the fabric of our daily lives, as a means through
which we express our own otherwise unspoken
fears, desires and memories.

Television, in this way, serves as company not
simply for the lonely but in its sense of familiarity
within the home. Alongside the proper disquiet
at the dangers inherent in television's role as "the
keystone in consumer capitalism", we do well to
remember that, as critic David Marc points out,
"Television is made to sell products but is used
for quite different purposes by lonely, alienated
people, families, marijuana smokers, born-again
Christians, alcoholics, Hasidic Jews, destitute
people, millionaires, jocks, shut-ins, illiterates,
hang-gliding enthusiasts, intellectuals…in spite of
all demographic odds."

Critics of the media often see the audience as
passive consumers in a one-way communication
process. Television executives, who live in terror

◀ **Director Francis Ford
Coppola wanted** *Apocalypse
Now* **(1979) to be "a film
experience that would give
its audience a sense of the
horror, the madness, the
sensuousness, and the moral
dilemma of the Vietnam
war." Nearly three years in
production, the film was
spectacular, extravagant, and
incoherent, reveling in its
surreal images of the war as
the biggest show on earth,
and displaying Hollywood's
inability, at the end of the
1970s, to come to terms with
defeat.**

▼ **Was it his rabid
anti-communism or his
ape-like masculinity that
made John Rambo popular
enough to have a bar named
after him in Lhasa, Tibet?
The character who had begun
life as the inarticulate victim
in an anti-war novel became,
in the hands and pectorals of
Sylvester Stallone, an
Italian-American Tarzan,
a strutting, muscle-bound
apologist for American
foreign policy in the Reagan
presidency. Rambo was
as brutal an image of the
warrior-savage as any
culture had produced.**

◀ **By the late 1980s, the
Vietnam war had become
history, and Vietnam war
stories could be told
according to the conventions
of earlier war movies.**
Platoon **(1986), which
advertised itself as the first
film to tell "the truth" about
the war, in fact told a familiar
story about a young man's
education in the hell of war. It
was as much about only the
American experience of the
war as every other Vietnam
movie had been; the
Vietnamese were merely
extras to be raped, killed,
pitied and not understood.**

◀ For a brief period in the mid-1970s Hong Kong television production included some of the most innovative programming in the world, but when the writers and directors responsible for the innovations moved back to film, the television stations reverted to the production of formula costume drama serials that proved more popular with the viewing public. Ironically, the innovators found their film work was equally restricted by a combination of censorship and the conservative tastes of their audience.

The soap-opera formula – the serial drama with a small cast and limited studio sets – was an almost inevitable choice for any television service aiming to attract large audiences with low-cost programming. Latin American soap operas, called *telenovelas*, originated in Mexico and Cuba in the 1950s and were later also produced in Brazil and Puerto Rico. Daniel Filho, Brazil's most prolific maker of popular drama, suggested that, under military rule in the 1970s, his soap operas provided, with football, the only permitted topics of conversation: "In Brazil we believe in miracles, and all soap operas have a character who is going up in the world, making it." Like their Indian and Chinese equivalents, these variations on the basic American formula could easily accommodate local cultural requirements. However, the *telenovela* formula was devised to fill time cheaply – and this need itself arose from the adoption of the values of the multi-channel all-day commercial television, suitable for a rich country, by a much poorer one.

In the developed world further expansion of the media involved the exploitation of increasingly specialized markets for higher-priced media commodities such as financial information or "quality" television. These appealed to the more privileged social groups. A 1979 survey identified 14 separate audience groupings among the consumers of American television. MTM sustained

of the hand on the channel switch, envisage a much more active viewer who chooses to watch something else, or not to watch at all. They may, perhaps, be closer to the truth.

The new communications media
The first worldwide television satellite link-up opened in 1967, with the Beatles performing their new song *All You Need is Love*. Benign promises about the "Third Age of Broadcasting" were made in the early 1970s – about the ways in which the media might change the world, or in which the media themselves might change – but few were kept. Other promises, concerned with developments in communications technology, took their place. Computer data processing, electronic news-gathering equipment and satellite transmission made the Global Village that media theorist Marshall McLuhan had heralded in the early 1960s a reality; by the mid-1980s the news agency Visnews expected to have a news story from the other side of the world on American television within 90 minutes of its happening.

The revolutions in information technology expanded the media and made their impact more immediate. In the West, network broadcasting reached its maximum potential in the mid-1970s, as watching took up more time than any other activity apart from sleeping and working, on average six hours a day per person in the United States. But there were more possibilities of expansion for the media companies than increasing the consumption of Western audiences. One involved the development of television services in the Third World. In 1986, 83 percent of Chinese households had a television set, and the most popular programs drew audiences of 100 million. In 1975 an Indian experiment in educational broadcasting to the rural population made use of direct broadcasting by satellite (DBS) for the first time anywhere in the world. But Indian broadcasting otherwise followed the familiar Western pattern: introduction of color in 1982, commercial sponsorship of programs in 1984. The audience encompassed 70 percent of the population but programming was aimed at the middle-class audience sought by the advertisers. One result was the development of Indian soap operas.

Indian Cinema and Television

the most impressive record among American producers of "quality" television, aiming series such as *Lou Grant* and *Hill Street Blues* at a liberal professional audience, who preferred programs that they felt were more sophisticated, stylistically complex and psychologically "deep" than ordinary television fare. "Quality" programs such as M*A*S*H* could reach "quality" social groups (the metropolitan, the upwardly mobile, the wealthy), and this offered advertisers an alternative strategy to the constant quest for a larger share of the ratings.

What such systems of scheduling demonstrated is that in an increasingly diverse media economy there can be profit in supplying products aimed specifically at the upper end of the market. As the hardware costs of broadcasting continue to increase, however, many analysts argue that only the pursuit of international mass audiences can sustain the investment in both equipment and programming. This leads to the prospect of a diet of least objectionable programming, sport, music, videos, news and reruns. They point to the Italian experience, where deregulation of broadcasting multiplied the number of stations, lowered program quality and drastically reduced cinema attendance. The introduction of commercial television in France has similarly been held reponsible for the decline in film production, while some Indian filmmakers

Doordshan, the single government channel of Indian television, remained highly resistant to American imports, but its emphasis on low-budget development programming led to frequent complaints about its dullness.

The story in Indian cinema is strikingly different. Since 1930 India has been one of the four top film-making countries, and into the 1980s it produced 800 films a year, in 23 different languages. Adapting the conventions of traditional mythology, literature, theater, dance and music, Indian films developed quite different narrative practices from Western films, telling their familiar stories through a system of stylized expressions and abrupt changes of mood and tone. These distinctive forms have kept the Indian cinema dominant in its home market and hardly known outside that market. The Indian cinema best known in the West is the "parallel cinema" of Satyajit Ray, Ritwaik Ghatak and Mrinal Sen, which, although rooted in Indian tradition, has taken much of its cinematic esthetics from European models, and has been acceptable in Western "art cinema" markets.

On the other hand, the Indian commercial cinema has demonstrated an adaptability comparable to that of Hollywood. Although their forms are rooted in Sanskrit drama, Indian films use plots which would not be out of place on American television.

G.P. Sippy's blockbuster production *Sholay* (*Embers*, 1976), the most successful movie in Indian film history, took elements of its plot from Westerns such as *The Magnificent Seven* and *Butch Cassidy and the Sundance Kid*.

◀ On location in the Himalayas.

argue that there, too, television will end the "parallel cinema" of Satyajit Ray, Mrinal Sen and others.

For those who can afford it, High Definition Television (HDTV), using twice the number of horizontal lines as the present 525-line and 625-line systems, will offer a sound and picture quality and size previously available only in the cinema. But, as with previous innovations in broadcasting and sound reproduction, rival systems compete to be adopted as a world standard, or tenaciously retain their share of the potential market. HDTV will appear first in Japan, the "television society" whose citizens watch more television than anywhere else in the world, and where most of the technology in HDTV is now being originated. Satellite distribution, dominated by powerful multinational corporations, may gradually change the nature of television, from a naturally regulated medium to one that is fundamentally unregulated. Whereas the

▲ Britain preserved its reputation for having the "least worst television in the world" through "quality television". Adaptations of literary classics have always played an important role in sustaining this image. But as the cost of production has risen, co-production deals have become more common. The British company Granada shared the cost of producing *Brideshead Revisited* with WNET, an American PBS station, Exxon and the German network NDR. British producers claim that their programs are made primarily for British audiences, but the content and format of quality television is moving closer to a predictable international norm.

VOICE OF AMERICA

▲ Novelist Gore Vidal called him "the Acting President"; more sympathetic observers "the Great Communicator". Ronald Reagan and his image-makers embraced radio and television as the media in which American politics were conducted.

▼ Television did what Hollywood had done before it – sold American culture around the world; but even on isolated Pacific islands, it did the job more cheaply and quickly than Hollywood ever could.

American Federal Communications Commission once upheld the Fairness Doctrine, which required broadcasters to provide balanced coverage of issues, this has been abandoned as the technology of international media distribution makes the effective regulation of the content of the broadcasts ever more difficult. However much the range of choice available to consumers is increased, the ever-higher costs of hardware will inevitably produce greater inequalities in access to electronic information, between nations as well as individuals. At the same time, fewer organizations, subjected to fewer controls on their activities, will determine what choice is offered to consumers.

In some respects the new technology has threatened the existing power structures of the media industry. American cable systems (whereby a consumer subscribes to a broadcasting service, which is then transmitted via an underground cable) and deregulation produced new rivals to the broadcast networks – among them Home Box Office, the first pay-TV channel in the United States, and Ted Turner, who expanded his Atlanta television station WBTS into an international operation based on the first 24-hour news channel, CNN.

Some of the new technology freed the audience from the control of distributors. Video made films

and television programs much more like books or records, objects to be enjoyed at will, and distributors strongly resisted this. Universal Studios and the Disney Corporation fought a prolonged but unsuccessful legal battle to have home video recorders declared illegal, because of their potential for encouraging breaches of copyright. Conglomeration of the new media companies with the old, and the merging of hardware and software concerns, provided a more circuitous remedy: in 1987 the Japanese electronic corporation Sony established a likely trend, reverting to the vertical integration practiced by Hollywood in the 1930s, by buying CBS records. By a combination of conglomeration and diversification the major American networks have protected themselves from demise.

Broadcasting and imperialism
Satellite television has presented issues of national sovereignty and censorship in Europe, but the impact of international broadcasting, whether radio or television, on areas of the Third World, has been considerably greater. By the late 1980s the Voice of America was broadcasting in 42 languages to an audience of 120 million, and building 66 "superpower" 500kW transmitters to extend its service. The Soviet Union had 32 such transmitters, France 12, West Germany 10, while

Britain, the only major power planning to cut back its overseas broadcasting, had eight. In all, 31 countries had external radio services spreading their ideologies beyond their borders cheaply and efficiently. The United States also transmitted *America Today* by satellite, providing two hours a day of arts and sports programming free to any cable-television system.

In 1984 there were 24 satellites providing programs for the domestic American market, and many of them cast their "footprint" over the Caribbean. The availability of American television asserted powerful cultural and political influences: much fuller coverage of American domestic politics was available to the islanders of St Lucia than news of their own internal political affairs. The fear was that dependence on American television would eventually displace national cultural values.

The concern was less with overt propaganda than with the proliferation of a transnational, homogeneous "world culture", produced by the politically and economically dominant countries and distributed as an instrument and badge of their dominance over the Third World. The argument has changed little in substance from the complaints against Hollywood's influence in the 1920s. As the mass audience in the West for radio and television began to fragment, broadcasting became internationalized through co-production arrangements, seeking its audience in many countries simply to pay the bills. The media have been important forces in maintaining Western influence and interests in Third World countries after independence from colonial rule: into the 1980s the majority of journalistic and technical staff continued to be trained by American or European agencies and partly as a result of this, to adopt Western values with regard to program content. Equipment and programs supplied at cut rates have made possible the establishment of broadcasting services, but have inhibited local production because of its high cost by comparison with American programs of much more ostentatious production qualities. These programs also cater to the status requirements of Third World metropolitan middle-class groups, the first consumers of the new media.

The availability of television is one of a number of attractions luring Third World populations to exchange rural poverty for a makeshift life on the edges of sprawling cities. Its main function even here, however, is to deliver viewers to advertisers. In most of South America television is entirely financed by advertising and sponsorship. In 1974 advertisements took up more than 35 per cent of programming time on Venezuelan television, while Brazilian TV Globo's *telenovelas* were often sponsored by manufacturing companies or banks as promotional devices.

The Third World is not only vulnerable to the economic power of the West, whose political authority insists on the "free market" in goods and television programs as evidence of the "democratic" nature of Third World governments. It is also subject to the tyranny of a largely one-way flow of information. The Associated Press news service transmits 90,000 words of

The News in East and West

Soviet television, strictly supervised by the state, constructed "news" as a quite different commodity from its Western counterparts. By comparison to Western news, its main news program *Vremya (Time)* was humorless and undramatic, emphasizing industrial or agricultural production achievements. Watched in 80 percent of Russian homes, Soviet television openly acknowledged its role in forming taste, opinion and ideology. It reflected the multinational and multilingual structure of Soviet society through cultural diversity, in contrast to the cultural homogeneity purveyed by American television; nevertheless its rigid moral standards, which excluded the representation of sex, violence or corruption, were regarded as excessively puritanical by many Russians.

In part Soviet news programming fulfilled functions carried out elsewhere in Western television. Some researchers have suggested that much of the pleasure viewers derive from television comes from, for example, the spectacle of large numbers of people enjoying themselves provided by game shows and sitcoms recorded before a live audience. In this Western experience of television, news is consumed for negative reasons, to make sure that nothing has happened which might affect the viewer's life adversely.

▼ Unlike Western news programming, Soviet television news was undramatic in its presentation, often reporting on achievements in agricultural or industrial production. Broadcasting is done in 70 languages within the borders of the Soviet Union, with 23 principal regional stations. Here workers at a Georgian steelworks broadcast the good news about their production figures.

news a day from New York to Asia, and receives 19,000 words back. News from the Third World is even more vulnerable to a process of stereotyping than domestic news output. In the West, events become television news according to a predictable set of criteria: they must be phenomena of the moment – dramatic events rather than trends, big, apparently unexpected, preferably negative in character, and if possible focused on an individual already known to the audience. By these criteria little that happens in the Third World qualifies as news except war, natural disasters, and political instability. Since this forms the image taken into the homes of countless Westerners, existing stereotypes about our neighbors in the Global Village are reinforced every night.

What is taking place quietly in the living rooms of thousands of Caribbean family units as they sit innocently before their television sets frightens us. It is a process of deculturization, which is painless, but also very thorough and long-lasting.

CARIBBEAN PUBLISHING AND
BROADCASTING
ASSOCIATION

THE ROYAL FAMILY AND THE MEDIA

In the 1930s the BBC began to manufacture a new image for the British royal family. In 1932 George V made the first Christmas broadcast to his people. John Reith, the BBC's Director-General, made suggestions about what royalty might say, and in 1936 personally stage-managed Edward VIII's abdication speech. The funeral of one king, the abdication of a second and the coronation of a third within 16 months provided the BBC with marvelous opportunities for pathos and pageantry. The coronation of George VI in 1937 was the most elaborate outside broadcast yet undertaken, and arguably the first large-scale "media event". A very few of the king's subjects, in southeast England, could watch it on television; for the next coronation, in 1953, more than a million television sets were sold. This was the world's first truly international television outside broadcast, relayed live to France, Holland and West Germany.

Some 500 million people around the world watched the investiture of Prince Charles in 1969, and 750 million witnessed his "fairytale wedding" in 1981. Although Britain has been most successful in exporting its royal occasions, the state ceremonies of other countries, too, particularly royal weddings, have been grand occasions for television around the world. The wedding of Crown Prince Akihito in Japan in 1959 became an occasion for the celebration of national unity. It also doubled the number of television sets in Japan in a year.

But television's place in our homes makes it an "unheroic" medium; its most appreciated personalities celebrate their "normality". In 1968, the BBC and ITV together produced a documentary, *Royal Family*, intended to "humanize" the monarchy. For the first time, viewers saw royalty talking to each other just as if they were ordinary people. Perhaps it was too successful. Since then, media treatment of the royal family in the television age has become less reverential. Increasingly, they have been cast in the public imagination as characters in a soap opera, barely different from *Dallas* and *Dynasty*, the prime-time sagas of endless internecine families.

▲▶ In 1981 Prince Charles married Lady Diana Spencer, the young and innocent ideal of the prospective British queen (main image), unlike the svelte American divorcee Wallis Simpson, for whose love Edward VIII was forced to abdicate in 1936 (inset).

▶ Like soap opera characters when the scriptwriters change, the royals' personae are occasionally subject to alteration by the media. Princess Anne was for her earlier career presented as the sulky kid sister (far right), but in the 1980s emerged as the caring charity worker rolling up her sleeves up for the sake of a good cause (near right).

▶▲ The woman who became Queen of England in 1937 was Elizabeth Bowes Lyon, with sweet English-rose looks. In her later career she was idolized as the nation's grandmother (opposite top). But the viciously affectionate animated puppets of Fluck and Law's television series *Spitting Image* brought her with the other royals down to the level of all other television characters.

▶▶ The coronation of Queen Elizabeth II in 1953, within days of news of the British expedition's success in climbing Mt. Everest, symbolized a rebirth for Britain after the war. Souvenirs of all kinds abounded.

SOUVENIR
CORONATION
SONG
BOOK
National Airs of The Empire

FULL
WORDS
AND
MUSIC

GOD SAVE THE KING

6d.

LONG MAY THEY REIGN

Datafile

In the 1980s sport became a business: the search for prize money and marketing opportunities drove the stars to greater achievement, while the appeal of many sports to a wider market lay in the television companies' ability to find an audience. In that respect, the 1988 Seoul Oympic were a disaster, with American and European television companies finding viewers – and advertisers – hard to come by.

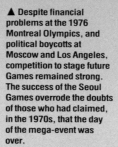

Olympic attendance

◀ Although the United States, the Soviet Union and East Germany (GDR) continued to bring home the bulk of the medals for those Olympics in which they chose to compete, the remaining medals were shared out between a much more diverse range of countries than previously, including many Third World nations.

▲ Despite financial problems at the 1976 Montreal Olympics, and political boycotts at Moscow and Los Angeles, competition to stage future Games remained strong. The success of the Seoul Games overrode the doubts of those who had claimed, in the 1970s, that the day of the mega-event was over.

Olympic Gold medals

- Others
- USSR
- GDR
- USA
- Poland
- Bulgaria
- Cuba
- Romania
- Hungary
- FRG
- Chile
- Italy
- S. Korea

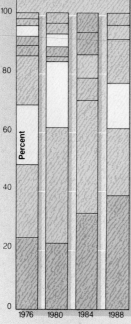

▶ The appeal of television brought sudden fortune to some sports that had previously existed with little public interest or money. Snooker, a game ideal for color television, received blanket coverage on British screens in the late 1970s and 1980s, and the prize money put up by the game's sponsors increased accordingly.

Snooker prize money in UK

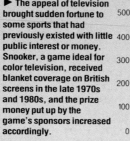

Participants of US recreational activities

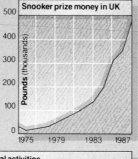

Ten-pin bowling

Softball

Tennis

Golf

▲ The 1980s was the age of physical fitness, with crazes for marathon running, aerobics and weight training. Despite the hype, traditional sports still occupied the bulk of the population: ten-pin bowling remaining by far the most popular. Similarly, in Britain, angling was unchallenged as the most popular participation sport.

Professional tennis players – top earnings

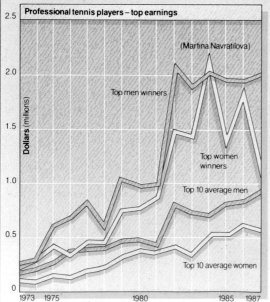

(Martina Navratilova)

Top men winners

Top women winners

Top 10 average men

Top 10 average women

◀ Tennis became highly professionalized from the late 1970s, with an established circuit, computer rankings and ever-growing prize money. Although men's winnings remained higher than those for the female game, the Czech-born Martina Navratilova achieved the record earnings of any player in a single year.

In the 1980s sport increasingly defined itself in every advanced industrial nation as part of a leisure industry, and passed this seductive description on to other, less affluent, countries. As the "leisure economy" expanded, sports-related consumer expenditure increased, on building sports halls and stadia, on participation, ticket admissions, gambling, clothing and equipment, food and drink, television rights and advertising. In the hands of multi-million-dollar corporations, and inextricably linked to the international television market, sport became big business. Together with television, advertising, sponsorship and modern marketing procedures transformed the character of sport.

Sport and commerce

The 1984 Los Angeles Olympics – "The Corporate Games" – celebrated with unashamed commercialism a notion of sport subservient to marketing requirements. Thirty corporate sponsors, including Coca-Cola, Levi Strauss, and McDonald's, each paid between $4 million and $15 million for the exclusive right to market their products under the Olympic logo. They refurbished the LA Coliseum, built the velodrome and Olympic pool, supplied equipment, communications, transport and the "official" clothing. For the first time since 1936, the host nation's commitment to staging the Games as a demonstration of its ideological superiority was not measured by the scale of its financial commitment. However, this represents more a recognition of the cultural, economic and even political authority of American multinational corporations than it does any easing of the entanglement of sport and politics. The government of South Korea, where the 1988 Games were held, was keen to use the Olympics not simply as a means of legitimizing its existence politically, but also for its long-term economic effects. As Lee Young Ho, South Korean Sports Minister, explained: "Hosting the Olympics gives us international recognition and a psychological boost for our next step up to join the advanced countries within the next decade. Look what happened to Japan after the 1964 Olympics."

The Los Angeles Games also promoted the idea of sport as a form of entertainment to be consumed passively by its spectators; it is not accidental that many of the leading corporate sponsors of sport are food, drink and tobacco companies, things to be consumed while watching rather than playing. Far more people are now involved in sport through the press and broadcasting than in any other way. The Los Angeles Olympics were watched by 2000 million viewers worldwide.

Sport has become central to the function of television as entertainment, acquiring the trappings of show business in its presentation. In the

THE INDUSTRY OF LEISURE

Sport and commerce

Sponsors and television audiences

Professionalism in modern sport

Sport and politics

Sport for all

United States there are now sports events organized specifically for television while the schedules of many other events are increasingly dictated by the need for sport to accommodate itself to the requirements of television. Other sports have been transformed into new forms of entertainment by changing their rules: shorter snooker matches, round-the-city cycle racing, World Cup athletics and World Cup rugby have all been developed to make these sports more attractive for television and sponsors.

The popularity of televised sport ensures that escalating sums of money are involved. At the 1976 Montreal Olympic Games, ABC acquired the American television rights for $25 million, and made three times that amount selling advertising. By 1984 American rights went to ABC at a cost of $225 million for the Summer Olympics and $90 million for the Winter Olympics; the sales of advertising netted over $300 million. The bulk of the income of the International Olympic Committee (IOC) derives from American television, whose networks also planned to spend $1.4 billion in television rights to the American National Football League between 1987 and 1990.

Similarly, in 1977 Australian television mogul Kerry Packer saw the potential of using traditionally popular sports with a mass following to increase the numbers of spectators, increase players' incomes and attract huge sponsorship. To do this he changed the traditional format of cricket, played floodlit matches for the first time and even abandoned the familiar white clothes of the cricketer. He contracted 35 of the world's top players, dubbed "Packer's Circus", to play a series of international matches in Australia to be shown exclusively on his Channel Nine television

▲ ▶ The more popular and profitable the sport, the higher the level of sponsorship in return for advertising space. Not only soft drinks' corporations and cigarette companies sponsored sport in the 1980s; the computer industry, banks and insurance companies all saw sports sponsorship as a good form of advertising.

▼ Every nuance of the athlete's experience of victory is captured by the camera, as British runner Sebastian Coe wins Olympic gold for the 1500m at Moscow in 1980. Its vicarious pleasures and sorrows have made sport an increasingly profitable form of entertainment, a development which the media have not been slow to exploit.

network. A crisis in international cricket was provoked by this injection of commercialism into its self-definition as a game for gentlemen; this was as severe, if not as long-lasting, as that engendered by the banning of South Africa from international cricket competition.

Sponsorship is attracted to already buoyant sports, which in turn encourage the creation of special events to attract media coverage and more sponsorship. Lack of media attention results in a relative lack of sponsorship; this is a common fate for minority and female sports. Only those minority sports with an obvious televisual appeal have broken through this barrier and television has artificially promoted interest in some sports, concentrating heavy coverage on them simply because they are easy and cheap to televise. One result of this is the "discovery" of sports by TV channels excluded from the most popular – sumo wrestling has been one such import to the West by television companies and sponsors anxious to catch the next wave of popular interest.

Sport's vicarious excitement, built on the controlled unpredictability of rule-bound competition, makes it an ideal television commodity. The agony and ecstasy of athletes, the gestures and facial expressions of the spectators, confrontations, accidents, victory and defeat, fill broadcasting time with spectacle and excitement. Sport becomes continuous drama, presenting heroes and villains, highlighting beauty and brutality. The techniques of presentation "construct" a game for us through the selection of camera angles, the use of close-ups and action replays to repeat and emphasize key moments. Together with this visual presentation, the commentators' analyses as well as their value judgments convert the television spectator into an armchair expert on players' technical abilities and on umpiring decisions.

Radio, newspapers, specialist magazines and books reinforced television's discourse on sport as entertainment, personalizing and dramatizing it. Popular sports journalism used the language of

▼ Canadian athlete Ben Johnson's victory at the 1988 Seoul Olympics was short-lived. His winning time of 9.79 seconds set a new world record for the 100m but within 48 hours he had been stripped of his gold medal for taking Stanozolol, an anabolic steroid. These drugs were used illicitly by many athletes during training to speed up the body's recovery rate, thus permitting extra-hard training. The use of potentially dangerous drugs to enhance performance has often been described as widespread. This is a measure of the immense pressure to win that the commercialization of sport has produced.

the battlefield, where rivals and enemies are demolished or humiliated by a blast or a charge. As sport has increasingly assumed the characteristics of other forms of television, its performers have been obliged to adopt the mannerisms of celebrity, and, equally, have become victims of its terminology of hyperbole: every top athlete becomes a "legendary superstar". Like pop stars and film stars, they are required to distill a lifetime of acquired skill into moments of consumable spectacle for sport competition and show business to procreate profit. The celebrity they acquire opens their personal lives to the prurient gaze of the secondary media of gossip columns and talk shows. "Superbrats" as well as superstars are manufactured for our consumption as an integral part of media sport. Individuals such as John McEnroe and snooker-player Alex Higgins are characterized as unstable and irascible, versions of an entertainment personality archetype identified as talented, unpredictable and ultimately self-destructive. For the entertainment such figures produce they are paid vast amounts of money: the Argentinian footballer Diego Maradona cost Napoli a staggering £6.9 million,

and his basic salary is a million dollars annually.

The complete integration of sport as entertainment into the leisure industry has finally rendered the "amateur" concept obsolete. The values permeating modern sport come from the commercial model and percolate down from top professionals. Sports organizations as substantial as the International Amateur Athletic Federation depend increasingly on sponsorship for their survival. Even "amateur" athletes, the exemplars of amateur sport, are now able to command enormous fees from sponsors, take what is required for "expenses", and invest the remainder in a trust fund, which is, at least, an improvement on a previous situation in which top sportsmen and women received under-the-table payments, prizes and gifts, or else were covertly sponsored by their governments. The 1988 Olympics were the first in which this sham amateurism was replaced by open professionalism for the athletes.

The commercial model of sport emphasizes competition, an obsession with winning and an endless quest for records, all of which puts tremendous pressure on individual players and athletes. The myth of "rags to riches" inducts

▶ British Olympic medallist Fatima Whitbread is among the many women who have been subjected to clichéd analysis at the hands of male sports journalists, who continue to churn out copy on the looks of female athletes rather than discussing their skill and technique.

▲ Synchronized swimming joined the official list of Olympic events in 1984. Other sports are still considered less than "ladylike" – female athletes are banned from the hammer, pole vault, triple jump and steeplechase.

▲ The massive amounts of money generated out of television coverage of sport have resulted in equally massive fees for exclusive rights, putting crowd-pullers such as baseball or boxing beyond the means of all but the largest and wealthiest of the television companies. The smaller channels have responded by generating interest in the more esoteric sports, such as Japanese sumo wrestling.

human physiology; champions are "produced" rather than "born".

Media sport remains one of the strongest bastions of male chauvinism. Televised sport belongs, almost exclusively, to the male gaze, and much of its appeal to sponsors and advertisers results from its being the form of television most likely to secure a male audience. In traditional male sports, such as American football and Australian-rules football, men are celebrated as 20th-century gladiators and warriors. In contrast, the most popular women's sports covered by the media are those seen as "feminine appropriate". A sportswoman is portrayed first as female, then as an athlete: popular journalism discusses her sexuality – how "lithe", "leggy", "pretty" or "graceful" she is, or her performance of other female roles – that she is a "housewife and mother of two" – as much as on her sports skill and technique.

Sport and politics

Such commentary is reserved for Western women: East European women athletes, particularly those from the German Democratic Republic (GDR), are castigated for their "masculine" appearance as well as their ideology. In 1972, the GDR competed in the Olympics for the first time, and by 1976 did so well that, together with the US and the USSR, it became one of the three "Olympic Superpowers". With a population of only 17 million, the GDR's performance is superlative, but if Olympic successes are calculated per capita of the population, Finland and

youngsters into a world of aggressive, competitive sport where most of them will not make it to the top. The ordinary rates of pay for sports professionals are unremarkable, and most professionals are bought and sold like commodities, with little control over their conditions of work. Abuse of the body is intensified by success: in order to enhance performance, sporting superstars are impelled to overtrain, to take dangerous drugs, and to undergo extreme diet manipulation. In the Eastern bloc, although the sports system is non-commercial, many of the pressures on athletes are similar. Contemporary athletes mock

Trinidad are outstanding as well, while the United States and Soviet Union actually fall below other countries.

The GDR's achievement results from the active intervention of the state in sports provision and promotion; it gives a higher priority to sport than anywhere else in the world. Its constitution guarantees the right of every citizen to participate in sport and it has ample facilities for those who participate for health and recreation, as well as those who wish to compete at a high level. As much official encouragement is given to women as to men, and East German women have been more successful in Olympic competition than women from any other country.

In contrast, in the West, among nations which have a liberal democratic ideology and where a market economy prevails, it is generally assumed that state intervention is minimal, and that individuals can participate without undue pressure and harmful effects. However, in all Western countries, there is greater government intervention than ever before, and sport is being managed now more consciously, though less overtly than in centrally organized societies. From the 1960s, commercialism has interacted intimately with nationalism and the role of the state. National governments have poured vast amounts of money into sport to gain international prestige. The 1976 Montreal Olympics highlighted the financial implications of hosting sports extravaganzas. Reputed to have cost a staggering $2 billion, they left massive debts for tax payers.

The Soviet intervention in Afghanistan, which led to the United States team withdrawing from the Moscow Olympics in 1980 and the subsequent refusal of the Soviet Union to go to Los Angeles in 1984, changed the character of the Games and demonstrated the hypocrisy of Western denials that sport was a form of international politics. Although, for the first time since 1952, the United States and Soviet Union were not confronting one another in Olympic competition, ironically, Cold War politics between East and West were accentuated.

Sport has also become a vehicle for protest by individuals against oppression by their own governments. The anti-apartheid sports movement has continued to use international sport as a means to oppose the South African government, despite the piecemeal amelioration of apartheid in sport through "multinational" sports events. It argues that black sportsmen and women are being used as puppets to prop up a political arrangement based on racism, brutality, and repressive laws which systematically ignores the human rights of the majority of South African citizens.

Racism and violence continue to be depressing features associated with some spectator sports, and nowhere more so than in Britain, where football hooliganism, insidiously linked to right-wing groups, has burgeoned in recent years. The simplistic explanation, couched in terms of moral outrage at the individual troublemaker and the need for firmer instruments of repression and punishment, has persisted as the political analysis, even in the face of the deaths of Italian fans as a result of the hooliganism of English football fans

◄ The distinctive appearance of Ruud Gullit, the Dutch soccer star of the mid-1980s, gave rise to a new cult image among his fans — a cult that emphasized the links between the position of the sporting star and the pop-star in modern society.

at the Heysel stadium in Brussels in May 1985. The dramatic and brutal nature of the Heysel disaster made it newsworthy, particularly since the scenes of the horror of the dying were seen live on television across the world. As a result English clubs were banned from international competition.

In the Western media, nationalism and sport seem to be linked when convenient, and separated when not. An athlete is always represented as winning for his or her country, but losing for him or herself. National rivalry between countries within the same political sphere and of comparable economic development – within Western Europe, for example – has been a useful way of retaining chauvinism without the need for military expense. The xenophobia evident in Britain during the Falklands/Malvinas war had been in part maintained and kept available by the displacement of nationalist sentiment into exchanges with bat or ball.

But one hopeful sign might be noted. If sport has now become "the continuation of politics by other means", as von Clausewitz described war, it is yet not war. If the gladiatorial combats between ideologies are played out in Olympic arenas, no-one dies in their enactment. Sacking the manager of a national football team for a humiliating defeat is less disruptive than overthrowing a government. When Diego Maradona scored a dubious goal for Argentina "with the hand of God and the head of Maradona" in a game which knocked England out of the 1986 World Cup, it did not prove necessary to resume the war between Britain and Argentina over the incident. Sport is neither innocent nor safe, but it is less dangerous, as well as more manageable, than war.

◄ Diego Maradona captained the Argentinian team to victory in the 1986 World Cup. Maradona's career has taken him to Europe, as one of the new breed of soccer superstars for whom their national clubs are no longer good enough – even though the national team is the best in the world. A "superleague" of clubs able to afford huge fees for the best players in the world has made soccer skill an internationally marketable commodity.

Sport For All

Despite the contemporary philosophy that sport is not a luxury, but an essential part of life, few Western governments recognize that flourishing grass-roots sport depends on state intervention, and that the best state policies are those that seek to ensure that sport is for everyone. Those who criticize sport under communism ignore that it is accessible to ordinary people free of charge. In comparison, in most Western countries many sports are still out of reach of the pockets of the majority. In America, the poor have few opportunities to participate in sport. One solution to the dominance of competition in sports ideology may lie in alternative forms of sport which stress co-operation and playfulness, such as fun-runs and mini-marathons.

In recent years many Western governments have channeled concern about national health into the promotion of fitness schemes and community sport. The Australian "Life – Be In It" campaign includes a light-hearted media promotion of new sports and fun for everyone, while the British Sports Council recruitment drive, "Ever Thought of Sport", identified groups with special needs, such as unemployed ethnic minorities and women.

► The Paraplegic Olympics, 1984.

Datafile

In the later 1970s and 1980s mainstream music has reverted to a formula dictated by the requirements of the international market-place: although the adult-oriented rock of the mid-1970s was much criticized, the music dominating the American charts 10 years later owed it a large debt. The radical drive of the rock bands of the sixties was much subdued; Bruce Springsteen, who took over the role of "the boss" of rock 'n' roll, was hailed by President Reagan as the embodiment of the ideal young American. Formula-driven disco dominated black music, although at least the work of Michael Jackson transcended many of the limitations of the formula while achieving huge international sales.

It remained true that American and, to a lesser extent, British music dictated style. After the passing of punk, a new breed of bands flourished that relied on synthesizers for their music and a high degree of marketing to promote them as image.

▲ Sales of recorded music in the United States failed to sustain the growth of the previous decades, as music became an ubiquitous but somewhat irrelevant adjunct to lifestyle, rather than a central means of defining attitudes to society and politics. The popularity of portable stereos brought a switch from records to tapes.

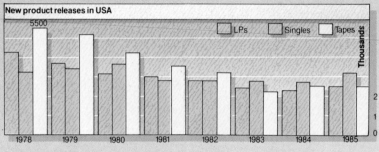

New product releases in USA

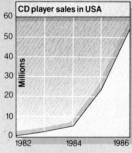

CD player sales in USA

◀▼ The development of the Sony Walkman brought new marketing opportunity for taped music, but sales of hardware remained static until the introduction of the compact-disk player, which was so attractive that record companies found they could sell new compact-disk versions of old favorites as well as new releases.

▲ The declining vitality of the popular music scene in the United States, and the domination of the larger record labels, made much of the music released seem anodyne. One result was the decline in the number of new releases, particularly for LPs as 12-inch singles allowed individual tracks to extend beyond three minutes.

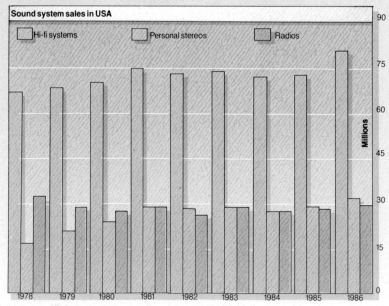

Sound system sales in USA

Popular music in the seventies and eighties was bewildering in its variety and rate of change and the critics frequently make the confusion even worse. But beneath the surface it may be possible to discern the broad movement – sometimes moving in parallel, sometimes in conflict – of two fundamental approaches to popular music. One, the "ecstatic", persisted from earlier eras: it continued to celebrate raw emotion and values inherent in the musical moment, and saw style as an expression of those values. Though still present in this period, its role was far less dramatic than before. The old confrontations with established authority and traditional values were not repeated (moral panic was directed to new regions of youth culture, rather than music) and their absence no doubt contributed to the appearance of a "steady state", which seemed to be reached by the late seventies.

The other approach, which might be termed "extrinsic", was rooted in the self-consciousness of postwar consumerism, in particular in the distinction between the commodity and its image. In music, this approach created a division between the art and the style. This separation seemed to permit some musicians cynically to exploit the popular music system, creating styles and fashions without being fully committed to them. More generally, though, it gave a new twist to some longstanding problems of expression in consumer culture – the relationships between "high" culture and "low", between authenticity and artifice, between creativity and commerce. Different solutions or part-solutions to such questions lay behind many of the constantly shifting patterns of much popular music in this period. In all of them, music seemed to serve style, not style music.

Adult-oriented rock

The early- to mid-1970s had seen a compromise between the two approaches. Earlier white rock had felt its way into the celebratory nature of black music (without fully reaching its spiritual core) and black music, in turn, had been influenced by the inventiveness of rock. Much music-making along these lines persisted, but elsewhere the so-called progressive rock of Emerson, Lake and Palmer or Jethro Tull, and singer-songwriters such as James Taylor or Carly Simon aspired to a Romantic ideal of art, which was interpreted as being true, first and foremost, to oneself. Preoccupied with the self, their "adult-oriented rock" (AOR) was ambivalent toward other functions of music. Although dependent on a notion of the need for "authentic" roots, and finding these in particular in rock's debt to the emancipating influence of black music, AOR musicians, critics and consumers began to regard

MUSIC, IDENTITY AND PROPERTY

Adult-oriented rock
The decline of black music
The challenge of punk
Style, image and art
Music from Africa

that music, and its derivatives, as emotionally and esthetically immature. Determined to appear equally stern toward commerce, they also looked askance at the growing tendency to celebrate consumer culture for its own sake. The irony of many rock stars, accumulating great wealth was not recognized; instead, their wealth confirmed them in the eyes of the public as independent, powerful figures, with whom consumers could identify.

These attempts to marginalize black music had relatively little impact on black music itself, or on its audience. But as the expressive power of black performers such as Curtis Mayfield or Marvin Gaye gave way to "formula soul" in the midseventies, there was a sense that black American music might, finally, have few more major revelations to make. Some looked to Africa or the Caribbean for a continued vitality in black music; others accepted the predictable and mechanical sound of the disco beat. In the past most changes in black music had come about either because of changes in the relationship between the black tradition and white approaches to culture and commerce, and in the subtle variations within that relationship, or because elements within black music reacted to each other in new ways. Soul had grown from the interaction of the sounds and rhythms of gospel, rhythm & blues and white pop, in the context of a successful black attempt to emulate white commercial ownership of the product. The Motown label, on which a special form of soul developed, produced the basis for the emergence of a closely related group

▼ In marked contrast to the drabness of the world outside, the strobe lights and impenetrable sound levels of the disco seem to create a special territory; and this territory helps to explain the music. Mechanical sounds and rhythms have little appeal in an everyday world itself marked by predictability; but in the disco that predictability is turned, temporarily, into a means of release. But what liberates the body in this context takes the music prisoner.

of highly charged musical styles. The Four Tops' 1966 hit single, *Reach Out, I'll Be There*, epitomized the way in which gospel message and secular emotion flowed into each other to produce a "utopia of feeling".

Although a utopia of urban life remained a remote prospect for blacks in the United States, music had helped to push the black consciousness movement into the public arena and into wider acceptance by blacks themselves. Following after this high point, the drift into formula soul, succeeded by the mechanical qualities of most disco music, seems almost inexplicable. It may have been that what black music represented had now become part of the musical common heritage and, as such, had forfeited something of its ability to surprise and shock.

The challenge of punk

Meanwhile in Britain – still the world's mainspring of popular music after the United States – developments were taking a different turn. Black music had developed its riches through being grounded in self-acceptance and affirmation, though paradoxically at its most intense it had opened up the possibility of self-surrender. By contrast, mainstream rock had become obsessed with the need for self-identification. Now came an entirely new approach in which the self contemplated itself, objectively, as "other". But in contrast to the classical legend of the self-absorption of Narcissus, the image of the self was not reflected in the comforting pastoral of water,

▲ The Eurythmics starred in the 1988 concert to celebrate African politician Nelson Mandela's 70th birthday. The problem for such specifically political events was to avoid becoming an oblique exercise in consciousness-raising.

▼ Live Aid – a high-tech concert staged simultaneously in London and Philadelphia in July 1985, to raise funds for famine relief in Africa – gave the audience the sense of a link between the public sharing of culture and a remedy for suffering.

but projected on to the cold, shiny surfaces of commercial artifice. What was important now was not the internal self, but the self as a construct of consumer capitalism.

The roots of this change can be traced in part to the sixties' Mods, who were fascinated with commodities and determined to undermine the most idealistic side of pop and rock culture. But the principal source was to be found in the art-school connection. Art schools had exerted a persistent and powerful influence on the course of British popular music in particular, from the late fifties on. In the fifties and sixties, art school had been the first to see that popular culture, especially rock 'n' roll, offered the chance to challenge the control

of high culture, either by demonstrating that rock, too, could be "high", or by a bohemian denial of the common assumption that "high" culture eventually touched everyone in some way. What distinguished the late sixties, and seventies, approach was the central perception that, in commodity culture, arguments about "high" and "low" were specious: all was commerce and all was art.

Although the central movement of thought and practice in this regard was most closely associated with Britain, an important impetus came from New York, from the ideas of Andy Warhol and the music of the Velvet Underground. In a society where mass communication ultimately appropriated and trivialized everything, and in which individual expression as the basis of art was irrelevant, what became important, in Warhol's view, was surface spectacle. For the Velvets, and especially for Lou Reed, that spectacle was urban decadence, viewed through the "streetwise cynicism of the Big Rotten Apple". The harsh, blighted New York sound of the Velvets contrasted most obviously with the optimism of the West Coast's counter-culture. But its celebration of impersonal urban monotony also obliquely challenged the fundamental principle of most of the century's popular music, which derived from the role of the offbeat – confidence in the existence of alternatives.

Ironically, their basis in what they saw as a value-free mass-culture esthetic failed to make Warhol and the Velvets commercially successful, and created instead a cult audience. In Britain, however, the situation was rather different. The familiarity of many musicians with pop art theories provided a more responsive environment for this idea. Equally important, however, was the fact that, from the consumer's point of view, in mid-seventies Britain the relentless march of commodity culture had affected everyone, but had left untouched many of the country's "traditional" inequities and done little to erase the increasing sense of the loss of historically rooted identity. The self in daily life seemed constricted socially and undernourished historically. A new self could be created, by using commercial culture in a way that seemed to erase all memory of social and historical inhibitions. The opportunity was widely accepted, in the deliberate artifice of "glam rock".

Through all the confusion caused, especially in the mass media themselves, by the glam rock of David Bowie, Brian Ferry and bands such as Queen, it was their way of affording this opportunity that provided the most persistent thread. Bowie became "a blank canvas on which consumers write their dreams, a media-made icon to whom art happened". These "dreams" largely revolved around ambivalent images of sexuality, and it was here that moral outrage, seeking an outlet for a renewed bout of authoritarianism, focused its attention. But glam rock's display of sexuality achieved a result far from the perversion in which convention hoped to see the final dénouement of the permissive society. Glam rock challenged the male heterosexual domination of conventional society and the counter-culture by pointing, not to female repression, so much as to the false premises of that masculinity. It also insisted that sexuality was not part of an individual's essential being, but a role that could be chosen and enacted: "A display that was intent on demonstrating that the assumed 'privacy' of

sexual matters ... was an illusion. Sexuality was as much part of the public domain as politics, class, and subcultures."

The disturbing qualities of glam rock were to some extent tempered in the public mind by its obvious artfulness; punk, on the other hand, which followed, in the short period beginning in 1976, seemed by contrast to be a systematic denial of the merit of any kind of skill. Yet punk, like glam rock, had a deep acquaintance with ideas of image and artifice.

The most common interpretations of punk proceed along the lines of a defiant outburst from frustrated proletarian youth, or of a resurgence of democratic culture in the face of commercial appropriation. But punk's many art-school connections placed it, too, in the tradition of art-school experimentation. More extensively than had been done before, punk applied avant-garde artistic concepts, with only limited previous exposure in the visual-arts world, in a much more public arena. When attempting to assess the overall effect of punk what stands out is the *knowing* employment of subversive concepts, the *calculated* assault on traditional expectations, and the *self-conscious* use of alienating effects to create conditions in which the process of commodity culture could be re-examined. Punk achieved its effects by confusing distinctions, by standing relationships on their heads, by turning codes of practice against themselves. Audience expectations of performers were negated: the Sex Pistols sang *You Don't Hate Us As Much As We Hate You*. Concepts of gender were undermined, not by extremes as much as by the removal of overt sexuality. Rock's worried

▲ Jamaican reggae star Bob Marley was known in the mid-sixties as a Kingston "rude boy", one of those whose ska records provided Britain's black youth with its first real chance to identify culturally with the Caribbean. In the seventies, reggae, linked with Rastafarianism, provided a sense of hope – and Marley symbolized this above all others. Reggae's impact on pop remained spasmodic. The success of rap in the eighties, however, owed much to the "dub" techniques of the ska and reggae "sound system" disk jockeys.

African Music

From Algerian rai to Zairean soukous to South African mbaqanga, Africa is home to an unparalleled diversity of popular-music styles. Deep in their history the complex meeting of cultures under conditions of colonial domination was crucial; no less important was the legacy of the slave trade. When the various sounds of exile transformed by their New World experience (into jazz, rumba, calypso) returned to Africa in the fifties, the effects were dramatic – not a fusion with indigenous styles, so much as a series of combustions.

The "discovery" of African music by the West has been one of the most distinctive developments of the eighties. Although European record companies were present in Africa from the 1910s, African music's popularity outside Africa had always been fitful. The changes in the eighties were due partly to determined efforts by individual African musicians to reach a wider audience, and partly to the increasing numbers of musicians basing themselves abroad. But "mainstream" success remained elusive. For many devotees this is not a matter of regret. They suspect the existing level of popularity as being a musical sightseeing trip with post-imperialist overtones – a tendency exemplified by Paul Simon's incorporation of *a capella* vocal sounds by Ladyship Black Mambazo in his best-selling album *Graceland* (1985).

▶ Nigerian juju band Sunny Adé in 1982.

compromise between art and commerce was vilified in the same breath as the industry itself; the Sex Pistols took EMI's handout, *and then* recorded a blast against the company. Meanings bestowed by history were systematically cut up, rearranged, re-used, just as punk fashion did with clothes. Musical "labels", like graphic symbols were stolen, divested of significance, often brutalized. Punk pointed to the failure of categorization to mean anything in contemporary commodity culture.

Music after punk

In punk, the position of music as sound was a paradoxical one. Music was no longer the energizing force behind change; the full effects, and effectiveness, of the "extrinsic" depended on the role of visual images, or of their memory. Yet, for the vast majority of customers, aural perception still provided the foundation of their likes and dislikes, and hence of their ability to respond in any creative way. For all its sophisticated approach, glam rock had been, by its own admission, a musical thief; while "the biggest mistake of the punks was that they rejected music" (according to ex-punk musician Mick Hucknall, in 1987). The comparatively short life of both may be attributed above all to the audience's boredom with the sounds.

Pure punk lasted only for a year or two after 1976, but its influence was out of all proportion to its longevity or its record sales. In the wake of punk a diversity of styles have co-existed. Various factors would appear to militate against this situation – corporations requiring a transnational product; commercial radio stations requiring the broadest possible audience to satisfy advertisers – yet, once again, it is the paradoxes which catch the eye. Swept up as never before in international commerce, popular music has become most valuable as a "property" not when it is sold itself, but when it helps to sell something else (sometimes, in charity festivals, even selling the needs of the poor in the Third World to the affluent Western young). But the success of music used this way depends entirely on its distinctiveness; put the other way, the commodity's success depends on a piece of music's individual autonomy.

Pop video, by contrast, which seemed intended to stake a claim for the absolute distinctiveness of each musical item, usually had the reverse effect. Whereas pop videos aimed to bring pop music into the realm of art, they more often drew attention to its kinship with advertising. Despite the global reach of the music business, and the transnational nature of the best-selling sounds, it remained true that the most successful musicians were American or British. Artists from France and Germany could break through their stranglehold briefly; musicians from other cultures were often condemned to an audience limited to their own countries.

In the late 1980s popular music could still be the arena where fundamental issues in mass culture and society were worked out. This is clearly seen in the changing "female iconography" of performers such as Madonna. For all its immediacy and contemporaneity, this reinterpretation was also historically articulate. Madonna's use of male backing groups, for example, had to be seen against the history of girl groups in pop music, while her turning of the stereotyped images of women to devastating advantage evoked the torch singers of the twenties and thirties.

Past and present interact, too, in one of the most remarkable figures of the eighties, Michael Jackson. Jackson drew on black dance rhythms of the street, on stylistic elements in soul and disco, and the use of video (not forgetting his ownership of the rights of many Beatles songs), all this pointing to a mastery of contemporary materials and a successful attempt to reach – and profit from – as wide an audience as possible. In the same vein, the alterations to his image in 1987 – lightening of the skin, plastic surgery on the nose – were an insurance policy for maintaining the breadth of his appeal in a transnational, transracial business. But other interpretations are possible, when historical factors are considered. One, more negative, suggests that skin lightening has disquieting echoes of hair straightening preparations by means of which many blacks in the twenties and thirties sought to ease their way in the white-controlled world. But a second interpretation, reaching still further back, is more positive. "Whiting-up" is a reversal of the "blacking-up" done by minstrels of the turn of the century (see page 44). In the context of his profoundly black music, Jackson in whiteface (white veneer on black body) draws attention to increasing black control in the white man's game.

At the same time, Jackson's knowing use of images and style suggest that more recent history has had its impact, too. In his minute attention to dress and to body language, in his confusion of sexuality and childishness, there are clear reminders of the seventies. Seen in this light, what may make Michael Jackson so unusual, therefore, is the interplay of the ecstatic and the extrinsic. Whether that encounter will be as productive as earlier ones in the popular music story remains to be seen.

▲ David Bowie has continually changed his image since the early 1970s, consciously challenging his audience's confidence in established stylistic boundaries. His music changed direction several times in the later 1970s and 1980s, allowing him to keep at one remove from his fans.

◄▼ The less dispassionate styles of Prince (opposite) and Michael Jackson, by comparison, seem to signify greater self-identification, but control is always there. So too is ambiguity. Even in the blatantly erotic performances of Prince, the puzzling combination of lust and piety leaves audiences both involved and removed. For Michael Jackson's even larger following there is a double enigma: of "funky" physicality and innocence; and of a pale face singing black music.

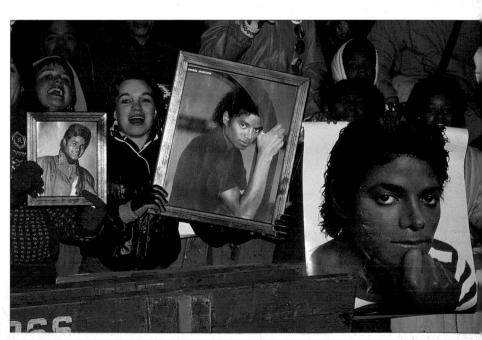

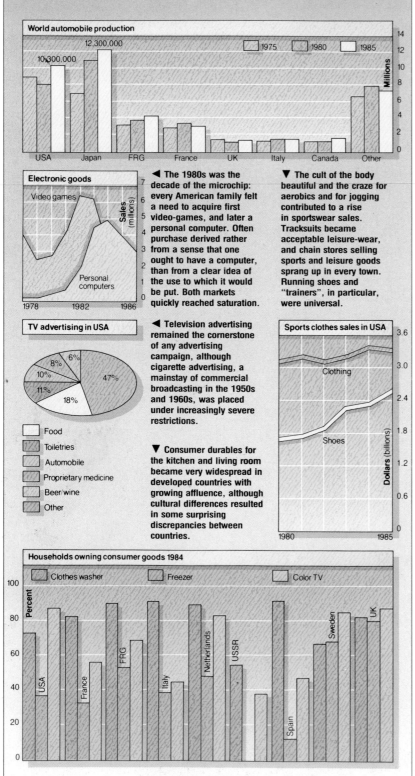

Datafile

The 1970s and 1980s saw the final creation of a "world style", with international companies marketing identical clothes and goods in identical stores throughout the world. The result was for design to move upmarket, to look for new ways of offering added value by adding "style" to goods, whether by putting the designer's label on the outside of clothes, or by making the element of style ostentatiously visible.

▼ In the 1970s and 1980s the United States finally lost its pre-eminence in automobile manufacture to Japan. The motor trade throughout the world adapted to rising oil prices and fears of oil shortages by building smaller, cheaper and more fuel-efficient cars.

World automobile production

12,300,000
10,300,000

1975 1980 1985

USA Japan FRG France UK Italy Canada Other

Millions

Electronic goods

Video games

Personal computers

Sales (millions)

1978 1982 1986

◀ The 1980s was the decade of the microchip: every American family felt a need to acquire first video-games, and later a personal computer. Often purchase derived rather from a sense that one ought to have a computer, than from a clear idea of the use to which it would be put. Both markets quickly reached saturation.

▼ The cult of the body beautiful and the craze for aerobics and for jogging contributed to a rise in sportswear sales. Tracksuits became acceptable leisure-wear, and chain stores selling sports and leisure goods sprang up in every town. Running shoes and "trainers", in particular, were universal.

TV advertising in USA

47%
6%
8%
10%
11%
18%

- Food
- Toiletries
- Automobile
- Proprietary medicine
- Beer/wine
- Other

◀ Television advertising remained the cornerstone of any advertising campaign, although cigarette advertising, a mainstay of commercial broadcasting in the 1950s and 1960s, was placed under increasingly severe restrictions.

▼ Consumer durables for the kitchen and living room became very widespread in developed countries with growing affluence, although cultural differences resulted in some surprising discrepancies between countries.

Sports clothes sales in USA

Clothing

Shoes

Dollars (billions)

1980 1985

Households owning consumer goods 1984

Clothes washer   Freezer   Color TV

Percent

USA France FRG Italy Netherlands USSR Spain Sweden UK

In the 1950s and even the 1960s high fashion, for all its caprice and change, had given the impression of a world of stability and consensus. As the West became increasingly crisis-ridden in the 1970s, first politically and then economically, this was reflected in the turbulence and confusion of fashion. Now, fashion originated on the streets, in art colleges and on student campuses.

A confusion of styles

It became a fashion cliché to say that *haute couture* was dead, that a pluralism of styles meant that everyone could wear "their own thing". In fact it was more complicated than that. There were very definite looks, and equally definite ways not to look. Fashion manufacturers and designers on the one hand, and consumers on the other, were becoming more sophisticated and more aware of the fragmentation of society into more subtly defined social groupings; the old identifications of class and generation gave way to definitions that no longer indicated just status, but also the sort of person you thought you were.

Artists and bohemians of the 19th century had originated the habit of dressing *against* the dominant mode, but by the 1970s the practice was so common that the notion of a dominant mode itself seemed to lose all meaning. Even "classic" styles – the Burberry raincoats, tweeds, tartans and cashmere cardigans of the British upper class – could be rejuvenated by the self-parody of Sloane or, in the United States, Preppie fashions. Hippy fashions, "clone" fashions (the new macho look for gay men), punks, new romantics, "Dallasty" dressing, Laura Ashley (a very middle-class style) and even feminist fashions all challenged the dominance of Paris. With the return, however, of a more open and flaunting smartness in the second half of the 1980s, the predictions of the death of Paris appeared to be premature, though contemporary designer dressing seems a marker primarily of money rather than class or status.

The fashion industry was also changing to meet these changed circumstances. At one end, mass-produced fashion was increasingly monopolized by a few huge firms who spread their production processes across many countries, exporting labor costs in particular to the Third World. At the other end, sweatshops began once more to proliferate in London, New York and other Western fashion centers. The old "middle-class couture" firms of the mid-century tended to be squeezed out, but there was room for new designers who created advanced looks and manufactured in relatively small quantities. At the consumer end, despite the proliferation of styles, the market was increasingly dominated by a few very large multiple chain stores.

THE NEW NARCISSISM

Men's fashions were increasingly drawn into the carousel of changing styles; the new narcissism expressed itself both in the bizarre designs of Jean-Paul Gaultier, who claimed that his Parisian styles were inspired by the King's Road, Chelsea, and in the smartening up of men's high-street shops, where designer sweaters, baggy trousers and Lacoste and Ralph Lauren style shirts were now to be seen.

The creation of lifestyles

Bombarded with mass-media images, both men and women with aspirations to style have been increasingly encouraged to perceive fashion as a performance and a game. In the 1950s the fashion magazines constantly advised women to "know your type and stick to it", whereas today their advice is more likely to be on how to create a whole variety of "looks". Fashion as performance, masquerade and play ties in with a greater eclecticism in fashion; it also fits with the continuing

▼ The eighties have seen the shopping malls of the United States spread around the world where "consumer choice" turns out to mean branches of the same chain stores in whichever shopping precinct you happen to be.

thirst for "retro-chic". This recycling of fashions from the recent past has become a particularly significant element in mass-media representations. The global successes of television series such as *Brideshead Revisited* and *The Jewel in the Crown* relied in part on the meticulous reproduction of the fashions of the 1920s and 1930s respectively. What fashion took from these productions was an often romantic, indeed sentimental imagery of modes and manners which were in reality rigidly class-bound, imperialist and racist. By vaguely aping the styles of a decadent aristocracy, the British were able to justify their national past while transforming themselves into the heroes and heroines their grandparents might conceivably have been.

The recreation of such fashions gives the consumer a more distanced and ironic attitude to fashion. The consumption of fashion still relates to the identity of the wearer, but also increasingly to chosen "lifestyles". We no longer announce our

membership of a class or status group with our clothes; rather, it is common to invent a "lifestyle", while "personality" and "identity" are less stable than used to be believed.

The slow evolution of fashion lines is therefore to some extent displaced by fads that can be easily discarded, and some of these fads originate in the costumes of public figures: stars, royalty and television characters. The French designer Claude Montana thought up the fashion for wide shoulders bulked out with heavy shoulder pads, but it was American soap opera and Britain's Princess Diana that popularized it. On the other hand, the original Boy George look – Hasidic hat and curls, vivid makeup, and a kind of tent-like robe over baggy trousers – was the pop star's very own street style, widely copied by young *female* fans. The same was true of the 1985 Madonna look of sleaze, tousled locks tied up with rags, and heavy "fifties" lipstick.

The varying reception of these various fashions reinforces generation gaps at the same time as it narrows some gender ones, just as the youth fashions of the 1950s and 1960s did. But 1960s fashions aimed to make *everyone* look youthful, and how far to raise your hem was a source of intense discussion among women over 30 years old at that time. Few people over 20 have ever wanted to look like Boy George or Madonna.

Although students of the eighties may wear black in the manner of the Parisian existentialists of the late forties, it is without their politics, and while they may revitalize the dress and music of fifties' beatniks, it is often minus the social protest of the earlier time. Style has come to replace content. Is it the case, then, that in the end the use of clothes to express dissidence does, as British critic and jazz musician George Melly once suggested, turn "revolt into style"?

Revolt or style?

One counter-cultural fashion at least retained its power to shock for a decade: punk. A peculiarly British phenomenon, punk was born in the hot summer of 1976. It was an onslaught on all received notions of beauty, taste and decency, a fashion of *objets trouvés* and "made ups", usually the refuse of daily life – safety pins, plastic dustbin liners, lavatory chains, torn jeans, ocelot fur fabric, PVC and sex-shop satin – to create a look that exploded into the washed-out aftermath of the hippy scene, ousting kaftans, smocks, bell-bottom trousers, curls and natural faces in favor of shaved heads, rag-wrapped limbs and faces scarified with fright make-up of black lips and reddened eyes. One unusual feature of this "ugly" and shocking look is that, at the same time that it permeated mainstream fashion – every high-street hairdresser in the eighties could turn out young women and men with spiked hair and shaved necks – it has also remained a hard-line counter-cultural fashion, used by sections of the young to express their profound alienation from contemporary society. At the same time, in its esthetic connections with surrealism and the avant garde it operated to question what is meant by "beauty" or "ugliness", and brought the practice of art into the performance of everyday life.

Although punk influenced mainstream fashion, by the late 1980s that influence was waning, overtaken by the materialist ethos of the decade. Counter-cultural groups, often using forms of dress to express views of the world, have frequently been fashion innovators. But in a more general way 20th-century fashions have to a large extent abandoned the hierarchical meanings they once carried. Fashion was once attacked as the living symbol of wealth and privilege, now it is more often feared as emblematic of a mass consciousness, of conformity, and a metropolitan uniformity without uniforms.

The designer culture

Once the whole of Western society had begun to participate in consumer culture, lifestyle became not only a phenomenon that affected subcultures but a commodity available to all. A range of manufactured lifestyles, each advertising its unique qualities, dominated the market-place and dictated consumption choices in the 1970s and 1980s. The boutique idea provided a basis on which countless retail set-ups were subsequently established. In Britain the success of the Laura Ashley and Next retail chains consolidated the role that the promotion of a complete lifestyle – clothing, furniture and interior decoration – played in selling goods to a particular group of customers. Whether nostalgic or modern, each consumer style functioned on the level of its visual and symbolic identity. In the second half of the 1970s one option emerged which emphasized the role of the designer in creating style. The "designer-jeans" phenomenon, launched in the United States as a marketing ploy to help individualize and put added value into otherwise anonymous, mass-produced artefacts, quickly spread. Hairdressers became hair-designers, and designer-shops appeared selling ranges of "designed" products, from paper-clip holders to chairs. The goods were united less by their function than by the claim to individuality in the esthetic sensibility which had created them and

▲ The pop star Madonna's image of 1985–86 deliberately made cultural bricolage and style sleaze into an ambiguous image of a femininity which vaguely suggested defiance and rebellion.

► Punk took anti-fashion dressing just about as far as it could go – only to be gobbled up by mainstream fashion, where it emerged in the spike hairstyles, unisex earrings and omnipresent black of the mid-1980s. Punk was the ultimate urban style – the violence and decline of the inner city reinterpreted in anarchistic terms on the human body.

▼ Madonna attracted imitators among pre-teen girls. Style and image are reaching younger age groups; and the marketers of the Madonna image welcome this, seeing in the nine- and ten-year-olds an easily manipulated market.

◀▲ Two couture influences dominated the 1980s: the Italian and the Japanese. In the early 1980s Japanese *haute couture* wrapped women in body-disguising shrouds in colors of black, mud and porridge. Issey Miyake, a truly innovative designer, modified these into garments which are still fluid and have immediate appeal and sensuousness (left). The Italians created a business-woman's mode which re-appropriated a certain masculinity and rendered it bold and alluring. The origins of the big shoulder pads of the mid-1980s was also to be traced to the American soap operas *Dallas* and *Dynasty* (above) but the Italians Armani and Versace brought the power-dressing look to *haute couture*.

▲ Swatch watches are just one example of the extension of style and design into more and more accessories; or the extension of gadgets and machines into the total outfit of the individual. The Filofax, the Walkman, the watch, the personal calculator — are they part of one's outfit or part of one's interior decor; more like a garment or more like a telephone or more like a handbag? Either way their style, shape and color form part of the total look which marks the wearer out as designer style, yuppie, high street or avant-garde.

which would, by implication, consume them.

Conran's Habitat principle (see page 166) lost its appeal to the "knowing minority" by moving downmarket. Something else was needed to re-inject added value into those products which courted an elite, taste-conscious market. The answer lay not only in selling "good taste" but in creating a whole design culture to surround and guarantee it. The use of the designer label served this function, isolating those objects to which it was attached from the mass of undifferentiated artefacts.

The design esthetic of the 1980s

The designer-shops of the early 1980s, in New York, Milan, Paris, Tokyo, Copenhagen, London, sold the same artefacts that had won prizes for good design in the 1950s. The same esthetic, characterized by geometric simplicity and mono-chromes, was present. Good taste required a return to the safe, well-trodden path of inter-national Modernism. A cult-object movement developed in the 1980s. It suggested that only a small group of cognoscenti had enough know-ledge and refined taste to identify these special objects. "Classic" objects from the near past such as the Zippo lighter, Arne Jacobsen's ash-trays and Alvar Aalto glass were re-appropriated and set alongside "new classics" such as Richard Sap-per's Tizio light, and simple black alarm clocks and radios from the Braun company, which set out to emulate their qualities of timelessness and functional good taste.

Many manufacturers participated in the growing international fashion for designer goods. Richard Sapper's kettle designed for Italian metalwork manufacturer Alessi immediately became a cult object *par excellence*. Italy had been the first coun-try in the postwar years to identify its upmarket products – mostly furniture, plastic products and electronic goods – with designers' names and as a result, men such as Archille Castiglioni, Vico Magistretti, Mario Bellini, Ettore Sottsass and Marco Zanuso became well known figures in the design world. Even automobile design, until then the most anonymous of areas, created its own designer heroes in the 1970s. The Italian Giorgio Giugiaro became well-known internationally as the designer of the Volkswagen Golf and Fiat Panda. Italy experienced a second wave of design-related success in the 1980s, associated this time with an extension of the alternative ideas it had pioneered in the late 1960s.

The Italians had been the first to understand the limitations of the Modernist design esthetic, but by the late 1970s the rest of the design world had realized that the concept of "ultimate form" was obsolete. Now the radical designers of the 1960s emerged again to question conventional design values.

The Italian Post Modern movement centered on the work of a small number of designers as-sociated with two experimental groups – Studio Alchymia and Memphis. From 1979 they held regular exhibitions to coincide with the Milan Furniture Fair, borrowing the concept of the an-nual show from fashion designers, with whose philosophy they sought to identify themselves.

▼ The association between pop stars and fashion continued beyond the rebellious individuality of Madonna: here British pop group Madness are dressed in Mod revival style – though with 1980s coloring – by Jasper Conran.

Furniture and interior design were seen to be linked more with the concept of image than with ideal forms, and to be more part of the general process of mass communication and mass culture than ever before. This attempt to align design with mass culture became the hallmark of the New Design. Ironically, however, the experimental nature of the new movement meant that work was generally limited to the prototype stage and therefore became, in real terms, somewhat exclusive and expensive. This failure to achieve in practical terms what was envisaged in theory had often previously foiled attempts to inject a level of popular culture into the designed artefact.

The work of Ettore Sottsass, which had been so influential in the earlier period, continued to inspire much of the radical Italian design of the 1980s. His pieces emphasized the use of surface pattern, were banal in nature and appropriated from what he called "non-culture": the mosaic on the floor of suburban bars and the spongy pattern on the covers of government account books. References to imagery from the 1950s abounded, but this was less a conscious reference to the past than a use of imagery still found in the Italian suburbs. Decorated plastic laminates covered the surfaces of the oddly shaped bookcases, chairs, tables and stools that made up Sottsass' contribution to the collection.

Alessandro Mendini, who also provided items for the Studio Alchymia collections, was pre-occupied with the concept of "kitsch" produced by

▲ With its steel girders and glass top, the "Mainframe" desk, manufactured by Bonomi Design Limited, epitomized the "High-Tech" movement of the 1980s.

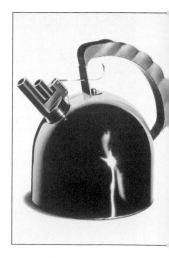

◄▲ The thinking behind Ettore Sottsass' bookcase – Carlton, which was designed for the first Memphis exhibition held in Milan in 1981, contrasts dramatically with Richard Sapper's whistling kettle, manufactured by Alessi in 1984. While the former represents a direct threat to the essentially "chic" values of the Italian design establishment, the latter confirms its ideals by becoming a "cult" object.

technical reliability and low price, joined the bandwagon producing goods, such as the Sony Walkman, the Olympus camera and the Sharp hand-held calculator, which quickly became new design classics. Although in the area of technological goods it did not name its designers, the creators of Japanese fashion design, among them Issey Miyake and Yohji Yamamoto, became well-known names in the 1980s, influencing the minimal nature of fashion at this time.

As in the 1960s, fashion in the 1980s was still at the forefront of design, influencing other goods which formed part of the same lifestyle. While in the 1970s design culture had succeeded in providing lifestyle accompaniments for an elite, international set, by the following decade it was becoming democratized, mainly through the efforts of the mass media which set out to spread their sphere of influence across a much wider social spectrum. Product advertising, Sunday supplements, magazines and High Street retail outlets began to use the words "design" and "designer" to provide added value for a wide range of goods. Along with good health and male narcissism – two inventions of the advertising industry in the 1970s and 1980s – design became a popular catchword, guaranteeing added value for the consumer and increased sales and profits for the manufacturer.

the mass dissemination of images in the contemporary environment. He used fine-art imagery – from Kandinsky and Seurat, for example – to stress the fact that even high culture, once duplicated, became part of the world of the banal. While Sottsass remained optimistic about the possibility of designs making significant cultural statements, Mendini's more pessimistic work communicated the impossibility of combating fundamental social and economic laws by means of design.

In 1981 Sottsass launched his own design collection called "Memphis". Less esoteric than Alchymia, but still covered in brightly patterned plastic laminates, Memphis furniture soon became well-known images, disseminated by the mass media and used in countless advertising campaigns. Images which had their origins in the mass media were recirculated. While, superficially, Memphis initiated an international style revolution which penetrated fashionable quarters worldwide, on a deeper level it stood for the final demise of the European Modern Movement as the arbiter of taste and good design.

The free-for-all encouraged by the Memphis experiment became one of the characteristics of the 1980s and the problem of establishing criteria for evaluating design became increasingly difficult: "Appropriate" replaced "good" and the consumer moved to the center of the picture, displacing the earlier emphasis upon production and technology as the major determinant of good design. The link between design and ethics was broken and the possibility emerged of design embracing popular values.

By the 1980s, design culture had become part of international trading. Japan, which had hitherto sold its high-tech products on the basis of their

▼ The main contribution of Japan to international design culture was that of a "high-tech" esthetic, visible in the sophisticated audio equipment which is sold to the whole world. Rather than encouraging a "user-friendly" approach to these new, complex machines, it opted for a "value-for-money" philosophy which suggested that the most complicated-looking equipment offered the most advanced technology at an affordable price.

◄ The Olympus OM-1 camera was just one of the many "high-tech" products to emerge from postwar Japan and penetrate international market-places. It offered sophisticated technology at a reasonable price and epitomized the Japanese interest in encouraging advanced technology rather than innovative design for its own sake. Japan opted for the manufacture of small consumer machines because of the ease with which such goods could be exported in large numbers.

THE LIGHT FANTASTIC

► Computer graphics manipulating the image for advertising, graphics and art, (this page).

►► The video game (far right) offered a simple, logical world to get lost in; rides in sophisticated fairgrounds (center right) often sought to reproduce the experiences.

► Jean-Michel Jarre played a concert in London in 1988, combining the most up-to-date computer technology in sound and visuals with the evergreen appeal of fireworks.

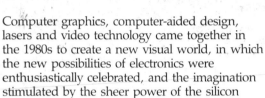

Computer graphics, computer-aided design, lasers and video technology came together in the 1980s to create a new visual world, in which the new possibilities of electronics were enthusiastically celebrated, and the imagination stimulated by the sheer power of the silicon chip.

The development of video technology, with its simple techniques of stopping the image, recoloring it, inverting or distorting it, digitizing it and easily intercutting it, provided pop music with a visual counterpart to the ephemeral, studio-created three-minute single; and the pop video became the new expressive form of the 1980s. Meanwhile, a combination of silicon-chip logic and video graphics had created a multitude of simple, bounded but highly seductive alternative worlds, to be reached for the price of a small coin in any video parlor around the world. The programmers created universes in which dragons sat on hidden treasure, voracious monsters pursued you around mazes and aliens attacked in ever more exotic space ships. The iconography of the B-movie and the cartoon comic reigned supreme, though often modulated by a quirky sense of self-deprecating humor.

Computer graphics were turned to far more serious ends in all kinds of industrial uses, yet they became omnipresent, particularly in high-profile graphics such as television company logos and ads. The possibility of producing solid three-dimensional images, through computer graphics or through holography, which could produce a free-standing 3-D image, added new opportunities. Film producers experimented with ways of integrating the conventional photograph with the new image.

Finally, the new imagery was used simply for visual delight. Light shows became an essential element in tourist attractions throughout Europe and America, and the laser beam, with its pencil-thin beams of intensely colored light, was used to more and more grandiose effect in rock concerts. As musicians such as Jean-Michel Jarre developed greater sophistication in the use of computer technology within their music, they found ways of combining sound and light into enormous spectaculars.

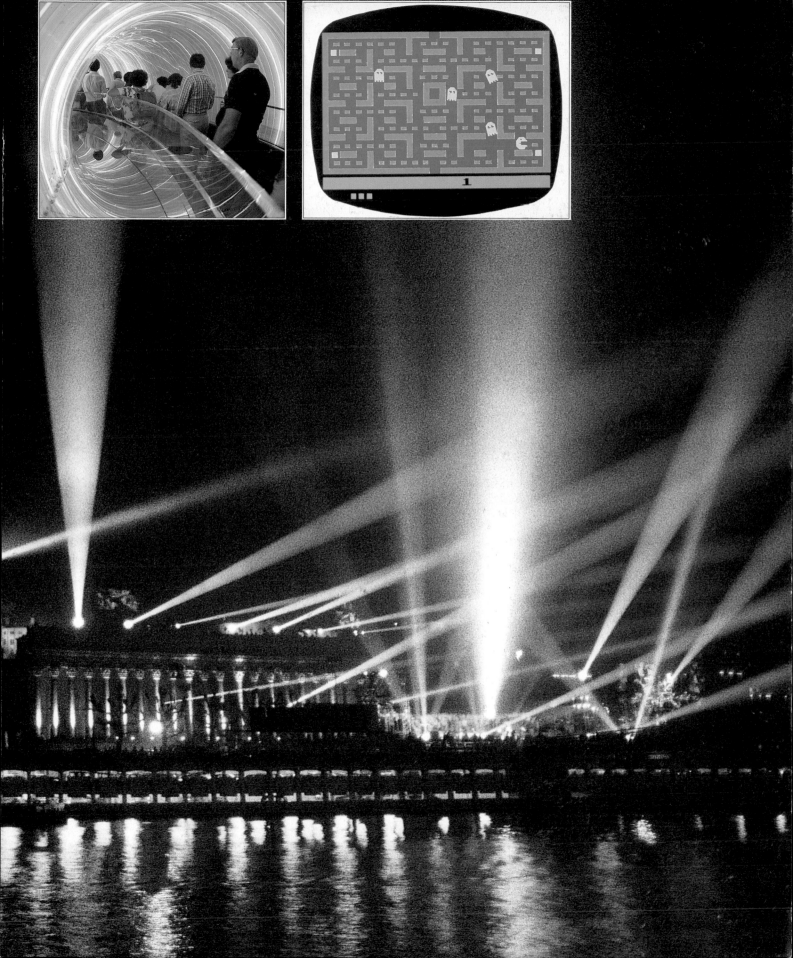

BIOGRAPHIES

Louis Armstrong (center)

Roger Bannister

Theda Bara

Aalto, Alvar 1898–1976

Finnish architect, city planner and furniture designer. His mature work was informal and personal – with an imaginative use of free forms, indigenous materials and the ability to "fit" buildings to their sites. The Saynatsalo town hall, set in a forest clearing, is his masterpiece. Three commissions undertaken in 1927–28 established his international reputation, especially his use of wood and spatially complex interiors in the Viipuri library.

Aaron, Hank 1934–

US baseball player. One of the best hitters in the game, over 23 professional seasons he established several records. Turning professional in 1952, in a total of 3298 games his totals include 775 home runs, 1477 extra-base hits and 2297 runs batted in 12364 times at bat. With a lifetime batting average of 0.305, his 3771 hits and 2174 runs scored were at that time exceeded only by Ty Cobb. Most of his career he played for the National League Boston (later Atlanta) Braves. His last two seasons (1975–6) were with the American League Milwaukee Brewers.

Agnelli, Giovanni 1866–1945

Italian industrialist. Educated at military academy and an officer in the 1880s, he founded FIAT in Turin in 1899. FIAT quickly became the biggest motor company in Italy and the major supplier of arms to the Italian forces in both World Wars. He was a staunch anti-communist during the Fascist period, elevated to the Senate by Mussolini in 1923.

Aldrich, Robert 1918–83

US film director and producer. He began as a production clerk in Hollywood in 1941 and had assisted several directors and written and directed episodes of TV series before directing his first picture, *The Big League*, in 1953. He set up his own production company in 1954. His style was typically dynamic, full of movement, with climaxes of brutality and chaos. Credits include *The Big Knife* (1955), *Whatever Happened to Baby Jane?* (1962) and *The Dirty Dozen* (1967).

Allen, Woody 1935–

US film actor, director, screenwriter, playwright and jazz clarinetist. His cynical, self-deprecating humor was a dominant influence on American humor in the 1970s. *What's New Pussycat?* (1965) was his first screen credit (writer/actor), followed by other parodies, including *Bananas* (1971) and *Love and Death* (1975). Greater success came with *Annie Hall* (1977) and *Manhattan* (1979), and in the eighties his subject matter broadened, in films like *Midsummer Night's Sex Comedy* (1982), *Stardust Memories* (1980) and *Hannah and Her Sisters* (1986).

Arbuckle, Roscoe "Fatty" 1887–1933

US film actor, director and screenwriter. Vaudeville preceded comedy one-reelers for Selig Polyscope, from 1907. In 1913 came the move to Sennett's Keystone Cops and starring roles with Chaplin, Conklin and Mabel Normand. By 1916 he was writing and directing himself; in 1917 he went independent. A large, baby-faced, remarkably agile man, he was one of Hollywood's most popular stars when his career ended in a brutal sex scandal (1921). He later directed pseudonymously but his attempts to perform were doomed.

Arden, Elizabeth 1878–1966

Canadian-born US businesswoman. Born Florence Nightingale Graham, she studied nursing before opening her first beauty salon on New York's Fifth Avenue in 1909. She eventually became one of the world's leading producers of beauty aids, selling over 300 different items and owning two luxury beauty resorts at her death. She was a pioneer in the advertising of cosmetics.

Armstrong, Louis 1900–71

US jazz trumpeter, vocalist and composer. The greatest jazz trumpeter ever, he joined Joe Oliver's band in 1922, leaving for New York in 1924. By 1930 he was a star with some great recordings (including *Potato Head Blues* and *West End Blues*) behind him and he had invented scat singing. In 1935 Mafia man Joe Glaser became his agent, and until 1947 he played with big bands. His final line-up, the six-piece All Stars, produced classic albums such as *Plays Fats* and *At the Crescendo*.

Astaire, Fred 1899–1987

US actor, dancer and choreographer. After a successful stage career with his sister Adele, he turned to films in 1933. His partnership with Ginger Rogers lasted through 10 films, including *Roberta* and *Top Hat* (both 1935), *Swing Time* (1936) and *Carefree* (1938). His sophisticated, yet apparently casual style was based on matchless technique. Later partners included Rita Hayworth, Eleanor Powell and Cyd Charisse. He also had a light, charming, singing voice.

Atlas, Charles 1893–1972

Italian-born body builder. He was the creator of a popular body-building course marketed by mail order. A young, skinny immigrant, he suffered the famous sand-kicking humiliation when a lifeguard stole his girl at Coney Island, but by 1922 he had improved his physique so much he was described as "America's Most Perfectly Developed Man." In 1929 he and a young advertising man, Charles Ronan, began marketing a program of isotonic exercises and advice on nutrition.

Bailey, David 1938–

British photographer and film-director. A self-taught photographer, his first pictures were accepted by *Vogue* magazine in 1959, when he was only 21. His method was to work with only one model – at first, Jean Shrimpton, and later Marie Helvin – and his fresh lively style of fashion portraiture has made him one of the most successful and most durable British fashion and beauty photographers. He has several books to his credit, most notably *Nudes*.

Baker, Josephine 1906–75

US-born dancer and singer. A flamboyant entertainer whose beauty and vivacious personality made her the toast of Paris in the late twenties and thirties, she joined a touring company at 16, later working in Boston and New York. On Broadway she rose through the ranks of *Chocolate Dandies*, also making an impression in the floor show at Harlem's Plantation Club. In 1925 she went to Paris for *La Revue Negre* and stayed, taking French citizenship in 1937; at the height of her success she was the highest-paid entertainer in Europe.

Ball, Lucille 1911–

US actress. In the fifties the star of one of TV's most successful comedy shows, *I Love Lucy*, she was America's greatest female clown but major Hollywood stardom evaded her. She had begun playing bit parts in films in 1933, later graduating to support and co-star roles with Bob Hope and Red Skelton. The TV production company she and husband Desi Arnez created eventually controlled RKO, and on divorce in 1960 she became president of a business grossing an annual $25 million. She eventually sold to Gulf and Western, and continued starring on TV, in *The Lucy Show*.

Bannister, Roger 1929–

British athlete. First to run a mile in under four minutes (6 May 1954), he trained systematically to break what was regarded as the ultimate psychological barrier in running. He ran while training to be a neurologist and took the title for the mile at the British (1951 and 1953-4) and Empire (1954) championships and for the European 1500 metres (1954). He published *First Four Minutes* (1955).

Bara, Theda 1890–1955

US film actress. Her first big role, as a femme fatale in *A Fool There Was* (1915), brought instant stardom. Born Theodosia Goodman of Cincinnati, she was marketed as the child of a French painter and his Egyptian mistress, born in the Sahara and named after an anagram of "Arab Death". From 1914 to 1919 she appeared as the vamp in more than 40 films.

▲ Brigitte Bardot

▲ Franz Beckenbauer

▲ Chuck Berry

Bardot, Brigitte 1934–

French film actress. She made the cover of *Elle* at 15 and was spotted by Roger Vadim, an aspiring film director. Her film career began that year, but it was in 1956 that *And God Created Woman*, the first film directed by Vadim, by then her husband, that established her as the first "sex kitten", a sensual, innocently responsive young woman. Her spontaneous private life excited as much interest internationally as her films, which included *Love is My Profession* (1958), *La Verité* (1960) and *Viva Maria* (1965).

Basie, Count 1904–84

US jazz pianist and organist. With Bennie Moten's band from 1929 to 1933, he began forming Kansas City groups, taking with him several fellow members, from 1934. By late 1936 he had moved to New York, gained a record contract and enlarged to a 12-piece. His style relied on a uniquely cohesive rhythm section which functioned like a sextet. Through the forties the line-up changed a lot and the band shrank to an octet, but in 1952 he established a 16-piece and in 1954 made the first of many European tours.

Beaton, Cecil 1904–80

British photographer and stage designer. His decorative portraits of celebrities were his most important work. He worked as a staff photographer on *Vogue* and *Vanity Fair* in the twenties and continued his portrait work, using elaborate backgrounds that subordinated the sitter to an overall pattern. He was a war photographer in World War II. Many of his portraits are published in *The Book of Beauty*, *Persona Grata* and *It Gives Me Great Pleasure*.

Beckenbauer, Franz 1945–

West German football player. Captain of the national team that won the European championships in 1972 and the 1974 World Cup, he also captained Bayern Munich to win three European Cups and four national titles. From 1976 to 1980 he played for the New York Cosmos. Returning to West Germany, he played for Hamburg until 1982. In the late 1980s he was manager of the West German national team.

Bellini, Mario 1935–

Italian industrial designer. Graduating from the Milan Polytechnic in 1959, he has collaborated with Olivetti since 1963, and also worked with various motor companies, such as Fiat, Lancia and Renault. His most outstanding contribution to modern design is the Olivetti ET101 electronic typewriter – allegedly modeled on the shark. His Praxis typewriter was modeled on the angled lectern used by Roman scribes.

Bergman, Ingmar 1918–

Swedish film and TV director. It was with *Smiles of a Summer Night* (1955) and *The Seventh Seal* (1957) that his reputation was established. His themes are metaphysical, agonizing examinations of his own inner world or the human predicament, or studies in human psychology with the interior life of women a dominant concern. He created a troupe of actors with whom he has worked for many years. Among his greatest works are *Wild Strawberries* (1957), *The Silence* (1963), *Persona* (1966), *Cries and Whispers* (1972) and *Fanny and Alexander* (1982).

Bergman, Ingrid 1915–82

Swedish film actress. Her radiant vitality brought rapid success in Swedish films and in 1939 she went to Hollywood. She was enormously popular until 1949 when her private life shattered the wholesome image her studio had pushed hard. It was 1956 before America welcomed her back in *Anastasia*. Credits include *Casablanca* and *For Whom the Bell Tolls* (both 1943), *Gaslight* (1944), *Notorious* (1946), *Joan of Arc* (1948), *Murder on the Orient Express* (1974) and *Autumn Sonata* (1978).

Berkeley, Busby 1895–1976

US choreographer and film director. One of Broadway's leading dance directors, his film break came when Warners hired him to choreograph *42nd Street* (1933). Lavish, erotic, vulgar, his set-pieces for massed girls delighted audiences, and his inventive camera shots – from above, below, diagonal or traveling – and rhythmical cutting multiplied the pleasure. Credits include *The Gold Diggers of 1933*, *Fashions of 1934* and *Dames* (1934).

Berlin, Irving 1888–

US song writer. In a long career which spanned the jazz age through to the fifties, he wrote over 800 songs. Graduating from street singer and singing waiter to song plugger, he began writing lyrics and later his own music. He wrote for Broadway revues, musical comedies – his most popular was *Annie Get Your Gun* (1946) – and the film scores for his stage successes, notably *Top Hat* (1935), *Easter Parade* (1948) and *Call Me Madam* (1953). Among his standards are *Alexander's Ragtime Band*, *God Bless America*, *There's No Business Like Show Business* and *White Christmas*.

Berry, Chuck 1931–

US singer, composer and guitarist. As a black artist influencing white musicians, he earned the title "king of rock 'n' roll", and his style – Chicago blues spiked with country – bridged the gap between blues and pop. His first disk, *Maybellene* (1956), sold a million. Other hits include *Roll Over Beethoven* (1956), *Sweet Little Sixteen* and *Johnny B. Goode* (both 1958). Charged under the Mann Act (1959), it was 1964 before he recorded again.

Bertoia, Harry 1915–78

Italian-born sculptor and designer. He studied at Michigan's Cranbrook Academy, then taught painting and metalwork there for six years from 1937. After a period with Charles Eames, he joined Knoll Associates in 1950, for whom he designed the steel-wire Diamond or Bertoia chair (1952). He produced numerous monumental architectural sculptures, and a sound-sculpture fountain for Chicago's Standard Oil building.

Bertolucci, Bernardo 1940-

Italian film director. A leader of Italy's younger generation of directors, most of his films have a political dimension. He was Pasolini's assistant on *Accattone!* (1961) and directed his first feature in 1962. The second (1964) had a critical success, but it was 1970 before *La Strageia del Ragno* and *Il Conformista* established his reputation. Later films include *Last Tango in Paris* (1972), *1900* (1976), *La Luna* (1979) and *The Last Emperor* (1987).

Beiderbecke, Bix 1903-31

US jazz cornet player, pianist and composer. Jazz's first great lyricist and the first white jazzman admired by black musicians, his style, with its delicate, thoughtful phrasing, was influential after his death. His most famous solo is *Singing the Blues*. He began playing cornet at 15, influenced by riverboat music, and worked in New York, Chicago, St Louis and Detroit, before joining Paul Whiteman (1928-30). His piano composition was influenced by Debussy, the most famous piece being *In a Mist*.

Bikile, Abebe 1932–78

Ethiopian marathon runner. He was the first black African athlete to win an Olympic Gold medal. Trained as a member of Haile Selassie's Imperial Guards he had only run two marathons in his life before taking the gold in record time at the Rome Olympics in 1960 – barefoot. He won the marathon again in 1964, after only six weeks training, but a leg injury forced him to drop out of the Mexico City Olympics. A car accident in 1969 left him unable to walk, and he took up paraplegic sport.

Humphrey Bogart

Bjorn Borg

Clara Bow

Bogart, Humphrey 1899–1957

US actor. Unlikely star material – a slight, tight-lipped man with a lisp – he was Hollywood's antihero: self-reliant, cynical, sardonic. He made a hit on Broadway as the gangster in *The Petrified Forest* (1935), transferring successfully to film. Five years of gangster roles followed. In 1941 he had his next big chances in *High Sierra* and *The Maltese Falcon*: his great popularity continued until his death and revived in the sixties. Credits include *Casablanca* (1943), *The Big Sleep* (1946), *The Treasure of the Sierra Madre* (1947) and *The African Queen* (1952).

Boone, Pat 1934–

US singer and actor. The hottest property on disc after Presley in the late fifties, he was the safer face of rock 'n' roll. Wholesome, softspoken and religious, his wins on TV talent shows earned him a recording contract with Dot Records. He made 13 singles which sold over a million, including *Ain't That a Shame* (1955), *Friendly Persuasion* and *Remember You're Mine* (both 1956), and *Love Letters in the Sand* (1957).

Borg, Bjorn 1956–

Swedish tennis player. The first man to win the Wimbledon singles title five times in succession (1976–80) since the 1900s, he began playing very young and turned professional in 1972. He won the Italian Open at 17, the French at 18, and by 1975 he had broken the record for consecutive cup singles wins. His most powerful shots were his serve and the two-handed backhand. He won the French Open six times (1974–5 and 1978–81) and the World Championship three times (1978–80), retiring in 1983.

Botham, Ian 1955–

British cricketer. He made his debut for Somerset Country Cricket Club in 1974 and first played for England three years later. An all-rounder of exceptional power and ability, he almost single-handedly saved England from losing the Ashes in 1981. His ebullient character has often led him into trouble off the pitch. He became one of the leading wicket-takers in Test cricketers.

Bourke-White, Margaret 1906–71

US photographer. One of the first to create photo essays, she became an industrial and architectural photographer in 1927. By 1929 she had been snapped up for *Fortune*. In 1936 she was one of the first four staff photographers on the new *Life* magazine and covered World War II. Thereafter her assignments included the partition of India, unrest in South Africa and the Korean War.

Bow, Clara 1905–65

US film actress. Winning a fan-magazine beauty contest took her to Hollywood, but her break came in 1925 when the producer she was under contract to joined Paramount. Molded by the studio publicity machine with her swinging bob and cupidbow lips, she became the ultimate flapper: vibrant, liberated. *It* (1927) confirmed her status, but scandal, a shift in taste, mental instability and the coming of sound quickly put an end to her career.

Bowie, David 1947–

British singer, musician and actor. Born David Hayward-Jones, he had been working with a mime troupe, studying at a Buddhist monastery in Scotland, and running an arts laboratory before the major success of his album *The Man Who Sold the World* in 1970. The most articulate and provocative of the "glam-rock" artists of the early 1970s, he abandoned the style mid-tour in 1973, going on to explore other musical idioms, notably soul and electronic music. He has also starred in films such as *The Man Who Fell to Earth* (1976) and *Merry Christmas, Mr Lawrence* (1982).

Bradman, Don 1908-

Australian cricketer. The greatest batsman ever, he set an unequaled Test record with an average of 99.94 runs per innings. His perfect eye and timing were acquired early. He scored 334 runs in a Test innings in 1930, during his first English tour, a record which no Australian has equaled, and he scored 19 Test centuries against England from 1928 to 1948. In later years he was involved with cricket administration in Australia.

Brando, Marlon 1924–

American actor. A Method actor, schooled at the Actors' Studio, his first stage success was on Broadway, with *A Streetcar Named Desire*. His naturalistic film performances in *The Men* (1950), *A Streetcar Named Desire* (1951), *Viva Zapata!* (1952) and *On the Waterfront* (1954) won admirers and detractors. No one could deny his charisma and young audiences saw him as a icon of their generation. His own non-conformity (and age?) made finding parts difficult in the sixties but *The Godfather* and *Last Tango in Paris* (both 1972) confirmed his comeback.

Brel, Jacques 1925–78

Belgian-born French singer and songwriter. He began writing *chansons* in 1950 and was performing at the Trois Baudets theater in Paris by 1954. He soon became an international star, and in the 1960s toured both the USA and the USSR. His lyrics contained a mordant satire on modern morals, set to sophisticated melodies far removed from formulaic pop or folk. He also wrote an opera called *Le Voyage dans la lune*.

Brown, James 1928–

US singer. A dynamic, highly influential rhythm & blues artist and great showman, he was touring with the Famous Flames when their self-financed disk *Please, Please, Please* (1956) became a hit and won him a contract with King; *Try Me* (1958) was another million-seller. In 1964 he began touring with the electrifying James Brown Show. By 1968 he was seen as a black leader, appealing for calm after the death of Martin Luther King, but his message was simply "soul power".

Brundage, Avery 1887–1975

American industrialist and sports administrator. After training as an engineer, in 1915 he set up the Avery Brundage Company, a construction firm based in Chicago. But he is chiefly remembered for his involvement with the International Olympic Committee, which he joined in 1936 and led from 1952 to his retirement in 1972. A keen amateur sportsman in his youth, he struggled to keep the Olympic Games free from professionalism and political interference.

Bugatti, Ettore 1881–1947

Italian automobile manufacturer. A designer for several small companies before setting up a factory at Molsheim, Alsace, in 1909, his first production model, the Type 13, was raced successfully in 1911. Two of his other racers, the Brescia and the Type 35, were outstanding, the latter being the only car capable of winning grand prix while priced for amateurs. A passionately meticulous man, his great folly was the Type 41 (La Royale), designed to be the ultimate supercar: only six were ever built and three sold. He used the redundant engines in high-speed railcars in the thirties.

Carson, Johnny 1925–

American television personality. He worked as a magician in the 1940s and wrote comedy routines in the 1950s. His humorous monologues in *The Johnny Carson Show* led NBC to give him a spot on *The Tonight Show* in 1962, after which his naughty boy image and his "desk sofa" interview technique made him one of the nation's most popular television personalities.

Cash, Johnny 1932–

US singer. In 1954 Sun Records gave Johnny Cash and the Tennessee Two a tryout. It was a hit and others followed, including *I Walk the Line*: they had a unique, hard, rockabilly sound. In 1958 he signed with Columbia; in time his popularity waned but with the unconventional Tijuana brass sound on *Ring of Brass* (1963) he was big again. The first major artist to record before a prison audience, with his *At Folsom Prison* album (1968) he landed an ABC-TV series.

▲ David Bowie

▲ Donald Bradman

▲ Jim Clark

Castiglione, Achille 1918–
Italian industrial designer. Born into a family of designers, he was a founder of the Italian Association for Industrial Design in 1966. His style is influenced by the theories of the surrealist artist Marcel Duchamp. His "Toio" lamp for Flos, for example, used a car head-lamp. His wit is also evident in the "Arco" lamp, with its tiny arc-and-reflector light supported by a massive marble base.

Castle, Vernon (1887–1918) and Irene (1893–1969)
US husband-and-wife dancing team. They were married in 1911 and achieved world fame, creating the one-step and the turkey trot and bringing the glide, hesitation waltz, tango and bunny hug to a wider audience through their exhibition dancing and a book, *Modern Dancing* (1914). Vernon was killed training cadet pilots during World War I.

Chanel, Coco 1883–1971
French couturier. She persuaded women to look for casual, understated elegance and introduced several classics, including the jersey dress, trench coat, turtleneck sweater, and little black dress, as well as costume jewelry and bobbed hair. Her empire grew from a tiny hat shop opened in 1913 and included a textile business, perfume laboratory and jewelry workshop. The perfume Chanel No.5 was introduced in 1922 and financed many of her enterprises. She retired in 1938 but made a comeback in 1954, introducing another classic, the cardigan suit.

Chaplin, Charlie 1889-1977
British actor, director, producer and screenwriter. A childhood music-hall artiste, he created one of the world's greatest screen clowns, Charlie the Tramp – pathetic, heroic, naively full of impossible aspirations and yet finally triumphant – pantomimic performances of balletic delicacy. His masterpieces include *The Tramp* (1915), *The Kid* (1921), *The Gold Rush* (1925), and two silents made after sound *City Lights*, (1931) and *Modern Times* (1935).

Chevalier, Maurice 1888–1972
French entertainer and actor. He specialized in Gallic roguery: charm, swagger and joie de vivre. Partnering Mistinguett at the *Folies-Bergère* in 1909 was his break and after 1918 he starred on the halls, earning international fame. His Hollywood career began in 1929, and he won popularity in romantic comedies like *The Love Parade* (1929), *One Hour with You* and *Love Me Tonight* (both 1932). Filming in Europe from 1935 to the late fifties, he returned to entertaining, but made a Hollywood comeback, his most successful appearance in *Gigi* (1958).

Christie, Agatha 1890–1976
British detective novelist. Her international popularity was based on ingenious plotting, the brilliant use of suspense and misdirection and an excellent ear for dialog. Her chief detectives are Hercule Poirot and Miss Marple, and she wrote 67 novels, among them *The Murder of Roger Ackroyd* (1926), *Murder on the Orient Express* (1934) and *Ten Little Niggers* (1939). She also wrote several plays (including the long-running *Mousetrap*, 1952), six pseudonymous novels and an autobiography.

Cimino, Michael 1943–
US film director and screenwriter. He co-scripted *Silent Running* (1972) and Clint Eastwood's *Magnum Force* (1973) before scripting and directing Eastwood's *Thunderbolt and Lightfoot* (1974). His next was *The Deer Hunter* (1978), which won critical success. *Heaven's Gate* (1980) became a benchmark for Hollywood extravagance.

Clair, René 1898–1981
French film director and screenwriter. One of the innovators of early sound, he explored ways of using sound, image and movement, writing or collaborating on almost all his films. His sequence of musicals – *Sous Les Toits de Paris* (1930), *Le Million* and *A Nous la Liberté* (both 1931) and *Quatorze Juillet* (1932) – were among the most original early sound films. His second film, *Entr'acte* (1924), demonstrated a brief involvement with surrealism, but many of his films were fantasies: he was a humanist, using satire or irony to make his points.

Clark, Jim 1936–68
Scottish racing driver. He won the world championship twice: in 1963 with a record seven of the 10 events (equaled in 1984 by Alain Prost), and in 1965 with six, plus Indianapolis. Entering racing in 1956, he first competed on the international circuit in 1960 for the Lotus team. Both his victories were in Lotus-Fords.

Clark, Ossie 1942–
British fashion designer. He began designing for Quorum, one of the most popular Chelsea boutiques, whilst still a student at the Royal College of Art, and joined the firm as a full-time designer in 1966. Although one of his most celebrated early designs was a high-fashion leather motorcycle jacket, he is chiefly remembered for ultra-feminine garments created from delicate fabrics such as silk, jersey and chiffon.

Connolly, Maureen 1934–69
US tennis player. In 1953 she became the first woman to win tennis's grand slam: the Wimbledon, US, Australian and French championships in one year. She had also won the Wimbledon singles in 1952 (then the second youngest woman to do so) and she won again in 1954. A serious riding accident ended her competitive career in 1954; she became an instructor.

Conran, Terence 1931-
British retail entrepreneur. After setting up a holding company in the mid-1960s, he came to prominence after the foundation of the Conran Design Group and the Habitat Group, both in 1971. Habitat stores made available a well-coordinated collection of stylish articles for the home, forerunners of the "designer" items of the 1980s. In the mid-1980s his activities included the running of high-street stores, and he also became involved in the running of museums, being founder of the Boilerhouse Project in London.

Cooper, Gary 1901-61
US film actor. One of Hollywood's most popular stars, his laconic style and lanky looks appealed to men and women: he was the strong, silent man of adventure and romance. He went to California with hopes of a career in cartooning and drifted into extra work in 1925. His break came quickly, as replacement second lead in *The Winning of Barbara Worth* (1926). In the thirties Capra and Hawks extended his range into comedy. Credits include *The Virginian* (1929), *A Farewell to Arms* (1932), *Mr Deeds Goes to Town* (1936), *Ball of Fire* (1941) and *High Noon* (1952).

Coppola, Francis Ford 1939-
US film director, screenwriter and producer. He got his first directing job from Roger Corman. The success of his second film, *You're a Big Boy Now* (1967), won him *Finian's Rainbow* (1968), which crashed. Another failure had his production company near bankruptcy, but then came *Patton* (1970), script only; *The Godfather* (1972); *American Graffiti* (1973), production only; *The Conversation* and *The Godfather*, Part II (both 1974); and *Apocalypse Now* (1979). His policy of fostering young talent suffered when financial problems loomed again and thereafter success has been fitful.

Joan Crawford

Babe Diedrikson

Sacha Distel

Courrèges, André 1923–

French couturier. He made his name in the mid-sixties with futuristic, mostly white designs after working for Balenciaga for 11 years. In 1961 he opened his own salon and by 1964 he had found youth-oriented style – a simple, trapezoid, short-skirted line. Other fashion originals include hipster pants, sequined jump suits and vinyl trimming on coats and suits.

Coward, Noel 1899–1973

British actor, director, librettist and playwright. He was an excellent actor, taking the lead in many of his plays, memorably *The Vortex* (1924) and *Private Lives* (1930). His comedies won admirers and detractors in the twenties and thirties: sophisticated, technically brilliant and frequently defying moral convention. *Hay Fever* (1925) and *Blithe Spirit* (1941) are among his most accomplished works. In 1942 he wrote, produced, co-directed and starred in the wartime sea drama *In Which We Serve*.

Crawford, Joan 1904–77

US film actress. She was the most durable Hollywood star. Not particularly pretty or sexy, she had glamor; no brilliant actress, she worked hard. Mostly she was ambitious and adaptable: a flapper to rival Bow in the twenties; working girl in the thirties; melodramatist in the forties; mature femme fatale in the fifties; and horror star in the sixties. Credits include *Our Dancing Daughters* (1928), *The Women* (1939), *Mildred Pierce* (1945), *Johnny Guitar* (1954) and *Whatever Happened to Baby Jane?* (1962).

Cronkite, Walter 1916–

American broadcast journalist. After dropping out of the University of Texas in 1935 to work for the Houston Post, he covered World War II and the Nuremberg Trials. He was taken up by CBS in 1950 and gained respect and popularity in the "You Are There" series. From 1962 to 1981 he was the anchor-man of his own nightly newscast, and his low-key broadcasting earned him the title of "The Most Trusted Man in America".

Crosby, Bing 1904–77

US vocalist. Signed by Paul Whiteman in 1927 as one of the Rhythm Boys, it was with the trio's booking at the Coconut Grove that his solo career took off. A nationwide CBS hookup in 1931 caused him to lose his voice and find fame: his unique sound was attributed to nodules on the vocal cords. The relaxed, casual style was much imitated. He made many films – musical romances in the thirties, "Road" movies in the forties and later took some dramatic roles. With over 2600 records released (among them 22 million-sellers), by 1975 he was estimated to have sold over 400 million discs.

Davis, Bette 1908–

US film actress. She has something rarer than looks – a powerful screen presence compounded of emotion and intelligence – but she had to fight for good material. *Human Bondage* (1934) was equal to her talent and the decade beginning 1938 shows her at her peak in films like *Dark Victory* (1939), *The Little Foxes* (1941) and *Now Voyager* (1942). *All About Eve* (1950) revived her flagging career, but since then chances have been rarer: *Whatever Happened to Baby Jane* (1962) and *Hush Hush…Sweet Charlotte* (1965) were notable.

Davis, Miles 1926–

US jazz trumpeter, keyboards and composer. He has a unique capacity for conceptual development. After three years with Charlie Parker (1945–8), he began leading nine-piece bands and found a sound epitomized by *Birth of the Cool* (1949/50). 1954–60 produced influential recordings from his five- and six-piece, including *Miles Ahead* and *Kind of Blue,* and established modal improvization. After 1965, his improvizations were more abstract; in 1968 he switched from song structures to extended pieces and launched jazz-rock with *In a Silent Way* and *Bitches Brew*. In the eighties his live performances gained new power.

Day, Robin 1915– and Lucienne 1917–

British designers. A chair by Robin Day won first prize in the Museum of Modern Art's "International Competition for Low-Cost Furniture" in 1948, and he produced the ubiquitous "Polypropylene" chair for Hille in 1962. Lucienne Day has designed dress and furnishing fabrics, carpets, wall-paper, table-linen and china.

De Coubertin, Pierre 1863–1937

French educationalist. He was responsible for the revival of the Olympic Games. One of the first Frenchmen to see the need for physical education, he studied educational methods in Europe and the USA. He visited the excavations of the Olympic site in Greece, and in 1892 began proposing a modern revival, believing international competition among amateurs would lessen world tension. He was president of the Olympic Committee from 1896 to 1925.

De Mille, Cecil B. 1881–1959

US director, producer and screenwriter. A co-founder of the Lasky company, later to become Paramount Pictures, he pioneered the switch to feature-length films, developed his own regular players and concentrated on improving production values. His early romantic comedies and later epic spectaculars demonstrate the same successful formula: explicit visual (largely sexual) detail allied with verbalized Christian values.

Dean, James 1931–55

US film actor. A symbol for rebellious youth in the mid-fifties and thereafter, his death in a car crash aroused the type of mass grief only Valentino's death had paralleled. His film career was brief – a few bit parts (1951–53) and three starring roles in *East of Eden* and *Rebel Without a Cause* (both 1955) and *Giant* (1956).

Dempsey, Jack 1895–1983

US boxer. World heavyweight champion between 4 July 1919 and 23 September 1926, he attracted bigger gates than any previous fighter. He began boxing professionally in 1914 and took the title at the first attempt, knocking his opponent down seven times in round 1. His title defence against Firpo in September 1923 was typical of his courage: knocked out of the ring in round 1, he came back to win in round 2. He failed to recover his title, retiring in 1940. He won 62 of his 84 bouts, 31 by knockouts.

De Sica, Vittorio 1902–74

Italian film director and actor. His name as a neo-realist is based on *Sciuscia* (1946) and *Bicycle Thieves* (1948), on which he collaborated with Cesare Zavattini. An actor from 1923, he played suave, comedy roles on stage and in films with great success. His later credits include three weightier pieces: *La Ciociara* (1960), *The Garden of the Finzi-Continis* (1971) and *Una Breve Vacanza* (1973).

Diaghilev, Sergei 1872–1929

Russian impresario. His vision of a ballet which integrated the best of music, painting, drama and dance revitalized an almost moribund art. In 1906 he left Russia for Paris, and in 1909 opened his first Ballets Russes season with Pavlova, Nijinsky and Fokine. His choreographers, Fokine and Massine, found a style of action ballet which relied heavily on mime. *The Firebird* (1910), *Petrushka* (1911) and *The Rite of Spring* (1913) were his major achievements.

Diedrikson, Babe 1914–56

US sportswoman. She excelled in basketball, baseball, softball, swimming, figure skating, track and field events and as a golfer. A member of the women's All-America basketball team in 1930–1, in the 1932 Olympics she won gold medals in the 80m hurdles and javelin. From 1934 she concentrated on golf, winning the US Women's Amateur in 1946 and 17 championships in 1947, including the British Ladies' Amateur, the first American to do so. Turning professional for the second time in 1948, she earned more than any other woman golfer in 1948–51, taking the US Women's Open in 1948, 1950 and 1954.

▲ Thomas Edison

▲ Sergei Eisenstein (second from left)

▲ Duke Ellington

Dietrich, Marlene 1901–

German-born film actress and entertainer. Joseph von Sternberg's *The Blue Angel* (1930) brought prominence. Signed to Paramount, she made six of her first seven films with Sternberg, most notably *Shanghai Express* (1932) and *The Scarlet Empress* (1934), wonderfully indulgent pieces with her as a sexual icon, alluring in fur and feathers or drag. In 1935 the Svengali partnership ended, and her best later work was with Borzage, Lubitsch, Wilder and Lang.

Dior, Christian 1905–57

French couturier. He re-established Paris's lead in Western fashion after World War II and his marketing methods spread Parisian fashion worldwide. After working for designers Robert Piguet and Lucien Lelong, he opened his own salon with the backing of textile manufacturer Marcel Broussac and began ten uniquely successful years with the New Look (1947) followed by the Sack in the fifties.

Disney, Walt 1901–66

US film animator, producer and executive. In 1928, with Ub Iwerks, his artist-collaborator, he created Mickey Mouse. Other characters followed – Minnie Mouse, Donald Duck, Goofy and Pluto – and the *Silly Symphony* series, matching action to pre-recorded sound. A leader in the technical field, he was using Technicolor by the mid-thirties, developed a multiplane camera which improved perspective and action shots, and produced the first feature-length cartoon, *Snow White and the Seven Dwarfs*, in 1937. In 1950 he made his first pure live-action film, *Treasure Island*. In 1954 he opened the fantasy park Disneyland in Anaheim, California.

Distel, Sacha 1933–

French singer. A champion schoolboy swimmer, he went on to become the *Jazz Hot* magazine Guitarist of the Year from 1953 to 1958. But it was chiefly as a singer that he made his mark, recording more than 200 songs in several languages. Following the success of his song *Raindrops Keep Fallin' On My Head* (1970), he became one of the most popular performers in Europe.

Dorsey, Tommy 1905–56

US jazz bandleader and trombonist. Work with, among others, Paul Whiteman preceded the shortlived Dorsey Brothers orchestra, formed with Jimmy Dorsey (1934). He took over Joe Haymes's band, buying star talent throughout the thirties. An ambitious perfectionist, he created a versatile, disciplined swing orchestra, and made a series of hits, including *I'm Getting Sentimental Over You* and *The Sunny Side of the Street*. He added strings in 1942.

Dylan, Bob 1941–

US folk rock composer, singer and guitarist. The leader of American folk/protest in the sixties, he was, after the Beatles, the most influential person working in rock. Woody Guthrie was his own most formative influence. His surrealistic lyrics raised the consciousness of a generation, personally and politically. Early classic tracks include *A Hard Rain's A Gonna Fall* and *Blowin' in the Wind* (both 1963). His later career has shown several changes of direction and uneven work.

Eames, Charles 1907–78

US designer and architect. His most famous work is a series of molded plywood chairs created in the thirties and forties, some of them with Eero Saarinen. Exhibited successfully at New York's Museum of Modern Art in 1946, his plywood chairs were later mass-produced by the Herman Miller Furniture Co. Subsequent designs used plastic reinforced with glass-fiber and wire mesh.

Earl, Harley 1893–1969

American industrial designer. He was born into a Hollywood coach-building family which produced customized car-bodies for the stars and even supplied the film industry with chariots for epics. When the firm was bought out by Cadillac, he introduced the now-standard method of sculpting body-work designs in clay. He was invited to join General Motors in 1925. His major success were the 1927 la Salle and the 1937 Buick Y Job, but he also introduced two-tone paint, chromium painting, and tail-fins.

Eastwood, Clint 1930–

US film actor, director and producer. One of the actor-producers of the seventies, he won fame by starring in Sergio Leone's spaghetti Westerns (1964–6). His image as the laconic hero under pressure brought worldwide popularity and in the eighties contributed to his election as mayor of his Californian hometown, Carmel. His credits include *A Fistful of Dollars* (1964), *Coogan's Bluff* (1968), *Magnum Force* (1973) *Escape from Alcatraz* (1978) and *Pale Rider* (1985).

Edison, Thomas 1847–1931

US technologist. Patentee of 1093 inventions, he was a self-taught man who became a folk hero. A telegrapher until his improved stock-printer caused him to turn to manufacture, in 1876 he sold up to establish the first industrial research laboratory. He chose projects which satisfied popular needs and his success was phenomenal: in 1876, the carbon transmitter; 1877, the phonograph; 1879, the carbon filament lamp; 1900, an operational motion-picture camera and projector. In 1887 he began manufacturing his inventions.

Eisenstein, Sergei 1898–1948

Russian film director and theorist. His reputation derives from a vigorous editing technique based on the theory of montage – that two conflicting images produce a third element, and that such elements can induce predetermined emotions in an audience. *Strike* (1925), *The Battleship Potemkin* (1925) and *October* (1927) explored and developed work, *Alexander Nevsky* (1938) and *Ivan the Terrible Pt I* (1945) and *Pt II* (completed 1946), follow his reprieve after a period out of favor for his deviation from Socialist Realism.

Ellington, Duke 1899–1974

US jazz composer, arranger and pianist. With his embryonic sextet, The Washingtons, formed in 1924, his extraordinary career took off. Using ten (later most commonly 15) pieces, he appeared at New York's Cotton Club, toured regularly in the USA and worldwide. No one else has been creatively involved in so many stages of jazz development. He wrote extended pieces and simple ballads, and his song-writing had the universality to produce numerous standards.

Evert, Chris 1954–

US tennis player. The top money-earner in the women's professional game, by 1988 she had earned over $60 million in prize money and sponsorship deals. A popular and respected player, her game was characterized by powerful volley shots. She came to prominence in 1970, when she beat Margaret Court, reaching the semi-finals of the US championships in 1971, then the youngest to do so. She won the US Open (1975-8, 1980 and 1982), the Wimbledon singles (1974,1976, and 1981) and the French Open (1974-5, 1979-80, 1983 and 1985).

Fairbanks, Douglas 1883–1939

US actor. Despite an on-off early career as a stage actor, he was starring on Broadway by 1910. A contract with Triangle took him to Hollywood in 1915. He found instant success: cheerful, athletic, courageous – the American male ideal – he played tongue-in-cheek comedies, then swashbuckling roles. In 1916 he set up his own production company, joining other big names to form United Artists in 1919. His appeal survived the coming of sound but not of age.

Fangio, Juan 1911–

Argentinian racing driver. The winner of the world championships in 1951 and 1954-7, he dominated automobile racing throughout the fifties. Admired for the skill and safety of his driving, he won the title for Alfa Romeo, Mercedes-Benz, Ferrari and Maserati. When he retired in 1958, he had taken 16 Grand Prix titles, including four consecutive German championships.

F. Scott and Zelda Fitzgerald

Aretha Franklin

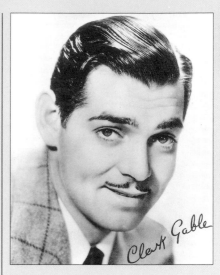

Clark Gable

Fellini, Federico 1920–

Italian director. An internationally famous director, many of whose films have a kaleidoscopic quality — part fantasy, part autobiographical — major credits include *I Vitelloni* (1953), *La Strada* (1954), *Le notti di Cabiria* (1957), *La Dolce Vita* (1960), (1963), *Giulietta degli Spiriti* (1965), *Roma* (1972) and *Amarcord* (1973). Work as a reporter, with a touring company of actors, and as a scriptwriter preceded collaboration with Rossellini (1945–48), and his debut with *Luci dei Varieta* (1951).

Ferrari, Enzo 1898–1988

Italian automobile manufacturer. A test driver in 1919, he joined Alfa Romeo in 1920, racing for them until he formed an agency in 1929, which from 1930 to 1932 was in reality Alfa's works team. In 1939 he set up a company to make racing cars, but war halted production. His first postwar cars were racers, one forming the basis of his earliest road car, the 166 Inter (1947). The successful 250 Europa series (1954) suggested a commitment to road cars, but his heart was in racing and that has shaped the company's technical and commercial development.

Feuillade, Louis 1873–1925

French film director. He directed over 800 films, scripting many of them and writing about 100 others, but he is most remembered for the dreamlike quality of fantasy serials such as *Fantomas* (1913–14), *Les Vampires* (1915–16) and *Judex* (1916). His ability to create mystery and suspense from the most everyday surroundings commended him to the surrealists.

Fitzgerald, Ella 1918–

US jazz vocalist. For 45 years America's greatest interpreter of popular song, she is best known for the songbook recordings of Gershwin, Mercer, Kern, Porter, Berlin and Ellington she began in the late fifties. High-speed scat improvizations on numbers like *Lady Be Good* and *Flying Home* were equally brilliant. She sang with Chick Webb's band from the mid-thirties, leading for two years before going solo in 1941. From the forties her international reputation grew as she honed an increasingly cabaret-style performance.

Fitzgerald, F. Scott 1896–1940

US novelist and short–story writer. *This Side of Paradise* (1920), his first novel, won instant fame. With his new wife, Zelda, he began living life in the fast lane. His later work chronicles the mood of the times and his sense of impending disaster; it includes the novels *The Beautiful and Damned* (1922), *The Great Gatsby* (1925), *Tender Is the Night* (1934) and *The Last Tycoon* (unfinished).

Ford, Henry 1863–1947

US industrialist. He built his first experimental car in 1896, but it was 1903 before he was ready to go into production. The Model T (introduced 1908) was made for 19 years and total sales represented half the world's auto output. By 1913–14 he had introduced the first assembly-line system. By 1927 he had integrated production, assembly and transportation at a plant in River Rouge. But he had lost his market lead through his refusal to change his product, and the Model A (1927) did not have the same success.

Ford, John 1895–1973

US film director. An instinctive artist, his work has a folk quality, the Westerns in particular demonstrating a nostalgia for America's past which draws on evocative musical scoring and images of men within landscape. A director since 1917, two silents merit attention: *The Iron Horse* (1924) – the film that inspired a new wave of popular Westerns – and *Four Sons* (1928). His reputation rests on films such as *The Lost Patrol* (1934), *Stagecoach* (1939), *The Grapes of Wrath* (1940), *How Green Was My Valley* (1941), *They Were Expendable* (1945), *My Darling Clementine* (1946), *She Wore a Yellow Ribbon* (1949), *The Quiet Man* (1952), *The Searchers* (1956) and *The Man Who Shot Liberty Valance* (1962).

Fox, William 1879–1952

Hungarian-born film executive. Starting with the purchase of a penny arcade in 1904, by 1915 he had set up the Fox Film Corporation, merging a production company, motion-picture theater chain and distribution business. The business grew and by the end of the twenties the company (estimated value $200m) was making about 50 films each year. On the brink of a series of important takeovers, the stockmarket collapse, the cost of converting his cinemas to sound, anti-trust laws and a car crash forced him into sale and eventual bankruptcy.

Franklin, Aretha 1942–

US singer. "Lady Soul" was steeped in gospel music, touring as a soloist with her evangelist father. At 18 she turned to blues and was signed by Columbia. It was with her Atlantic signing (1966) that she took off. She delivered eight consecutive million-selling singles — among them *I Never Loved a Man* and *Baby I Love You*" (both 1967) and *I Say a Little Prayer* (1968) — the first female soloist to do so.

Freed, Alan 1922–65

US disk jockey. Born in Philadelphia, he moved to Cleveland in 1950 and worked in radio. He was introduced to rhythm & blues in 1952 and began promoting it on his radio program *Moondog's Rock 'n' Roll Party*, thereby naming the music for the new white audience. He appeared in several rock 'n' roll movies and wrote songs (including co-writing Chuck Berry's *Maybellene*), but was involved with a payola scandal in 1960, accepting bribes to play records.

Fuller, Buckminster 1895–1983

American industrial designer and futurist. He was twice expelled from Harvard before becoming a self-styled "explorer in comprehensive anticipation design". He turned his immense inventiveness – he held over 2000 patents – to the solution of social problems, such as the "Dymaxion" house, designed to meet the housing shortage of the inter-war years. Without formal training, he designed the famous geodesic dome, providing the maximum of space with the minimum of materials, most notably in his construction of the translucent US pavilion at Expo 67 in Montreal.

Gable, Clark 1901–60

US film actor. His name spelt sex appeal – he was a man's man and a woman's dreamboat. The thirties were his great decade: his third wife's death (1942), active service in World War II and age seemed to take the edge off later work. Signed by MGM in 1931, he played mostly brutes and gangsters, in films like *Possessed* (1931) and *Red Dust* (1932), before *It Happened One Night* (1934) softened the image. *Gone With the Wind* (1939) brought his most important role, but his best performance was his last: *The Misfits* (1961).

Garbo, Greta 1905–

Swedish film actress. The protegée of Mauritz Stiller, she was part of the deal when he signed with MGM. Her first film, *The Torrent* (1926), took them and the public by storm. Among her other silents, those made with John Gilbert did particularly well, and after sound her greatest roles were *Queen Christina* (1933) and *Camille* (1936). She retired in 1941. She always protected her private life jealously.

Gardner, James, 1907–

British designer. After an early career which led him to design jewelry for Cartier and camouflage for the British Army, he became associated with British exhibition design, starting with the *Britain Can Make It* Exhibition of 1946. He also designed the Festival Gardens at Battersea in 1950, and the British pavilions at Brussels in 1958 and at Expo 67 in Montreal. He was responsible for the visual design of the ocean liner QE2.

Greta Garbo

Bob Geldof

Dizzy Gillespie

Garland, Judy 1922–69

US film actress and singer. One of those performers who attract devotion, her appeal rests as much on the spectacle of her personal life as her talent. Signed by MGM at 13, she was teamed with Mickey Rooney for nine films. *The Wizard of Oz* (1939) brought world fame, and *Meet Me in St Louis* (1944) did well. MGM fired her in 1950, but she struggled back to make a successful, sporadic concert career, and notched memorable performances in *A Star Is Born* (1954) and *Judgment at Nuremberg* (1961).

Gaye, Marvin 1939–84

American singer and composer. Under long-term contract to Tamla Motown from 1962, he helped pioneer the Motown sound. The son of a church minister (who killed him), he grew up in the gospel tradition, and his mature work revealed a remarkably flexible voice. As well as the exceptional *What's Going On* (1971), his greatest hit was *I Heard It Through the Grapevine* (1968).

Geldof, Bob 1954–

Irish singer and song-writer. After forming the pop group The Boomtown Rats in 1975, he accused English punk musicians of hypocrisy in rejecting wealth and stardom. His own philosophy was expressed in the group's first single, *Looking After No. 1* (1977). He earned worldwide admiration for his organization of Band Aid in response to the Ethiopian famine of 1984. Live Aid, the concert staged simultaneously in London and Philadelphia in July 1985, raised over £100 million.

Gershwin, George 1898–1937

US composer. His mixing of classical, popular and jazz forms was highly influential. A song plugger from 1914, several of his own were used on Broadway in 1918–19, including the hit *Swanee*. He wrote for George White's *Scandals* (1920–24) and *Rhapsody in Blue* (1924) for Paul Whiteman. In 1924 he teamed with brother Ira in his first big success, *Lady Be Good*, and they became one of Broadway's great song-writing teams; credits include *Strike Up the Band* and *Funny Face* (both 1927), *Girl Crazy* (1930) and *Porgy and Bess* (1935). He also wrote works for piano and orchestra, including *An American in Paris* (1928).

Gibson, Charles Dana 1867–1944

US illustrator and artist. His pen-and-ink drawings of girls defined America's ideal woman around 1900. Based upon his wife, his immensely popular and much imitated line drawings usually concerned comic or sentimental themes of current interest. He first published in the humorous magazine *Life*. *Collier's Weekly* later paid him $50,000 for 52 double-page drawings.

Gillespie, Dizzy 1917–

US jazz trumpeter and composer. One of the major figures of jazz, the forties was his most creative period. During that decade he redefined the technical limits of the trumpet, established bebop (with Charlie Parker) and taught and encouraged talented young musicians. Most of his greatest work was written then, including *Night in Tunisia, Groovin' High, Salt Peanuts* and *Blue 'n' Boogie* – all now jazz standards. He formed his first big band in 1945; reformed in 1946, it toured and recorded until 1950, since when he has most often led small groups.

Gish, Lillian (1896–) and Dorothy (1898–1968)

US actresses. Child stage performers, their film break came in 1912 when they met D.W. Griffith at the Biograph offices: they acted in their first film that day. They became members of his repertory company, often appearing together at first. Lillian, deeply dedicated to her work, was the greatest dramatic actress of the silent screen — her fragility masking an extraordinary emotional and spiritual power. Her greatest roles for Griffith include *Broken Blossoms* (1919) and *Orphans of the Storm* (1922); later high points were *La Bohème, The Scarlet Letter* (both 1926) and *The Wind* (1928). Dorothy's best roles were in light comedy. Both concentrated on stage work from the thirties.

Giugiaro, Giorgio 1938–

Italian industrial designer. After studying at the Turin Academy of Fine Arts, he started work for Fiat at the age of 17, and later for Bertone and Ghia. He set up his own firm, ItalDesign, in 1968, and has been the most active figure in Italian car design since producing the Alfa Romeo Alfasud in 1971, the Volkswagen Golf in 1974, and the Fiat Panda in 1980. More recently, he has switched his attention to exhibition dream-cars. He also designed sewing-machines for Necchi, cameras for Nikon and watches for Seiko — and even created a new design for pasta in 1983.

Givenchy, Hubert de 1927–

French couturier. Best known for his separates and international chain of ready-to-wear boutiques, opened in the sixties, he was apprenticed to Jacques Fath at 17, later designing for Piguet, Lucien Lelong and Schiaparelli until he opened a shop in 1952. His first collection was colorful, feminine and beautifully tailored and he slashed overheads to keep prices down. In 1954 he helped launch the Tube; in 1957, the Sack. His designs for Audrey Hepburn in *Breakfast at Tiffany's* (1961) popularized the sleeveless, high-waisted Princess line.

Gleason, Jackie 1916–87

US actor and comedian. A rounded, jovial man, he was one of the most popular TV performers of the fifties, starring in comedy series such as *The Life of Riley, The Honeymooners* and *The Jackie Gleason Show*. He had worked in vaudeville and nightclubs before Warners signed him to a film contract in 1940. After his TV success Hollywood gave him comic and dramatic leads, including in *The Hustler* (1961); nothing clicked like TV had.

Goldwyn, Samuel 1882–1974

Polish-born film producer. His first foray into films, *The Squaw Man* (1913), with newly formed Lasky was a big success, but it was 1923, when he formed an independent company, Samuel Goldwyn Productions, before he had the freedom to prove his instincts as a showman. He went for the best talent, knew how to put a team together and was ready to spend money.

Goodman, Benny 1909–86

US jazz clarinetist. Professional at 13, by 1925 he was Chicago's greatest clarinetist, featuring for Ben Pollack. After five years' studio work, he had his own band, broadcasting weekly on NBC. His swinging jazz was noticed, reports of student riots lit the touch paper and in Chicago and New York (1934–9) he won an international reputation; his small group introduced another new sound, the electric guitar. He swung through the forties, embracing bebop, but also becoming involved with classical music. He toured successfully into the eighties.

Grange, Red 1903–

US footballer. He made his reputation in the collegiate game: while playing for the University of Illinois, he scored 31 touchdowns and gained 3637 yards in 20 games. On 19 October 1924 he scored five touchdowns, four in the first 12 minutes of the game against the University of Michigan. After college, he played for the Chicago Bears from 1925 and attracted a considerable following to the professional game. Latterly, with the Bears, he excelled as a defensive back, retiring in 1934.

Grierson, John 1898–1972

British film producer, director and theorist. The founder of the British documentary movement, he established a film unit at the Empire Marketing Board, where he directed *Drifters* (1929). He was a fine organizer and his team of trainees made about 100 films with social-reformist content. In 1933 the unit transferred to the GPO; improved facilities led to experiments in form and technique: *Song of Ceylon* and *Night Mail* are prime examples. Appointed Film Commissioner of Canada in 1939, he created the National Film Board of Canada.

Lionel Hampton ▲

Jean Harlow ▲

Jimi Hendrix ▲

Griffith, D.W. 1875–1948

US film director, the first to use film techniques creatively. It was a talent demonstrated even in his earliest shorts for Biograph – using close-ups, full shots, dramatic lighting, camera movement, parallel action, intercutting and rhythmical editing to convey narrative. He also sought a subtler style of performance, establishing a stock company of young actors. His major works were the epics *The Birth of a Nation* (1915) and *Intolerance* (1916).

Hagen, Walter 1892–1969

US golfer. Almost single-handed, he changed the status of the professional golfer: dressing and living well, he demanded to be treated like a gentleman. A caddie at nine, he gained his first major championship title when 21. He won the US Open twice (1914 and 1919), the British Open four times (1922, 1924 and 1928–9) and the US PGA five times (1921 and 1924–7). He led the US Ryder Cup team six times and played over 2500 exhibition matches worldwide.

Hammerstein, Oscar 1895–1960

US lyricist, writer and producer. Best known for his collaboration with Richard Rodgers, he wrote or part-wrote about 45 musicals for theater, film and TV between 1920 and 1959. In 1943 he began working exclusively with Rodgers. Previously he worked with Youmans, Friml, Romberg and Kern; credits for that period include *Rose Marie* (1924), *The Desert Song* (1925), and *Show Boat* (1927). His work with Rodgers includes *Oklahoma!* (1945), *Carousel* (1945), *South Pacific* (1949), *The King and I* (1951) and *The Sound of Music* (1959).

Hampton, Lionel 1909–

US jazz vibes, drums and vocalist. In 1986 leader of the oldest big band, his formula – attacking brass and strong rhythm – produced near hysteria. He worked in Chicago and Los Angeles and studied theory before setting up on his own, featuring on vibes. Benny Goodman snapped him up in 1936. A RCA recording contract signed in 1937 gave him a free hand and he made 90 sides capturing the best of swing. He formed his own band in 1940; it became a university for young talent.

Handy, W.C. 1873–1958

US jazz composer, bandleader and cornet player. Possibly composed, was certainly the first to set down on paper, numerous classic blues themes; his credits include *Memphis Blues*, *St Louis Blues*, *Beale Street Blues* and *Old Miss Rag*. He set up a publishing company in Memphis after his early successes, moving the company to New York's Broadway in 1918. He pursued his publishing career throughout the twenties and thirties.

Harlow, Jean 1911–37

American film actress. Born Harlean Carpenter, she eloped from her native Kansas City with a millionaire at the age of 16 and became a film extra in Hollywood. Frank Capra's *Platinum Blonde* in 1932 established her as the archetypal Blonde Bombshell of that decade; brassy, wise-cracking, ineluctably female. After a brief period playing the "man's woman" opposite Clark Gable in films such as *Red Dust* (1932) and *China Seas* (1935), she died of a cerebral edema at the age of 26.

Harmsworth, Alfred Charles 1865–1922

Irish newspaper magnate and politician. With his brother Harold, he built a publishing empire, initially issuing periodicals, and buying the *Evening News* in 1894. In 1896 he started the *Daily Mail;* selling for 1 penny, its bold headlines and racy style had a great impact on British journalism. He founded the *Daily Mirror*, the first exclusively women's interest newspaper, in 1903. In 1908 he became chief proprietor of *The Times*.

Hart, Lorenz 1895–1943

US song lyricist. During his 25-year collaboration with Richard Rodgers, they produced about 1000 songs. Among them are *My Heart Stood Still* (1927), *With a Song in My Heart* (1929), *Lover* (1933), *Blue Moon* (1934), *My Funny Valentine* (1937), *Falling in Love with Love* (1938) and *Bewitched, Bothered and Bewildered* (1940). In contrast to Rodgers, his attitude towards work remained that of the determined non-professional, but his lyrics were as well crafted as serious poetry.

Hawks, Howard 1896–1977

US film director, screenwriter and producer. A professional craftsman and untricksy storyteller, involved in every aspect of his films and working in every genre, he made some of Hollywood's best films. Credits include *Scarface* (1932), *Bringing Up Baby* (1938), *Ball of Fire* (1942), *The Big Sleep* (1946), *Red River* (1948), *Gentlemen Prefer Blondes* (1953) and *Rio Bravo* (1959).

Hearst, William Randolph 1863–1951

US newspaper publisher. His methods polarized the American press. He turned his father's *San Francisco Examiner* to profit (1887–9) and then bought the ailing *New York Morning Journal* (later *Journal-American*) in 1895. He reshaped the paper, using copious illustration, color-magazine sections, bold headlines and a sensation-seeking approach. By 1925 he owned newspapers and magazines all over the USA. In the thirties his empire was depleted by the Depression and his own extravagances (in film production and the purchase of antiques for his castle at San Simeon) but it thrived from World War II onwards.

Hefner, Hugh 1926–

American publisher. Raised a strict Methodist in the American Midwest, he graduated in 1949 and started work in the subscriptions department of *Esquire* magazine. Four years later, he started *Playboy*, a magazine combining nude photography, glosssy advertising and "serious" features, aimed at young, affluent, urban males. He himself led the hedonistic permissive lifestyle his magazine advocated.

Henderson, Fletcher 1897–1952

US pianist, arranger and composer. The first to use written arrangements without losing jazz's essentially improvisational spirit, he became recording manager for a black label after university, working with Bessie Smith among others, but by 1924 he was leading his own band. His contrapuntal use of sections of the orchestra and his technique of setting soloists against an amplified orchestral backing foreshadowed the thirties' big bands. After a serious car crash in 1928, he was known mostly as Benny Goodman's arranger.

Hendrix, Jimi 1947–70

US rock guitarist, and composer. An appearance on British TV gave the Jimi Hendrix Experience its first hit single, *Hey Joe*, and his impact was phenomenal. The power of his blues playing seemed to re-create the electric guitar – it was the heaviest rock around – yet his vocals were cool. In 1969 he disbanded the group and formed Band of Gypsies. His most highly rated albums include *Are You Experienced* (1967), *Band of Gypsies* (1970) and *Soundtrack from Jimi Hendrix* (1973).

Heston, Charlton 1923–

US actor. His splendid physique and presence ensured epic roles once he made Hollywood, in *Julius Caesar* (1949). Credits include *The Ten Commandments* (1956), *Ben-Hur* (1959), *El Cid* (1961), *The Greatest Story Ever Told* and *The Agony and the Ecstasy* (both 1965) and *Antony and Cleopatra* (1972), which he adapted and directed. Away from the spectacle, he turned in other good performances, including *Touch of Evil* (1958). In the eighties he starred in a popular TV soap-opera, *The Colbys*.

Hines, Earl 1903–83

US jazz pianist. He rivaled Armstrong as Chicago's brightest star in the twenties: duets like *Weatherbird Rag* (1928) are plainly competitive. He got his own band and 12-year tenure at the mob-controlled Grand Terrace in 1928, expanding to big band later. Another big band followed (until 1947) and another unsatisfactory teaming with Armstrong, (until 1951). It was 1964 before concerts for Stanley Dance put him back with the greats.

◄ Charlton Heston

◄ Harry Houdini

◄ Michael Jackson

Hitchcock, Alfred 1899–1980

British-born film director. He was a meticulous planner with a superb visual sense. His films were thriller-dramas which explored, and aroused, profound metaphysical anxieties. After a brilliant career in Britain – most memorably *Blackmail* (1929), *The Man Who Knew Too Much* (1934), *The Thirty-Nine Steps* (1935) and *The Lady Vanishes* (1938) – he went to Hollywood in 1939, where the period 1954–60 was particularly rich, featuring *Rear Window*, *Vertigo*, *North by Northwest* and *Psycho*.

Hobbs, Jack 1882–1963

English cricketer. The world's greatest batsman in his time, he first played first-class cricket in 1905, scoring a century in his second game. He was a professional cricketer for 30 years, scoring a record 61,237 runs (including 197 centuries) and playing for England in 61 Test Matches. His greatest innings was against Australia in 1926, when his century helped England keep the Ashes. He was the first professional cricketer to be knighted, in 1953.

Holiday, Billie 1915–59

US jazz vocalist and composer. The greatest jazz singer of the thirties, her small, bell-like voice was ecstatic, sensual and vulnerable. She first recorded with Benny Goodman, hitting real form with Buck Clayton, Lester Young and Teddy Wilson in 1935. Segregationism on tour for the Glaser organization (1935–9) forced her to go solo but heroin devoured her talent and she ceased to trust her audiences. By 1952 (two cures on) she was working the clubs and recording again; interest in her personal life kept the career alive till 1957 but heroin finally claimed her.

Holly, Buddy 1936–59

US singer. His legendary status came after the aircrash which killed him, and the memorial album – *The Buddy Holly Story* (1959), containing all his biggest hits with The Crickets – has sold consistently. The Texican-Mexican beat and vocal style derived from country and gospel music. His most popular singles include *Peggy Sue* and *That'll Be the Day* (both 1957) and *It Doesn't Matter Anymore* and *Maybe Baby* (both 1958).

Hope, Bob 1903–

British-born film actor and entertainer. Fast gags and topical wisecracks brought success on film, TV specials and worldwide tours, making him possibly the richest ever entertainer. He began in vaudeville, and became a radio star. His film break came in *The Big Broadcast* of 1938, and *The Cat and the Canary* (1939) was his first hit. The hugely popular "Road" series, with Crosby and Lamour, began in 1940. Of the rest, *The Paleface* (1948), rates best.

Houdini, Harry 1874–1926

Hungarian-born conjurer. His father, a rabbi, took the family to the USA and the child became a trapeze artist. By the early 1900s his amazing ability to extricate himself from shackles, ropes, handcuffs, straitjackets and locked containers, sometimes while weighted and submerged in water or suspended head down 23m (75ft) above the ground, had brought world fame. Also a successful conventional illusionist, he denounced mind readers and mediums as charlatans, arguing his case in two books published in the twenties.

Hulanicki, Barbara 1936–

British fashion designer and retailer. Born in Palestine of Polish parents, she moved to England in 1948 and worked as a commercial artist, illustrating fashions for magazines such as *Vogue* and *Tatler*. She set the Biba boutique in 1964 in London's Kensington, and her glamorous yet inexpensive designs – from vamp dresses to demure sweet-heart neck-lined T-shirts – together with the lush 1930s' romanticism of the store's furnishings, made her boutique a mecca for fashion-lovers of the 1960s.

Huston, John 1906–87

US film director, screenwriter and actor. He drifted through acting, cavalry life, journalism, scriptwriting, busking and painting before settling for screenwriting in 1937. He made a brilliant directorial debut with *The Maltese Falcon* (1941) and scored several hits early in his career, notably *The Treasure of the Sierra Madre* (1948), *The Asphalt Jungle* (1950) and *The African Queen* (1952). Later work was more variable, but included high points such as *The Misfits* (1961), *Fat City* (1972) and *Wise Blood* (1979). He was also a considerable cameo actor.

Ikuba, Massura 1908–

Japanese industrialist. After serving as a research physicist in the Second World War, he co-founded the Tokyo Telecommunications Engineering Corporation (1946) – with an investment of only $500. Twelve years later the company changed its name to Sony (with a practical reference to "sound" and a patriarchal hint of "sonny"), now one of the largest producers of electronics equipment in the world. He took part in the development in some of the most important areas of popular electronics, such as the transistor radio, the pocket-radio, the all-transistor and trinitron colour television, the video tape-recorder, the videocassette recorder, and the digital audio system.

Ince, Thomas 1882–1942

US film producer, director, screenwriter and actor. Tight shooting scripts, organized production and procedures, spectacular action (using trained horses and buffalo), authentic cowboys and Indians, and a 20,000-acre desert lot won his Westerns at NYMP a fine reputation. By 1916 he was concentrating on scriptwriting and supervising the studio's stars and directors. In 1918 he built his own studios at Culver City, merging with First National in 1922.

Issigonis, Alec 1906–88

British industrial designer. Born in Smyrna (now Izmir in Turkey), he trained as an engineer in London and spent almost all of his career in the British firm variously known as Morris Motors, the British Motor Corporation, and British Leyland, which he directed from 1961 to 1972. Two of his designs, both involving radical departures from conventional construction, became classics: the "Morris Minor" (1948), and the "Mini" (1959), one of the most remarkable symbols of the Swinging Sixties.

Jackson, Michael 1958–

US popular singer. He began his career with the Jackson Five in 1969, and in the early 1970s recorded his first solo hits *Got To Be There* (1971) and *Rockin' Robin* (1972). His album *Off The Wall* (1979) launched him into the big time. This was followed up by *Thriller* (1982), which marked the start of his preoccupation with video packaging, and *Bad* (1987). In 1988 he released a quasi-autobiographical film *Moonwalk*.

Jacobsen, Arne 1902–71

Danish architect and industrial designer. The theory that economy + function = style informed his stark architectural designs. He began working as an architect in 1928 and most of his commissions were based on his industrial design, especially the three-legged stacking chair (1952) and the egg chair (1959).

Jagger, Mick 1943–

British rhythm & blues vocalist. The charismatic lead vocalist of the Rolling Stones could claim to have made androgyny fashionable. He was spokesperson when press cast the group as anti-establishment trouble makers and later fronted their long-running career of "jet-set debauchery and chic demonic postures". The group's greatest albums include *The Rolling Stones* (1964) and *Beggars' Banquet* (1968). His film career's most notable success is *Performance* (1970).

Al Jolson

Shashi Kapoor

Jessel, George 1898–1981

US comedian, actor, composer, writer and producer. A professional at nine, he developed a popular vaudeville act which mixed comedy, nostalgia and sentimentality. Through the twenties and thirties he composed, wrote and produced musicals, starring in several, including *The Jazz Singer* (1925). Moving to Hollywood in 1943, he spent 10 years producing films, among them *The Dolly Sisters* (1945).

Johnson, Amy 1903–41

British airwoman. She became interested in flying while working as a secretary in London. She caught the public imagination when, with no long-distance experience, she made an unsuccessful attempt to break the record for a light-aeroplane solo flight to Australia in May 1930; her time to Karachi (6 days) was a record. Later she established other records flights, including Siberia to Tokyo (1931); London to Cape Town (1932); and London to the Cape return (1936).

Johnson, Jack 1878–1946

US boxer. The first black world heavyweight champion (26 December 1908 to 5 April 1915), his professional career lasted from 1897 to 1928. He fought 114 bouts, winning 80 (45 by knockouts). His victory over a white increased his fight opportunities as white America sought a challenger. Conviction under the Mann Act forced him to flee abroad and he defended the title outside the USA several times, losing in 1915 in the belief the charge would be dropped. In 1920 he surrendered to serve sentence, working in vaudeville after his release.

Jolson, Al 1886–1950

Russian-born singer and actor. Remembered as the star of Hollywood's first sound feature, *The Jazz Singer* (1927), he had been a black-faced Broadway hit in Shubert Brothers' shows since 1911 and in *La Belle Paree*. He found his style earlier in circus, café and vaudeville spots. Films, then rather more stage work, followed the 1927 success as musical tastes changed. He made a comeback, dubbing Larry Parks's singing in *The Jolson Story* (1946).

Jones, Bobby 1902–71

US golfer. An amateur player, he was the first to win golf's grand slam: in 1930, the British and US Open and Amateur championships. It was 1973 before his record of 13 wins in those championships between 1923 and 1930 was equaled. He won the US Amateur five times (1924–25, 1927–28 and 1930); the US Open four times (1923, 1926, 1929 and 1930); the British Open three times (1926–27 and 1930), and the British Amateur once (1930).

Joplin, Scott 1868–1917

US ragtime pianist and composer. A saloon-bar player in St Louis, he was later based in Sedalia, in whose red-light district his music was a hit, and, after enrolling at a black academy (1896), he began to write down the rags he heard. In 1899 his *Maple Leaf Rag* was published, selling 75,000 copies in the first year. Other successes include *Easy Winners*, *Elite Syncopations* and *The Entertainer*.

Kapoor, Shashi 1938–

Indian film actor and producer. Hailing from a family with a strong cinematic tradition, he worked for the Prithvi and Shakespeareana theatrical companies before appearing in his first film, *Char Diwari*, in 1960. He came to international notice through a series of films by James Ivory and Ismail Merchant, begining with *The Householder* in 1963. He began producing in 1978, with the award-winning *Junoon*.

Keaton, Buster 1895–1966

US film actor, director, producer and screenwriter. An accomplished child acrobat, he began making comedy shorts in 1917. *One Week* (1920), *The Boat* (1921) and *Cops* (1922) helped establish his deadpan persona: using only tiny facial movements to indicate emotion, he outfaced chaos. In 1923 he turned to feature-length material, including *Our Hospitality* (1923), *The Navigator* (1924) and *The General* (1927).

Kelly, Gene 1912–

US dancer, actor, choreographer and director. Master of an athletic, spontaneous style, he succeeded Astaire as Hollywood's leading dancer and as a choreographer revitalized film dance. He worked his way to Broadway, starred in *Pal Joey* (1940) and choreographed a Broadway show (1941) before his screen debut in 1942. His first outing as choreographer came in *Cover Girl* (1944); other star/choreo roles include *Anchors Aweigh* (1945), *On the Town* (1949), *An American in Paris* (1951) and *Singin' in the Rain* (1952); the two latter he co-directed.

Kelly, Grace 1928–82

American film actress and Princess of Monaco. Born into a wealthy Philadelphian family, she starred in a number of Hollywood films in the mid-1950s. Although she won an Oscar for her unusually down-beat performance in *Country Girl* in 1954, she established her popular image as a superficially cool yet latently passionate woman in three films directed by Alfred Hitchcock; *Dial M for Murder* (1954), *Rear Window* (1954), and *To Catch a Thief* (1955). After making *High Society* in 1956, she married Prince Rainier of Monaco.

Kern, Jerome 1885–1945

US composer. His work often had a melodic, folk quality. He began studying music in 1903 and worked as a pianist and music-publishing salesman from 1905, writing for European operettas. His first musical was produced in 1912. Stage credits include *Oh! Boy* (1917); *Show Boat* (1927), the first "serious" musical derived from a literary source; *Music in the Air* (1932) and *Roberta* (1933). Moving to Hollywood in 1930, he began writing film music. His best-known songs include *Ol' Man River, Smoke Gets in Your Eyes* and *They Didn't Believe Me*.

Killy, Jean-Claude 1943–

French skier. Top male international alpine skier from 1965 to 1968, his irreverent attitude won wide popularity. Success came quickly: in 1964 he won the French alpine events, in 1965 the European championship, and in 1966 the combined world title. He held the World Cup for the most international wins in 1966–7 and 1967–8 and in 1968 was the second skier to win all the alpine events at the Olympics. He retired from amateur competition in 1968 and turned professional in 1972, becoming the world professional champion.

King, Billie Jean 1943–

US tennis player. Her campaigning and play raised the status of women's tennis. Winner of the most Wimbledon titles, she took the singles six times (1966–8, 1972–3, 1975), women's doubles nine times (1961–2, 1965, 1967–8, 1970–3 and 1979) and mixed doubles four times (1967, 1971 and 1973–4). She also won the US singles four times (1967, 1971–2 and 1974) and the French title in 1972. Turning professional in 1968, she was the first woman athlete to win more than $100,000 in a season. She helped form a separate tour for women and was co-founder of the Women's Tennis Association.

Kubrick, Stanley 1928–

US film director. A meticulous worker who has lately taken years to make each film, he keeps tight control at every stage. His first two, low-budget features were almost one-man shows; the next two – *The Killing* (1956) and *Paths of Glory* (1957) – critical successes. It was with *Dr Strangelove* (1964) that his mordant vision really found expression. Even his detractors, who find him self-indulgent, cannot deny that his later films – *2001: A Space Odyssey* (1968), *A Clockwork Orange* (1971), *Barry Lyndon* (1975), *The Shining* (1979) and *Full Metal Jacket* (1987) – have been visually stunning.

▲ Gene Kelly with Judy Garland

▲ Billy Jean King

▲ Suzanne Lenglen

Kurosawa, Akira 1910–

Japanese film director. The best-known of Japan's directors, he has worked in all genres. He has a virtuoso style (using rapid, complex travelling shots in his action films) and a humanism which makes even his period dramas socially aware and sometimes sentimental. Credits include *Stray Dog* (1949), *Rashomon* (1950), *Living* (1952), *Seven Samurai* (1954), *Throne of Blood* (1957), *Yojimbo* (1961), *Dersu Uzala* (1975), *Kagemusha* (1980) and *Ran* (1985).

Laemmle, Carl 1867–1939

German-born film studio boss. Investment in nickelodeons caused him to set up a distribution network in 1907 and by 1909 he was challenging the monopolists. He founded a production company, the Independent Motion Picture Company (IMP), to evade their pressure and by skilfully manipulating publicity invented the star system to establish his studio's image. In 1912 he effected a series of mergers to create Universal.

Lang, Fritz 1890–1976

German film director. He fled Nazi Germany in 1933 after critical and commercial successes which included *Der Müde Tod* (1921), *Dr Mabuse der Spieler* (1922), *Metropolis* (1927) and *M* (1931). He worked for over 20 years in Hollywood, often frustrated by studio interference. After three social-concern films, *Fury* (1936) being the most powerful, he turned to commercial material. Credits include *Man Hunt* (1941), *The Woman in the Window* (1944), *Rancho Notorious* (1952), *The Big Heat* (1953) and *While the City Sleeps* (1956).

Lauder, Harry 1870–1950

Scottish music-hall comedian. The first music-hall artiste to be knighted (1919), he specialized in Scottish songs and always wore a kilt and glengarry and wielded a crooked stick. His most popular songs included *I Love a Lassie, Roamin' in the Gloamin* and *Stop Yer Ticklin', Jock!*.

Laver, Rod 1938–

Australian tennis player. He was the second man to win the Grand Slam and the first to win twice (1962 and 1969). He began taking major titles in 1959 and won seven Wimbledon titles: the singles (1961–62 and 1968–69); the mixed doubles (1959–60) and the men's doubles (1971). Turning professional in 1963, he dominated the game, winning Wimbledon again after open championships were introduced. In 1971 he was the first professional to total over $1 million in prize money.

Lawrence, Florence 1886–1938

US film actress. She was the Biograph Girl, the most popular of that studio's players and the star of D.W. Griffith's early films. It was 1910 before the public knew her name. Carl Laemmle persuaded her to join IMP and, with a cunning press campaign of false rumor and denial, announced that she was joining his studio to make *The Broken Oath* (1910). After 1914 her career dipped until a brief reappearance in the early twenties.

Lean, David 1908–

British film director. He is perhaps best known for lavish epics: *The Bridge on the River Kwai* (1957), *Lawrence of Arabia* (1962), *Doctor Zhivago* (1965), *Ryan's Daughter* (1970) and *A Passage to India* (1984). Earlier work included several skillful adaptations, such as *Blithe Spirit* and *Brief Encounter* (both 1945), *Great Expectations* (1946) and *Hobson's Choice* (1954). He had made his debut (co-directing with Noel Coward) on *In Which We Serve* (1942).

Leigh, Vivien 1913–67

British actress. She was an extraordinarily beautiful woman whose career was largely dominated by her relationship with Laurence Olivier: in the late forties and early fifties they were British theatre's leading couple. In films she had her greatest successes in *Gone With the Wind* (1939) and *A Streetcar Named Desire* (1951), the former being her first Hollywood role, the latter revealing previously unseen depth.

Lenglen, Suzanne 1899–1938

French tennis player. A volatile player with enormous flair, she was among the first personality players in tennis. One of the greatest ever women on grass and hard court, she lost only one match between 1909 and 1925. She dominated tennis from 1919 to 1926, winning the Wimbledon singles and doubles six times and the mixed doubles three, and the French singles six times and both doubles titles twice.

Lennon, John 1940–80

British pop composer, singer, guitarist and writer. One of the Beatles, the legendary group whose global career took off in early 1963 with *Please Please Me*, he and Paul McCartney were brilliant co-writers. Many rate *Strawberry Fields Forever/Penny Lane* and *Sergeant Pepper's Lonely Hearts Club Band* (both 1967) the group's best single and album. His career after the break-up (1970) was musically the most innovative, and the *Imagine* album (1971) its high point. He was murdered by a "fan".

Leone, Sergio 1921-

Italian film director and screenwriter. The originator of the spaghetti Western spent years assisting Italian and American directors before making his first feature *Il Colosso di Rodi*, in 1961. His highly successful series of Italian Westerns began in 1964 (with him co-scripting) and comprised *A Fistful of Dollars, For a Few Dollars More* (1965), *The Good, the Bad and the Ugly* (1966) and *Once Upon a Time in the West* (1968). *Once Upon a Time in America* (1983) was an impressive return to direction.

Lindbergh, Charles 1902-74

US aviator. He made the first nonstop solo flight across the Atlantic. Experience as a stunt pilot and with the airmails preceded his attempt in "Spirit of St Louis" on 20-21 May 1927. Retained as technical advisor by two airlines, he pioneered many routes. The kidnap and murder of his son in 1932 attracted so much attention that the family moved to Europe for some years. Criticized for his neutrality in 1940–41, he served as technical advisor and flew combat missions in World War II.

Linder, Max 1883-1925

French director and actor. His highly original style of screen comedy anticipated Sennett and Chaplin and by 1910 he was the most popular comedian in Europe and the USA, writing, supervising and (from 1911) directing his own films. He made over 400 for Pathé. Their humor depended upon the contrast between his elegant self-possession and the ridiculous situations in which he found himself.

Lloyd, Harold 1893-1971

US film actor. With Chaplin and Keaton the third silent comedy great, his films were often more popular than theirs and he became Hollywood's highest-paid actor. An extra in 1912, his friendship with director Hal Roach was crucial. They developed several characters before finding the go-getting, all-American boy whose dotty optimism saw him through. Slapstick gave way to careful plotting and features such as *Safety Last* (1923) and *Girl Shy* (1924) are classics.

Lloyd, Marie 1870-1922

British music-hall artiste. Immensely popular, she was cheerful, alluring, fashionable, frank, witty and crammed full of vitality. Her best-known songs include *Oh, Mr Porter!, My Old Man Said Follow the Van, A Little of What You Fancy Does You Good* and *I'm One of the Ruins That Cromwell Knocked Abaht a Bit*.

Harpo, Groucho and Chico Marx

Curtis Mayfield

Loewy, Raymond 1893–

French-born industrial designer. Trained as an engineer, he went to New York in 1919. He founded a design company in 1929 and designed many household products to be made by unskilled labour as part of the New Deal. He designed Studebaker cars, Greyhound buses and Lucky Strike cigarette packaging as well as electric shavers, office machines, soft-drink bottles and radios. In the sixties and seventies he worked in aerospace, designing for Apollo and Skylab.

Lombardo, Guy 1902–77

Canadian-born dance-band leader. The conductor of "the sweetest music this side of paradise" formed his band, the Royal Canadians, in Ontario in 1925 and soon won representation by MCA. His first national broadcast was from Chicago in 1927 and from 1929 he was booked each winter for New York's Roosevelt Grill, moving to the Waldorf-Astoria when that closed. For 48 years his broadcasts were part of America's traditional New Year's Eve celebrations. He introduced more than 300 new songs and sold over 100 million records.

Louis, Joe 1914–81

US boxer. The longest reigning world heavyweight champion (22 June 1937 to 1 March 1949), he defended the title 25 times (with 21 knockouts), and lost it only on his first (brief) retirement. He turned professional in 1934, peaking in the years 1939–42, when he defended the championship seven times during the December 1940 to June 1941 period. He failed to recover the title in 1950 and retired again in 1951.

Lubitsch, Ernst 1892–1947

German film director. His American comedies of manners were acute satirical studies of society's preoccupation with sex and money. He crystallized narrative in a series of shots or tiny scenes which wittily defined character or theme. Internationally successful when he left for Hollywood in 1923, his German credits include *Die Austernprinzessin* and *Madame Du Barry* (both 1919). Among his American successes were *Kiss Me Again* (1925), *The Student Prince* (1927), *The Love Parade* (1929), *Monte Carlo* (1930), *The Smiling Lieutenant* (1931) and *Ninotchka* (1939).

Lucas, George 1945–

US film director, screenwriter and producer. One of Coppola's protégés, he observed on *Finian's Rainbow* (1968) and *The Rain People* (1969), documenting the latter. His first feature, *THX-1138* (1971), expanded one of his prize-winning student shorts. *American Graffiti* (1973) won critical success; the public liked it too but his next, *Star Wars* (1977), dwarfed everything in sight.

Lumière, Louis 1864–1948

French director. With his brother Auguste, he developed a camera-projector, the cinematographe. Their first film, *La Sortie des Usines Lumière* (1895), showed their employees leaving work, and another early film *L'Arrivée d'un Train en Gare de la Ciotat* excited spectators with shots of a train speeding towards them. By 1900 staff photographers had amassed 2000 titles, mostly news shorts shot worldwide. Thereafter he turned his attention to photography.

Lynn, Vera 1919–

British vocalist. After residences with pianist Charlie Kunz and Ambrose and His Orchestra, she began her solo career in 1941, launching a radio series, *Sincerely Yours*. Immensely popular with troops worldwide, she was nicknamed the Forces' Sweetheart, and toured extensively; the song *The White Cliffs of Dover* dates from this period. *Auf Wiedersehen Sweetheart* (1952), the first big hit of her comeback career, was the first British disc to top the British and US charts.

MacEnroe, John 1959–

American tennis player. He came to the world's attention in 1977 when he reached the semi-finals of the Wimbledon Men's Singles at the age of 18. Four years later he took the title and established himself as the premier figure in men's tennis, winning Wimbledon again in 1983 and 1984. His skills and strength won him many tournaments, but his fits of temper on-court and tendency to swagger off-court won him few friends. Since then his performance has been more erratic and in 1985 he took a sabbatical from tennis, re-emerging in 1988.

Magistretti, Vico 1920–

Italian industrial designer. Graduating from the Milan Polytechnic in 1945, he has since become one of Italy's leading furniture designers, creating the first Italian plastic chair, the "Selene", in 1962. His best-known chair is perhaps the "Modello 115", with its classic frame and traditional rush seating. An important design consultant in Italy, he also teaches at London's Royal College of Art.

Marciano, Rocky 1923–69

US boxer. The world heavyweight champion from 23 September 1952 to 27 April 1956, he had a powerful punch and immense stamina. Turning professional in 1947, he fought 49 bouts and retired unbeaten after defending his title six times, having scored a total of 43 knockouts.

Marx Brothers, The

US comedy team: brothers Chico (1886–1961); Harpo (1888–1964); Groucho (1890–1977) and Zeppo (1901–79). All but Zeppo had a separate comic persona and their style was an almost surrealistic blend of slapstick, boisterous vitality, insult, anarchy and logic-chopping. After a tough apprenticeship in vaudeville, they made Broadway in *I'll Say It Is* (1924); then *The Coconuts* (1925) and *Animal Crackers* (1928). The last two were filmed (1929–30) and ten more movies followed. Even weak direction and weaker plots could not lessen their impact in classics such as *Duck Soup* (1933) and *A Night at the Opera* (1935)

Mayer, Louis B. 1885–1957

Russian-born film executive. In 1907 he bought a rundown cinema, soon owning New England's largest theater chain. In 1914 he entered distribution. After experience with Alco, he founded a production company in 1918. In 1924 Mayer merged with Metro and Goldwyn, and until 1951 maintained control. A hardworking tyrant, his nose for popular taste, willingness to spend money and ability to pick personnel made him the most powerful studio boss in the thirties and forties.

Mayfield, Curtis 1942–

American singer, song-writer and guitarist. He began in his grandmother's Travelling Soul Spiritualist Church Choir, and the influence of gospel music is discernible in his music as a soloist and with The Impressions, formed in 1956; he confronted social problems in the anti-drugs lyrics for the film *Superfly* (1972).

McCormack, Mark 1930–

American entrepreneur. Educated at Princeton and Yale Universities, rose to prominence with the formation of the International Management Group in 1962, creating the industry of sports management and sports marketing. He handles sporting celebrities such as Chris Evert and Martina Navratilova. The television division of IMG has represented not only sporting bodies but also the Nobel foundation and the Vatican.

McLuhan, Marshall 1911–80

Canadian communications theorist. He became Professor of English Literature at Toronto University in 1952 and director of its Center for Culture and Technology in 1963. He prophesied that printed books would become obsolete, killed off by television and electronic information technology, and that our thought processes would be reshaped by these phenomena. His books include *Understanding the Media* (1964) and *The Medium is the Message* (1967).

▼ Eddy Merckx

▼ Mistinguett

▼ Robert Mitchum

McQueen, Steve 1930–80

US film actor. One of the most popular stars of the sixties and seventies, his supercool, loner, pragmatic style suited the times. A drifter until 1958 there was TV stardom in *Wanted: Dead or Alive*, star billing in the film *The Blob* and the film part that gave him his break, *Never So Few*. He did well in *The Magnificent Seven* (1960), but *The Great Escape* (1963) confirmed his stardom. The best of his later credits were *The Cincinnati Kid* (1965) and *Bullitt* (1968).

Méliès, Georges 1861–1938

French director and producer. In 1888 he sold his share in the family business to buy Robert Houdini's theater and earned a name as an imaginative illusionist. He began projecting shorts on a Bioscope in 1896, but was soon making films with a camera of his own design, building Europe's first film studio in 1897. His fantasy films, with their original use of optical and mechanical effects, were the most influential, particularly *Voyage to the Moon* (1902) and *À la Conquête du Pole* (1911).

Mendini, Alessandro 1931–

Italian industrial designer. Having worked as an architect for the Milan firm Nizzoli until 1970, he became the editor of the design magazine *Casabella*, and later *Modo,* and the highly influential *Domus.* Finding his inspiration in "banality" – employing, for example, the designs and materials of everyday objects from 1950s suburban "non-culture" – he has made furniture for the avant-garde Studio Alchymia. His most famous piece is a post-Modernist coffee-set.

Merckx, Eddy 1945–

Belgian cyclist. He became the amateur world champion in 1964, winning the professional title three years later and again in 1971 and 1974. He dominated the world of cycling in the early 1970s, taking first place in the Prix de France in all but one of the six races between 1969 and 1974. Six times awarded the title of Sportsman of the Year in his native Belgium, he did much to bring cycling to public attention throughout Europe.

Miller, Glenn 1904–44

US jazz trombonist, arranger, composer and band leader. His was the most successful big band ever, producing music which swung harder than any other white band of the time. By 1939 RCA singles and a radio series were confirming his success, and his films, *Sun Valley Serenade* (1941) and *Orchestra Wives* (1942), found a worldwide audience. Drafted into the US Army in 1942, he re-formed his band using several key men from his previous line-up and wowed Britain before being lost in a plane over France in 1944.

Minnelli, Vincente 1910–

US director. A child performer, he was a theatre designer before directing several successful Broadway musicals from 1935. Arthur Freed persuaded him to join MGM in 1940 and he was trained in film technique before his 1943 debut. He developed a lavish visual style and made some of Hollywood's greatest musicals, including *Meet Me in St Louis* (1944), *An American in Paris* (1951) and *The Band Wagon* (1953). Other credits include *Father of the Bride* (1950), *The Bad and the Beautiful* (1952) and *Lust for Life* (1956).

Mistinguett 1875–1956

Flemish-born music-hall artiste. Although she almost never appeared outside Paris, she won an international reputation as a symbol of the city for over 50 years. In her youth she performed Parisian low-life character sketches; later she mostly sang and danced – she had marvellous legs, saucy looks and a good line in repartee. She appeared at the Moulin Rouge, which for a time she co-owned, and later the Folies-Bergère, with Maurice Chevalier.

Mitchum, Robert 1917–

US film actor. A popular leading man from the late forties, his tough heroics appealed to men, his brooding sexuality to women. He began acting in 1942 and started appearing in films in 1943. *The Story of GI Joe* (1945) was his big break. His best performances include *The Night of the Hunter* (1956), *The Sundowners* (1960), *Two for the See-Saw* (1962), *El Dorado* (1967), *Ryan's Daughter* (1970) and *The Friends of Eddie Coyle* (1973).

Mix, Tom 1880–1940

US film actor. His faster, more exciting format ousted the "authentic" film Western. His military career a publicity fiction, he got early experience in Wild West shows between 1906 and 1910. Selig hired him to herd cattle in 1911, but he was soon starring, directing or producing his own films. By 1917, when he joined Fox, his vehicles were action-packed two-reelers full of stunts he performed himself. Fox's top directors and cameramen made him the silents' cowboy star.

Miyake, Issey 1935–

Japanese fashion designer. After graduating from Tama University in 1964, he studied fashion in Paris and worked for Laroche and Givenchy before going to New York. His first show was held in that city in 1971, and two years later he held a second in Paris, by which time he had already established his own style: bold, sometimes quirky designs, using linear and geometric shapes, wrapped and layered around the body. He has continued to be one of the most innovative designers, combining elements of West and East in his garments.

Mizoguchi, Kenji 1898–1956

Japanese film director. One of Japan's finest directors, his *The Life of O-haru* (1952) and *Ugetsu Monogatari* (1953) are consistently rated among the masterpieces of world cinema. Directing his first film in 1922, a constant theme was women's status in Japanese society: his sister was sold to be a geisha when he was a child. Other titles include *Sansho Dayu* and *Chikamastu Montogatari* (both 1954).

Monroe, Marilyn 1926–1962

US film actress. Born Norma Jean Baker, she had an unhappy childhood, shunted from orphanages to foster homes, badly treated and sexually molested. She married at 16, began modelling in 1945, and in 1946 was signed up with Fox. By 1952 Fox began pushing her into films such as *There's No Business Like Show Business* (1954), *Niagara* (1952) and *How To Marry A Millionaire* (1953), which established her as the archetypal screen sex goddess. In 1954 she married the baseball hero Joe DiMaggio, but this was not a success and in 1956 she married again for the last time, an unlikely match with the writer Arthur Miller. Her most famous films were: *The Asphalt Jungle* (1950) *Gentlemen Prefer Blondes* (1953), *The Seven Year Itch* (1955) and *Some Like it Hot* (1959). After a period of profound self-doubt she committed suicide by an overdose of barbituates when fired from her last movie.

Montana, Claude 1949-

French designer. After leaving school, he came to London and began designing Mexican-style papier-mâché jewelry for the street markets. He returned to Paris in 1972 and launched his first collection under his name five years later. His styles tend towards machismo, with strong hard lines and bold aggresive colors. He typically uses leather (he worked for the leather manufacturers MacDouglas in the mid-1970s), and likes chains, buckles, and other metal adornments.

Morton, Jelly Roll 1890–1941

US jazz pianist, composer, arranger and vocalist. He explored the limits of the small band and many of his New Orleans stomps and blues are classics. Doing anything from pimping to pool, boxing promotion to running a tailor's shop while playing piano (1906–23), his hour came in 1923 in Chicago: published by the Melrose brothers, recording for Gennett and touring with his own groups. In 1926 he made his greatest recordings, the Red Hot Peppers sessions. By 1928, in New York, the big bands were catching on and he was old hat.

Paul Newman

Yoko Ono

Jesse Owens

Murnau, F.W. 1888–1931

German film director. One of the most talented of silent directors, his reputation rests on three films: *Nosferatu* (1922), an expressionist film shot uniquely on real locations; *The Last Laugh* (1924), visually so powerful that it needed no titles; and *Sunrise* (1927), his first American film, a lyrical, pessimistic work which suffered a hastily applied moral ending.

Navratilova, Martina 1956–

Czech-born American tennis-player. After winning the Women's Singles title in Czechoslovakia from 1972 to 1974, she came to the notice of the Western public when she reached the semi-finals of the women's singles at Wimbledon in 1976, having defected to the USA the previous year. A player of extraordinary power and skill, particularly in serve-and-volley play, she won the Wimbledon title eight times in the 1980s. She is probably the wealthiest sportswoman ever, amassing no less than $2,173,556 from prize-money alone in 1984.

Nelson, George 1917–

American industrial designer. He graduated from Yale School of Fine Arts in 1931 and after spending the early 1930s in Europe, imported European modernism into America, introducing, for example, Mies van der Rohe to his home country. He founded the magazine *Architectural Forum* and prompted corporate modernism in his office-designs, such as the *Storage Wall* and the *Action Office*. Like so many other leading designers, he has done work for Olivetti, designing their Editor 2 typewriter in 1968.

Newman, Paul 1925–

US film actor, director and producer. A graduate of the Actors' Studio, he is intelligent, athletic, handsome and he has intensely blue eyes. Hollywood snapped him up after a Broadway hit and despite a terrible debut in *The Silver Chalice* (1955) he was soon getting good roles, giving good performances. In the sixties and early seventies he was America's top male lead. Credits include *The Hustler* (1961), *Hud* (1963), *Cool Hand Luke* (1967), *Butch Cassidy and the Sundance Kid* (1969) and *The Verdict* (1982).

Nicholson, Jack 1937–

US film actor. A versatile, charismatic character who first won notice in *Easy Rider* (1969), he had been starring in B-movies since 1958, writing and co-producing too. Thereafter most of his films have been good and his notices great. He excels in outsider roles. Credits include *Five Easy Pieces* (1970), *The King of Marvin Gardens* (1972), *The Last Detail* (1973), *Chinatown* (1974), *Profession: Reporter* and *One Flew Over the Cuckoo's Nest* (both 1975) and *The Witches of Eastwick* (1987).

Nicklaus, Jack 1940–

US golfer. With natural talent, power, asuteness and iron nerve, he dominated world professional golf in the sixties and seventies. Turning professional in 1962, he won the Masters six times (1963, 1965–66, 1972, 1975 and 1986), the US Open four times (1962, 1967, 1972 and 1980), the PGA championship five times (1963, 1971, 1973, 1975 and 1980) and the British Open three times (1966, 1970 and 1978). He was the first golfer to win over $300,000 in a year (1972).

Noguchi, Isamu 1904–

US sculptor and designer. He studied in New York, then worked as Brancusi's assistant in Paris, where he was influenced by abstract sculptors and the surrealists. His first exhibition was in New York in 1929. His sculpture often represents elegant, abstract organic forms, and his instinctive awareness of the interrelationship of bone and rock evolved into a sense of "oneness with stone." As a designer, he worked on several environmental projects, including the UNESCO garden (1958), a Hawaiian playground and a fountain for the Detroit Civic Center (1975).

Oliver, Joe "King" 1885–1938

US jazz cornetist and composer. His skill took time to build but by 1917, with volume and plenty of muted effects, Kid Ory was billing him "King". Shrewdly, he followed the flow from Orleans to Chicago in 1919. His Creole Jazz Band (1922–4) with Armstrong on second trumpet was the hottest thing around, featuring the pair's complex "ad-libs" in classics like *Mabel's Dream* and *Riverside Blues* (recorded in 1923). In 1925 he formed the Dixie Syncopators, with a new saxophone team.

Olivetti, Adriano 1901–60

Italian industrialist. Trained as an industrial chemist, he inherited a small typewriter factory and turned it into one of the world's largest producers of office machinery. An ardent anticommunist, he nevertheless pursued a "Christian Socialist" industrial policy, providing employee benefits and allowing for a degree of worker participation in management.

Olivier, Laurence 1909–

British stage and screen actor. The son of a clergyman, his first role, at the age of 15, was in *The Taming of the Shrew*. He became a Hollywood star by playing romantic leads in *Wuthering Heights* (1939) and *Rebecca* (1940), and later directed himself in film versions of *Hamlet* (1948), *Richard III* (1955), and *Othello* (1965). Although usually associated with tragic and romantic roles, he has also taken off-beat parts, like that of seedy vaudeville artiste Archie Rice in John Osborne's *The Entertainer* (1957).

Ono, Yoko 1933–

Japanese-born artist and singer. Raised in Tokyo by her wealthy family, in 1953 she went to New York where she got involved with avant-garde conceptual art. In 1966 she met John Lennon, and they were married in 1969. In that year they held their first "Bed-in for Peace" at the Amsterdam Hilton, and a year later began releasing their *Plastic Ono Band* LPs.

Oshima, Nagisa 1932–

Japanese film director. A leader of Japan's new wave, his films often attack traditional mores, offering radical alternatives, and feature sex and/or violence. His technique has been equally innovatory, mixing fantasy and reality. He made his first feature, *A Town of Love and Hope*, in 1959. *In the Realm of the Senses* (1976) made world headlines with its realistic portrayal of sexual obsession. Other credits include *Death by Hanging* (1968), *Diary of a Shinjuku Thief* (1969), *The Ceremony* (1970) and *Merry Christmas Mr Lawrence* (1982).

Owens, Jesse 1913–80

US athlete. His record in the long jump, set in 1935, stood for 25 years and he won four gold medals in the 1936 Berlin Olympics – for the 100- and 200-meter runs, the long jump and the US 400-meter relay team – to the fury of Adolf Hitler, who had hoped to demonstrate Aryan superiority. But his most remarkable feat was on 25 May 1935, when he equaled the world record for the 100 yards and broke those for the 220 yards (and 200 meters), the 220-yard (200-meter) low hurdles and long jump.

Ozu, Yasujiro 1903–63

Japanese film director. Many of his films are compassionate, drily humorous studies of middle-class Japanese family life and most are shot with great simplicity. He evolved a quiet style which depended upon long takes using a static, low-angle camera, subtle editing rhythms, realistic settings and repertory players. Credits include *The Only Son* (1936), *The Munetaka Sisters* (1950), *Tokyo Story* (1953) and *Early Autumn* (1961).

Packer, Kerry 1937–

Australian media baron. He started his long and successful career in the press as a trainee executive in the Australian Consolidated Oven and Compress Printing in 1955, and since the mid-1970s has established a dominant influence in the Australian press and in broadcasting. He caused a controversy in 1977 when he contracted 35 of the world's top cricketers to play a series of matches in Australia, televised exclusively by his own Channel Nine network.

◄ Charlie Parker

◄ Gary Player

Palmer, Arnold 1929–

US golfer. The leading figure in world golf from the late fifties to the mid sixties, he became a professional in 1954. He was the first to win the US Masters four times (in 1958, 1960, 1962 and 1964) and to win $100,000 in prize money in one year. Other titles include the US Open (1960) and the British Open (1961–2). He built a business empire and negotiated the construction of China's first golf course.

Papanek, Victor 1925–

American design theorist. As professor of design at the University of Kansas, he wrote his polemical study, *Design for the Real World* in 1967, a book which attacked the preoccupation of modern designers with "concocting trivia" and their neglect of the more pressing needs of good design for the Third World. His energetic lecture-touring and his emphasis on the need to use diminishing resources wisely made him a cult figure in the ecology movement of the 1970s.

Parker, Charlie 1920–55

US alto-sax player and composer. His daring harmonic structures, explorations of rhythm and unique tone were charismatic and vastly influential. Born in Kansas City, he did his apprenticeship mostly around town, then some big-band work, before helping to establish bebop on New York's 52nd Street (1944–45). He formed an excellent five-piece in 1947, but after 1950 he gigged with pick-up groups or toured with Herman and Kenton. Heroin addiction and alcohol killed him.

Pasolini, Pier Paolo 1922–75

Italian film director. A novelist and essayist, he began writing screen plays in 1954. *Accattone!* (1961), his first feature, was based on one of his novels and brought instant recognition. He mined world literature and the contemporary scene, often exciting charges of blasphemy. A committed Marxist and a profoundly mystical Christian and a Freudian, his work was always controversial. Credits include *Il Vangelo Secondo Matteo* (1964), *Teorema* (1968), *Il Decamerone* (1971), *I Racconti di Canterbury* (1972) and *Sale le Centoventi Giornate di Sodoma* (1975).

Pelé 1940–

Brazilian football player. A folk hero, the most famous, best-paid athlete of his time, he had a powerful kick, great accuracy and terrific anticipation. He joined Santos in 1956 as inside left forward; in 1962 the club won its first world championship. He led Brazil to victory in the World Cup in 1958, 1962 and 1970. Following retirement (1974), he accepted a contract with the New York Cosmos to promote the US game, led them to league victory in 1977 and retired again.

Penn, Arthur 1922–

American director. After acting and university he became an NBC floor manager in 1951 and by 1953 was writing and directing drama. In 1958 he had a Broadway success, *Two for the See-Saw*, and directed his first film, *The Left-Handed Gun*, with little impact. Other Broadway hits followed before he filmed one of them, *The Miracle Worker* (1962). His subsequent sixties films – *Mickey One* (1965), *Bonnie and Clyde* (1967) and *Alice's Restaurant* (1969) – were socially and/or stylistically influential, especially for his theme of violence. Other credits include *Little Big Man* (1970) and *Night Moves* (1975).

Piaf, Edith 1915–63

French singer and entertainer. A tiny woman, shabbily dressed, with a powerful, strident voice, her style was personal and seemingly simple. She packed an emotional punch fueled by her audience's knowledge of her tragic childhood and adult life. A street singer when very young, she became a popular cabaret and music-hall performer – touring Europe and the USA – and the intellectuals' darling, starring in Cocteau's *Le Bel Indifferent* (1941). Her most famous songs were *Je ne regrette rien* and *La vie en rose*.

Pickford, Mary 1893–1979

US film actress. The most popular film star ever, she had a natural, radiant child-woman appeal: she was "America's Sweetheart" and no one wanted her to change. So she played lovable little girls and was 28 before she insisted on cutting off the curls. The career went downhill. A shrewd negotiator, in 1909 she was earning $40 a week; in 1916 $10,000, plus bonus and profit share. In 1919 she, Chaplin, Fairbanks and D.W. Griffith formed United Artists, and in 1920 she married Douglas Fairbanks, to the public's delight.

Player, Gary 1935–

South African golfer. After turning professional in 1953, he won the British Open six years later and became a leading competitor of the 1960s and early 1970s. A small and slightly-built player, he relied on fitness, diet, and a somewhat mechanical technique rather than the traditional qualities of power and swing.

Poiret, Paul 1879–1944

French couturier. Paris's most fashionable dress designer before World War I, his most influential design was the hobble skirt. After working for Worth, he opened his own small shop in 1903. He revived the Empire line and a flowing style based on the classical Greek tunic. But many of his clothes are theatrical; employing strong colours and decorated with pearls and feathers, they are much influenced by the Ballets Russes and Eastern art.

Poitier, Sidney 1924–

US actor and director. Hollywood's "token" black star for almost two decades, he was a charismatic personality with an impressive acting talent. He first made Broadway in 1946 in an all-black production of *Lysistrata*. He made his first film appearance in 1949; major credits include *The Blackboard Jungle* (1955), *The Defiant Ones* (1958), *To Sir With Love*, *In The Heat of the Night* and *Guess Who's Coming to Dinner* (all 1967).

Porsche, Ferdinand 1875–1952

Austrian automobile manufacturer. In 1899 he joined Jacob Lohner to develop electric and petrol-electric cars, moving to Austro-Daimler in 1905. In 1930 he opened his own design studio and in 1936 fulfilled Hitler's request for a "people's car", the Volkswagen. After two years' internment, he sold a prototype sports car to the Swiss in 1948. Production of the first streamlined coupé body began at the end of 1948 and Porsche entered competition racing in 1951.

Porter, Cole 1892–1964

US composer and lyricist. His songs are witty, subtle, civilized, detached: everything he was himself. He had his first Broadway musical in 1916, then military service and a playboy lifestyle kept him busy. But after *Fifty Million Frenchmen* (1929) he was a major force on Broadway. Credits include *The Gay Divorce* (1932), *Kiss Me Kate* (1948), *Can-Can* (1953) and *Silk Stockings* (1955). He also worked in films, and among his most successful film songs are *I Get a Kick Out of You* (1934), *Begin the Beguine* (1936) and *In the Still of the Night* (1937).

Porter, Edwin S 1869–1941

US film director. Initially a designer and builder of projectors and cameras, he became a director/cameraman for Edison in 1899, making the first cutting-room assembly, *The Life of an American Fireman* (1903); the first epic, *The Great Train Robbery* (also 1903), which influenced the Western genre profoundly; and a stop-motion animation film, *The Teddy Bears* (1907).

Presley, Elvis 1935–77

US singer and actor. The rock 'n' roll idol of the fifties, he was the first to notch massive sales over a short career. The first broadcast of his first single for Sun (1955) attracted real attention and RCA bought his contract. In 1956 he had the then greatest sales in a year (10 million), with a disk at No.1 for 25 weeks (24 in 1957); between 1956 and 1962 he totaled 18 No.1 hits. *Love Me Tender* (1956) was his film debut clearing costs three days after release, he went on to make 32 more, all custom-built vehicles; his popularity declined in the sixties, but he had a successful cabaret and concert comeback in the early seventies.

Viv Richards

Babe Ruth

David Sarnoff

Pulitzer, Joseph 1947–11

Hungarian-born newspaper editor and publisher. One of the USA's most influential journalists, he began his career on a German-speaking newspaper in 1868. By a dynamic series of purchases and mergers, he established St Louis's Post-Dispatch and New York's The World, founding the Evening World himself. He was sympathetic to labor interests and established the Pulitzer Prize, awarded annually to Americans for excellence in literature, music and journalism.

Quant, Mary 1934–

British dress designer. The leader of the sixties youth-oriented fashion movement which usurped the power of the couturiers, she set up a cosmetics business in 1955 and spent two years designing millinery before opening a boutique in the King's Road, London, in 1957. In seven years she was mass-producing designs which sold throughout Europe and the USA. The miniskirt and hot pants were her most original designs. Early in the seventies she ceased manufacture but continued to design clothes, furs, linen and spectacles and to run her cosmetics business.

Rank, J. Arthur 1888–1972

British film magnate. The founder of an empire which controlled every aspect of the British film business from production and processing to distribution and exhibition, in 1935 he began the series of takeovers which by the mid-forties gave him ownership of 1000 cinemas and over half Britain's studios. In the sixties the company began to diversify. Its gong logo and the Charm School, a training ground for young talent in the forties and fifties, are fondly remembered.

Redford, Robert 1937–

US film actor and director. The most popular Hollywood star of the seventies, his strong-jawed, blond looks commended him to all. He made Broadway in 1959 and won the lead in Barefoot in the Park in 1963. From 1965 he had regular film work but it was Butch Cassidy and the Sundance Kid (1969) which hit gold. Credits include The Candidate (1972), Three Days of the Condor (1975) and All the President's Men (1976). He directed Ordinary People (1980) and The Milagro Beanfield War (1988).

Reed, Lou 1942–

American singer, song-writer, guitarist. It was with the formation of the Velvet Underground in 1964 that he first made his mark. His songs depicted the empty debauchery of New York street-life with a mixture of lyricism and violence. He found more solo success with Transformer (1972) and Rock and Roll Animal (1974).

Reeves, Jim 1924–64

US singer. A country-music star whose great popularity survived his death in a plane crash, he had been forced by an early leg injury to give up a career as a professional baseball player. He began recording in 1945, also writing songs and playing guitar. Among his greatest hit singles were Mexican Joe (1953), Four Walls (1957), He'll Have to Go (1959) and I Love You Because and I Won't Forget You (both 1964).

Reith, John 1889–1971

Scottish creator of British public-service broadcasting. Trained as an engineer, he was appointed general manager of the newly formed BBC in 1922. He aimed to bring purpose and status to broadcasting, including cultural, educational and religious programmes alongside information and entertainment and demanding high standards of behavior from his staff. When the company was made a corporation, he became its director-general, pursuing the same policy while keeping technical standards high. In 1936 he inaugurated British TV. He left the BBC in 1938 to serve as a wartime minister and peacetime administrator.

Richards, Gordon 1904–

British jockey. He was the most successful jockey through 26 British flat-racing seasons he rode in from 1925 to 1954. In May 1950 he became the first to ride 4000 winners. His total score – 4870 – was a world record, not broken until 1956. He won the St Leger five times, the 2000 Guineas three times but the Derby only once. He retired after injury to become a trainer and racing manager.

Richards, Viv 1952–

West Indian cricketer. He made his debut for the island of Antigua in 1971, and captained Somerset from 1974 to 1986, and led the West Indian team in 1985. Widely considered one of the finest batsmen of the century, he used his sporting celebrity to promote cultural solidarity in his native West Indies.

Riefenstahl, Leni 1902–

German film director and actress. She learned basic film technique while starring in semi-documentary films which extolled the beauty of nature. She wrote, produced (and starred in) her first directorial credit, The Blue Light, in 1931. In 1934 Hitler asked her to film the "Nuremberg Party Convention", and she produced a powerful piece of propaganda, Triumph of the Will. Olympia (1936), a record of the 1936 Berlin Games, seems in reality to have been dedicated to the human body.

Robeson, Paul 1898–1976

US singer and actor. The son of a slave, he turned down a football career to read law. Unable to get work, he became an actor. He had a big hit in Emperor Jones (1924), but it was in the film version of Show Boat (1936) that he won world fame. His other greatest success was as Othello (1930 and 1943). Film credits include Sanders of the River (1935) and King Solomon's Mines (1937).

Robinson, Bill 1878–1949

US singer and dancer. A professional at eight, he became one of the world's greatest tap dancers and a star of vaudeville. He created the much-imitated stair tap-routine and had outstanding stage success in the revue Blackbirds (1927) and The Hot Mikado (1939). His cheerful personality earned him the nickname "Bojangles" and he reached a wider audience in films, teaming several times with Shirley Temple. Film credits include The Little Colonel (1935) and Rebecca of Sunnybrook Farm (1938).

Rockne, Knut 1888–1931

Norwegian-born football coach. He made Illinois's University of Notre Dame team one of the twenties' most successful collegiate teams. He entered Notre Dame at 22, playing end, and with Gus Dorais popularized the forward pass. He became head coach in 1918, and through 13 seasons the team won 105 games, losing 12 and tieing 5. His technique of substituting whole teams during games foreshadowed the "platoon" system.

Rodgers, Richard 1902–79

US musical-comedy composer. His most successful collaborations were with Lorenz Hart and Oscar Hammerstein II. He met Hart at university and they put on the varsity show in 1920. Their first professional success was a revue, in 1925; their later, increasingly sophisticated musical comedies included Babes in Arms (1937), The Boys from Syracuse (1938) and Pal Joey (1940). After Hart's death, he worked with Hammerstein on eight musicals, including Oklahoma! (1945), Carousel (1945), South Pacific (1949), The King and I (1951) and The Sound of Music (1959).

Ross, Harold 1862–1951

US journalist. Founder of The New Yorker magazine, he was a major influence on reportage, humor and fiction in the USA. He edited the servicemen's newspaper in France during World War I before establishing his weekly in 1925. He aimed to encapsulate the contemporary scene in a light-hearted yet rigorous style, an approach which allowed satire and parody and attracted new writers and artists. Humorist James Thurber and cartoonists Helen Hoskinson and Mary Petty made their reputations there.

◄ Jean Shrimpton

◄ Frank Sinatra

◄ Bessie Smith

Rossellini, Roberto 1906–77

Italian film director. One of the neo-realists of post-World War II cinema, his trilogy – *Roma Citta aperta* (1945), *Paisa* (1946) and *Germania Anno Zero* (1947), compelling drama set convincingly in real locations – was an arthouse hit. From 1938 to 1942 he had co-scripted or directed Fascist-commissioned films. His affair with and marriage to Ingrid Bergman produced several films, none of which were well received; *Stromboli* (1949) is best known but *Viaggio in Italia* (1953) is highest rated. Post-Bergman *Il Generale della Rovere* (1959) was admired.

Rubinstein, Helena 1870–1965

Polish-born cosmetician. She left Poland in 1902 to visit Australia, where she opened a beauty salon, offering free consultation and a cream she had taken with her. An instant success, she studied dermatology in Europe, opening salons in London (1908) and Paris (1912). In 1914 she immigrated to the USA and set up salons in New York and other cities. By 1917 she was distributing products wholesale and after World War II she manufactured on all five continents. Constantly improving and developing new lines, she was the first to introduce medicated skin-care products.

Ruth, Babe 1895–1948

US baseball player. The holder of a record 60 home runs in a 154-game major-league season (1927), he became a professional in 1914. He pitched 29 consecutive scoreless innings for the Boston Red Sox in the 1916 and 1918 World Series. Sold as an outfielder to the New York Yankees for $125,000 in 1920, he stayed there until 1934. In 1930–31 he was the game's top earner with a salary of $80,000. He led the American League in home runs for 12 years, hitting in 22 major-league seasons a total of 714 from 8399 times at bat.

Sapper, Richard 1932–

German-born Italian industrial designer. Having studied mechanical engineering, he went to work for Mercedes-Benz in Stuttgart, but in 1958 moved to Milan to collaborate with Marco Zanuso. Together they produced a number of prized cult objects, such as the Brion Vega folding radio in 1965 and the Italian "Grillo" telephone in 1969. On his own account, he designed the stork-like "Tizio" low-voltage lamp in 1978, a triumph of Italian elegance and German engineering – the current runs through the slim flexible screwless bodywork. Later work showed a tendency towards formalism. His stylish kettle for Bollitore in 1983 could not be used to make a cup of tea because the handle became too hot to hold before the water had boiled.

Sarnoff, David 1891–1971

US broadcasting pioneer. Using his first wages to buy a telegraph machine, he became a radio operator for Marconi, picking up the Titanic's distress signal at the world's most powerful radio station on top of a Manhattan store in 1912. In 1916 he proposed the marketing of home radio-receivers to Marconi; in 1921, by then at RCA, he broadcast the Dempsey-Carpentier bout to demonstrate the idea's potential. In 1926 he formed NBC, launching research into TV in 1928.

Sassoon, Vidal 1928–

British hair-stylist. He opened his first salon in Bond Street, London, at the age of 26 and soon became the favorite of British pop stars and models. After developing techniques such as blow-drying and the blunt cut, he created numerous new styles for women, such as "The Shape" (1959), the "Nancy Kwan" (1963), the geometric "Five-Point-Cut" (1964), and later the "Feather Cut" (1977), for men and women.

Schiaparelli, Elsa 1896–1973

Italian-born couturier. Like Dior, she commercialized Parisian fashion. Settling in Paris in the late twenties, she toyed with writing and sculpture before opening a small salon. By 1935 she was a leader of fashion: in 1932 she introduced the padded shoulder. Her designs were simple yet eccentric and she used color flamboyantly, introducing shocking pink and ice blue and designing fur bedjackets and rhinestone-trimmed lingerie. After 1935 she expanded into jewelry, perfume, cosmetics and swimsuits and in 1949 opened a New York branch.

Scorsese, Martin 1942–

US film director. A highly regarded filmmaker whose most successful films emphasize character rather than dramatic plot, his first major film was *Mean Streets* (1973). The disturbing vision of urban life and jumpy camerawork were typical of his work in *Taxi Driver* (1976) and *Raging Bull* (1979). His more "commercial" projects have included *Alice Doesn't Live Here Anymore* (1975) and *New York, New York* (1977).

Selznick, David O. 1902–65

US film producer. He set up his own company in 1936 and produced the immensely profitable *Gone With the Wind* in 1939, writing and directing parts of it: his involvement was always detailed and highly creative. Earlier he had worked on productions at MGM, Paramount and RKO, including *King Kong* and *Dinner at Eight* (both 1933) and *Anna Karenina* (1935). He brought Ingrid Bergman and Alfred Hitchcock to Hollywood, for *Intermezzo* (1939) and *Rebecca* (1940) respectively.

Sennett, Mack 1880–1960

Canadian-born director, producer and actor. A co-founder of the Keystone Studios in 1912, he soon made it a leader in the slapstick comedy genre. The early films were uninhibited one-reel farces which defied convention; sustained by the energy of their visual gags, they were improvised, then brilliantly edited by Sennett. The "Keystone Cops" were quintessential Sennett and among his stars were Mabel Normand, "Fatty" Arbuckle and Chester Conklin.

Shrimpton, Jean 1942–

British fashion model. "La Shrimp" was discovered by the rising star of British fashion photography, David Bailey, whose first pictures of her appeared in *Vogue* in 1961. Three years later, her face had appeared on the cover of 17 Condé Nast glossies within a year and her earnings had risen to £25,000 per annum.

Sinatra, Frank 1915–

US vocalist and film actor. After signings with Harry James and Tommy Dorsey, he went solo and a spot on radio's "Hit Parade" series in 1943 brought stardom. His style was casual, the way he phrased a lyric was anything but. The first vocalist to inspire teenage adulation, he had his first big film role in 1943 also. Dramatic roles, in particular *From Here to Eternity* (1952), revived his career in the early fifties, and he found even better form as a singer. Imputations of underworld connections have featured throughout his career.

Sirk, Douglas 1900–87

Danish-born director. A successful German-based theater director, he turned to films in 1933, becoming known for the visual power of his work. Still finding Nazi interference unacceptable, he left for Hollywood in 1937. Much of the material he was given was absurdly weak and his budgets minute. Nonetheless he contrived to create some memorable films, including *Magnificent Obsession* (1954), *All That Heaven Allows* (1955), *Tarnished Angels* (1957), *A Time to Live and a Time to Die* (1958) and *Imitation of Life* (1959).

Smith, Bessie 1895–1937

US jazz vocalist. The greatest blues singer ever, by 1920 she had a show in Atlantic City and in 1923 she moved to New York and signed with Columbia. By 1925 she was star of a hugely successful summer touring show, Harlem Frolics, and in 1927 she was earning more than any black artist anywhere. A second show, Mississippi Days, followed in 1928, but tastes began to change and her career declined. Her hard-living lifestyle was a prototype for women who sang the blues.

Gloria Swanson

Rudolph Valentino

Thorstein Veblen

Smith, Mamie 1883–1946
US blues vocalist. Her second record, *Crazy Blues* (1920), opened the market for black blues recordings aimed at black audiences, selling 7500 copies the first week. It was her big break: she formed the Jazz Hounds and made a fortune. By the mid-twenties she owned three luxury homes in New York. Tastes changed and her career waned through the thirties and early forties. Finally poverty and arthritis overtook her.

Sottsass, Ettore 1917–
Austrian-born Italian industrial designer. A graudate of the Turin Polytechnic, he set up office in the city in 1946. Since 1957 he has been closely associated with Olivetti, but has always maintained a quirky independence. In the 1960s he dabbled in Pop, and more recently produced bizarre furniture designs for the Studio Alchymica. In 1981 he formed the radical "Memphis" group, where he has continued his career as a designer of witty and outrageous furniture.

Sousa, John Philip 1854–1932
US bandmaster and composer. After leading the Washington Marine Band, he formed his own band in 1892 and began touring the world, winning an international reputation and helping to raise band standards throughout the USA. He wrote over 100 marches and his most successful – among them *The Stars and Stripes Forever*, *El Capitan* and *The Washington Post* – were judged vigorous, optimistic, patriotic and tremendously stirring.

Spector, Phil 1941–
US record producer. Originally with Atlantic, he set up Philles Records in 1961, creating a uniquely rich orchestral rhythm & blues sound using massed pianos, strings and percussion and cascading riffs in a style which recalled gospel singing. His early recordings were with the Crystals and the Ronettes: notably *Then He Kissed Me* and *Be My Baby* (both 1963). But the Righteous Brothers single *You've Lost that Loving Feeling* (1964), Ike and Tina Turner's *River Deep, Mountain High* (1966) sum up his mature style.

Spielberg, Steven 1947–
US film director and producer. He shot his first film at 12, won a contract with Universal after college. Unafraid of sentiment, he shows childhood as a constant preoccupation in his work. The most successful American director of the seventies and eighties, his box-office smashes include *Jaws* (1975), *Close Encounters of the Third Kind* (1977), *Raiders of the Lost Ark* (1981), *E.T.: The Extra-Terrestrial* (1982) and *The Color Purple* (1985).

Stallone, Sylvester 1946–
US film actor, screenwriter and director. He decided early that acting was for him but met with no encouragement. He landed bit parts in films and then the lead in a low–budgeter which led to support roles in majors in 1975. He wrote his own star part, *Rocky* (1976), sold the rights and made a fortune at the box office. All his later roles have depended upon his muscular physique and right-wing politics. With *Paradise Alley* (1978) he began directing as well as writing. Credits include the *Rocky* and *Rambo* series.

Steiger, Rod 1925–
US actor. He is a gifted, versatile actor, one of the greatest Method actors to emerge from the Actors' Studio. He had his early successes on stage and more particularly TV, notably in *Maty*. After one film appearance in 1951, he made a big impression with his second, *On the Waterfront* (1954). Credits include *Jubal* (1956), *The Pawnbroker* (1965), *Doctor Zhivago* (1966) and *In the Heat of the Night* (1967).

Sullivan, Ed 1901–74
US TV master of ceremonies. He entered journalism as a sports reporter and joined New York's *Daily News* in 1932. He began writing the paper's Broadway column and gained a reputation for spotting new talent. CBS hired him and he hosted two popular shows offering an extraordinary mixture of variety acts and well-known personalities: *Toast of the Town* (1948–55) and *The Ed Sullivan Show* (1955–71). His terse, reserved style earned him the nickname "Great Stone Face".

Swanson, Gloria 1897–1983
US film actress. Romantic comedy and tearjerkers for Triangle filled most of 1916–19. She joined De Mille at Paramount and found stardom in suggestive bedroom farces like *Don't Change Your Husband* (1919). In the mid- twenties, mostly in drama, she was America's ultimate glamor queen. Stroheim's extravagance broke an independent venture, *Queen Kelly* (1928), and she retired in 1934. Of her three comebacks, the second was the most memorable – *Sunset Boulevard* (1950).

Teague, Walter Dorwin 1883–1960
US industrial designer. The pioneer of industrial design as a profession, he worked first in advertising as a designer. In 1926 he set up an office specifically to design exhibitions, interiors, corporate graphics and product. Important early work included the design of two Eastman Kodak cameras (1927) and the Marmon 16 automobile (1930). He also designed railway coaches, office machines, filling stations and the Boeing 707 interior.

Temple, Shirley 1928–
US film actress. The most popular and most talented child star ever, she appeared in one-reelers before she was four. Fox put her under contract in 1934 and that year she won a special Academy award. Cute, dimpled and precocious, she could sing, dance and act. In 1938 she was the top box-office attraction and the focus of a thriving spin-off industry. By 1940 adolescence loomed and her career was almost over. In her forties she found a second career in public life, as an ambassador.

Thompson, Daley 1958–
British athlete. He left school – and home – at the age of 16 to concentrate on the decathlon, and three years later, with the aid of a government stipend, he became the youngest man to get 8000 points in the event. He won the Gold Medal in the decathlon at both the 1980 Olympics in Moscow and the Los Angeles Games in 1984. An ebullient, sometimes aggressive personality, he became one of the "superstars" of 1980s' sport.

Thorpe, Jim 1886–1953
US athlete. Judged the greatest American all-round athlete and footballer of the first half of the century, he was primarily of American Indian descent. He played semi-professional baseball in 1909–10, was chosen for the All-America football team in 1911–12 and won gold for the decathlon and pentathlon at the 1912 Olympics. A relatively unsuccessful National League baseball player (1913–19), he was a star of professional football from 1919 to 1926. Basketball, boxing, lacrosse, swimming and hockey were other sports in which he was outstanding.

Tilden, Bill 1893–1953
US tennis player. A powerful stroke-player with a great sense of theater, he was one of the game's greatest ever players and one of its first personalities. He was slow to develop, not reaching the finals of the US singles until 1918, but he went on to win the title seven times (1920–25 and 1929) and the Wimbledon singles three times (1920–21 and 1930). He also won several other singles, doubles and mixed-doubles titles in the USA, Italy and France.

Twiggy 1949–
British model and performer. Born Lesley Hornby, she acquired the name "Twiggy" as a result of her slender, boyish figure. Under the tutelage of entrepreneur Justin de Villeneuve, she was launched as "The Face of 1966" appearing in fashion magazines such as *Elle* and *Vogue*. She was the most sought-after and most imitated model for the next five years. Later, she appeared in several films, most notably *The Boy Friend* (1971).

Andy Warhol

John Wayne

Johnny Weismuller

Valentino, Rudolph 1895–1926

Italian-born film star. After four years as a Hollywood bit-part player, he won the lead in *The Four Horsemen of the Apocalypse* (1921) and was instantly a star. To his American female audiences he represented exotic sensuality, mystery and illicit eroticism in a potent compound of passion and melancholy. His subsequent box-office hits were *The Sheik* (1921), *Blood and Sand* (1922) and *Monsieur Beaucaire* (1924). News of his death met with unequaled fan hysteria.

Van Doren, Harold 1895–1957

American industrial designer. After an artistic career in Paris which encompassed translation, novel-writing and even film-acting, he returned to the USA to become the director of the Minneapolis Institute of Arts, later resigning in the belief that design was a more effective means than art of contributing to the modern world. His first major design, for the Toledo Scale Company in 1934, initiated the use of large-scale lightweight plastic molding, and his designs were always geared to the development of new materials. An innovative but practical designer, his work ranged from Maytag washing-machines to Goodyear tires.

Veblen, Thorstein 1857–1929

American economist and social critic. Hailing from an impoverished family of Norwegian immigrants, he took his PhD at Yale University in 1884. After several years of penury, he was finally given a teaching post at the University of Chicago from 1892 to 1906, where he produced his critique of capitalism, *The Theory of the Leisure Class* (1899). This study came to have great significance for later theorists such as Galbraith, particularly in its identification and critique of "conspicuous consumption".

Vidor, King 1894–1982

US film director. After a feature debut with Universal and a stint with his own studio (Vidor Village), his reputation began building when he joined MGM. The anti-war film *The Big Parade* (1925) established him. *The Crowd* (1928), *Hallelujah* (1929), *Street Scene* (1932) and *Our Daily Bread* (1934) had an equally humanistic, if sentimental, tone; in individual scenes he manipulated camera and sound brilliantly. From 1935 to the late fifties his work was more commercial: *Duel in the Sun* (1947) is the high point of this period.

Warhol, Andy 1930–87

American artist and film-maker. He was the greatest pop-artist of the 1960s, mass-producing images of items of popular consumption, such as his *Campbell's Soupcan* (1961) in his studio, "The Factory". His screen-prints of *Marilyn Monroe* (1962) likewise revealed the star as a cleverly packaged commodity. He was also the maker of many underground films, such as *Empire* (1965), or *Chelsea Girls* (1966), depicting aimless bohemian life of sex and drugs.

Warner, Jack L. 1892–1978

Canadian-born film executive. With his three brothers, he dabbled in film distribution and production before setting up the Warner Bros studio in 1923 and later expanding into distribution. The breakthrough came in 1927 when they launched the first sound film, *The Jazz Singer*. Their thirties' pictures – gangster movies, social dramas, biographies and musicals – reflected the mood of the Depression years.

Wayne, John 1907–79

US film actor. After 10 years of bit parts and B-movie vehicles, his big break came in 1939 with John Ford's *Stagecoach*. Many of his best roles were in Ford movies – *Fort Apache* (1948), *She Wore a Yellow Ribbon* (1949), *The Quiet Man* (1952) and *The Searchers* (1956). He became a folk hero: audiences saw him as the "spirit of America", and his off-screen fundamentalist, hawkish, patriotic style, coupled with bravery during illness, seemed to confirm their view.

Weissmuller, Johnny 1904–84

US swimmer and film actor. He totaled five gold medals in the 1924 and 1928 Olympics and set many freestyle world records. Film stardom came with his custom-built role in MGM's *Tarzan* series. Between 1932 and 1948 there were 12 films, starting with *Tarzan the Ape Man*, and various co-stars (Maureen O'Sullivan the most sultry pairing).

Welles, Orson 1915–85

US director, producer, screenwriter and actor. He co-founded the Mercury Theatre in 1937, going on air in 1938 and engineering a notorious panic with his broadcast of *The War of the Worlds*. RKO gave him artistic control for his Hollywood directing debut: *Citizen Kane* (1941). Many of its startling effects were not original but he clearly had a brilliant organizing vision. Judged as bad box-office, his later work was hampered by studio interference or finance problems. Credits include *The Magnificent Ambersons* (1942), *The Lady from Shanghai* (1948), *Othello* (1952), *Touch of Evil* (1958), *Chimes at Midnight* (1966) and *F for Fake* (1975). He was also a magnetic screen actor.

West, Mae 1892–

US actress. An entertainer at five, she wrote, produced and directed her first stage play, *Sex*, in 1926. Jailed for obscenity, she went on to direct several more of her own plays before going to Paramount. She was a shrewd woman with a talent for innuendo and *double entendre*, and her blowsy persona made her both a sex star and a parody of that image. Her witticisms became folklore, and in 1935 she was the highest-paid woman in the USA. Her films include *She Done Him Wrong* and *I'm No Angel* (both 1933).

Whiteman, Paul 1890–1967

US bandleader and violinist. His major contributions were to publicize jazz, to make it "respectable" and to popularize it; indeed he promoted the first prestige jazz concert – at New York's Aeolian Hall. He devised the band show and his own band presented spectacular, bowdlerized versions of jazz typified in the Universal film *The King of Jazz* (1930).

Wills, Helen 1905–

US tennis player. She was the world's top woman player from 1927 to 1935, with powerful serves and overhead shots which compensated for her lack of speed. A deeply committed competitor, she was nicknamed "Little Miss Polar Face". She won Wimbledon eight times (1927–30, 1932–33, 1935 and 1938), the US singles seven times (1923–25, 1927–29 and 1931) and four French singles and 12 US, Wimbledon and French doubles titles between 1923 and 1939. She also won the singles and doubles titles at the 1924 Olympics.

Yamamoto, Yohji 1943–

Japanese fashion designer. After studying at Keio University and the Bunka College of Fashion in Tokyo in the late 1960s, he worked as a freelance designer before forming his own company in 1972, his first collection being shown in Japan four years later. His designs typically swathe the body in loose, shapeless garments, often decorated with flaps, pockets, and straps.

Zanuck, Darryl F. 1902–79

US film executive, producer and screenwriter. He joined Warner Bros as a screenwriter in 1923; by 1929 he was in charge of production and responsible for the studio's successes in the early thirties. With Joseph Schenck he formed 20th Century Pictures in 1933, merging with Fox in 1934, to become a major force in Hollywood. In 1956 he went independent, having his only real success with *The Longest Day* (1962). In 1962 he went to the rescue of 20th Century-Fox after *Cleopatra*, becoming president and later chairman with his son also on the board. Both left during 1970–71, with his management style under attack.

GLOSSARY

Alienation
The sense of estrangement and lack of meaningful connection between the individual and his or her surroundings, thought by many to be the defining condition of modern existence.

Amateur
In sport, someone who does not compete for money. The definition has broadened this century, as athletes who are funded by educational colleges or governments may still be considered amateurs for selection purposes.

Anti-establishment
Opposed to rightwing or conventional values and opinions, typically those reflecting tradition and authority; see also **Counter-Cultural.**

Apartheid
The policy of racial segregation, enforced by the South African government, whereby the country's white minority dominates and exploits its non-white majority.

Applied arts
The design or decoration of functional objects.

Art deco
Style of decorative art fashionable in the 1920s and 1930s, which takes its name from the Exposition Internationale des Arts Décoratifs et Industriels Modernes (Paris, 1925); typically expressed by geometric or stylized shapes.

Art nouveau
A decorative style that flourished from the 1890s to the outbreak of World War I; a sinuous line based on plant forms was characteristic.

Avant-garde
The vanguard; those who create or support innovation or experimentation in any field, but particularly in the arts.

Bauhaus
Founded by Walter Gropius in Germany in 1919 (and closed by the Nazi party in 1933), a school of architecture and **applied arts**, which attempted to marry fine design with the commercial and technical requirements of industrial production.

Beat generation
A Term coined by American novelist Jack Kerouac, to identify an **anti-establishment** element in US society of the late 1940s and 1950s.

Bebop
Also bop; a **jazz** style which flourished in the 1940s and 1950s. Compared to earlier jazz, bebop's rhythms were more subtle and complex; melodic improvization was stressed.

Blues
"A state of mind and a music which gives voice to it", the blues evolved from the **folk music** of black Americans. Usually slow and melancholy, and with a 12-bar structure, most blues are sung laments on living and loving.

Boogie-woogie
A style of **blues** piano, at the height of its popularity in the 1930s. Fast and energetic, it featured a rolling left-hand bass pattern.

Cable television
Transmission via cable, commonly paid for by the user.

Chain store
One of a group of shops under the same company name, ownership and management.

Consumer society
One that sets very high value on the consumption of goods and services.

Convention
The agreed or customary method by which something is represented; for example, that "white" is "good" and "black" is "bad".

Counter-cultural
Opposed to the **mainstream**, different to the usual or the expected, and often subversive; see **anti-establishment, hippy.**

Cover version
In popular music, a remake of an earlier recording, often adapting the musical style to contemporary taste.

Cultural imperialism
Spreading or imposing a foreign culture (usually white, European or American) and its values at the expense of an indigenous culture.

Culture
Often assumed to refer only to what is called "high culture" in this book, culture is here used to indicate a particular way of life, and the non-utilitarian objects through which people living that way of life identify themselves. This sense is most easily recognized in the term subculture, which describes the culture of a distinguishable smaller group.

Decorative arts
The creation of ornaments and other decorative objects, such as pottery, furniture, carpets; an **applied art**.

Director
In film production the person responsible for staging the script and orchestrating actors performances, usually seen as the most important creative role.

Disk jockey
Also DJ; someone who introduces and plays recorded music (especially popular music) on radio or television, or in a discothèque.

Disco music
From "discotheque", a musical style characterized by insistent thumping bass patterns; enormously popular in the late 1970s.

Disposable income
The part of a person's income left over after tax has been deducted.

Documentary
Factual depiction of actual events or real peoples' lives, in a film or in a radio or television program.

Entertainment
Commercial **leisure** activity, produced by professional performers for sale to an audience, who consume it for pleasure, relaxation or amusement. Usually expected to be undemanding of its audience, entertainment, in such forms as cinema, music, literature and television has become a major industry in the 20th century.

Feminism
The belief that women are men's equals, and that society should embody that equality.

Film noir
A term coined to describe Hollywood **thrillers** of the 1940s and 1950s, which portrayed the dark underworld of crime and corruption.

Flapper
A young woman of the 1920s, often one who defied social conventions. Flappers cut their hair short and wore short skirts.

Folk music
Traditional songs, dance or music; in the 1960s applied to the work of Bob Dylan and others who revived traditional forms and wrote new words to old ballads to express contemporary social consciousness.

Franchise
Permission to sell a company's goods or sevices, usually within a particular geographical area, under that company's name.

Futurism
A movement in the visual arts, music and literature, which originated in 1909 with the publication of the Italian poet F.T. Marinetti's *Futurist Manifesto*. Its adherents made a cult of speed and the machine.

Generation gap
A lack of communication and understanding between people of different age-groups.

Genre
The common term given to a particular type or group of paintings, books, films or music, distinguished from others by their specific style or content: eg Western films.

Gospel music
A style of sacred singing which developed in the Protestant churches of black America; the main song is often freely improvised, and accompanied by a chorus of chanting and clapping.

Haute couture
High-quality fashion; the clothes designed and made by couturiers.

Hedonism
The doctrine that pleasure is the sole and the proper aim of human action.

High-tech
A movement in architecture and interior design dating from the 1970s, which employs industrial objects and imagery.

Hillbilly music
The traditional songs (largely of European origin) of rural communities in the southern United States; first recorded in the 1920s, usually to the accompaniment of a banjo, fiddle or guitar.

Hippy
Colorfully dressed in flowing ethnic styles, this **anti-establishment** group in 1960s society succeeded the beatniks as rebels against middle-class values.

Icon
Originally a religious image to be revered, now used to refer to an established and immediately recognizable image to which considerable cultural or symbolic weight is attached: eg to refer to John Wayne as "icon of American masculinity".

Iconography
A system of grouping of **conventional** visual signals by which audiences identify the **genre**, period or other classification to which an object in popular culture belongs: eg the clothes and settings specific to the Western film.

Ideology
The system of beliefs, perceptions and feelings in a particular **culture**, much of it so deeply ingrained in the forms, structures and **myths** of that culture that people regard it as common sense.

Jazz
Any of the various 20th-century styles of rhythmical, **syncopated** music, mainly instrumental and often improvised; the black American musicians of New Orleans are usually credited with its origination. See also **bebop, boogie-woogie, ragtime, rhythm & blues, swing.**

Jazz age
The decade between the end of World War I and the Wall Street Crash of 1929.

Kitsch
A German term for "vulgar trash"; something considered blatantly slick, pretentious or sentimental.

Leisure
Time spent not working, and the activities that occupy that time.

Lifestyle
The way a person or a group choses to live, expressed in opinions, behavior, home environment, and so on.

Market economy
One in which resources are allocated according to supply and demand, uncontrolled by government regulation.

Mainstream
The dominant or chief trend of opinion in society.

Mass media
Communication systems such as radio, television and newspapers, which reach large numbers of people.

Materialism
Devotion to the acquisition of material possessions, in preference to inner fulfilment.

Media
The different technological means of communication: the printed word, mechanical and electronic forms of reproduction.

Melodrama
A form of dramatic production which exaggerates emotions, particularly those concerned with **romance**. The dominant mode of most popular **fiction**, including Hollywood's.

Merchandising
The particular selling techniques brought to bear in advertising and marketing a product.

Mersey beat
Musical style combining elements of **folk music** and **rock 'n' roll**; it originated in the late 1950s in the northern English port of Liverpool and its most famous exponents were the Beatles.

Modernism
A movement across art-forms beginning in the late 19th century, which rejected traditional assumptions of order and value in favor of doubt, relativism, and a self-conscious concern with the formal organization of the artwork.

Monopoly
The exclusive control or possession of something; the effective domination of a market or trade.

Myth
A story that a **culture** tells to account for a contradiction at the centre of its existence; the Western myth, for instance, tells the story of the bringing of "civilization" to America through the extermination of its indigenous peoples.

Narcissism
The excessive (and often anxious) concern with self, to the exclusion of the social; believed by many to be a particular malady of Western society ("the Me generation") in the later 20th century.

Neo-realism
An Italian film movement of the 1940s and early 1950s characterized by realistic, almost **documentary-like**, portrayal of contemporary social problems.

Network
In radio or television, a group of affiliated broadcasting stations.

New Look
A romantically feminine fashion introduced by the designer Christian Dior in 1947; busts were exaggerated, waists were tiny, and, in contrast to wartime economies, skirts were extravagantly full and long.

New Wave
Initially, an innovative movement in French cinema among directors who entered the industry in 1959-62. The term has since been used also to describe surges of creative filmmaking in other countries.

Nickelodeon
In the USA, an early moving picture theater; from the admission price of a nickel (5 cents).

Nuclear family
The minimal family unit in 20th century Western culture, of husband, wife, and children.

Offbeat
Unusual or unconventional.

Permissive society
One that is sexually and morally tolerant; used to typify the 1960s, when a number of moral and social conventions were relaxed.

Planned obsolescence
Changing the appearance or performance of an everyday commodity, such as a refrigerator or a motor car, to encourage consumers to buy new models before the old ones have worn out.

Pluralism
The belief that two or more ideas, opinions or styles can coexist without necessarily conflicting. In culture, as in politics, pluralism implies a preference for toleration and adaptability rather than rigid adherence to established practice, and is inherently opposed to all forms of authoritarian control.

Pop art
Flourishing from the late 1950s to the early 1970s, artworks drawing inspiration from the imagery of consumerism and popular culture.

Pop music
Commercially oriented tunes or songs; term used from the 1950s to describe music aimed at the developing youth market.

Popular
Of the people; widely appreciated. But **popular culture**, as used here, also identifies a range of products and **entertainment**, primarily for **leisure** consumption, that are produced via industrial processes and sold in a **market economy**; features that distinguish them from folk or **vernacular culture.**

Prime time
Peak viewing hours on television, when the highest rates are charged to advertisers.

Producer
In filmmaking, the person responsible for the financial and administrative aspects.

Product variation
Also product differentiation; using advertising, packaging and so on to create differences between products of the same type such as cigarettes.

Professional
In sport, people for whom playing is their livelihood, or who compete for money prizes.

Prohibition
The years 1920-33 in the United States, when manufacturing, selling or transporting alcoholic drinks for general consumption was forbidden by law.

Psychedelic
Resembling the distorted visual and sound effects caused by hallucinogenic drugs.

Public service broadcasting
Non-commercial use of radio and television, generally supported by government funding, frequently broadly educational in character.

Punk
An anarchic youth movement in music and fashion which arose in Britain in the mid-1970s.

Ragtime
Tightly composed piano **jazz**, which combined **syncopation** with march forms, dating from the late 19th century.

Ratings
In television or radio, a system of measuring a program's success, which is based on assessing audience size.

Realism
A 19th-century movement in the arts which strove to depict accurately the worlds it represented, and to show things as they actually existed. Although the feasibility of this goal was questioned by **modernism**, the accusation that **melodrama**, for example, is not "realistic" has remained one of the principal arguments for dismissing popular culture from serious examination and appreciation.

Retro-chic
The revival of fashions from an earlier era.

Rhythm & blues
Also r & b; an up-tempo musical evolution from the **blues**, widely popular as dance music by the 1940s; bands usually featured a tenor saxophone; see also **rock 'n' roll.**

Rock 'n' roll
Popular dance music originating in the 1950s as an offshoot of **rhythm & blues**; most pieces have a 12-bar **blues** structure, and a heavily accented rhythm.

Romance
In popular culture, the representation of heterosexual love as the predominant subject matter. White popular music frequently depicts the failure of romantic love, romantic narratives more usually conclude with a happy ending that marks the foundation of a new **nuclear family**.

Sitcom
A situation comedy; humor based on everyday events and the interaction of a small group of characters.

Soap opera
Serialized radio or television fiction dealing melodramatically with the daily traumas and often highly charged love-lines of a group of characters; so called because originally sponsored by American soap manufacturers.

Soul music
Commercially successful black American music of the 1960s on, which combined **gospel** with **blues** styles.

Status symbol
Any obvious sign of a person's wealth or social prestige.

Streamlining
Fluid shaping, which increases performance by reducing water- or air-resistance; in the 1930s it was employed as a style on a wide range of objects.

Street fashion
Avant-garde styles, which originate on the city streets and not in fashion salons.

Swing
Smooth and rhythmical, dance-oriented orchestral **jazz**, popular from the mid-1930s to the mid-1940s, usually arranged for big bands.

Syncopation
The stressing of normally unaccented beats, in music such as **jazz**.

Syndication
The sale of a story or program for simultaneous release by a number of different media outlets.

Thriller
A book, play or film that creates excitement or suspense; especially one dealing with mystery or crime.

Tin Pan Alley
Until the 1950s, the composers and publishers of the popular music industry in the USA.

Underground
Term adopted in the 1960s to describe **anti-establishment** or **counter-cultural** beliefs and activities.

Vaudeville
Variety shows or revues, featuring singers, dancers, comedians and acrobats.

Vernacular culture
Like folk culture, the functional and artistic productions of people outside their involvement in the economic sphere; those things, from music to clothes to houses, that people make for themselves.

FURTHER READING

Film and the Media

Balio, Tino, ed *The American Film Industry* (Madison, 1986)

Barthes, Roland *Mythologies* (London, 1972)

Bordwell, David; Staiger Janet and Thompson, Kristen *The Classical Hollywood Cinema: Film Style and Mode of Production to 1960* (London, 1985)

Braudy, Leo *The Frenzy of Renown: Fame and Its History* (New York, 1986)

Chambers, Iain *Popular Culture: The Metropolitan Experience* (London, 1986)

Curran, James, Gurevitch, Michael and Wollacott, Janet, eds *Mass Communication and Society* (London, 1977)

Czitrom, Daniel *Media and the American Mind: From Morse to McLuhan* (Chapel Hill, 1982)

Dyer, Richard *Stars* (London, 1979)

Evans, Harold *Front Page History* (Harmondsworth, 1985)

Ewen, Stuart & Elizabeth *Channels of Desire: Mass Images and the Shaping of American Consciousness* (New York, 1982)

Finler, Joel, W *The Hollywood Story: Everything You Always Wanted to Know About the American Movie Business But Didn't Know Where to Look* (London, 1988)

Fox, RW and Jackson, TJ, eds *The Culture of Consumption: Critical Essays in American History 1800-1980* (New York, 1983)

Gomery, Douglas *The Hollywood Studio System* (London, 1986)

Holme, Bryan *The Art of Advertising* (London, 1985)

Horne, Donald *The Public Culture: The Triumph of Industrialism* (London, 1986)

Inge, M, Thomas *Concise Histories of American Popular Culture* (Westport, 1982)

Izod, John *Hollywood and the Box Office 1895-1986* (London, 1988)

Jowett, Garth *Film: The Democratic Art* (New York, 1976)

Katz, Ephraim *The International Film Encyclopedia* (London, 1980)

Lasch, Christopher *The Culture of Narcissism* (London, 1979)

Lazere, Donald, ed *American Media and Mass Culture: Left Perspectives* (Los Angeles, 1987)

Lewis, Peter and Pearlman, Corrine *Media and Power: From Marconi to Murdoch* (London, 1986)

Maltby, Richard *Harmless Entertainment: Hollywood and the Ideology of Consensus* (Methuen, NJ, 1983)

Mast, Gerald *The Movies in Our Midst: Documents in the Cultural History of America*

May, Larry *Screening Out the Past: The Birth of Mass Culture and the Motion Picture Industry* (New York, 1980)

McLuhan, Marshall *Understanding Media: The Extensions of Man* (London, 1964)

Meyrowitz, Joshua *No Sense of Place: The Impact of Electronic Media on Social Behaviour* (New York, 1985)

Modleski, Tania, ed *Studies in Entertainment: Critical Approaches to Mass Culture* (Bloomington, 1986)

Neale, Steve *Cinema and Technology: Image, Sound, Colour* (London, 1985)

Peiss, Kathy *Cheap Amusements: Working Women and Leisure in Turn-of-the-Century New York* (Philadelphia, 1986)

Rhode, Eric *A History of the Cinema from the Silents to the Seventies* (Harmondsworth, 1978)

Rosten, Leo *Hollywood, the Movie Colony, the Movie Makers* (New York, 1940)

Schatz, Thomas *Hollywood Genres: Formulas, Filmmaking, and the Studio System* (New York, 1981)

Short, KRM, ed *Film and Propaganda in World War II* (London, 1983)

Sklar, Robert *Movie-Made America: A Cultural History of American Movies* (New York, 1975)

Steinberg, Cobbett *Reel Facts* (Harmondsworth, 1981)

Susman, Warren *Culture as History: The Transformation of American Society in the Twentieth Century* (New York, 1984)

Thompson, Kristin *Exporting Entertainment: America in the World Film Market 1907-1934* (London, 1985)

Tunstall, Jeremy *The Media are American: Anglo-American Media in the World* (London, 1977)

Vestergaard, Torben and Schroder, Kim *The Language of Advertising* (Oxford, 1985)

Wheen, Francis *Television* (London, 1985)

Popular music

Bronson, Fred *The Billboard Book of No.1 Hits* (New York, 1985)

Cable, Michael *The Pop Industry Inside Out* (London, 1974)

Chapple, Steve and Garofalo, Reebee *Rock & Roll is Here to Pay* (Nelson-Hall, 1977)

Dixon, Robert, MW and Godrich, John *Recording the Blues* (London, 1970)

Eberly, Philip *Music in the Air* (New York, 1982)

Ewen, David *All the Years of American Popular Music* (New York, 1977)

Feist, Leonard *An Introduction to Popular Music Publishing in America* (New York, 1982)

Gillett, Charlie *The Sound of the City* (London, 1983)

Murrells, Joseph *Million Selling Records from the 1900s to the 1980s* (London, 1984)

Oakley, Giles *The Devil's Music* (Ariel, 1983)

Oliver, Paul *The Story of the Blues* (London, 1969)

Sanjek, Russell *From Print to Plastic* (New York, 1979)

Tirro, Frank *Jazz: A History* (New York, 1977)

Ward, Ed et al *Rock of Ages* (Rolling Stone, 1987)

Whitburn, Joel *The Billboard Book of Top 40 Hits* (New York, 1985)

Zalkind, Ronald *Contemporary Music Almanac, 1980/81* (New York, 1983)

Design

Aslin, E *The Aesthetic Movement: Prelude to Art Nouveau* (London, 1969)

Bayley, Stephen *Harley Earl* (London, 1989)

Douglas, M and Isherwood, B *The World of Goods: Towards an Anthropology of Consumption* (Harmondsworth, 1980)

Forty, Adrian *Objects of Desire: Design and Society 1750-1980* (London, 1986)

Fraser, W, Hamish *The Coming of the Mass Market* (London, 1981)

Heskett, John *Industrial Design* (London, 1980)

Hillier, Bevis *The Style of the Century, 1900-1980* (New York, 1983)

Hine, Thomas *Populuxe: The Look and Life of America in the '50s and '60s* (London, 1987)

Hounshell, DA *From the American System to Mass Production* (Baltimore, 1985)

Lucie-Smith, Edward *A History of Industrial Design* (Oxford, 1983)

Marchand, Roland *Advertising the American Dream: Making Way for Modernity 1920-1940* (Los Angeles, 1985)

McCarthy, F *A History of British Design 1830-1970* (London, 1979)

Meikle, Jeffrey *Twentieth-Century Limited: Industrial Design in America 1925-1939* (Philadelphia, 1979)

Papanek, Victor *Design for the Real World: Making to Measure* (Harmondsworth, 1972)

Pirlos, A *The American Design Ethic* (Cambridge, Mass, 1982)

Sparke, Penny *An Introduction to Design and Culture in the Twentieth Century* (London, 1986)

Sparke, Penny *Ettore Sottsass Jnr* (London, 1983)

Sparke, Penny *Japanese Design* (London, 1987)

Sudjic, Deyon *Cult Objects* (London, 1986)

Veblen, T *The Theory of the Leisure Class* (New York, 1899)

Fashion

Bell, Quentin *On Human Finery* (London, 1947)

Carter, Angela *Nothing Sacred* (London, 1982)

Charles-Roux, Edmonde *Chanel* (London, 1975)

Cunnington, Cecil Willet and Cunnington, Phillis *The History of Underclothes* (London, 1951)

Delbourg-Delphis, Marylene *Le Chic et le Look: Histoire de la Mode Féminine et des Mœurs de 1850 à nos jours* (Paris, 1981)

Etherington Smith, Meredith *Patou* (London, 1983)

Ewing, Elizabeth *Dress and Undress: A History of Womens Under-wear* (London, 1978)

Fraser, Kennedy *The Fashionable Mind: Reflections on Fashion 1970-1982* (Boston, 1985)

Hebdige, Dick *Subcultures: The Meaning of Style* (London, 1978)

Hollander, Anne *Seeing Through Clothes* (New York, 1975)

Konig, René *The Restless Image* (London, 1973)

Laver, James *A Concise History of Costume* (London, 1969)

Lurie, Alison *The Language of Clothes* (London, 1981)

Melly, George *Revolt into Style: The Pop Arts in Britain* (Harmondsworth, 1972)

Packer, William *Fashion Drawing in Vogue* (London, 1984)

Squire, Geoffrey *Dress Art and Society 1560-1970* (London, 1974)

Wilson, Elizabeth *Adorned in Dreams: Fashion and Modernity* (London, 1985)

Sport

Baker, William, J *Sports in the Western World* (New Jersey, 1982)

Guttmann, Allen *A Whole New Ball Game: An Interpretation of American Sports* (Chapel Hill, 1988)

Guttmann, Allen *From Ritual to Record: The Nature of Modern Sports* (New York, 1978)

Mandell, Richard, D *Sport: A Cultural History* (New York, 1984)

ACKNOWLEDGEMENTS

Picture Credits

1 Charlie Chaplin: CP
2–3 Drive-in movie: Winston Link
4 Busby Berkeley *Gold Diggers of 1933*: APL
6 The New Look: Magnum/Robert Capa
20–21 The Paris Exhibition, 1900: Roger Viollet
54–55 The Beach at Deauville: John Hillelson Agency
88–89 Finale of *Broadway Melody*, 1938: KC
122–123 Ten-Pin Bowling, 1959: National Bowling Hall and Museum of Fame
156–157 The Pranksters' Psychedelic Bus: Gene Anthony
190–191 Live Aid, 1985: Retna/Sam Wix

9 CP 10–11 Museum of Modern Art, New York/Film Stills Archive 12 CP 15 AP 16–17 RF 18–19 Andrew Driver 25 Popperfoto 26–27b CP 27t EA 28l Mander and Mitchenson Theatre Collection 28r Missouri Historical Society 29, 30t MEPL 30–31b Bulloz 31t EA 31br MEPL 33 W.H. Smith 34 FPG International 35t EA 35c FP 35b Museum of the City of New York 36t Michael Holford 36b CP 37t NFA, London 37c KC 37b Museum of Modern Art, New York/Film Stills Archive 38–39, 39b KC 39t EA 40 National Film and Sound Archive, Australia 40–41 CP 41t APL 42t CP 42–43b CP 42–43c EA 43 Süddeutscher Verlag 44l The Circus World Museum (Wisconsin) 44tr, 44br HPC. 44 (background) Mander and Mitchenson 45t Liverpool, Walker Art Gallery 45b Süddeutscher Verlag 46–47 KC 46t EA 46b NFA, London 47l National Archives, Washington 47cr CP 47br KC 49t Le Comité International Olympique, Switzerland 49b, 50 HPC 50–51 John Hillelson Agency 51t CP 52t HPC 52b CP 53t Library of Congress, USA 53b Colorsport 58–59 The National Motor Museum, Beaulieu 60l FP 60cr Olivetti, Milan 60br AGE Fotostock, Barcelona 61l EA 61r Time Inc, New York 62t MEPL 62c Geffrye Museum, London 63 John Frost Collection 64 Brown Brothers 64–65, 65r The National Motor Museum, Beaulieu 65tl, 66 HPC 66t Roger Viollet 66–67 Chicago Historical Society 67c FPG International 67t CP 68t, 68–69 HPC/The Bettmann Archive 68b UP/Bettmann Newsphotos 69tr CP 69br Roger-Viollet 71t, 71b CP 72–73 Ramsey Archive 73l, 73cl, 73r EA 73cr CP 74t Süddeutscher Verlag 74b EA 75t Mander and Mitchenson 75b Roger-Viollet 76, 77t MEPL 77c Süddeutscher Verlag 77b Barnaby's Picture Library 78 MEPL 79l, 79br Bridgeman Art Library 79tr, 79cr Angelo Hornak 81 CP 82 EA 82–83 Novosti Press Agency 83t KC 84t, 84c CP 84b NFA, London 85t KC 85b Barnaby's Picture Library 86–87 Dick Busher 86t KC 86b Museum of Modern Art, New York/Film Stills Archive 87tl APL 87r CP 93t EA 93b Chicago Historical Society 94 CP 95 Metropolitan Museum of Art, New York 96 APL 97t FP 96–97b Süddeutscher Verlag 98l Topham Picture Library 98r Roger Viollet 99 Freemans Ltd 100–101 John Smallwood/FP 100bl, br, bc EA 101t CP 101c KC 101b EA 103 CP 104 Popperfoto 105tl, 105tr CP 105b HPC 107 Süddeutscher Verlag 108, 109, 110–111b KC 110 CP 111t APL 112t Wisconsin Center for Film and Theater Research 112b NFA, London 113t, 113b KC 114 APL 115t KC 115r National Film Archive, London 116–117, 116bl, 117tl, 117tr, 117br RF 119 Hulton Deutsch Collection 120t Saturday Evening Post 120l MEPL 120–121 Popperfoto 121t Süddeutscher Verlag 127 Magnum/Robert Capa 128t Popperfoto 128b Cecil Beaton photograph courtesy of Southeby's, London 129l Popperfoto 129tr, 129br HPC 130t Yulsman/Globe Photos 130–131 Popperfoto 131l, 131r NFA, London 132 Popperfoto 133t The Design Council, London 133l, 133r EA 134t The Design Council 134–135, 135t, 135cr Popperfoto 135br Freemans Mail Order 136, 137t EA 137b Topham Picture Library 138t CP 138c EA 138br Hutchison Library 138bl, 139tr, 139c, 139b RF 141 Michael Ochs Archives/Venice, California 142l Popperfoto 142r EA 143l Sotheby's, London 143r Val Wilmer 144t EA 144b Victoria and Albert Museum 145 Pictorial Press Ltd 147, 148b Popperfoto 148t RF 149l, 149r EA 150t APL 150bl FP 150bc, 150br EA 151 Winston Link 152t APL 152b, 153r

EA 153l NFA, London 154b Magnum/Bruce Davidson 154t Bridgeman Art Library 154–155 KC 155t RF 155b John Frost Collection 161, 162l Pictorial Press Ltd 162r, 163t Popperfoto 163b Victoria and Albert Museum, Fashion Department/John French Estate 164t Telegraph Colour Library 165b Whitmore-Thomas 165t EA 165b Malcolm Lewin/Architectural Press 166l Arcaid/Richard Einzig, 166r John Rose and John Doyle 167t Rosenthal Group 167b Bang and Olufsen 169 EA 170tl KC 170b EA 170tr APL 171 KC 172t Pictorial Press Ltd 172b, 173b AP 173t RF 175 Novosti Press Agency 176t Popperfoto 176b RF 177t Topham Picture Library 177b Colorsport 178–179 RF 179t AP 179cr Popperfoto 179br All-sport 181 RF International/ Mary Englander 181 inset AP 182 Pictorial Press Ltd 183t Retna/Bob Freeman 183b Val Wilme 184t Retna/Joel Axelrod 184b Pictorial Press Ltd 185l Michael Ochs Archives/Venice, California 185r Retna/Barron Wolman 186 Hulton Deutsch Collection 186–187 RF 187t EA 188t Michael Ochs Archives/Venice California 188b Lisa Law 188–189 RF 189tr, 189cr Michael Ochs Archives, Venice, California 189cl Jak Kilby 195, 196l EA 196–197, 197b KC 197c Popperfoto 198t NFA, London 198c NFA, London 198–199, 199tl KC 199r Kerstin Rogers 200t HK TVB International Ltd 200b Barnaby's Picture Library 201 Granada Television 202t Hulton Deutsch Collection 202b Hutchison Library 203 Novosti Press Agency 204t Hulton Deutsch Collection/Sotheby's 204b, 204–205, 205tr, 205bl RF 205cr Central Independent Television 205br EA 207t Colorsport 207b Popperfoto 208 RF 209tl Sporting Pictures 209tr Colorsport 2009b All Sport/Vandy Staat 210–211, 210b Sporting Pictures 211 Colorsport 213 Retna/John Jacques 214r Retna/Paul Rider 214b Retna/Adrian Boot 215t RF 215b Jak Kilby 216 Retna/Michael Putland 217t, 217b RF 219 Zefa/Clive Sawyer 220 Retna/John Bellissimo 220b Retna/Scott Weiner 221 RF/Brendan Beirne 222l RF 222tr Pictorial Press Ltd 222br Swatch Watches 223 RF 224l, 224br The Design Council 224–225 Bonomi Design Ltd 225cr Topham Picture Library 225br Olympus 226tl Zefa 226cr, 227l RF 226–227 Retna/Michael Putland 227r Amidei & Co 228l CP 228c AP 228r KC 229l NFA, London 229c, 229r RF 230l EA 230c Sylvan Mason 230r CP 231l, 231r RF 231c EA 232l KC 232c FPG International 232r RF 233l APL 233c Novosti Press Agency 233r Val Wilmer 234l CP 234c RF 234c NFA, London 235l EA 235c RF 235r EA 236l EA 236c KC 236r Val Wilmer 237l, 237r RF 237c HPC 238l KC 238r, 239c RF 239l APL 239r Roget-Viollet 240l NFA, London 240r RF 241l Colorsport 241c Roger Viollet 241r KC 242l APL 242c RF 242r Süddeutscher Verlag 243l Michael Ochs Archives/Venice, California 243r Colorsport 244l RF 244c FPG International 244r CP 245l Cecil Beaton Photography courtesy of Southeby's, London 245c Michael Ochs Archives/Venice, California 245r CP 246l KC 246c APL 246r CP 247l, 247c RF 247r KC

Abbreviations

APL	Aquarius Picture Library
AP	Associated Press
CP	Culver Pictures
EA	Equinox Archive
FP	The Futile Press
HPC	Hulton Picture Company
KC	Kobal Collection
MEPL	Mary Evans Picture Library
NFA	National Film Archive
RF	Rex Features

Abbreviations

t = top, tl = top left, tr = top right, c = center,
b = bottom etc.

Author's Acknowledgements

Every book is a collaborative production, but this one more than most. Editing it has been an exhilarating process, as I have watched in develop its argument about how we can take our everyday escapism seriously. Many people have taken part in that argument; some of the most important are mentioned only in the Further Reading list. My friends and colleagues at Exeter – Karen Edwards, Anthony Fothergill, Mick Gidley, Judith Higginbottom, Edwyna Prior, Peter and Luisa Quartermaine, Ron Tamplin, Michael Wood, and especially Ruth Vasey – have listened with forebearance to its growth and nurtured it through its growing pains.

The talents of my co-authors turned the tasks of editing into a pleasure, and I am grateful to all of them. But writing is only half the story in a book like this, and people at Equinox have added enormously to what merits it has. In particular, thanks are due to Graham Speake for initiating the project; to Ayala Kingsley and John Ridgeway for the imagination that has gone into the book's design; to Jan Croot for finding the pictures; and especially to Peter Furtado for his patient and careful editorial supervision of the book, and for managing to keep me just the right side of jargon.

This book, which tries not to be nostalgic, is for remembrance.

Equinox Acknowledgements

Editorial and research assistance
Monica Byles, Mary Davies, Jackie Gaff, Louise Jones, Mike Pincombe

Design Assistance
Cyndy Gossert, Nicholas Rous, Dave Smith, Del Tolton, Michelle Vonahn

Artists
Alan Hollingbery, Kevin Maddison, Colin Salmon

Photographs
Shirley Jamieson, Alison Renney, Christine Vincent

Typesetting
Anita Rokins, OPUS Ltd

Production
Clive Sparling

Color Origination
Scantrans, Singapore

Index
Ann Barrett

INDEX

Page numbers in italics refer to illustrations or their captions and to datafile captions. Bold numbers refer to the subjects of special or ancillary text features

For individual films *see under* films; for individual songs and albums *see under* popular music.